Napoleon, France and Waterloo

In loving memory of Irene Collins, colleague, friend, mentor and fellow labourer in the Napoleonic vineyard.

Napoleon, France and Waterloo

The Eagle Rejected

Charles J. Esdaile

Pen & Sword
MILITARY

Copyright © Charles J. Esdaile 2016

ISBN 978 1 47387 082 6

A CIP catalogue record for this book is available from the British Library

Typeset in Ehrhardt by
Mac Style Ltd, Bridlington, East Yorkshire
Printed and bound in the UK by CPI Group (UK) Ltd,
Croydon, CRO 4YY

Pen & Sword Books Ltd incorporates the imprints of Pen & Sword Archaeology, Atlas, Aviation, Battleground, Discovery, Family History, History, Maritime, Military, Naval, Politics, Railways, Select, Transport, True Crime, Fiction, Frontline Books, Leo Cooper, Praetorian Press, Seaforth Publishing and Wharncliffe.

For a complete list of Pen & Sword titles please contact
PEN & SWORD BOOKS LIMITED
47 Church Street, Barnsley, South Yorkshire, S70 2AS, England
E-mail: enquiries@pen-and-sword.co.uk
Website: www.pen-and-sword.co.uk

Contents

List of Illustrations

Preface

Two hundred years on from the fall of Napoleon, one thing is certain, and that is that the Napoleonic legend is as strong today as it ever was. Although many figures in the academic world are critical, indeed even fiercely critical, within its portals there are still those – Mike Broers, Alan Forrest and Stephen Englund – who at the very least see Napoleon as a reformist who was genuinely committed to building a new social and political order, and, what is more, a new social and political order that was in many respects wholly admirable. Meanwhile, beyond the ivory tower Napoleon remains a figure who continues to be associated not just with such personal qualities as romance, heroism and adventure, nor even with military genius, but also with freedom, progress, democracy and all the advances of the modern world: for a recent example of such thinking, one has only to turn to Andrew Roberts' *Napoleon the Great* (London, 2014). In brief, then, in many eyes the emperor remains, if not the very epitome of the French Revolution, at the very least its instrument. Of course, just how far such a popular view of Napoleon can be said to exist cannot be measured with any certainty without the benefit of substantial market research, but what is certainly the case is that the past half-century has not shown any let-up in the flood of books and other materials that has kept the legend of Napoleon alive. In 1970, in the feature film, *Waterloo*, Dino de Laurentis gave us a version of the climactic battle of the Napoleonic Wars that was as emphatic in its presentation of the emperor as a man of 1789 as it was deficient in its history, whilst in 1977 the writer, Vincent Cronin, produced a biography so hagiographic that it might as well have been dictated to him on Saint Helena. In 1993 David Hamilton-Williams published *Waterloo: New Perspectives – the Great Battle Re-Appraised*, this being followed very closely by a second volume entitled *The Fall of Napoleon: the Final Betrayal*, the general tenor of these two works being to present the emperor as a great champion both of France and of the values of the Revolution who had been brought down only by the unremitting hostility of the *ancien régime* (and, more particularly, Britain) and the treason of a variety of trusted subordinates. To quote the peroration of *The Fall of Napoleon*:

> To the people of France he was Napoleon, their emperor, created by their will and unbeaten in war. Betrayed in 1814 by Talleyrand's conspiracy

aided by Marmont and Augereau and the senators. Betrayed again in 1815 by Fouché, Lafayette, Davout and the members of the chambers. Betrayed by his father-in-law, the emperor Francis ... But not by the people of France – not by the nation.[1]

Nor is Hamilton-Williams isolated in his rhetoric. On the contrary, across the Channel such romanticism is also alive and well. For a good example, one has only to turn to the pages of F.G. Hourtoulle's *1814: the Campaign for France – the Wounded Eagle* (Paris, 2005). Sumptuously illustrated with endless depictions of overwhelming Allied numbers on the one hand and heroic French defenders on the other, not to mention a greatcoated and grim-faced Napoleon, this is essentially a straightforward military narrative whose numerous maps make it extremely easy to follow (in this respect, it is greatly to be preferred to F.L. Petre's *Napoleon at Bay, 1814* [London, 1913]). Yet the level of analysis is, at best, woeful. Thus, coverage of Napoleon's attempted reconstruction of the *Grande Armée* in the wake of Leipzig is restricted to a brief recapitulation of the measures that he took to bring in fresh recruits with no reference to the extent to which he was successful.[2] Of the response of France to the new *levée en masse*, then, we hear nothing, Hourtoulle instead falling back on the tired old argument of the stab in the back:

> The top dignitaries thought that the empire was dying and were putting out feelers to the Bourbons so that they would have their place in a restored monarchy. But the exhaustion and discouragement affected most those whom Napoleon had raised highest: the marshals. These men were tired of the unending wars and the setbacks they had suffered, they wanted to be able to enjoy their possessions and fortunes ... Marmont fought like a lion but ... his sorry *ragusade* [is] the only thing by which history will remember him.[3]

In fairness, Hourtoulle does not let Napoleon off scot-free. On the contrary, it is recognized both that Napoleon was repeatedly offered very favourable terms and that, as he puts it, the emperor 'hedged, still believing he could win a decisive victory, enabling him to negotiate from a position of strength and to obtain an even more favourable armistice', the fact being that '[the emperor] was ... plagued by an illness which has hit many great men, conquest', not to mention a 'narcissism [that] grew with each success, nourished by the servility of his underlings'.[4] Unfortunately, such caveats count for very little. Truly, then, Napoleon may be said to have won the peace. As Hamilton-Williams writes, indeed, 'Napoleon's last struggle, for posterity and martyrdom, like the majority of his campaigns, was a resounding victory.'[5] With the coming of the bicentenary of the battle of Waterloo, meanwhile, that victory is being reinforced still further. Visit the field of Waterloo, and it will be discovered to be a shrine to Napoleon's glory – to judge by the merchandise in the gift shops, it might even be thought that the struggle was one of his greatest triumphs, whilst the stars of the great re-enactment that was staged to re-enact the battle were not the British and the Prussians, nor still less the Dutch-Belgians, but rather the soldiers of Napoleon. Equally, the dominant theme is clearly not the commemoration of the sacrifices that were made by the soldiers who fought for Wellington and Blücher but rather the continued exaltation of the emperor. Already forthcoming, meanwhile, have been many books that have at the very least sought to examine the battle from a French point of view, a good example being Andrew Field's *Waterloo: the French Perspective* (Barnsley, 2006).

Is, however, the battle of Waterloo a subject that deserves to be commemorated? In a number of works the current author has in effect expressed some doubt as to whether this is really the case, going so far as to refer to the battle as a 'glorious irrelevance'. As we shall see, it is easy enough to suggest any number of ways which might have secured a victory for Napoleon on 18 June 1815, but the question then arises as to what would have happened next. For admirers of Napoleon, the issue is simple enough: in the opinion of Hamilton-Williams, for example, victory at Waterloo would have enabled the emperor to capture Brussels and then turn back against Blücher's Prussians. Enveloped from the north, the latter would have been forced to retreat, thereby exposing the Russian, Austrian and south German forces that were currently massing beyond the Rhine. With these troops forced to retreat in turn, the chances were that, notwithstanding its earlier condemnation of Napoleon, the coalition would have crumbled, thereby giving the emperor both the time that he needed to make good his promises of a 'liberal empire' and the opportunity necessary to show that, as he claimed, he really was a man of peace.[6] This scenario, however, is at the very least open to doubt. In brief, such was the emotion that the French ruler now stirred in the breast of his opponents that it is very difficult to believe that winning not just Waterloo but a subsequent battle against the Prussians would have gained him a favourable peace. What is far more likely is that Schwarzenburg and the other Allied commanders would have trusted to their superior numbers and once more thrust across the French frontier, thereby recreating the circumstances of 1814. At this point, however, Napoleon would have had no option but to make fresh demands on the people of France. Thus far, these had been kept to a minimum: the army that had invaded Belgium in June 1815 had been raised not from fresh conscripts, but rather the soldiers of the Bourbon army, augmented by the 120,000 men who were either absent without leave or on furlough at the time of Napoleon's return from Elba.[7] But even in the event of victory in Belgium, losses would have been heavy, whilst the numerical odds facing Napoleon would have been worse than ever, the fact being that there would have been absolutely no chance of avoiding another levy on the scale of the ones that had been attempted in 1813 and 1814.

In brief, it is this situation which the proposed work seeks to examine. To take just two or three salient questions, what was the state of relations between Napoleon and the citizens of France in the last years of the empire; to what extent was the emperor himself capable of captaining the sort of fight which he now faced; and, finally, what actually happened in France in 1814 and 1815? What is proposed, then, is not an exercise in counter-factual history, but rather the scholarly examination of a series of concrete situations from which certain conclusions may be drawn as to the likelihood of what would have transpired had Napoleon triumphed at Waterloo. That the emperor could have beaten Wellington is not denied, but could he then have withstood the retribution of an entire continent? The answer is at the very least doubtful.

What makes this study all the more necessary is the fact that the English-language literature on France in 1815 is surprisingly thin. Books on the Waterloo campaign, of course, are numerous: the last year alone has seen the publication of general volumes on the subject by Gordon Corrigan, Gregory Fremont-Barnes, Bernard Cornwell, Tim Clayton, Peter and Dan Snow, Robert Kershaw, Martyn Beardsley, Tristan Clark, Gareth Glover, David Crane and John Grehan, while, setting aside Hamilton-Williams, older works that are still widely available include those by David Howarth, Jeremy Black, Andrew Roberts, Ian Fletcher, David Chandler, Alessandro Barberi, Peter Hofschroer and Jacques Logie. Yet these works are overwhelmingly based on military narrative and show little desire to engage with the political and social situation in France, preferring for the most part to accept the simplicities of such Bonapartist apologists as Henri Houssaye, a veteran of the Franco-Prussian War who between 1888 and 1905 produced four substantial volumes on the last period of Napoleon's career, namely *1814: Histoire de la campagne de France* (Paris, 1888); *1815: la première abdication, le retour de l'ile d'Elbe, les cent jours* (1893); *1815: Waterloo* (Paris, 1899); and *1815: la seconde abdication [et] la terreur blanche* (Paris, 1905), all of which were translated into English in the early years of the twentieth century. Yet Houssaye's message, which is effectively cribbed in such populist works as Paul Britten-Austin's *1815: the Return of Napoleon* (London, 2002), is deeply misleading: in brief, the people of France are made out as having been solidly behind Napoleon, when more scholarly studies – for example, Munro Price's admirable *Napoleon: the End of Glory* (London, 2014). – have shown very clearly that by 1814 popular support for Napoleon was all but non-existent.

It would be tempting to apply this logic to the situation that pertained in France in 1815, and the only anglophone scholars who have in recent years written works that have attempted to go beyond the legend on the one hand and the military narrative on the other, namely Gregor Dallas, Alan Schom and Stephen Coote, have, in fact, done just this.[8] It is evident, however, that none of their works is based on the same weight of archival research as *Napoleon: the End of Glory*, whilst the fact is that there is no scholarly English-language study of France in 1815, though it should be pointed out that Malcolm Crook has done a great deal to improve our understanding of the plebiscite by which Napoleon sought to legitimize his return to power.[9] Indeed, even works that examine the topic of war and society in Napoleonic France in general are few and far between. Setting aside specialized (though very useful) works on such matters as conscription, one can only point to the general account offered by Marie-Cecile Thoral and the regional work of Gavin Daly, though there is also some useful material in such studies of France in the Revolutionary and Napoleonic era as that written by Donald Sutherland.[10] As for lives of Napoleon, even the best of these, such as the magisterial two-volume study written by Phillip Dwyer, are too much caught up in the narrative of the emperor's life to be able be much more than suggestive.[11] This is not to say that there are not other things in the extensive historiography that may not be read without profit – one thinks here of the contributions of such eminent scholars as Geoffrey Ellis, Georges Lefebvre and Jean Tulard – but the fact remains that the domestic background to the Hundred Days has gone surprisingly unnoticed, and, further, that current French research on the subject has not been incorporated into the English-language historiography. In stating this point, the author would be remiss if he did not mention R.S. Alexander's *Bonaparte and Revolutionary Tradition: the Fédérés of 1815* (Cambridge, 1991). However, important though this work is, its focus is restricted to a handful of major cities, whilst the author cannot show that the neo-Jacobin movement that he describes was capable of influencing public opinion in favour of the régime, let alone of functioning as a an effective political militia.

A further point to note here is that even the most obvious and easily accessible of primary sources have often gone unused. The Napoleonic Wars, as is well known, constitute one of the first conflicts whose participants left behind a substantial eyewitness record, and the British army was no exception in this respect: on the contrary, counting published work alone, British soldiers generated more than 400 diaries, memoirs and collections of correspondence. Of these, many deal with the subject of the Waterloo campaign, and their authors very often make more or less perceptive comments on the state of public opinion in France (it should be remembered here that, following Napoleon's defeat, Wellington's army joined the Prussians in marching on Paris and therefore had some first-hand experience of the matter). Still more interesting, meanwhile, are the accounts of a number of British civilians who for one reason or another found themselves in France at the time of the return of Napoleon, names that crop up here including those of the later historian of the Revolutionary and Napoleonic era, Archibald Alison, and Byron's crony, John Cam Hobhouse.

To conclude, then, this is a book that has never yet been written, and, further, a book that seeks to meld two very different traditions of historical writing, namely the so-called 'old' military history and the new. At the same time, of course, it is one more contribution to the Napoleon debate, though doubtless one as forlorn in its own way as the last desperate charge of the Imperial Guard on the slopes of Mont Saint Jean: the Napoleonic era, alas, is very much an exception to the rule that history is written by the victors. That said, it has been a book worth writing: it is not just the dead of the First World War who sleep in Flanders fields.

*   *   *

As usual, my debts are many. First of all, Rupert Harding and all his team at Pen and Sword have been their usual admirable and patient selves, not to mention a pleasure to work with. Second of all, Rory Muir, Alan Forrest, Munro Price, Gavin Daly and Zack White have all read sections of the text and provided me with much helpful advice and encouragement. Third of all, the staff of the Sydney Jones Library at the University of Liverpool and all the other institutions where I have worked have been as patient and professional as ever. And, fourth of all, my family has put up with yet another summer taken up by long hours at my desk: now that Boney has finally been defeated, I do pray that they will see some something more of me and hope that they know just how grateful I am to them.

Overleaf: The early stages of the attack of the Old and Middle Guard as it was actually delivered: note the very dispersed manner in which the troops concerned moved forward and contacted the Allied line. And note, too, how a concentrated approach via the low ground beside La Haye Sainte would have been protected by the high ground to its left and directed straight at the weak brigades of Kielmansegg, Vincke and Ompteda. Not shown on the map, but still present in considerable numbers were the remains of the French cavalry, a force still fearsome enough to have discouraged the much stronger forces of Adam and Maitland from wheeling left and taking the Guard in the flank.

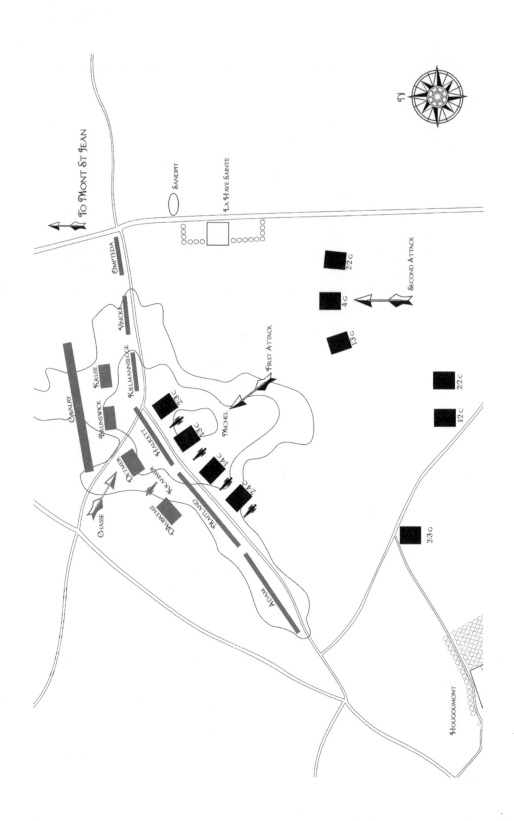

Chapter 1

Victory at Waterloo

Lying flat on the ground a few yards in the rear of the crest in a desperate attempt to shelter from the rounds of canister being discharged every few minutes by the French guns posted in the lee of the battered farm barely 200 yards away, not to mention the roundshot shrieking in from the enemy batteries out in the valley beyond, the weary redcoats raised their heads and looked at one another. Amidst the deafening cacophony of battle it was impossible to exchange a word even with a man's nearest neighbour, but the questioning looks on the men's faces told their own story. One and all, they had sensed it as much as heard it, a dull, reverberating rhythm that somehow penetrated the cannonade and caused the ground to tremble beneath their mud-smeared knees and elbows. A few more seconds ticked by, and now it was unmistakeable: the tramp of thousands of booted feet and the rolling of hundreds of drums. A-rum-dum! A-rum-dum! A-rummadum, rumma-dum, dum-dum! '"Old Trousers"', croaked a grizzled veteran. 'It's "Old Trousers."'[1] Instinctively, the men reached for their muskets and pulled them closer, checking that the edges of the flints that set off their charges were still sharp and scraping away the crusted powder from touch holes and priming pans. They would, they knew, need them very soon.[2]

Less than half a mile away the French infantry came inexorably onwards. In all, there were twelve battalions, seven of *chasseurs* and five of grenadiers, all of them crack troops who had seen much service in the campaigns of 1812–14 and some of them in the long war in Spain and Portugal as well, whilst initially they were headed by the emperor himself, the latter having left his command post near La Belle Alliance to spur them on. An eyewitness was an officer of Napoleon's personal staff named Octave Levavasseur, who had just arrived back at La Belle Alliance fresh from a mission on which he had been sent to spread the entirely false news that Grouchy had come:

> General Drouet rode up, shouting, 'Where is the Guard, where is the Guard?' I pointed them out to him: they were approaching to cries of 'Form square!' Just then, the emperor rode past me followed by his officers; he was on the other side of the road. Arriving before the Guard,

he said, 'Follow me!', and led them down that road swept by a hundred pieces of artillery. Immediately behind him came 150 bandsmen playing the triumphal marches heard on the [Place du] Carrousel. Very soon the road could not be seen for guardsmen marching in serried ranks in the wake of the emperor: the cannon balls and spherical case that raked it bestrewed it with dead and wounded. A few paces more and Napoleon would have been alone at their head.[3]

In terms of their uniforms, for the most part hastily assembled especially for the campaign from drafts contributed by other units, they were a motley crew – only a handful wore the famous bearskins of the Old Guard, the remainder sporting battered shakos or even forage caps – but, having thus far sat out the battle safely in the rear, they were the freshest troops on the field, while to the last man they were dedicated to the emperor. As they crossed the valley bottom, meanwhile, they had glimpsed cavalry forming up to support them, while to right and left the shattered remnants of infantry divisions that had been repulsed earlier in the day edged forward to flail the defenders with their musketry, if not actually to go in with the bayonet. And, finally, with them rumbled a battery of horse artillery. It was a wonderful moment, even the wounded strewn on the slopes of the French ridge and in the valley bottom dragging themselves to their knees to cheer and wave as they passed.[4] An eyewitness was Sergeant Hyppolyte Mauduit of the First Grenadiers of the Imperial Guard:

Formed in columns of attack by echelon with two guns loaded with canister positioned in the intervals between them, each one of them firmly supported by all the rest, these [twelve] battalions set out to attack the enemy. Headed by Comte Friant, the first battalion of the Third Grenadiers took as its alignment the left-hand verge of the main road, while the other units followed *au pas de charge* in the best of orders, taking care to maintain their proper distances … Meeting with Marshal Ney near the farm [of La Haye Sainte] the emperor gave him command of the column which already possessed such commanders as Lieutenant-Generals Friant, Roguet and Michel, Brigadiers Cambronne, Poret de Morvan and Harlet, and Colonel Michel … One and all, they marched to their deaths to repeated cries of 'Vive l'empereur!'[5]

Nor were the Guard on their own. Spurred on by Marshal Ney, who one French officer glimpsed galloping along the line shouting, 'Courage! The army is victorious: the enemy is beaten at every point!', not to mention the efforts of Octave Levavasseur, the weary men of the corps of Generals Reille and Drouet gathered themselves for one last effort, and pressed forward in the hope that they might at least tie down the defenders and prevent them from moving to the threatened sector.[6] Of particular interest here is the remark of Hyppolyte Mauduit: 'Comte Reille [*sic*] received orders to form all the men of his corps who were disposable in column to the right of the wood of Goumont [i.e. Hougoumont] without delay and to advance upon the enemy.'[7] At the same time officers stationed on the Anglo-Dutch left wing also report that the French also moved troops forward. As Kevan Leslie, in 1815 a lieutenant in the Seventy-Ninth Foot, wrote to William Siborne, 'At the period to which you allude, the enemy in front of us seemed [to be] moving forward a fresh column for a simultaneous attack to that on the right of our line. This was checked by the appearance of the Prussians breaking from the wood on the left of our position.'[8] Finally, John Kincaid of the First Battalion of the Ninety-Fifth reports that just at this point the French infantry who had been holding the knoll across the road from La Haye Sainte since just after the latter's capture made a charge that carried them to within twenty yards of the hedge behind which the riflemen were now sheltering and then engaged in a fierce fire-fight.[9]

Just shy of La Haye Sainte the column veered off the highroad and headed into the corpse strewn fields to the left. That said, they did not seek to ascend the broad watershed that ran from just above Hougoumont to La Belle Alliance and connected the features held by the two armies, but rather kept to the hollow occupied by the farm, thereby protecting themselves from the flanking fire that would otherwise have come their way from the troops holding the crest of the ridge above Hougoumont.[10] Shells and roundshot thinned their ranks, whilst Marshal Ney, who had ridden forward to take personal charge of the attack, had his fifth horse of the day killed under him, but still the infantry kept going, sensing, perhaps, that the rate of fire from the British guns was dropping away: despite Wellington's strictures against wasteful long-distance counter-battery fire, some batteries were running short of ammunition while others were being shot to pieces.[11] Amongst these last was the Royal Horse Artillery unit commanded by Captain Cavalié Mercer:

We suddenly became sensible of a most destructive flanking fire from a battery which had come, the Lord knows how, and established itself on a knoll somewhat higher than the ground we stood on, and only about 400 or 500 yards a little in advance of our left flank. The rapidity and precision of this fire were quite appalling. Every shot, almost, took effect, and I certainly expected we should all be annihilated. Our horses and limbers, being a little retired down the slope, had hitherto been somewhat under cover from the direct fire in front, but this plunged right amongst them, knocking them down by pairs and creating horrible confusion. Then drivers could hardly extricate themselves from one dead horse before another fell or perhaps themselves. The saddle-bags in many instances were torn from the horses' backs and their contents scattered over the field. One shell I saw explode under the two finest wheel horses in the troop: down they dropped ... The whole livelong day had cost us nothing like this. Our gunners too – the few left fit for duty of them – were so exhausted that they were unable to run the guns up after firing; consequently at every round they retreated closer to the limbers ... The fire continued on both sides, mine becoming slacker and slacker, for we ... were so reduced that all our strength was barely sufficient to load and fire three guns out of our six.[12]

The fact was that, even as it was, Wellington's army was already in severe trouble. Following the fall of La Haye Sainte at around six o'clock, the French had brought up a battery of artillery – the very guns, in fact, that did such damage to Mercer's battery – and positioned it in part in the garden of the farmhouse and in part on the knoll that projected from the hillside just across the road, while elements of the units that had stormed the farm crept forward and subjected the defenders to a heavy fire of musketry. Captain John Kincaid was with the first battalion of the Ninety-Fifth Regiment just a few yards away across the main road:

The loss of La Haye Sainte was of the most serious consequence as it afforded the enemy an establishment within our position. They immediately brought up two guns on our side of it and began serving out some grape to us, but they were so very near that we destroyed their artillerymen before they could give us a second round ... For the two or three succeeding hours, there was no variety with us but one continued blaze of musketry. The smoke hung so thick about that, although not more than eighty yards asunder, we could only distinguish each other by the flashes of the pieces. A good many of our guns had been disabled and a great number more rendered unserviceable in consequence of the unprecedented close fighting ... I felt weary and worn out, less from fatigue than anxiety. Our division, which had stood upwards of 5,000 strong at the commencement of the battle, had gradually dwindled down into a solitary line of skirmishers. The Twenty-Seventh Regiment were lying literally dead in square a few yards behind us ... I had never yet heard of a battle in which all were killed, but this seemed likely to be an exception as all were going by turns.[13]

Kincaid's fears, of course, were not fulfilled: even in the units that were hardest hit, plenty of men survived to claim the famous Waterloo medal. That said, the hour or so following the fall of La Haye Sainte was a grim time for the riflemen. The initial commander of the battalion, Colonel Andrew Barnard, was wounded by a sniper ensconced in the garden; his replacement, Major Alexander Cameron, soon after was taken to the rear following a severe wound to the neck; and Lieutenants Johnston and Simmons were both shot down as the battalion evacuated the sandpit that was its initial position, yet another officer who may have been hit at this time being Captain Edward Chawner.[14]

To return to the oncoming French, in front were four battalions of *chasseurs*, behind them three battalions of grenadiers, and finally, behind them again, a third echelon consisting of two battalions of grenadiers and three of *chasseurs*. Unusually, no chain of skirmishers marched ahead of the columns: instead, all was to be risked on one desperate burst of speed and energy designed to break through an enemy line that was clearly on its knees. Indeed, never had such a gambit been more necessary. For the past two hours more and more Prussians had been debouching onto the field and attempting to storm the village of Plancenoit deep in the French right rear. Thanks to a determined counter-attack by the infantry division constituted of the Young Guard, the Prussian commander, Von Bülow, had been temporarily fought to a standstill, Napoleon saw all too clearly that this was not a moment for finesse and had ordered Ney to press home his assault without delay. As Marshal Ney later remembered, 'Around [six] o'clock in the evening General Labédoyère came to me and told me on behalf of the emperor that Marshal Grouchy was arriving on our right and attacking the left wing of the united British and Prussian armies ... A little while afterwards I saw four regiments of the Middle Guard coming up in my direction headed by the emperor himself. The latter wanted me to renew the attack by forcing the enemy centre, and ordered me to place myself at their head alongside General Friant.'[15]

On the ridge above La Haye Sainte the few officers of the waiting troops who still possessed horses stared down from the ridgeline in consternation at the oncoming columns. Behind them, their men were still hugging the ground but a certain shuffling was evident in their ranks: clearly they were nervous and ill at ease. At a sign from the battalion commanders, the sergeants got the men on their feet and started putting them through the manual of arms in a desperate attempt to steady their nerves, but each movement saw more men fall to roundshot, shell or canister, and the gaps in the ranks were becoming ever harder to fill. Unfortunately the defenders were for the most part not seasoned redcoats of the sort that had repulsed the corps of General Drouet earlier in the day on the other side of battlefield in the famous action that culminated in the great charge of the Household and Union brigades. Beside the highroad and therefore directly above La Haye Sainte stood the sad remnant of the brigade of Christian von Ompteda: a King's German Legion formation, this was in itself a force of high quality, but over the course of the day it had been used most cruelly. Thus, of its four battalions, the Second Light had constituted the original garrison of La Haye Sainte and had within the past hour been finally been driven from its buildings in some disorder, having lost some 200 men, whilst the Fifth and Eighth Line had both been terribly cut up by French cavalry when the Prince of Orange had misguidedly ordered them to attempt to drive the French from their gains, this being an episode that had cost the life of Ompteda; other than a handful of men who had escaped the massacre at the hands of the enemy cavalry, all that was left, then, was the First Light, and even that had seen two of its companies suffer heavy losses when they were sent to the help of their fellow riflemen.[16]

If Ompteda's brigade was now little short of being a broken reed, the two other formations in the sector most threatened by the Guard had scarcely attained the status of a reed in the first place, both of them being made up of very raw troops with little experience or training. Thus, first came the Fifth Hanoverian Brigade under Colonel von Vincke, a fresh unit brought over in haste from the left flank, but this was composed entirely of militiamen or *landwehr* and had lost two of its four battalions when an order to withdraw to a position of greater safety a few hundred yards in rear of the ridge was, so it seems, deliberately misunderstood by their officers as a means of marching off the battlefield altogether.[17] And, finally, and a little further to the west came the First Hanoverian brigade of Count Friedrich von Kielmansegg, this consisting of three *landwehr* battalions, two light battalions and a rifle company. The record of this force was somewhat better in that they had stood their ground all day under heavy fire, but the result had been terrible casualties, not least when a lucky French roundshot had struck down an entire face of the square formed by the Bremen and Verden Battalions, while another battalion had been lost earlier in the day when it had been sent down into the valley to clear the west face of La Haye Sainte only to be destroyed by French cavalry. Something of the plight in which the brigade found itself is conveyed in the report submitted after the battle by its commander. Thus:

The enemy cavalry reformed again ... and sent a mass of skirmishers ahead to lure us into firing our weapons: they cost us some losses in our squares. The enemy then advanced two light artillery pieces to several hundred paces before the left square under the cover of infantry and cuirassiers. We had no means to defend ourselves against the murderous fire of case shot because our artillery had been out of ammunition for some time and was therefore sent to the rear ... At this time ... the lieutenant colonel commanding the [Bremen Field Battalion], the brigade major and many officers and men had been killed or wounded.[18]

Beside Kielmansegg's men came the only British troops in the area, namely the left wing of the brigade commanded by Sir Colin Halkett. Yet this was yet another force that was in a bad way. Caught in line by French cavalry at Quatre Bras, it had suffered such terrible losses that its four battalions had been combined into two composite units. Closest to the French attack was the ad hoc formation composed by the Thirtieth and Seventy-Third Regiments of Foot, and, like the battalions around it, this had been severely pounded by the French artillery. Thomas Morris was a private in the ranks of the Seventy-Third:

On their next advance they brought some artillerymen ... and fired into us with grapeshot, which proved very destructive, making complete lanes through us ... On looking around I saw my left-hand man falling backwards, the blood gushing from his eye; my poor comrade on the right, by the same discharge, got a ball through his right thigh of which he died a few days afterwards. Our situation now was truly awful: our men were falling by dozens with every fire. About this time a large shell fell just in front of us, and while the fuse was burning out we wondered how many of us it would destroy. When it burst ... seventeen men were killed or wounded by it: the portion which came to my share was a piece of rough cast-iron about the size of a horse-bean which took up its lodging in my left cheek; the blood ran down copiously inside my clothes and made me rather uncomfortable.[19]

Nor were things any better with the Thirtieth. As an officer called Tincombe recalled, 'At length, the French brought artillery within range of us and poured grape, canister and everything they could think of into our square and nearly cut us to pieces.'[20] Amongst the dead were Ensign Henry Beere and Captain Thomas Chambers, a diminutive man shot dead by a French sniper only moments after observing that, as the smallest man in the regiment, he was entirely safe. Such were the losses, indeed, that fears began to grow that the battalion would simply disintegrate, the commander of the Thirtieth therefore resolving to send its two colours to the rear.[21]

The men facing the French assault, then, were already in a bad way, and they now visibly quailed before the sight bearing down upon them, and all the more so as the commander of the division to which Halkett, Kielmansegg and Ompteda all belonged, Karl von Alten, was badly wounded. Having cleared the constriction represented by the La Haye Sainte and its attendant garden and orchard, the leading French troops shook out their formation a little, the two battalions in the centre deploying into line so that they could if necessary make use of musketry to clear the way, but the formation showed no signs of halting and pressed on up the slope. This was too much. In brief, Kielmansegg's men broke and fled, as did the survivors of Ompteda's brigade – according to some accounts, indeed, this had already disintegrated[22] – while Vincke's two battalions did not last much longer, though at least their discipline held to an extent sufficient for the retreat to be made in good order, while two companies even sacrificed their lives in a heroic counter-attack.[23] As for Morris and his fellow redcoats, at first they did very well, checking and even driving back the battalion initially opposed to them, but they found themselves under heavy artillery fire from close range and were ordered to return to the sunken road to take shelter. An eyewitness was Ensign Edward Macready of the light company:

> Late in the day the French brought up two guns on the crest of our position which fired grape into our square … with very deadly effect. Someone in authority must have thought that the bank of a hedge which ran a very short distance in our rear would afford us some cover, and in an evil moment we received the command to face about and march down to it. You may readily conceive that the fire would not slacken on a body effecting such a movement, but, though suffering sadly and disordered by our poor wounded fellows clinging to their comrades thinking they were being abandoned, our little square retained its formation.[24]

As Macready suggested in a separate account, all was carnage and confusion: 'Prendergast … was shattered to pieces by a shell [and] McNab killed by grapeshot, and James and Bullen lost all their legs by roundshot … As I recovered my feet from a tumble, a friend knocked up against me, seized me by the stock, and almost choked me, screaming (half maddened by his five wounds and the sad scene going on), "Is it deep, Mac, is it deep?"'[25] All might yet have been well, but then disaster struck. To quote Macready again:

We had all but reached the hedge, when a body of men (British) rushed in upon us, turned us altogether into a mere mob, and created a scene of frightful confusion. Nothing could be more gratifying than the conduct of our people at this disastrous period. While men and officers were jammed together and carried along by the pressure from without, many of the latter, some cursing, others literally crying with rage and shame, were seizing the soldiers and calling on them to halt, while these admirable fellows, good-humouredly laughing at their excitement, were struggling to get out of the mêlée, or exclaiming, 'By God, I'll stop, Sir, but I'm off my legs.'[26]

Reaching an irregularity of ground which gave them gave them some protection, the survivors were rallied by a captain named Garland who made a gallant attempt to organize a counter-attack at the head of the light company, only for the men concerned to be shot to pieces in an instant. Wrote Thomas Morris, 'About a dozen of us responded to the call, and such was the destructive fire to which we were opposed, that it was not long before every one of our party, except me and my brother, was either killed or wounded.'[27]

Within minutes, then, a massive hole had been torn in Wellington's centre. The nearest troops available to plug the gap were a single regiment of green-coated German troops from the principality of Nassau under a Colonel August von Kruse.[28] Unlike the wretched Hanoverian militiamen, most of whom were undergoing their baptism of fire, at least some members of this unit – the First Infantry Regiment – were veterans of the Peninsular War, and had already proved their worth earlier in the day: several companies, for example, had taken part in the defence of Hougoumont. Since then, however, they had come under the same heavy fire as the rest of Wellington's centre, and begun to buckle under the strain: desperate to reduce his losses, Kruse ordered his men to strip the linen covers from their shakos in the hope that this would render the regiment a less conspicuous target.[29] At the same time, the men who had fought in Spain and Portugal had been padded out with new recruits who were no more steady than their Hanoverian fellows. As Baron Constant de Rebecque, who was serving as chief-of-staff to the commander of I Corps, the Prince of Orange, afterwards complained: 'I was regularly required to go ... to rally the three squares of the Nassau contingent, which were composed of young soldiers under fire for the first time and often retired: I brought them back several times. At one point one of these battalions was put into complete disorder when a shell exploded amidst their ranks. I rode ahead of them and fortunately managed to bring them back.'[30] In the circumstances, it was a wonder that anything was got out of them at all, but the prince, still only eighteen and otherwise known as 'Slender

Billy', was well liked by his men and was able to inspire them sufficiently to get them to advance upon the enemy. Just at the crucial moment, however, their commander was hit by enemy fire. To quote the same observer, 'In that instant … the Prince of Orange's horse was wounded and he was struck by a piece of grapeshot which pierced his left shoulder and threw him to the ground … Several *aides de camp* arrived and led him from the field of battle and carried him in a blanket to Waterloo.'[31] The story of what happened next is recounted in the report submitted after the action by Von Kruse:

> Napoleon's Guard reached the plateau with our infantry withdrawing only 100 paces. A violent fire fight broke out, and showing as much courage as foresight, the Crown Prince … attempted to put an end to it with a bayonet charge. For this honour he thought of the Nassauers. Thus, he brought up the second battalion and led it in column. The remainder of the first battalion joined up with them and the attack was carried out with great bravery. I saw one side of a square of the French Guard start to waver when, perhaps because the Prince of Orange was wounded, a wave of panic hit the young soldiers, and at the moment of their greatest victory, the battalion fell into confusion and retreated. The remaining battalions in the first line soon followed, leaving only small bodies of brave men on the plateau. I had the *landwehr* battalion and the remainder of the second battalion join them, but in such a way that the enemy fire could have little effect on them.[32]

The situation for the Anglo-Dutch army was now bleak in the extreme. On the other side of the crossroads, the nearest troops available were in no state to mount a counter-attack: the first battalion of the Ninety-Fifth, now under the command of a mere captain, was under severe pressure from the French troops who had seized the knoll where they had originally been stationed, while, famously, the Twenty-Seventh Foot had been standing in square under such heavy fire that they had lost over two-thirds of their strength.[33] As for the other shoulder of the breakthrough, the troops here consisted of the second of the two composite battalions which Halkett had headed at the start of the day, and this was if anything in an even worse state than its fellow, one of its two constituent units (the Sixty-Ninth Foot), having suffered the indignity of losing a colour at Quatre Bras and the other (the Thirty-Third Foot), being commanded by Lieutenant-Colonel William Elphinstone, a dithering incompetent who had risen through the ranks entirely by purchase and went on to lose an entire British army in the First Afghan War of 1839–42. When Halkett ordered his men to advance by wheeling to the left to take the Guard in flank, then, the result was not impressive. Initially, some success was achieved: there are even reports of French troops in the path of Halkett's men running away, though it is probable that these were not soldiers of the Imperial Guard but rather some of the French skirmishers who had spread out from La Haye Sainte in the wake of its capture. However, the composite battalion was caught by a terrible discharge of canister and brought to a halt, while Halkett was brought down by a musket ball that struck him in the mouth. Losing his nerve, Elphinstone immediately ordered a withdrawal to the shelter of the sunken lane, and this produced a panic which led to the entire battalion rushing in upon Macready and Morris and their fellows in the manner we have described and completely disrupted their efforts to regain their order.[34]

Thus far, Wellington had fought his battle extremely well, having almost always contrived to be at the proverbial right place at the right time, but, perhaps misled by a French deserter who had galloped up to a unit stationed on his centre right shouting that the Imperial Guard was about to attack, he was currently several hundred yards away with the Guards brigade of Sir Peregrine Maitland.[35] So thick was the smoke that at first he does not seems to have realized what was happening. Finally advised of the crisis by a staff officer named James Shaw-Kennedy who had witnessed the French breakthrough, he ordered the five battalions of Brunswick troops present on the field to plug the gap and sent other officers to find out the exact situation. Though stiffened by a cadre of Peninsula veterans, most of the Brunswickers, too, were very raw, whilst they had also suffered many hundreds of casualties at Quatre Bras. Indeed, so unsteady had they appeared during the French cavalry charges that, finding himself in their vicinity, Alexander Mercer had elected to fight his guns to the end rather than letting his men take shelter in the squares behind them, for fear that the sight of the crews sprinting for safety would cause panic in their ranks. His words, indeed, are worth quoting:

The Brunswickers were falling fast, the shot every moment making great gaps in their squares, which the officers and sergeants were actively employed in filling up by pushing their men together, and sometimes thumping them ere they could make them move. These were the very boys I had but yesterday seen throwing away their arms and fleeing, panic-stricken, from the very sound of our horses feet. Today they fled, not bodily to be sure, but spiritually, for their senses seemed to have left them. There they stood ... like so many logs ... Every moment I feared they would again throw down their arms and flee.[36]

Like all the other defenders, then, the Brunswickers did not prove equal to the crisis, and that despite the fact that Wellington himself had ridden forward to lead them into battle. As William Siborne later wrote, albeit in a tone that was clearly designed to cause as little embarrassment as possible:

> The reinforcement which Wellington had provided for this part of the line, consisting of five battalions of Brunswick infantry, moved rapidly into the interval between Kruse's Nassau and Halkett's British brigades. But so unexpectedly did the Brunswickers find themselves placed under a most destructive fire, and so suddenly were the columns assailed, that they were unable, in the midst of the thick smoke in which they became involved, from the partial irregularities, by which, under such circumstances, their advance was accompanied, to form up in sufficient order before they came in close contact with the enemy, whose vigorous attack compelled them ... to fall back about 100 paces.[37]

What this account does not make clear is that the Brunswickers' flight was only checked by the efforts of the thin line of British light cavalry that formed Wellington's last line of defence, the latter literally damming the torrent of fugitives with horseflesh. The potential role of the British cavalry at this point is worth considering. Earlier in the day the attack of Drouet's corps had been smashed at what appeared to be the moment of victory by the famous charge of the Household and Union Brigades. However, allowed to gallop out of control deep into the enemy positions, the troops concerned had suffered such terrible casualties that they were in effect out of action for the rest of the battle. As for the rest of Allied cavalry, this had not distinguished itself. Beginning with the Germans and Dutch-Belgians, many units had either refused to charge at one moment or another, fallen into complete disorder or decamped from the field altogether. That this was so is evident even from accounts emanating from the regiments concerned. Willem van Heerdt, for example, was a staff officer attached to the General Charles de Ghigny's Second Netherlands Cavalry Brigade, whilst his account comes from some point late in the afternoon:

> As the brigade had suffered severely from the heavy cannonade and was threatened by a superior cavalry, it was ordered to take a position further to the rear, which was complied with accordingly in the most gallant manner, yet the moment it retook its positions in front of the enemy, the second line got into disorder and left the field. The general instructed Colonel Duvivier, who was present with some men of his regiment, to do his

utmost to find and collect his men. Of the Eighth Hussars, Captain Ducha was killed [while] those who were wounded included Major de Villiers, Second Lieutenants Gérard, De Bailler and De Villers, plus numerous men and horses.[38]

If this was to be expected – the Dutch-Belgian cavalry at Quatre Bras had taken a heavy beating at the hands of their opponents and therefore had little confidence in themselves – even some of their British comrades had proved extremely unsteady. To such an extent was this the case, indeed, that after the battle it was a matter of common gossip, this being particularly clear from the journals and correspondence of James Stanhope. Thus, a lieutenant-colonel in the First Guards, in a letter to Lady Stanhope he complains that 'our light cavalry made no head' against the 'most immense body of cavalry' which assailed Wellington's centre-right in the course of the afternoon and, in general, showed 'a lamentable inferiority', whilst elsewhere we learn that the light cavalry 'did very little', 'behaved infamously', and even 'might as well have been in England', and that at one point he saw 'Lord Uxbridge riding about in the most gallant manner, heading everything but lamenting that the cavalry had all deserted him'.[39] In his account of the battle Sir Walter Scott suggested a possible reason for this – in brief, he suggests that the problem was that, being almost entirely composed of light cavalry armed only with sabres, the British horsemen found themselves overmatched by the French cuirassiers and lancers[40] – but on the desperate afternoon of 18 June 1815 such questions counted for little. As one infantryman in a beleaguered square was heard to shout, 'Where are the cavalry?'[41]

The disorder, then, was spreading by the moment. Further along the ridge towards Hougoumont the brigades of Maitland and Adam were still relatively intact, but they dared not abandon their positions for fear that a fresh wave of French cavalry would burst out of the smoke and take them in flank as they marched on the crossroads (that this was a real danger, there can be no doubt: despite the terrible casualties suffered by the enemy horsemen in the long series of attacks they had launched in the course of the afternoon, to the very end the survivors continued to make themselves felt; more than that, indeed, in retrospect it is clear that, even if the French did not break through, they did succeed in tying down a large part of Wellington's best troops and confining them to formations that rendered manoeuvre impossible). As the staff officer who had ridden to warn Wellington of the crisis later wrote, then, the situation was becoming increasingly desperate:

La Haye Sainte was in the hands of the enemy, also the knoll on the opposite side of the road, also the garden and the ground on the Anglo-Allied side of it … Ompteda's brigade was nearly annihilated and Kielmansegg's so thinned that [it] could not hold [its] position. That part of the field of battle, therefore, which was between Halkett's left and Kempt's right was unprotected, and, being the very centre of the Duke's line of battle, was consequently that point, above all others, which the enemy wished to gain. The danger was imminent.[42]

However, the Anglo-Dutch were not quite finished. In brief, one last force of infantry remained to Wellington in the form of the Dutch-Belgian division commanded by David Chassé, a hard-bitten veteran who had served for many years in the French army prior to 1814. Originally stationed on the extreme right of the defending line near the village of Braine l'Alleud, these troops – formally speaking, the Third Netherland Division – had a little while before been brought over to support the tottering Allied centre, and, without waiting for orders from Wellington, Chassé now launched his men at the triumphant Guard in a desperate counter-attack that was spearheaded by the Belgian artillery battery of Captain Krahmer and the Dutch infantry brigade of General Detmers. As he later wrote:

When I saw that an English artillery battery positioned on the left … of my division had stopped firing, I went … to enquire the reason and learned that there was no ammunition. At the same time I saw the Garde Imperiale advancing, while the English troops were leaving the plateau en masse and moving in the direction of Waterloo. I immediately ordered the battery of horse artillery under the command of Major van der Smissen [sic] to advance, to occupy the height and to direct an emphatic fire upon the enemy column. At this time I also ordered Major-General d'Aubremé to have the brigade he commanded form two squares in echelon and to form a reserve with the foot artillery. I [then] positioned myself at the head of the First Brigade and advanced in close columns at attack pace against the French.[43]

An eyewitness to the scene was Ensign Macready of the Thirtieth Foot. As he wrote, 'A heavy column of Dutch infantry … passed, drumming and shouting like mad with their shakos on the top of their bayonets.'[44] Amongst the soldiers charging the enemy, meanwhile, was Chassé's chief-of-staff, Leonhard van Delen: 'After having made a short but very zealous and appropriate speech, [His

Excellency] ... assembled all the battalions of the First Brigade and advanced towards the enemy, while the drums beat the attack ... [To the accompaniment] of shouts of "Long live the King!", the ... brigade moved forward against the heavy enemy musket fire, and ignored the fact that it was now threatened by a cavalry charge.'[45] As a private in the Fourth Militia named Adriaan Munter wrote in a letter to his family dated 22 July 1815, 'We fought like lions. The general shouted, "Keep courage children!", and this gave us new courage so as to continue.'[46] It was a brave effort, but it was not enough. Three of Detmer's five battalions were raw militia, and, inevitably, they quailed in the face of the disciplined volleys to which the troops they were attacking subjected them. Amongst the casualties was yet another senior officer, this time the Prince of Orange's chief of staff, Constant de Rebecque: 'At this very moment a cannon ball ricocheted off the ground and hit my horse in the girths, covering me with mud and stones, and I received part of the blow on the fleshy part of my left leg. The very next instant ... a grapeshot hit the steel scabbard of my sabre and forced it against my leg so that it was folded in half so that I could only sheath half the weapon.'[47] Even then all might not have been lost – Chassé had only committed half his force, and might yet have at least checked the French – but just at the moment the fortunes of war finally turned against the Allies. Determined to do everything he could to save the day, accompanied by the commander of his cavalry and, indeed, second-in-command, Lord Uxbridge, Wellington had joined the Dutch general, and was just in the process of ordering Uxbridge to send in the relatively fresh light cavalry brigades of Vivian and Vandeleur, when he suddenly stopped in mid-sentence and turned very white. The exchange that followed has gone down in history as a classic example of British understatement. Thus, Wellington: 'By God, sir, I have lost my leg'; Uxbridge, 'By God, sir, so you have.'[48]

Swaying in the saddle, Wellington was escorted from the field to have his leg amputated by a hard-pressed surgeon in a cottage at Waterloo, from where he was evacuated to Antwerp and finally a Britain that turned its collective back upon him and left him to live out the many years that were left to him in an increasingly embittered retirement on his family estate in Ireland. Behind him, meanwhile, he left a scene of chaos. Hearing that the Duke was down, Detmer's brigade were gripped by panic, and, as one man, turned and fled. Present in the front ranks of the Imperial Guard was an anonymous sergeant who evidently wrote the letter to an old friend that follows at a time when he was still unaware of the drama that had occurred a few score yards away:

They came within 100 yards of us and ported arms to charge, but we advanced upon them in quick time and opened a brisk file fire by [three] ranks. They allowed us to come within thirty yards of them: they stood till then looking at us as if panic-struck and did not fire. They then, as we approached, faced about and fled for their lives in all directions ... They ran very fast, but many of them fell while we pursued, and with them one stand of colours.[49]

As for Uxbridge, though utterly unprepared for the task which he now faced – prior to the battle, Wellington had rebuffed his every attempt to discuss his plans – saw clearly enough that the day had been lost. The headquarters was a shambles – almost all of the Duke's personal staff had fallen – many divisional and brigade commanders had been killed and wounded, there were no reserves of infantry left in a fit state to fight, much of the army's artillery had been silenced, ammunition was running short, and the last news he had had of the Prussians was that, while unknown numbers had penetrated Napoleon's right rear, there was still no sign of the troops who had been supposed to link up with Wellington's left wing. It was a grim situation, by far the worst, indeed, that any British general had faced since the battle of Saratoga in 1777. Uxbridge bowed his head and sighed wearily – it would be the end of his career, for sure[50] – but there was nothing for it: summoning up several *aides-de-camp*, he gave orders for all units to fall back and rally on the edge of the forest of Soignies beyond Waterloo; at least, he thought, there should not be much in the way of a pursuit, the vast bulk of the French cavalry having been used up in the fighting of the afternoon.[51]

Fantasy? Well, of course, but nonetheless fantasy that is by no means implausible. The battle of Waterloo, as the Duke of Wellington famously observed, was 'a near-run thing'. Contained in this observation is a simple truth that might easily be overlooked, namely the fact that the French could easily have won. Had matters been handled differently, there was a very real possibility that Wellington's 'infamous army', as he called it, could have been driven from the field before the Prussians arrived: speaking in part for effect though he certainly was, Napoleon's famous pronouncement to his staff over breakfast at Le Caillou on the morning of 18 June to the effect that the French had ninety chances in their favour as opposed to only ten against does have a certain ring of truth to it.[52] Famously enough, of course, to the end of his days the beaten emperor was insistent that he actually did triumph over Wellington at Mont Saint Jean. To quote the recollections of the surgeon who attended to him on Saint Helena, Barry O'Meara, of a conversation he had with the exiled emperor one evening, 'I ... took the liberty of asking whether, if neither Grouchy nor the Prussians had arrived, it would have been a drawn battle. Napoleon answered, "The English army would have been destroyed. They were [already] defeated at midday."'[53] Meanwhile, many of the men who fought under him were still more explicit in their analysis. Here, for example, is Captain Paul Lemmonier-Delafosse's summary of the events of 18 June: 'It was an extraordinary battle, the only one in which we have an instance of the two opponents both being beaten, the English first and then the French! A battle that the Prussians won themselves by arriving on the field of struggle fresh and ready to fight at a moment when the French oppressed by fatigue, by twelve hours of combat.'[54]

It has to be said, of course, first, that what has been described here is essentially a tactical victory, and, second, that to believe that anything more could have been achieved is simply deluded. We have left Wellington's army in disarray, certainly, but also with a safe line of retreat into and through the forest of Soignies, and, what is more, an opponent that had suffered heavy casualties, was devoid of the means of launching an effective pursuit, and, finally, had become increasingly embroiled with the oncoming Prussians. One scenario, then, is that the Army of the Netherlands could have rallied during the night. Providing the Prussians had not themselves pulled back, the combat could then have been resumed the next day with the assistance of the 17,000 men whom Wellington had left to protect the main Paris-Brussels highway at Hal, this being a scenario that might even have plucked victory from the jaws of defeat.[55]

Much more likely, of course, would have been a Prussian retreat: several of the Prussian generals, including, not least, Blücher's chief of staff, August von Gneisenau, had never been entirely comfortable with the decision to stay in touch with Wellington, and it is impossible not to suspect that their opinion would have prevailed. Yet, even had the Prussians fallen back in the direction of the Rhine, this would not necessarily have been a prelude to a great French victory. Once again, we return to the devastation that Ney's foolhardy behaviour had unleashed on the French cavalry: to reiterate, no effective pursuit was possible in so far as Napoleon's wing of the Army of the North was concerned. In the first place, then, Uxbridge would almost certainly have been able to get clear with his army in one piece: Brussels would have had to be abandoned, certainly, but beyond the Belgian capital lay the massive fortress of Antwerp, and with it a sure refuge in which the Anglo–Dutch forces would have been completely safe. Indeed, the idea that Wellington might evade him and take refuge in Antwerp was a thought that had caused the emperor much concern the night before the battle. 'Our first surprise as the day broke', wrote one French soldier, 'was that the English had not only ... resumed their position, but seemed ... resolved to defend it. Bonaparte, who had no apprehension during the night but that they would escape the punishment he had designed for them, was animated by a most sensible joy at seeing them at their post: he was too fond of the game of war, and thought that he played it too well, to have any pleasure in a game only abandoned to him. He could not restrain the expression of his feeling to those who were around him. "Bravo!", said he. "The English! Ah, je les tiens donc!"[56] To return to the situation in the wake of the battle, the Anglo–Dutch could almost certainly have got away, whilst the same applies to the Prussians. Having gained a partial victory in the fierce fighting that had broke out far too late around Wavre, Grouchy had secured a bridgehead across the River Dyle at Limale and was therefore threatening Blücher's line of retreat, but, with his rear protected by the same belt of hills and woods he had traversed the day before and his forces as yet but little damaged, the Prussian commander could probably have fallen upon him and driven him back across the river before heading for the safety of the Rhine. The potential for a serious disaster existed, then, but assured it most certainly was not.

This long preliminary essay, of course, covers only the battle of Waterloo itself, and then only in the context of the situation as it stood on the morning of 18 June. Broaden the analysis out so as to cover the campaign of 15–18 June as a whole, and the possibilities of Allied failure become greater still. As we shall see, on at least three occasions decisions could have been taken that would have at the very least materially altered the course of events in Napoleon's favour. In the words of one anonymous French soldier:

> The most unlimited confidence in the talent and fortunes of the emperor, the annihilation or embarkation of the English, our arrival at the Rhine amidst the acclamations of the Belgians, the treasures of kingdoms poured into our military chests, and nations rising in mass to recruit and assist us, all these were the dreams of the night of the 15th [of June]. It seemed as if one kind of temper possessed everyone and that the madness of the emperor had passed in contagion through every individual of the army. Upon this very verge of most extraordinary events, it is impossible not to reflect how very near all these extravagant hopes were to [being] realized, how very little was wanting that the Emperor Napoleon had obtained as usual a victory as he sustained a defeat.[57]

Meanwhile, what nobody can deny is that the emperor's plan of campaign was both exactly what was needed given the military situation that he faced and meticulously prepared. To quote David Chandler, indeed, 'The original strategical conception was as brilliant as anything Napoleon ever devised.'[58]

Before moving on to the campaign, however, let us think a little more about the battle. Laid out in this chapter is only one of the many ways in which the struggle could have ended in a French victory. First, and most obvious, there is the question of the time at which the battle started. In reality, this was about half an hour before midday, but supposing it had instead, done so at, say, nine o'clock? Even if the battle had played out exactly as it did in reality, the result could have been very nasty indeed, as the final crisis of the battle would have come well before the Prussian intervention in the fighting had reached such an extent that Napoleon was forced to reinforce Mouton's VI Corps with the whole of the Young Guard. On such small issues do great things turn. As Chandler has pointed out, in fact, the decision to postpone the assault (or perhaps, more accurately, the failure of so many troops to reach the battlefield in good time), 'proved the most fatal one of the day for the French, for even had an inadequately supported infantry attack been launched against Wellington during the morning, the French must surely have won, for Blücher would have been too late arriving on the field to affect the issue'.[59] Nor, of course, was an early French attack the only means of securing victory. Just as perturbing for Wellington was the question of what would have occurred had the Prussians taken any longer to get into action than was actually the case (something that was all too possible: the commander of the first corps to reach the field, Bülow, was a rather cautious character who showed much reluctance to commit his forces to the fighting before every last man had come up, and eventually had to be chivvied into action by a curt message from an irate Blücher)?[60] As for the idea of the Prussians not arriving at all, thanks, presumably, to a more effective performance on the part of Marshal Grouchy, from the Allied point of view it does not bear thinking about: not for nothing, then, has that commander ever since been heaped with opprobrium by all those who have bought into the Napoleonic legend.[61]

To reiterate, then, the battle of Waterloo could easily have been won by the French, but it has to be said that, as witness our earlier discussion, this does not mean to say that Napoleon's triumph would have been anything like as sweeping as the sort he would have needed to have even the remotest chance of putting an end to the war, if, that is, such a chance ever existed. For such a victory, we have to look not to 18 June, but rather the three days of marching and fighting which went before. The story of these events is well enough known, but, in brief, on 15 June the 125,000-strong Army of the North struck across the River Sambre into Belgium. Quickly capturing Charleroi, the troops pushed north along the main road to Brussels, thereby threatening to drive a wedge between Wellington's Army of the Netherlands and Blücher's Army of the Lower Rhine, the one a mixture of British, Dutch-Belgian and German troops, and the other solidly Prussian, even if many units hailed from other areas of Germany such as the Rhineland, for example. This was, of course, precisely the effect Napoleon wanted to achieve, for, having driven the two armies facing him apart, he could then have turned upon them one after another from the safety of the so-called 'central position' and defeated them in detail. It was a classic Napoleonic formulation. 'The Army of the North', writes David Chandler, 'was to move in three parts – two wings and a reserve. The traditional central position would then enable the French ... to pin or mask each Allied army and destroy them one by one. Each wing would engage the attention of the enemy in its vicinity while the emperor manoeuvred the reserve and any other disengaged troops to fall on each foe in turn.'[62]

Faced by this threat, once they had finally grasped the emperor's intentions, Wellington and Blücher made haste to concentrate their forces, which for reasons of supply had been scattered over many miles of country. There quickly followed, then, the double battles of Ligny and Quatre Bras, these two actions marking a day of missed opportunities for the French. Let us begin at Quatre Bras, a strategic crossroads which was the key to maintaining contact with Blücher, who had decided to make a stand some miles to the south–east in a strong position at Ligny. In the former sector the commander of the French left wing, Marshal Ney, had a substantial force at his disposal in the form of two corps of infantry and one corps of cavalry. A vigorous attack on his part early in the day could at the very least have inflicted serious damage on Wellington's forces, the vast majority of which were still trudging towards the crossroads: indeed, until well into the afternoon the only Allied troops in the vicinity were a handful of Dutch and German units. Yet no such attack was forthcoming, the reason for this being that for a long time Napoleon had no idea that Wellington was heading for Quatre Bras, and therefore failed to issue Ney with orders to advance until quite late in the morning, matters then being further delayed by the fact that many of his troops were still strung out along the road to the frontier.[63] Not until some time around two o'clock in the afternoon, by which time the first of Wellington's British troops were arriving on the battlefield, did the attack go in, and then it was eventually forced back to its starting point. Winning a decisive victory would never have been a possibility for Ney with the troops that he actually had available to him, but even so he might easily have been able to achieve a result that would have seriously undermined his opponent's ability to stand firm two days later. In the circumstances, then, the complaint voiced by Ney to Napoleon in the wake of the battle does not seem unfair. Thus: 'I have attacked the English position at Quatre Bras with the greatest vigour, but an error of Count d'Erlon's deprived me of a fine victory.'[64]

A few miles away at Ligny, the situation was rather similar. Contrary to the claims of tendentious authors with an axe to grind that the Prussians were tricked into facing the French there by a Wellington desperate to rescue his army from the difficulties into which it had been placed by his failure to anticipate Napoleon's plans, Blücher had long since been planning to fight the French at Ligny should they attack in the Charleroi sector, and had concentrated three of his four corps there within twenty-four hours of the Army of the North crossing the frontier. However, though Napoleon appears to have believed that Blücher, a notoriously wilful and headstrong commander, was at least capable of concentrating his troops in a dangerously advanced position, it was not for some time that he discovered that he had the bulk of the Army of the Lower Rhine in his grasp. Here too, then, the French attack was delayed until the early afternoon of 16 June, the result being that an even greater opportunity was squandered than the one that was lost at Quatre Bras. In the words of a modern British study of the battle:

> The battle of Ligny is one of the great might-have-beens of history ... If [Drouet's] corps had come up along the Nivelles–Namur road, then a large portion of the Prussian I and II Corps would have been outflanked by [Drouet], cut off from the Prussian III Corps by the Imperial Guard's storming of the village of Ligny and eventually annihilated or forced into surrender. The rest of the Prussian army would have speedily retired from Belgium, leaving the Duke of Wellington facing the full weight of Napoleon's entire army.[65]

What made 16 June still more unfortunate for the French was that either Quatre Bras or Ligny could still have been turned into a smashing victory notwithstanding the delay in taking the war to the enemy. We come here to the strange case of the corps of General Drouet. Consisting of some 20,000 troops, this had originally been assigned to Marshal Ney. However, after having made an extremely tardy start, as it marched northwards along the axis of the Charleroi-Brussels highway, it was suddenly directed to wheel to the right without delay and join the French forces attacking the Prussians at Ligny. Making reasonably quick progress, within less than two hours Drouet's men had just reached the outskirts of the battlefield, when, just as suddenly as before, they received a summons to return from a Marshal Ney outraged that they had been taken from his command, or so he believed, without the proper protocols having been followed (Ney being the commander of the wing of the Army of the North to which I Corps belonged, any orders to Drouet should have been transmitted via his headquarters, but, the fortunes of war having placed what he believed to be Napoleon's instructions in Drouet's hands before they reached the marshal, he elected to act upon them straightaway, whilst covering his back by sending his chief of staff to inform Ney of what he had done). Having performed a hasty 'about face', the corps was soon heading back to Quatre Bras, only to discover that, by the time it finally arrived within striking distance of Wellington's forces, the guns had fallen silent, the result being that it did not fire a shot in either action.[66] What makes all this all the more odd, meanwhile, is Napoleon's own behaviour. In brief, if he felt he needed more troops, why did he not send to Charleroi and call up the corps of General Mouton, the latter having been left entirely without orders? There is here but one conclusion. To quote the widely respected nineteenth-century commentator, Charles Chesney, 'Viewed in any light, the Napoleon who left Lobau [i.e. Mouton, who had been ennobled as the Comte de Lobau] to choose which wing of the army he would join was not the Napoleon of Rivoli, of Wagram or even of Lutzen.'[67]

The net result of the fighting of 16 June, then, was that the Allied cause had had a narrow escape. This good fortune, moreover, was extended into the hours of night in that the Prussian high command took the crucial decision to retreat not north-eastwards toward the river Rhine, but rather north towards Brussels, this event being yet another of the many 'might-have-beens' of the campaign of Waterloo. If Napoleon was unlucky in this respect, it has to be said that he then compounded his own misfortunes by failing to use his cavalry to discover the direction of the Prussian retreat, and assuming that Wellington must have pulled out in the night and headed north for Brussels or even Antwerp. In doing so, however, he lost yet another opportunity to win a great success. Thus, over at Quatre Bras Wellington had not the slightest idea of what had happened at Ligny, and had therefore allowed his exhausted troops to bivouac on the battlefield, whilst even counting the many reinforcements that had come up during the night, he still had only 45,000 men with him, the rest of his troops still being on the march from their cantonments. Vigorous action on the part of Napoleon might well have caught the Anglo-Dutch army at a terrible disadvantage, then – it was not till eight o'clock in the morning that news finally reached Quatre Bras of the Prussian retreat – but, by the time the emperor heard that he was in the vicinity, Wellington had long since pulled out. Once again, the British commander had had a narrow escape, an escape, moreover, that was, as before, wholly the fault of the emperor. As even the admiring Vincent Cronin was forced to admit, 'On the morning of the 17th Napoleon had a unique opportunity to crush Wellington ... while the Prussians were in full retreat. Instead of seizing it, he wasted the morning visiting the wounded ... That morning Napoleon behaved not as a great general, but as a retired soldier who has just been recalled to the colours and is still adjusting to war. In so doing he "lost the favourable moment which ... decides everything".'[68]

Nor was this the inaction in respect of Wellington the only problem: Marshal Grouchy was sent to pursue the retreating Prussians, certainly, but this was done only after a considerable delay, whilst still more time was wasted by initially sending him in what proved to be completely the wrong direction. 'It is not true to say that with only a partial victory over the Prussians at Ligny', writes Andrew Field. 'A more effective pursuit of the Prussians that denied them the ability to intervene at Waterloo might well have given Napoleon the opportunity to have turned that battle into a victory.'[69] It was all of a piece with Napoleon's behaviour throughout the campaign. In the words of Gareth Glover, 'Napoleon was not so ill that it was preventing him from thinking straight; he was merely so complacent ... that he assumed the outcome was a foregone conclusion. His error lay in underestimating the drive and determination of his adversaries and discounting their abilities.'[70]

And so, at last we come to the morning of 18 June and, with it, the battle of Waterloo. Napoleon was not yet beaten, was still dangerous even, but his chances of winning had been much reduced by the mistakes and misfortunes of the previous two days. It is, indeed, the view of at least some commentators that, with the situation as it actually was, the odds were stacked against the emperor. As Andrew Uffindell has written, for example, 'The actual battle of Waterloo was far less of a near-run thing than the campaign as a whole. By ... 11.30 a.m. on 18 June, Napoleon's chances were unhealthy.'[71] However, let us set such reservations aside. Even if the actions at Quatre Bras and Ligny had not been marred from the French point of view by the catalogue of errors that was actually the case, some sort of victory could still have been gained at Mont Saint Jean, whilst it is even just conceivable that it could have been dramatic enough to allow Napoleon to enter Brussels. It is on precisely this assumption, of course, that the rest of this book rests. Exactly what would have happened is impossible to foresee, but the context of such a victory can be established clearly enough, and, on its different levels, it is to this that we must direct our attention.

Chapter 2

Europe Against Napoleon

I f we accept the possibility that Napoleon could have won the battle of Waterloo – that the evening of 18 June 1815 found him ensconced in Brussels with the Anglo–Dutch falling back on Antwerp, Blücher heading for the Rhine and Louis XVIII, so one must assume, hastily taking ship for the safety of England – the next question that arises is the impact that this would have had on the Allied coalition. That this is the most crucial feature of the situation, there is no doubt. Here we come to a fundamental plank in the Napoleonic legend. In the words of the emperor himself, 'If the Anglo-Dutch army had been destroyed at Waterloo, of what avail would have been the large armies which were preparing to cross the Rhine, the Alps and the Pyrenees?'[1] Needless to say, where the emperor led, his numerous supporters were only too happy to follow. In the opinion of the staunchly Bonapartist David Hamilton-Williams, for example, victory at Waterloo would have enabled the emperor to capture Brussels and then turn back against Blücher's Prussians. Enveloped from the north, the latter would have been forced to retreat, thereby exposing the Russian, Austrian and south German forces that were currently massing beyond the Rhine to a further offensive. With these troops forced to retreat in turn, the chances were that, notwithstanding its earlier condemnation of Napoleon as an outlaw who was to be brought down at all costs, the coalition would have crumbled, thereby giving the emperor both the time that he needed to make good his promises of a 'liberal empire' and the opportunity necessary to show that, as he claimed, he really was a man of peace.[2]

This sort of thing is only to be expected from apologists of the sort of Hamilton-Williams. Unfortunately, more balanced writers have also sometimes fallen prey to this line of thinking, albeit usually in rather less extreme forms. Here, for example, is Andrew Field: 'There is no doubt that if Napoleon had been successful in destroying these two armies [i.e. those of Wellington and Blücher], the morale of the allies would have been seriously affected … It could certainly be argued that the determination of the allies would have been shaken to the point where they were prepared to make an accommodation with France, but, at worst, it would still buy the emperor considerable time, the time he needed to secure his position. And it is certainly true to say that a great victory would have galvanised the majority of France behind him.'[3] The same view, meanwhile, is taken by Rory Muir. Thus: 'It has become customary to say that … even if Napoleon had triumphed, he would soon have been overthrown by the vast Austrian and Russian armies which were gathering against him. Perhaps so, but there seems little reason for confidence on such a hypothetical question.'[4]

As it is difficult to envisage even Napoleon triumphing over the massive Allied forces that were set to bear down upon him, the key point here is the one made by Field, namely the idea that one or more of the Allied powers would have been so shaken as to make peace. Of this prospect, it has to be said that still other historians have been extremely dismissive. 'The campaign of Waterloo', remarked the American historian, Owen Connelly, 'was unsurpassed for drama and left both sides bathed in glory.'[5] Accepting this proposition, however, did not preclude Connelly from laughing the idea that the emperor might somehow have come out on top to scorn. Thus; 'It would have made little difference if the Allies had lost. To argue that it would have, we must assume that the Allies would have quit if Wellington and Blücher had lost. And that was about as likely as Napoleon bodily ascending to Heaven, considering the Allies' enormous advantages.'[6] Ten years later or thereabouts, this was also the view of the British historian, David Gates: 'Even if Waterloo had ended in a triumph for France, it is hard to see how this could have brought her peace and security. Napoleon had won battles aplenty without achieving this, essentially because his military and political strategies had long since diverged … A defeat for the Allies at Waterloo could only have led to them making fresh endeavours to restore their ascendancy. That they possessed both the requisite political resolve and sufficient material resources to achieve victory in the long run cannot be seriously doubted: any ensuing campaign would, one suspects, have followed a similar pattern to that of 1813 with the Allies eventually reconquering France and restoring the Bourbons.'[7] And, finally, we have Munro Price's fine study of the period 1812–15: 'Even had he defeated the armies facing him, [Napoleon] could never have won the war. Though he refused to accept it, the Allies were determined to force him from his throne, and one French victory would not have shaken them … Had the war continued, thousands more soldiers and civilians would have died to no purpose.'[8] Meanwhile, writers of an earlier age were equally scathing. To quote Herbert Fisher, 'Even if the Waterloo campaign had been won by Napoleon, he could not have averted the inevitable catastrophe. The total mass of the Allied armies, of which the forces stationed in Belgium were but a fraction, was some 800,000 men, but behind them were the illimitable reserves of an indignant continent. The temper of Europe was such that even if France had retained the hot zeal of the early Revolution, and Napoleon the matchless vigour of his youth, the war must have gone against him.'9

Whilst these opinions appear extremely well founded, they cannot just be allowed to remain mere assertions. The place to begin here, perhaps, is the dark March morning when news arrived in Vienna of Napoleon's escape from Elba. Assembled in the Austrian capital to restore stability to Europe, the rulers of the great powers and their representatives were genuinely horrified by what had come to pass. In the words of Dominique Dufour de Pradt, an aristocratic French prelate who had served both as Napoleon's private secretary and French ambassador to the Grand Duchy of Warsaw, 'In treating of the Congress of Vienna we wish to remark ... the vigour and determination displayed in pursuit of the enemy who appeared in the month of March [1815]. The Congress did not show a moment's hesitation or division of opinion ... If, from the first appearance of the Revolution, such promptitude of action had been exhibited, what misfortunes would not have been prevented!'10 First to receive the news, it seems, was the Austrian chancellor, Prince Klemens von Metternich. Wakened from sleep at six in the morning of Tuesday 7 March by an aide who came to his bedside with a note emblazoned with the word 'urgent', he at first cast it aside, and, amusingly enough, turned over to return to his slumbers, having the previous night been putting the final touches to the settlement of the complicated Saxon question (see below) at a meeting that had kept him from his bed until a mere two hours earlier. Sleep, however, would not come, and at length the weary prince reached for the offending missive. Needless to say, within seconds he was on his feet and getting dressed. As he later wrote:

> Before eight o'clock I was with the emperor [i.e. Francis I]. He read the dispatch and said to me calmly and quietly ... 'Napoleon seems to wish to play the adventurer: that is his concern; ours is to secure that peace which he has disturbed for years. Go without delay to the Emperor of Russia and the King of Prussia and tell them that I am ready to order my army to march back to France. I do not doubt that both monarchs will agree with me.' At a quarter past eight I was with the Emperor Alexander, who dismissed me with the same words the Emperor Francis had used. At half-past eight I received a similar declaration from the mouth of King Frederick William III ... Thus war was decided on in less than an hour.11

The reasons why there should have been such promptitude in the councils of the great powers are not hard to divine. With news scarce as to where the emperor actually was, there was temporarily a mood of real panic, though Philip

Dwyer is probably to right to discount tales of monarchs and ministers sleeping fully clothed and booted with their scabbarded swords beside them (Talleyrand, indeed, was positively *blasé*, a letter that he wrote to a correspondent in Paris on the morning of 8 March giving news of the flight second place to an account of a visit to the theatre, and remarking that Napoleon's departure from Elba had rendered him little more than a brigand, the inference being that he would be dealt with in short order and without too much difficulty).[12] For a good example of the atmosphere that reigned in Vienna in the wake of the escape of Napoleon, we may turn to the memoirs of Auguste de la Garde-Chambonas, a French *émigré* who happened to be present in the city at the time that the news arrived:

> It would be impossible to depict the aspect of the Austrian capital from that moment. Vienna was like an individual who, lulled to sleep by dreams of love and ambition, suddenly found himself violently awakened by the rattle of the watchman or the clanging of the belfry warning him that his house was on fire. The various guests from all parts of Europe could not recall without dread the phases of the period that had just gone by. The constantly renewed disasters of a quarter of century of war, the invaded capitals, the battlefields bestrewn with dead; commerce and industry paralysed; whole families, nay, whole nations, in mourning, all this presented itself simultaneously to their minds ... The irritation in Vienna was at its height, and kept up by the prospect of a relentless war. The enthusiasm aroused by Napoleon's presence, the welcome given to him by the various populations, the rallying around him of the army, all these things combined caused the French nation to be looked upon as an accomplice to the breaking of the much desired peace. There was, moreover, the dread of a revival of the Revolutionary ideas, the delirium of which had struck terror throughout Europe.[13]

As a diehard *émigré*, La Garde-Chambonnas was wholly in favour of the resumption of hostilities. Admirers of Napoleon were far less happy, of course, but they could not but recognize that the mood of the moment was most unlikely to turn their way. Having travelled to the Austrian capital as part of the suite of the Empress Marie-Louise and her young son, the King of Rome, Napoleon's erstwhile private secretary Claud-François de Méneval had a privileged view of the situation:

> It was in the midst of a renewal of festivals and enjoyments that the unexpected news was thundered forth: the emperor has left the island

of Elba. It is impossible to describe the sensation which was brought by this news ... On the evening of the day an extraordinary spectacle was given at the court ... All were unanimous in the resolution to take energetic measures against Napoleon ... It would be difficult to describe the various impressions of stupor, fear, hope, in one word of the genuine or feigned feelings which were expressed by the lofty persons present at this assembly.[14]

Nor was Méneval the only Bonapartist to pick up on the anger and determination sparked by Napoleon's gambit. Here, for example, is a letter written by Lord Byron's close friend, the leading English radical John Cam Hobhouse, from Brussels on 8 April: 'Feeling no interest, and not thinking myself involved in the playing of this match ... I have resolved to pursue a journey I have long projected, and to revisit Paris in spite of the event which has driven so many of our countrymen with so much speed and so little urgency from that capital. I have still hopes of peace, but very little. A saying of the Duke of Wellington circulates at Brussels that he will be in Paris in three months and His Grace is not known either to boast or to threaten often in vain. The Prince of Orange has buckled on his armour and has forbidden the English officers under his command to say that Napoleon is a great man.'[15] Such resolution, meanwhile, was extremely common. In the words of the Prussian chief of staff, August von Gneisenau:

A most profound emotion and sentiment of depression were felt by everyone at seeing France once again fallen under the yoke of a military despot supported by a perjured army ... Those criminals who for twenty years had been employed in daily crimes, and their chief, who had acted as if there was nothing sacred on earth but what he pleased to call his will, hastened by their perfidious acts to receive that ample punishment for which their treasons and their treachery so loudly called ... The nations of Europe were driven to arms by the fearful apprehension of again seeing despotism and the sword extinguishing the rights of humanity. Their princes and their leaders had felt the dire consequences of the want of unanimity amongst themselves in former times, and with an unexampled coalescence of interests they once more took the field against the common enemy.[16]

With Francis, Alexander and Frederick William all resolved on war, it was not long before the main pieces of the jigsaw were in place. Some delay was occasioned by the fact that that very day Metternich, Castlereagh and Talleyrand had arranged to travel down the Danube to Pressburg to meet with the King of Saxony, and convey the news that he was to be stripped of a large part of his kingdom as part of the compensation it had been agreed that the Prussians should receive to make up for the territory which they in turn were giving up in Poland, but by 11 March they had returned and could therefore focus on the business of what to do about Napoleon. At this point the latter was not yet back in Paris, and there were, it seems, still some hopes that he would be detained before he got there, but the principle of common action was nonetheless established without the slightest equivocation. Just two days later, then, there emerged the famous declaration dethroning Napoleon as King of Elba (a move that presaged that his fate was likely to be removal to Saint Helena) and branding him an outlaw and a disturber of the peace and pledging to assist Louis XVIII and the French people in restoring order (it is not quite true, however, that the powers stooped, as is sometimes claimed, to outright incitement to murder, this being something that was opposed by both Metternich and Wellington). As yet there was no formal declaration of war, there still being hopes that the Bourbon régime could see off Napoleon by itself, but as the days passed it became more and more clear that troops were defecting to the emperor as fast as they could be sent against him. On 25 March, then, after some negotiation with the representatives of Britain with regard to the fresh subsidy agreement that the new struggle could not but require, the four great powers promulgated a new treaty of alliance in which they promised that they would wage war against France until such time as Napoleon had been overthrown once and for all – something which it should be noted did not necessarily amount to a promise to restore Louis XVIII: on 12 May, indeed, the Allies issued a joint statement promising that they would not put the Bourbons back on the throne against the will of the French nation[17] – and pledged to put armies of 150,000 men apiece into the field in the shortest time possible (for good measure, the British also promised a subsidy of £5,000,000).[18]

Europe, then was on the march. As for the idea that any of this was bluff, orders were soon going out establishing no fewer than five different armies: an Anglo-Dutch force in Belgium under the Duke of Wellington, a German and Austrian force on the Rhine under Schwarzenburg, an Austrian force in Italy under a commander who was as yet undesignated, and, finally, two substantial reserve forces that would stand ready to move behind the front-line forces in Germany, the one Prussian under Blücher and the other Russian under Barclay de Tolly. Under the surface, perhaps, mouths were dry and stomachs queasy: 'Beneath this seeming union and decisiveness ran tremors of doubt and apprehension. In vain did Pozzo di Borgo proclaim that within a few days Napoleon would be arrested and hanged. In vain did Metternich maintain his courtly smile of scepticism and Talleyrand confront the world with an impassive mask ... "It was not difficult", wrote Lord Clancarty, who succeeded Wellington as head of the British delegation, "to perceive that fear was predominant in all the imperial and royal personages."'[19] Yet the arithmetic was comforting enough. 'The army on the lower Rhine will be composed of Prussians under Marshal Blücher, on the upper Rhine, of Austrians, Bavarians, Würtembergers, etc, under Prince Schwarzenburg,' exulted the British ambassador to Vienna, Charles Stewart. 'In a short time the Allies will have 500,000 men on the Rhine.'[20]

Even before news of these moves in Vienna had reached him, Napoleon recognized that he was unlikely to face anything other than concerted hostility from the powers of Europe. That being the case, he embarked on a vigorous peace offensive. The moderate, pragmatic and thoroughly realistic Armand de Caulaincourt was re-appointed to the Ministry of Foreign Affairs. The many foreign visitors caught in France by 'the flight of the eagle' were not molested by the authorities and allowed to come and go at will: no more the detentions, then, of 1803. Equally, no sooner had the emperor entered Paris than he sought to reassure those members of the foreign diplomatic corps by giving them papers that allowed them leave for the frontiers whenever they wanted in the hope that this would persuade them to stay and talk, but most of the ambassadors left without stopping even for a word, while even those who did – notably the Austrian and the Russian – stayed only in effect to advise the emperor to give himself up without delay.[21] With this gambit rejected, Napoleon now tried a direct approach. On 4 April, then, the following address was directed to each of the rulers of Britain, Austria, Russia and Prussia:

You must have learned in the course of the last month of my return to the court of France, my entry at Paris and the departure of the Bourbon family. The true nature of these events must now be known to Your Majesty. They are the work of a restless power, the work of the unanimous will of a great nation, conscious of its duties and its rights. The dynasty which force had imposed on the French people was no longer made for them. The Bourbons would associate themselves neither with their sentiments nor their manners: France has, therefore, thought to separate herself from them. Her voice invoked a deliverer; the hope which induced me to make the greatest sacrifices had been deceived. I am come, and from the spot where I touched the shore the love of my people carried me to the bosom of my capital. The first wish of my heart is for peace is to repay so much affection with an honourable tranquillity. The restoration of the imperial throne was necessary for the happiness of the French people. My dearest hope is to render it useful at the same time to the peace of Europe. Sufficient glory has alternately illustrated the standards of all the nations and the vicissitudes of fortune have sufficiently repaid great successes with great reverses. A nobler career lies open to the sovereigns, and I am the first to enter it. After having presented to the world the spectacle of great battles, it will be sweeter to know no other rivalry than that of increasing the advantages of peace, no other struggle than a sacred contest to make the felicity of nations. France is pleased to proclaim, with frankness, this noble end of all its wishes. Jealous of its independence, the invariable principle of its policy shall be the most absolute respect for the independence of other nations. If such are, as I entertain ... the personal sentiments of Your Majesty, the general tranquillity is assured for a long time.[22]

This appeal, however, was ignored, whilst the best that an undercover emissary named Pierre Fleury de Chaboulon, whom Napoleon dispatched to a secret meeting in Basel with an agent of Metternich's in an attempt to secure a deal with his father-in-law, Francis I, could secure was a promise of, first, a comfortable exile (what was meant by this is not specified but suggestions that Francis would not have allowed him to be sent to Saint Helena are not unreasonable) and, second, the replacement of Louis XVIII by Napoleon's young son, guided though the latter would inevitably have to be by some sort of council of regency.[23] It would, of course, be easy enough to put this rejection of Napoleon down to a fixed determination to eliminate the French Revolution and, still more so, the man who had done more than anyone else to export it to the rest of Europe. However, on closer examination it appears that so simplistic an explanation is not tenable. This is not the place to discuss the war aims of the Allied powers, but the evidence that Napoleon could have had a lasting peace on many occasions prior to 1814 is overwhelming.[24] In brief, then, what confronted the emperor was not ideological hostility, but rather the legacy of many years of squandered credit. Yet it was not just the fact that over the period 1813–14 there had at last emerged a universal recognition that it was impossible to contain the French ruler within the established framework of international relations, and that neither neutrality, *détente* or treaties of alliance were of any avail in safeguarding state interests against him. To quote the highly respected diplomatic historian, Paul Schroeder:

Nothing Napoleon could have done would have secured [peace] ... Not only did his life-long record of lies and aggressions belie the profuse assurances he gave ... that he wanted peace and friendship with Europe and would honour the existing treaties and respect the independence of other states. From the moment he landed in France, his actions constituted a virtual declaration of war on Europe.[25]

Of course, the fact that, tempered though this was by promises that Napoleon would accept the frontiers of 1814 and even that the populace would sweep him from the throne at the first sign of military aggression, the response proferred via Fleury de Chaboulon to any suggestion that the emperor should abdicate was a flat refusal and, further, the insistence, in defiance of all the news coming out of France, that the emperor had the full support of not just the French army, but also the French people, was quite enough in itself to damn the peace offensive.[26] Yet this was not the end of it. Thus, for the simple reason that the only friends Napoleon had in France were on the one hand the army and, on the other, those elements of the masses that still entertained dreams of the sort of radical revolution that had briefly been on offer in 1793–4, the emperor reached out in directions that could not be more guaranteed to alienate the powers. No sooner was the emperor back in Paris, then, than he had organized a great review at the Tuileries in which he moved freely among the troops, greeting veterans he recognized and listening to their grievances, whilst he had scarcely landed in France before he had issued a proclamation to the army in which he told his soldiers that they had not been beaten in 1814 and promised them not just that the veterans of his wars would be restored to an honoured place in French society, but also that, or so the proclamation had it, victory would advance at the double.[27] If the army was to be favoured, so were the *sans culottes*. Faced by a situation in which the population of the rural areas through which he passed as he headed from the Mediterranean to Grenoble acclaimed him as the saviour of the revolutionary settlement, the erstwhile King of Elba evidently took a strategic decision to adopt the guise of a Jacobin. To quote Philip Dwyer, 'Napoleon caught on very quickly. He suddenly rediscovered his revolutionary roots, carried away by his own enthusiasm, imitating what he heard around him, pitting the poor against the rich, the peasantry against the local parish priests. He was now a man of the people, democratic, anti-Bourbon.'[28]

None of this was likely to endear Napoleon to the rulers and statesmen of Europe, but at least it was at one with the general perception of the emperor: warlord and Jacobin as he was, he could scarcely be expected to behave otherwise. However, the French ruler's re-invention of himself as a man of peace was if anything still more offensive, the fact being that this was imbued with the stench of frank hypocrisy. That this was the case, indeed, was recognized even by men who rallied to Napoleon, one such being General Jean Rapp, who was to go on to defeat an Austrian army at La Souffel. Thus, confronted by a Napoleon complaining bitterly that the Bourbons were accusing him of personal ambition when in fact they ought to be grateful to him for saving France from a dreadful revolution, Rapp was brave enough to point out that they were not the only ones who were likely to make such accusations. The result was an exchange that could not capture the situation more neatly. Napoleon: 'When people are ambitious are they as fat as I am?' Rapp: 'Your Majesty is joking.'[29] Equally unconvinced, meanwhile, was Napoleon's brother, Lucien. Though he claimed that he afterwards came to believe that the new ruler of France would willingly have surrendered the throne and gone into exile in the United States had Francis I only allowed Marie-Louise to travel to Paris and inaugurate a regency in the name of the infant King of Rome, he admitted that at the time he regarded the approach to Vienna as 'nothing but a means of sowing indecision in the march of our enemies'.[30]

Bad enough as all this was, matters were made still worse by Napoleon's efforts to stir up dissent in the coalition. This last, admittedly, was not the strongest of ensembles. Distrust of Britain was widespread, the Austrians and Prussians had a long history of hostility, and Austria was terrified of Russian expansion in Poland and the Balkans. In the period 1812–14, the glue holding Napoleon's opponents together had proved stronger than the centrifugal forces pulling them apart, but with the opening of the Congress of Vienna the underlying tensions had become all too apparent. In brief, the problem centred on the linked questions of Poland and Saxony. Motivated by a bizarre mixture of greed and idealism, Alexander I was proposing the restoration of Poland – interpreted as the Napoleonic Grand Duchy of Warsaw – in the guise of a Russian satellite state ruled by a Romanov prince and provided with a liberal constitution. To this, however, neither Britain, nor Austria, nor Prussia could agree, Britain because it would have left Russia far too strong; Austria because it would have left Russia far too strong, handed Prussia enormous gains in Germany as compensation, and stimulated Polish resentment elsewhere; and Prussia because she would have been left with an indefensible eastern frontier (in particular, she wished to regain the fortresses of Thorn and Posen). All three powers, meanwhile, were supported by France, for whom the issue was above all a means of re-inserting herself into the deliberations of the powers (that said, as French representative at the congress, Talleyrand was genuinely much concerned at the potential advance of the Russian frontier to the Oder, whilst, as British ambassador to Paris, Wellington believed that Louis XVIII might seize on the possibility of a war as a way out of the growing domestic difficulties which we shall detail in a later chapter). The result was a serious diplomatic impasse. Months of confused diplomacy ensued, but matters went from bad to worse and by December 1814 a variety of factors – Russian concessions and suspicion of the British – had caused the Prussians to join the Russians, whilst Britain, Austria and France were united in opposing them, going so far, indeed, as to sign a secret military alliance against them, this also being acceded to by Bavaria, Hanover and Holland. Chiefly at stake was the fate of Saxony, which was Protestant, exceedingly rich and populous, contiguous to Prussia, under Allied administration thanks to her failure to abandon Napoleon in 1813 whilst there was still time, and in consequence ideally suited to compensate Prussia for her Polish losses. For a brief moment it seemed that war might follow, but in the end sanity prevailed, a compromise being agreed whereby Galicia was returned to Austria, most of the Grand Duchy of Warsaw reconstituted as a semi-independent 'Congress Poland', and Prussia awarded Thorn, Posen and some two-fifths of Saxony, along with some extra territory in Hanover and on the frontiers of Holland.[31]

Severe though the problems in respect of Poland and Saxony had been, in reality they were unlikely to lead to war, there being little stomach for a fight: indeed, it has even been argued that all of the powers concerned were bluffing. That being the case, the fact that he saw it as something he could exploit is one more indication of the want of realism that marked Napoleon's outlook in 1815. However, let us accept that the emperor was not blessed with hindsight and that he sincerely believed that there was something to be gained from trying to play his opponents off against one another. Certainly there were elements of this in his table talk. Thus:

> If Austria chose it, everything might be arranged, but she has an expectant policy that loses everything ... The emperor is ill advised: he does not know Alexander, and is not aware how crafty and ambitious the Russians are: if once they get the upper hand, all Germany will be subverted. Alexander will set the good-natured Francis and all the little kings, to whom I gave crowns, playing at catch corners. Europe will not be sensible of my value till she has lost me. There was no-one but myself strong enough to tame England with one hand and restrain Russia with the other.[32]

What we are back with, then, is, if not quite the *grand empire*, then at the very least a Franco-Austrian league that could challenge, even dominate, the powers of the periphery – Britain, Prussia and Russia – from a strong central position. At all events it was precisely the necessary agreement with Austria which the emperor sought to negotiate. In his secret talks at Basel with Metternich's emissary, then, Fleury de Chaboulon took every opportunity that he could to stir up doubts in the minds of the Austrians and at the same time hold out the hand of friendship. For example:

> Though a Frenchman, I do justice to the strength of mind that the emperor has shown on this memorable occasion, but … it appears to me that the path which he now seems inclined to pursue will be as dangerous as it is impolitic. Austria, in the critical situation in which it is placed by the vicinity, ambition and alliance of Prussia and Russia has need of being protected and supported by a powerful ally, and no prince is more capable of succouring and defending it than Napoleon … Never perhaps was humanity threatened by a war so terrible: it will be a conflict to the death, not between army and army, but between nation and nation. The idea makes me tremble! The name of M. de Metternich is already celebrated, but with what glory would it be surrounded if M. de Metternich, in becoming the mediator of Europe, should accomplish its pacification.[33]

If poison and flattery failed, there was always the physical evidence of the diplomatic manoeuvres engaged in by Talleyrand to rescue France from the isolation in which she had found herself at the start of the congress. Pre-eminent among these was the secret treaty he had negotiated with Britain and Austria to block the Prussians and Russians in respect of Poland and Saxony, and the emperor was prompt to communicate this to Alexander I via the Russian ambassador to Louis XVIII, Count Budiakin. However, not least because the tsar was already well aware that some such deal had almost certainly been done, this move did no good whatsoever, and was, if anything, counter-productive, seemingly constituting yet one more proof of Napoleon's general duplicity: whilst confirmation of the news supposedly turned Alexander's ears red with anger, it did not turn him against a new war.[34] On the contrary, according to some accounts, Alexander was amongst the 'most animated' of the Allied leaders. To quote Méneval, 'This prince, who had been Napoleon's guest, whom he had loaded with apparent expressions of friendship, declared with the greatest vehemence … that he would let his last soldier be killed and would spend his last rouble to prevent Napoleon from ascending the throne of France once more.'[35]

A further question that needs to be raised here is that of what would have occurred had Napoleon won the battle of Waterloo. In brief, would defeat in Belgium have persuaded one or more of the Allies to make peace? For obvious reasons, no firm answer can be given to this question: we simply do not know, and cannot possibly do so. That said, it is difficult to imagine Alexander I, Francis I and Frederick William III caving in in such a situation themselves, and harder still to see what forces would have sought to coerce them into changing their minds. If anything, indeed, it can be assumed that defeat at Waterloo would have galvanised the Old Order into still greater efforts. At all events, the language that the three monarchs used could not have been more stark. Here, for example, is a proclamation that was promulgated by the Prussian monarch on 7 April:

A perfidious conspiracy has brought back to France the man who, for ten years together, has filled the world with sorrow. The people, confounded, have not been able to oppose his armed adherents. Though he himself, while still at the head of a considerable military force, declared his abdication to be a voluntary sacrifice to the happiness and repose of France, he now regards this, like every other convention, as nothing. He is at the head of perjured soldiers who desire to render war eternal. Europe again is threatened: it cannot suffer to remain on the throne of France the man who loudly proclaimed universal empire to be the object of his continually renewed wars, who confounded all moral principle by his repeated breach of faith, and who can, therefore, give the world no security for his peaceful intentions. Again, therefore, arise to the combat![36]

Before we conclude this summary of the position adopted by the monarchs of Europe, there is one matter that needs to be dealt with. Of this, the origins appear to lie in a curious exchange that the captain of HMS *Bellerophon*, Frederick Maitland, records that he had with the wife of General Bertrand in the wake of Napoleon's arrival on board his ship. Thus:

When I was conversing with Madame Bertrand, she said, 'Had the emperor gained the battle of Waterloo, he would have been firmly seated on the throne of France.' I answered, 'It certainly might have protracted his downfall, but, in all probability, he would have been overthrown at last, as the Russians were fast advancing, and he never could have resisted the combined forces of the Allies.' To [this] she replied, 'If your army had been defeated, the Russians would never have acted against him.' 'That I cannot believe', I said, 'as they were using every effort to join and support the Allies, and the assertion is ridiculous.' 'Ah', said she, 'you may laugh at it, and so may other people, nor will it perhaps now be discovered, but remember what I say, and be assured that at some future period, it will be proved that it never was Alexander's intention to cross the frontiers of France in opposition to him.'[37]

Desperate to maintain the fiction that somehow victory at Waterloo could have won the war for Napoleon, inveterate apologists for the emperor have sometimes attempted to make something of this point. According to Hamilton-Williams, then, both the Austrians and the Russians were unwilling to engage in a fresh campaign against France, in consequence of which their rulers were very slow to mobilize their forces for war, the fact being that, offered half a chance, they were in fact ready to do a deal with Napoleon in return for territorial gains at the expense of Prussia. Indeed, he goes so far as to claim that Alexander knew for certain that he could expect the whole of Poland in such a case.[38] However, no source is provided for these claims, while the fact that an army of 90,000 Russians was on French soil as early as 8 July suggests that they are at best exaggerated. As for their provenance, they seem likely to reflect a perception in Napoleon's camp that Alexander in particular was ambivalent about a second restoration of the Bourbons. In this, they were quite right – in the eyes of the tsar, if Napoleon was back in power in Paris, it was in good measure because of the incompetence and stupidity of the court of Louis XVIII, and he therefore began to investigate the possibility of replacing this last monarch with the more amenable Duke of Orléans[39] – but what they do not seem to have appreciated is that Alexander's thinking did not go nearly so far as they hoped: that Napoleon would have to go was never in the slightest doubt.

In the end, there was but one chance of survival. Alone among France's enemies, Britain possessed a substantial peace movement that was fiercely opposed to a resumption of hostilities, and, alone among France's enemies, too, she also possessed a political system that was responsive to public opinion and an opposition that could provide an alternative government. Suppose, then, Napoleon had somehow contrived to defeat Wellington at Waterloo before the Prussians had arrived, or, even better, gained the far more crushing victory that was very briefly on offer at Quatre Bras the day before. If not to the rest of the coalition, this would certainly have come as a hammer blow in Westminster, and it is just possible – *just* possible – that the result would have been a political crisis that would have brought the Whigs to power in place of the Tories and led to the withdrawal of Britain from the war, and, most crucially of all, the cancellation of the massive subsidies that Britain had agreed to make over to Austria, Russia and Prussia.[40] That, and that alone, might just have been sufficient to paralyse the massive phalanx of troops that was set to bear down on France and win

Napoleon a breathing space, but the chances are that even the Whigs could not have stomached the situation that would almost certainly then have resulted, and that, exactly as had been the case in 1803, Britain would sooner or later have been forced to resume hostilities. Yet a change of government was scarcely a likely prospect. In Parliament, true, a number of Whigs including Sir Francis Burdett, Samuel Whitbread, Francis Horner, George Tierney and Samuel Romilly attacked the Liverpool administration and opposed the successive moves that took Britain to war, whilst they were eventually joined by Lord Grey. That said, many Whigs either abstained or voted for the government, whilst, one or two mavericks aside, the Tories remained rock solid. Parliamentary approval for war, then, was assured and it is hard to see this changing even in the event of a major catastrophe.[41] As for extra-parliamentary opposition to the war, this was but a pale shadow of the intense activity of the period 1811–13. Social and economic unrest, by contrast, there was a–plenty – the country was reeling from the impact of demobilization and the industrial downturn brought by the end of the war, while the beginning of March saw the passage of the hated Corn Laws in the face of massive opposition and, with this event, serious rioting in London[42] – yet to move from here to the notion of political revolution is a long leap indeed. To quote H.T. Dickinson, 'Economic distress was certainly widespread in these years, but it was not successfully channelled into a mass movement for parliamentary reform. Popular radicalism … was not again to be a major force to be reckoned with until after 1815. Thus, popular conservatism and militant loyalism kept domestic radicalism at bay so long as it could be convincingly linked with the "anarchy" of the French Revolution and the military aggression of Napoleon.'[43]

All the more was this the case given the 'flight of the eagle'. Up until 1814 it had been possible to argue that the French people were as much the victims of Napoleon as anyone else, and that removing the emperor would be sufficient to lance the boil upon the body politic that France had become. Indeed, in declaring war in 1815, the Allies made specific use of this position, insisting that hostilities were directed solely against Napoleon rather than the inhabitants of France as a whole. Yet in the eyes of many British observers, the fact that a France restored to the prospect of peace and prosperity had seemingly rallied to Napoleon with such fervour had changed the situation beyond all recognition. Here, for example, are the views of Archibald Alison, a young Scottish graduate who had decided to celebrate the conclusion of his studies in the summer of 1814 with a long stay in France, and was therefore an eyewitness to the Hundred Days:

It is certainly a mistake to suppose that the military power of France was first created by Napoleon, or that military habits were actually forced on the people with the view of aiding his ambitious projects. The French have a restless, aspiring, enterprising spirit, not accompanied, as in England, by a feeling of individual importance and a desire of individual independence, and fitted, by the influence of despotic government, for the subordination of military discipline. Add to this the encouragement which was held out by the rapid promotion of soldiers during the wars of the Revolution ... and the general dissemination at that period of unbounded desire for pillage and rapine, and it will probably be allowed that the spirit of the French nation, at the time [Napoleon] came to head it, was truly and almost exclusively military. He ... was a great soldier, he rose to the supreme government of a great military people, and he availed himself of their habits and principles to gratify his ambition and extend his fame, but he ought not to be charged with having created the spirit which in fact created him, a spirit so powerful and so extensively diffused that, in comparison to it, even his efforts might be said to be ... waving with his fan to give speed to the wind. The favourite saying of Napoleon, 'Every Frenchman is a soldier, and, as such, at the disposal of the emperor', expresses a principle which was not merely enforced by arbitrary power, but engrafted in the character and habits of the French people ... A Frenchman does not regard war merely as the serious struggle in which his patriotism and valour are to be tried; he loves it for its own sake, for the interest and agitation it gives to his mind: it is 'his game, his gain, his glory, his delight' ... It is probable, however, that the effervescence of military ideas and feelings which arose out of the Revolution would have gradually subsided had it not been for the fostering influence of the imperial government. The turbulent and irregular energies of a great people let loose from former bonds received a fixed direction and were devoted to views of military aggrandizement under Napoleon. The continued gratification of the French vanity by the fame of victories and the conquest of nations completed the effect on the manners and habits of the people which the events of the Revolution had begun. Napoleon well knew that, in flattering this ruling propensity, he took the whole French people on their weak side, and he had some reason for saying that their thirst for martial glory and political influence ought to be a sufficient apology to them all for all the wars into which he plunged them.[44]

The coalition, then, was not going to crack: indeed, angered by the manner in which they had, as they saw it, been cheated of the whole of Saxony, and, still more so, the prize of the city of Leipzig, a target attractive not only on account of its economic potential (in the course of the Napoleonic Wars, it had become the nucleus of a thriving cotton industry), but also its association with the overthrow of Napoleon, the Prussians, at least, were very pleased to have been handed the chance of a fresh war that might well win them more territory. Such ambitions are understandable enough: the frontiers allocated Prussia under the Vienna settlement were so indefensible that it has been said that they looked like nothing so much as a practical joke perpetrated on Frederick William III and Hardenburg by their fellow monarchs and statesmen.[45] Told by Gneisenau that Napoleon had escaped from Elba, Blücher, for example, had been delighted at the news. Thus, 'It is the greatest piece of good luck that could have happened to Prussia! Now the war will begin again, and the armies will make good all the faults committed in Vienna!'[46] However, no longer could international relations be seen solely as a matter of courts and cabinets. From London to Saint Petersburg and from Stockholm to Naples, twenty-three years of war and political turmoil, not to mention the growing spread of literacy and the relaxation, indeed, in some instances, wholesale disappearance, of press censorship, had opened a pandora's box. In brief, even the most despotic of Europe's regimes had become aware that they could not engage in the levels of warfare characteristic of the Napoleonic epoch without making a conscious appeal to the élites, if not the masses as a whole, and they had therefore become ever more heavily engaged in a struggle not just to recruit bodies and rake in taxes, but also to win over hearts and minds, while in the French empire, too, the press had been used as a means of legitimizing and popularising the cause of Napoleon, even if the effect had often been largely counter-productive. For the first time, then, the journalist and pamphleteer had come to widespread prominence as a protagonist in national war efforts – one thinks here of Manuel Quintana in Spain and Friedrich von Gentz in Austria – and public opinion as a factor to be reckoned with. In Britain, then, a powerful political movement had emerged that favoured peace with France and succeeded in forcing the abolition of the hated Orders-in-Council, while in Spain, if the constitution of 1812 had been overthrown by the newly released Ferdinand VII in May 1814, it was in part because the national assembly that had been established in 1810 had completely failed to engage with the interests and necessities of an utterly impoverished populace. And, even if the crowd could be ruled out, there were always powerful interests in the courts and armies: in 1813 it is probable that had Frederick William not declared war on Napoleon, the Prussian army would have done it for him. The case he was making may well have been exaggerated, but when Fleury de Chaboulon's interlocutor – in reality, not the Monsieur Werner whom he knew him as, but rather an Austrian foreign-ministry official named Ottenfels – raised the matter, he certainly had a point: 'The prospect is no doubt extremely distressing, but ... nothing will alter the determination of the Allied monarchs. They have learned to know the emperor and will not leave him the means of disturbing the world. Even would the sovereigns consent to lay down their arms, their people would oppose it: they consider Bonaparte as the scourge of the human race, and would all shed their blood to the last drop to tear from him the sceptre and perhaps his life.'[47]

Having mentioned the people, we have to look at another possibility, and that is that, across Europe, populations that had experienced the Napoleonic Wars from the embrace of the *grand empire* but were now subjected to the restoration of a more-or-less reactionary and obscurantist Old Order might rally to Napoleon, the disadvantages of living under the empire having dramatically shrunk when viewed, say, through the lens of the Prussia of Frederick William III. This danger was certainly present in the minds of at least some statesmen, including not least Castlereagh, who specifically warned Wellington 'that Poland, Saxony and much Jacobinism are in our rear'.[48] In Paris, by contrast, it was a beacon of hope. To quote the deeply loyal Hortense de Beauharnais, for example, 'The emperor ... was convinced that the people [of Germany], having been moulded for ten years by institutions similar to our own, would remain on good terms with France; that their common needs and desires would render the decision of their rulers completely irrelevant.'[49] This, however, was so much wishful thinking. In one or two areas, certainly, the Napoleonic period had lain less heavily on society than in most others, and here there had been little resistance to French rule and even a degree of regret when it was swept away. One such region was the Rhineland where annexation to France had brought a certain amount of economic growth and the large-scale sale of *biens nationaux* – specifically, the lands of the area's many abbeys – in a manner that benefited the peasantry enormously.[50] As General Philipp von Muffling, a Prussian staff officer who experienced the battle of Waterloo at Wellington's right hand, later observed:

Amongst the inhabitants of the left bank of the Rhine we found a kind of stolid indifference prevailing towards Germany, her language and customs. All interests had turned to France: commercial relations were almost broken off with Germany; the line of customs houses and the difficulties of crossing that river contributed to this result ... The French government had carefully separated the province from Germany in order to transform it more surely and quickly into French departments. The officials, as well as those who aspired to become such, acquired the French language and customs: it was therefore no wonder that everything, from fashion down to domestic habits was brought from Paris. In this state of things the German language was almost forgotten. In 1814 we met with few natives ... who could write or speak German correctly. With German works, however important, which had appeared since the war of the Revolution, no-one was acquainted. Such were the fruits of French possession after hardly twenty years' rule. Ten years more and the German character would have perished forever.[51]

To regret Napoleon was not the same as to risk fire and destruction by rising in revolt in an attempt to support his cause, however. In consequence, although there were plenty of complaints of heavy Rhenish desertion from Blücher's army in the course of the campaign, even the most favoured part of Napoleonic Germany stayed loyal (this was something that was also true of particular elements in German society that had done well out of the empire, including not least the swarms of officers who had made careers and even names for themselves in the forces of such states as Westphalia: had Napoleon triumphed at Waterloo, it is possible – probable even – that such men would have rallied to Napoleon, but there is no evidence the Hundred Days was marked by any preparations for revolt).[52] Another area of Europe that might just possibly have gone with Napoleon in 1815 was Poland. Dismembered and finally wiped off the map by the partitions of 1772, 1793 and 1795, Poland had been restored in embryonic form by means of the creation of the Grand Duchy of Warsaw in 1807. Even before then many Poles had served in the French army in the various units that were formed from Polish prisoners of war who had been serving in the forces of either Austria or Prussia, and the period from 1807 to 1813 saw the army of the Grand Duchy fight bravely for Napoleon, a handful of lancers even having survived in his service to go into exile in Elba as part of his miniscule personal guard. Now, however, the future was far from clear, or, rather, all too clear: the whole of the Grand Duchy of Warsaw was under occupation by the forces of Austria, Russia and Prussia and a new partition was all but certain. 1815, however, was not 1807. The nobility – the only element of Polish society of any significance – had always been split on the question of Russia, and many of the magnates in particular believed that their privileges would be more secure in a Russian dominion, such as the one that was now on offer, than in a Polish state. In the glory years of empire such views had for the most part been overcome by the excitement of the moment, but now they returned with a vengeance, and all the more so as Napoleon had not only proved incapable of defending the Grand Duchy of Warsaw from the Russian forces which had poured across the frontier in January 1813, but also refused to augment its territory with Lithuania after he had overrun the latter region in the campaign of 1812. Ten or fifteen years on, perhaps, it would have been another matter: Congress Poland, as it was known, was not treated well by its Russian masters, and in 1830 Nicholas I found himself challenged by a major rebellion that took a year of fierce fighting to suppress. However, just as 1815 was not 1807, neither was it 1830, and thus it was that, if Napoleon entertained visions of hundreds of thousands of grateful Poles springing to arms, they proved wholly chimerical. On the contrary, so effectively did Alexander I cultivate figures like the highly influential Adam Czartoryski that, if anything, it was rather the reverse that was true: not only were there no moves in the direction of insurrection, but several articles appeared in the Warsaw press appealing for calm and begging nationalists to do nothing that would jeopardize relations with Russia. When news of Waterloo arrived, indeed, there were scenes of jubilation that suggest just how far the public mood had turned against the emperor. As one nineteenth-century commentator wrote, 'By persuading them that his great object was to confer on [the Poles] a national existence and liberal institutions, [Alexander] interested them so far in his views that they would willingly have armed to support those views as they had so often done those of Napoleon.'[53]

To write thus is assuredly to go too far, but what is quite clear is that the leaders of the Polish national struggle had lost faith in Napoleon and were not going to come to his aid. Elsewhere on the Continent, meanwhile, all the signs are that public opinion was even more estranged from the emperor. In Switzerland, for example, the general reaction was one of alarm. One eyewitness was Frédéric Rillier, an officer of Louis XVIII's personal bodyguard, who happened to find himself on leave in Geneva:

On the morning of the eighth [of March] I went out to find the streets full of anxious crowds. By dint of approaching a group of frightened-looking people, I discovered that the man whom everybody had believed to be wandering about on the Mediterranean coast had turned up at the gates of Grenoble, that is to say just thirty leagues away. Confirmed by every successive report, this news had a variety of effects ... Amongst some people fear led them to exaggerate the danger, but amongst others the idea of falling once more beneath a detested yoke filled them with noble sentiments, and, in particular, a determination to defend the independence that had so recently been regained.[54]

In Germany, anger was even more virulent. Doubtless conscious of the desires of its readers, the press was unanimous in its denunciation of Napoleon and the French people alike, and there were strident demands for the most savage of measures. To quote Stephen Coote, 'Newspapers across the Continent from the Rhine to the Oder took up the cry. So the French thought they weren't beaten they declared. Very well, then, they would have to learn that they were. The whole lot of them should be exterminated, declared the German-speaking press. The world could never be at peace all the time there was a French people. They should be shot like the mad dogs they were.'[55] Typical of German nationalists, at least, was the view of Heinrich vom Stein:

We are much excited by the news which arrives of the insurrection of the French army and the inert, inactive behaviour of the French people ... The revolution in France is a consequence of the deep corruption of the nation, which, actuated by revenge and rapacity, preferred the rule of a tyrant to the milder ... government of a rational, pious king, received the former everywhere with rapture and gladly made itself ready for wars of conquest and plunder. It forgot the oppression intellectual and physical under which it had lived, the arbitrary power that disposed of its life and property, the annihilation of trade, the waste of its children's lives, and only longed once more to fall on neighbouring nations and ... oppress them. And so the signal for a new contest is given. God will bless the arms of the Allies and chastise the corrupted nation for its crimes.[56]

Of course, the extent to which statesmen and newspapers moulded public opinion rather than merely reflecting it cannot be judged with any precision, but there is plenty of indication that it was not just ministers and diplomats who were exercised by the situation. In Prussia, in particular, the war of 1813–14 had called forth exertions of a sort that had simply never been seen in any of the numerous wars in which she had been involved up until 1806. Voluntary enlistment, for example, was widespread, while both Jews and women – groups that had in neither case ever played any part in public life before – threw themselves into support for the war, as witness, for example, the formation of no fewer than 600 associations, most of them local, but in at least some cases, national, of female patriots that devoted themselves to such causes as providing home comforts for the troops and caring for the wounded.[57] With large parts of

East Prussia, in particular, reduced to ruin by the impact of the war of 1812, the strength of feeling was entirely understandable, and it is therefore equally understandable that news of the escape from Elba provoked the strongest of reactions. Here, for example, is the British ambassador to Berlin, Sir George Jackson:

> The first news of the reappearance of Bonaparte was treated by the people of Berlin generally as a false report, and they were inclined to attribute it to the Saxons. But when the confirmation arrived, which it did on the very same evening, the whole city was in a state of agitation and alarm. Europe united, it was supposed, had really vanquished 'the invincible' and Prussia was fairly freed from the yoke of her oppressor, but here he was again, and the work of the last year and a half had to be gone through once more. Who should dare venture to predict its results? A calmer feeling now prevails; still, his successful advance causes considerable uneasiness in the public mind ... for Prussia already suffers from such widespread misery and poverty that half a century will hardly suffice for the restoration of the people and the state to their former condition of ease and prosperity ... However, the preparing for war is always animating, and, as already the first beat of the reveille is heard, Berlin is the livelier for it. Yet curses on the author of this new mischief are freely growled forth by many a man who has to take up the knapsack he has just cast forth, and to buckle on the sword he had hoped to turn into the much needed ploughshare and pruning hook.[58]

And here too is the later French prime minister, François Guizot, who experienced the Hundred Days as a senior official of the Ministry of the Interior:

> It was not alone governments, kings and ministers who showed themselves thus firmly determined to oppose Napoleon's return: foreign nations were even more distrustful and more violent against him. He had not only overwhelmed them with wars, taxes, invasions and dismemberments: he had insulted them as much as he had oppressed them. The Germans, especially, bore him undying hatred. They burned to revenge the injuries of the Queen of Prussia and the contempt with which their entire race had been treated. The bitter taunts in which he had often indulged when speaking of them were repeated, spread abroad and commented on, probably with exaggeration readily credited ... The universal feeling of the

people of Germany was as fully demonstrated at the Congress of Vienna as the foresight of their diplomatists and the will of their sovereigns.[59]

This is not to say that there were no frictions in Germany that might have been exploited by Napoleon in the long term. All along the Rhine, peasants were chafing at the heavy requisitioning to which they were subjected, not to mention the arrogant behaviour often affected by officers and men who were for the most part as least as foreign as the French troops whom they had displaced.[60] At the same time, as Jackson's words suggest, the Saxon affair was not without its impact. The decision to award some two fifth of the country to Prussia was anything but popular in Saxony. In mid-February, indeed, there had been significant anti-Prussian disturbances in the capital, Dresden, whilst at the beginning of May several regiments of the Saxon army mutinied rather than submit to being transferred to the Prussian service.[61] Given the fact that, according to Von Muffling, who was an eyewitness to the mutiny, the pro-Saxon party in the army 'thought they might reckon ... on Napoleon's assistance if fortunately he succeeded in re-establishing himself on his throne', there was at least a chance of sedition, but, with Saxony isolated far to the east amidst hordes of Prussian and Russian soldiers, to expect that the Saxons would have come out in favour of the emperor before he had actually won is clearly misguided.[62]

Given the fact that victory at Waterloo would have placed Napoleon in control of Belgium and dealt a heavy blow to the credibility of the newly established Kingdom of the Netherlands, many British writers have made a point of stressing that the soldiers mobilized by these countries in 1815, and more particularly the Belgians, who were in many instances French-speakers to boot, could not be trusted on the grounds that until very recently many of them had been fighting in the ranks of the French army. At the same time, the Belgians were increasingly disgruntled at the manner in which they were in general being treated as second-class citizens by the Orange régime. In the words of John Cam Hobhouse:

'His Majesty the King of the Netherlands' is a sound not yet familiar to Brussels ... If you mention the king, they ask you whether you allude to ... Louis XVIII. Yesterday, he was at the theatre: it was ill-lighted, and worse attended; not a person of apparent gentility was there to greet the new sovereign ... To an eye accustomed to the substantial shows of English royalty, the state of the Dutch monarch cannot but appear most pitiful, and, connected with the very general notion that, such as it is, it will dissolve at the first thunder of the French cannon, nothing can be less enviable than the position of William the First. I have not heard it even surmised that the Belgian troops will stand true to their allies in case the French should be fortunate in their first attacks ... The general disinclination of the Belgians to their union with Holland is acknowledged on all hands. It is not so clear that they are attached to France, but it is no less certain than reasonable that they would prefer annexation to any power sufficiently strong to carry the war into a foreign territory instead of fighting for their borders.[63]

These views, however, seem a trifle jaundiced. In fact, as many Belgians cannot but have recognized, being treated as second-class citizens by the Orange régime was as nothing compared with being treated as citizens by the régime of Napoleon Bonaparte.[64] For Belgium, indeed, the whole epoch of the Revolutionary and Napoleonic Wars had been a calvary. Invaded by the French in 1792, the then Austrian Netherlands and Bishopric of Liège had suffered heavily at the hands of French requisitioning, whilst at the same time seeing the dreams of independence encapsulated by the Brabant rebellion of 1789 crushed by an annexation supported by only by a handful of radicals who had been unable to make head in the short-lived 'United States of Belgium'. When annexation had been followed by conscription in 1798, the peasants of the south-east had risen in revolt, only to be put down amidst great bloodshed. There had followed fifteen years of comparative peace, but in late 1813 the Belgians had once again found themselves not just in the front line, but being treated as a conquered people. Following the Leipzig campaign, for example, Marbot had ended up at Mons. 'I found the spirit of the population changed. There was a regret for the old paternal government of Austria, and a keen desire for separation from France, and the perpetual wars which were ruining commerce and industry. In short, Belgium was only awaiting the opportunity to revolt ... From my hotel I could see every day 3,000 or 4,000 peasants and artisans assembling in the square and listening to the talk of certain retired Austrian officers ... All French officials left the department to take refuge at Valenciennes and Cambrai.'[65] In short, the days of Belgians marching off to do their duty for Napoleon were clearly numbered, while further harm was done by the determination of the Napoleonic régime to extract every last *franc* from its shrinking empire. 'When the French retreated out of Holland', wrote Edward Stanley, an English clergyman who passed through the area in the summer of 1815, 'the Duke of Tarentum [i.e. Marshal Macdonald] did the poor people at Liège the honour of making their town a point in the line of his march. He stopped one night, and because the inhabitants did not illuminate and express great joy at his illustrious presence he demanded an immediate contribution of 300,000 *francs*.'[66]

Even in normal times, life in the Napoleonic empire had been harsh enough. Some areas of the country, certainly, had enjoyed periods of growth – it was at this time that Liège emerged as a major industrial centre, for example[67] – but Belgian foundries and weaving sheds were no more proof against the vicissitudes of Napoleon's economic policy than those of any other part of the empire, whilst more traditional sectors experienced nothing but depression and decay. Like many other cities around the coasts of the *grand empire*, then, Antwerp had suffered very severely, and that despite the fact that Napoleon had poured immense resources into both improving its fortifications and giving its dockyards a major role in his never-abandoned attempt to restore French naval power. Thus, in the words of Archibald Alison, who visited the city late in 1814: 'Though ... extensive naval preparations had been going forward for years at Antwerp, there was not the slightest appearance of bustle or activity in the streets or on the quays of the city. These were as deserted as if Antwerp had been reduced to a fishing village.'[68] If regular commerce had been put an end to by the Continental Blockade, the smuggling that replaced it had proved a risky substitute. 'We were informed ... by eyewitnesses', the same observer continued, 'that they had seen £90,000 worth of English goods burned at once in the great square ... all of which had been bought and paid for by the Flemish merchants. The people ... spoke in great sorrow of the ruin which this barbarous policy had brought upon the ... countries in which it was carried into effect.'[69] Nor were things much better in the countryside. To quote Alison yet again, 'The peasants complained, in the bitterest terms, of the taxes and contributions of the French, stating that the public burdens had been more than quadrupled since they were separated from the Austrian government, of which they still spoke in terms of affection and regret. The *impôt foncière*, or land-tax, under the French, amounted to one-fifth of the rent.'[70]

Hardly had the campaign of 1814 begun, then, than Belgian soldiers fighting in the ranks of the French army began to desert in large numbers.[71] As for that of 1815, if the French were on occasion greeted with cheers in the border towns and villages, it would be dangerous to take such incidents at face value. As one veteran of the campaign remembered, 'We fell in with some groups of peasantry at the entrance of some villages who welcomed us with "Vive l'empereur!", but I cannot flatter myself that they appeared very sincere, or that there was a general sentiment in our favour. In truth, they rather seemed to deprecate us not to pillage them than to express their genuine feelings.'[72] Beyond the reach of French bayonets, meanwhile, public opinion did not give the slightest sign of swinging in favour of the invaders. Here, for example, is what Sir Walter Scott has to say in his account of his visit to France and Belgium in the summer of 1815:

> The anxiety of the inhabitants of Brussels was increased by the frightful reports of the intended vengeance of Napoleon. It was firmly believed that he had promised to his soldiers the unlimited plunder of this beautiful city if they should be able to force their way to it. Yet even under such apprehensions the bulk of the population showed no inclination to obtain mercy by submitting to the invader, and there is reason to believe that the friends he had in the city were few and of little influence. Reports of treachery ... were in circulation, and tended to augment the horrors of this agonizing period ... but, whatever might be the case with some individuals, by far the majority of the inhabitants ... regarded the success of the French as the most dreadful misfortune that could befall their city.[73]

Nor were views of the French any fonder in Holland. Whilst the Dutch army had fought for Napoleon and latterly been absorbed into the ranks of its French counterpart altogether, this did not make army officers eager to repeat the experience. In the words General van Dedem van der Gelder, for example:

> The French were to complain very bitterly when their allies deserted them during the famous days of Leipzig ... but I venture to ask them whether they would put up with humiliation and mistreatment at the hands of allies more powerful than them, whether they would absolutely not rise against men who had devastated their country, burning and pillaging everything, dishing out blows and raping women on all sides without offering the slightest reparation, let alone hearing complaints ... The French soldier is ... impregnated with the same pride as the Romans, the tendency, indeed, of believing themselves to be better than other people: believing that foreigners are inferior in everything, they regard them as having been put on this earth to be subjected to their will.[74]

If soldiers had experienced humiliation, civilians had experienced privation. As Alison tells us, 'Out of 200,000 inhabitants of [Amsterdam], more than one half, during the whole of that time, were absolutely deprived of the means of subsistence, and lived merely on the charity of the remainder, who were, for the most part, unable to engage in any profitable business, all foreign commerce being at an end ... The population of the town fell off about 20,000 during the time of its connection with France; the taxes, while the two countries were incorporated, were enormous; the income-tax, which was independent of the *droits réunis*, or assessed taxes, having been stated to us at one-fifth of every man's income.'[75] In the words of the same Edward Stanley we have recently quoted, then, 'War and slavery have quite reconciled the Dutch to the abdication of Napoleon. In answer to the question, "Êtes vous content de ces changements?", you meet with no doubtful shrug of the shoulders, no ambiguous "mais que, oui"; an instantaneous extra whiff of satisfaction is puffed forth, accompanied with the synonymous terms, "Napoléon et Diable."'[76]

If there is any doubt about Dutch views of Napoleon, one only has to turn to the situation that pertained in the erstwhile Kingdom of Holland. Annexed to France in 1809 after Louis Bonaparte had gone to ever greater lengths to resist Napoleon's demands in respect of the imposition of conscription and the Continental Blockade, since then the Dutch departments had been a hotbed of unrest. With the economic disruption brought by the wars increased to fresh heights by a fierce clampdown on smuggling, the inhabitants responded by wholesale tax strikes and draft evasion. With regard to conscription (an innovation that was particularly loathed), indeed, fewer than 20,000 men had been called up by 1812, while the process was accompanied by outbreaks of rioting that became steadily more frequent and more threatening alike, the French cause being done no good at all by the appalling losses suffered by the 14,000 Dutch troops who fought in the invasion of Russia (in one battalion of 500 men, over 400 died, while other units were wiped out altogether). As 1812 wore into 1813 so anti-Napoleonic posters and handbills became ever more common in many towns and cities, and in April a full-scale peasant rising took place in Leiden, the wave of executions to which this gave rise doing nothing other than to increase the anger of the populace. To political unrest, meanwhile, was added a fresh wave of economic misery, some eighty-seven firms collapsing in Amsterdam alone in the winter of 1811–12. With the notables on whom they depended to run the administration deserting their posts on all sides or at the very least keeping the lowest of low profiles, Napoleonic rule was little more than a shell by the time that the first Allied troops appeared on the eastern frontiers in November 1813.[77]

In the event, then, so far as is known, mobilization went very smoothly, while in the battles of Quatre Bras and Waterloo the many Dutch-Belgian troops who saw action conducted themselves no worse than most of the other Allied troops in the British array and that despite frequently suffering heavy casualties.[78] Just as staunch, meanwhile, had been the contingents supplied by the German states of Nassau and Brunswick, even though the troops of the former had fought on the side of the French ever since 1807. All this being the case, how much weight is it possible to put on Napoleon's hopes? Once again, one cannot be sure, but such had been the hatred of the French in most of the *grand empire* by the fall of the emperor that it is absurd to believe that there would have been any movement in their favour, the Army of the North proceeding to clinch matters by engaging in an orgy of pillage no sooner than it had crossed the Belgian frontier. As a colonel of the *gendarmerie* complained to Marshal Soult, 'Marauding and pillage are rampant in the army now: the Guard itself sets the example.'[79] Much the same opinion, meanwhile, can be found in the memoirs of the soldier we have just quoted in respect of public opinion in Belgium. Thus:

As soon as the troops had taken even a momentary position in the vicinity of a village, they rushed like water from a broken dam all over the country beneath; corn, cattle, bread meat, even household furniture, linen and clothes, disappeared in an instant. The village became a mass of ruins: empty houses, broken doors and the inhabitants flying into the woods and fields ... As our troops quitted these villages, the inhabitants, a most miserable spectacle, reappeared, and, viewing the ruin of their property, broke forth in intermixed sorrow and imprecations. It was really miserable to see them collecting their broken furniture, and, with their children in their hands, look woefully at the cornfields trodden underfoot ... One short hour had destroyed the labours of their life, and reduced them from comfort to extreme poverty.[80]

One last area that we need to discuss is, of course, is Italy. Here restoration of the Old Order had by no means been total. On the contrary, thanks to a last-minute decision to change sides, Joachim Murat had been allowed to remain on the throne of Naples, but he had felt increasingly under siege, the government of Ferdinand IV having spent the months that had passed since the abdication of Napoleon doing all that it could to harass him. Irregular troops were sent over from Sicily to form the nucleus of a fresh revolt in Calabria; traditional patterns of labour migration were exploited as a means of spreading disaffection, and everything possible was done to facilitate the operations of the numerous smugglers who were plying the coast with their ways. When Murat heard that Napoleon had escaped from Elba, he therefore resolved on a do-or-die exploit of his own. Mobilizing his army, he proclaimed a war of Italian liberation, and marched north to attack the Austrians. The latter, however, were ready for him. Any man who fled to the Austrian camp having been promised land, large numbers of Neapolitan soldiers deserted. What happened next, then, was hardly surprising. On 1–2 May Murat was beaten at Tolentino, the result being that he was forced to flee into exile in France.[81] The fact was that, as the British ambassador to the exiled Neapolitan court's Sicilian refuge, Lord William Bentinck, had already discovered, Italian nationalism was at best in its infancy.[82] Newly appointed as British ambassador to Tuscany, Lord Burghersh was scathing in his treatment of the subject, as witness a long dispatch that he penned to Castlereagh on 31 January 1815. Amongst some members of the élites, he conceded, there was much support for a united Italy, if only because the officers and officials who had served the Napoleonic administrations were frequently out of a job and unlikely to be satisfied even if they could find some appointment: 'In Tuscany to belong to an army which may amount to 3,000 or 4,000 men cannot flatter the pride of any man; in a civil line, the service required by the government is necessarily on so small a scale, and … the rewards so limited that neither the ambition of the rich man nor the wants of the poor man with talents will find their reward in devoting themselves to the service of their country.'[83] But the populace as a whole were a different matter. Wherever the Austrians had appeared, he admitted, 'the manner in which their officers, as well as men, have behaved themselves, as also the heavy contributions which have been raised by the generals, have given universal dissatisfaction, and, I fear, have totally alienated from them the minds of the Italian people'. But that did not equate to nationalism. As he continued:

> The glory of the ancient Italian name would excite some ardour in certain sections of the lower orders. It would, however, be confined to those who are exasperated against the German troops. For I am persuaded that, with the people of Italy, no measure could be so hurtful or unpopular as the forming of the country into one kingdom. The different states into which it has so long been divided have separated the feelings and interests of the people. The inhabitants of no separate country hate each other more thoroughly than those of the neighbouring states of Italy … The people are, besides, attached to their different capitals. They glory in the privileges they enjoy, and the inhabitants of Naples, Rome and Florence would be most unwilling to see their cities reduced to the state of provincial towns. With feelings such as I have described, the project of an Italian kingdom … might for a moment be established, but I doubt its being popular with the mass of the people: its after-details would encounter the greatest difficulties.[84]

To prove the point, one might here advert to the fate of King Joachim. An adventurer to the last, in October 1815 he landed in Calabria with a handful of followers and in the marketplace of Pizzo again proclaimed a crusade for a united Italy. Initially, the response was stupefaction – the people really did not seem to have any conception of what he was about – but then an old woman recognized him for who he was. Screaming that he had had four of her sons shot, she fell upon him, and it was only with the greatest difficulty that he escaped being lynched on the spot rather than immediately court-martialled and executed by the local *gendarmerie*.[85]

Had the war gone on, then, then, it really would have been a case of what Geoffrey Best called 'the French and the rest'.[86] No ruler, statesman or government was even remotely interested in negotiating with Napoleon, let alone confirming him on the throne of France, whilst each and every one of them willingly shouldered the burden of mobilization for what they could not rule out being a long and destructive struggle: quite simply, Napoleon was too great a threat to be allowed to remain in power, just as, by the same token, the coalition much too valuable to be squandered via petty squabbles over the division of the spoils. As for the peoples of Europe, whilst it is probably an exaggeration to imagine them panting for war against France, even nationalities that might have been expected to be restive were very far from taking up arms alongside the French. Like it or not, then, victory at Waterloo would not have resulted in victory in the war, a war in which, as we shall now see, Napoleon even in military terms would have been operating as a severe disadvantage. Indeed, from the moment that he was condemned by the powers assembled at Vienna, the game was almost certainly up. In the words of François Guizot:

> Napoleon, in quitting Elba, deceived himself as to the disposition of Europe towards him. Did he entertain the hope of treating with and dividing the Coalition? This has been often asserted, and it may be true, for the strongest minds seldom recognize all the difficulties of their situation. But, once arrived at Paris, and informed of the proceedings of the Congress, he beheld his position in its true light, and his clear and comprehensive judgement at once grappled with it in all its bearings … He understood, and accepted without a sentiment of anger against anyone, and perhaps without self-reproach, the situation to which the events of his past life had reduced him. It was that of a desperate gamester, who, though completely ruined, still plays on, alone, against a host of combined adversaries, a desperate game, with no other chance of success than one of those unforeseen strokes that the most consummate talent could never achieve, but that Fortune sometimes bestows upon her favourites.[87]

Chapter 3

The Military Balance

L et us assume, then, that Napoleon managed to win the Waterloo campaign, but that, even so, the coalition stayed rock solid. We now need to assess the military situation that the emperor would have faced in this eventuality. In brief, what would have been the issues and challenges that he would have had to confront, and what, too, would have been the chances of, first, he himself, second, his subordinate commanders, and, third, the reborn Napoleonic army, overcoming those issues and challenges? As we have seen, it is the opinion of many, if not most, military historians that all three would have been found wanting, that defeat, in effect, was inevitable, but it is important nothing is left to assertion. In this chapter, then, we shall subject the military context of a French victory at Waterloo to a detailed analysis. As will become clear, however, this will not be some exercise in fantasy. Whereas in the very narrow context of the late afternoon of 18 June 1815 it is possible to come up with a very clear sequence of events that might well have produced a victory for the French, thereafter the range of possibilities opens out once more, thereby rendering it impossible to do more than hazard a guess as to how things might have worked out. That said, even if some of them are not entirely absolute, we do have a series of 'givens' that allow us to come up with a series of conclusions that are, once again, less than favourable to Napoleon.[1]

So much for the basic thrust of this chapter. Before we move on to the discussion of commanders and commanded, however, we should first return to the very different 19 June 1815 that would have succeeded the victory brought about by the breakthrough effected by the Middle and Old Guard. In the course of the night, we can assume that both the Anglo-Dutch forces and the Prussians would have fallen back, with the former heading for Antwerp and the latter heading for the Rhine. For the former, in particular, this would not have been an easy process given the fact that the road from Brussels to Antwerp would also have been clogged with large numbers of terrified civilians in the form of well-connected onlookers such as Samuel Creevey and the Duke and Duchess of Richmond, and the many wives, children, servants and hangers-on who had followed Wellington's soldiers to Brussels. Particularly among the Dutch, Belgian and German units, desertion would have been heavy (the facts, first, that many men of these nationalities were long gone from the field even before the French finally prevailed, and, second, that at least 8,000 Prussian soldiers deserted the night after the battle of Ligny, mean this can be said without fear of accusations of national bias). Caught in a country that had overnight suddenly become potentially hostile, British units would not have been hit by this scourge nearly as badly, but even so exhaustion, the need to find food and the propensity to drunkenness that was the redcoats' besetting sin mean that straggling could not but have been a serious issue. However, given that the French army would have been too exhausted and disorganized to pursue Uxbridge's battered forces even had it not lost the bulk of its cavalry in the futile attacks of the afternoon, we may assume that the Anglo-Dutch would have made it to safety, albeit at the cost of a proportion of its baggage, perhaps half its guns, all of its wounded (other, that is, than a few senior officers). and as many as 20,000 deserters, stragglers and prisoners of war: aside from anything else, Napoleon would have been further delayed by the need to stage a triumphal entry into Brussels, receive the surrender of the city authorities and issue the decrees announcing the restoration of Belgium to the frontiers of France.

What, then, would have been the situation in military terms? Safe behind the defences of Antwerp would have been as many as 55,000 Anglo-Dutch troops (in the absence of an effective French pursuit, it may be assumed that the 17,000 men who had sat out the battle watching Wellington's right flank at Hal would have joined Uxbridge at Brussels and very possibly been allotted the task of rearguard). Given the enormous losses – as many as 30,000 men – that this implies, such a picture is hardly one to inspire much in the way of confidence, yet it should be remembered that the men who stuck it out and reached Antwerp would have contained a high proportion of disciplined veterans of a sort who were unlikely to be fazed even by the worst privations. Still relatively intact, meanwhile, were most of the old Peninsular battalions, including Maitland's Guards, Adam's Light Brigade and Pack's Highlanders. That said, this was an army whose commander-in-chief was dangerously wounded, whose general staff had been all but wiped out and which had lost a proportionate number of corps, divisional and brigade commanders. In short, it was a force which was in desperate need of rest and re-organization and one that would not be able to fight offensively for some little time.

In so far as the Army of the Netherlands was concerned, then, Napoleon had won himself a breathing space. Yet even so it should be recognized that there were limits to his success. Secure in Antwerp, Uxbridge could receive unlimited supplies and reinforcements by sea, whilst, with the remainder of the troops who had been fighting in the War of 1812 now coming home in large numbers, there was no shortage of men to send him. At the same time, however battered it may have been, the force that had stood its ground at Waterloo remained very much an army in being, not least because its British component, at least, was spoiling for a fight: given the spot at which the final French attack had hit Wellington's line, the only redcoats directly involved in the *débâcle* had been a single understrength brigade, the result being that a compelling narrative had emerged of British heroism let down by Belgian, Dutch and German cowardice. Yet if the British were eager for a resumption of the fight, so also were plenty of their allies: the haughty attitude of the redcoats having caused much resentment, there were many Dutch officers in particular who were anxious for an opportunity to vindicate themselves. Prince Carl-Bernhard of Saxe-Weimar, for example, was the commander of the Regiment of Orange-Nassau, and, as such, had fought very well at both Quatre Bras and Waterloo. Writing in 1841 to a Dutch officer named Ernst van Löben Sels who was collecting material for a Siborne-style account of the campaign, he expresses a bitterness that would have doubtless been still more acute had the French won the day. Thus:

> Of course, my dear captain, you may have noticed that the officers in our army who served in the campaign of 1815 do not like to discuss it, and, when they can no longer avoid this conversation, they do so with a bitter feeling in memory of the wrong and half measures that preceded the outbreak of hostilities, the confusion which characterized the operations and the lack of care and well-being afforded our army ... In addition, [there is] the very little due recognition the Duke of Wellington rendered in official reports about our army during the campaign [and] the brutality that he ... used in his relations with our chiefs in accusing them of not knowing how to make their troops march, but without actually having taken care of assuring [their] subsistence ... Here, my dear captain, are some of the reasons why the memory of this campaign leaves us as cold as a review of the camp at Beyen.[2]

At some point, then, the Army of the Netherlands was likely to take the field again. Ideally, of course, Napoleon would have loved to subject it to a knockout blow, but this was simply not within his grasp: not for nothing did he imply at Saint Helena that a British retreat to Antwerp was his worst fear. In brief, Antwerp was a formidable fortress that had taken the Spaniards a year to take in the siege of 1584–5 and had defied the Allies for three months in 1814, having only surrendered when it received news of the fall of Napoleon. Situated on the outside or eastern bank of a great bend in the river Scheldt, it was protected by a double line of bastions, which enclosed not just the city but also its capacious docks, and dominated by a massive citadel, whilst several detached forts commanded the river approaches from north and south alike. With all the resources of the considerable fleet built there by Napoleon in the past fifteen years to draw upon, it was also bristling with guns, whilst Wellington had ordered the construction of a number of outworks designed to strengthen the defences still further, the works involved being so significant as to give employment to no fewer than 20,000 labourers. All too clearly, even to think of taking the city was out of the question: to do so by escalade would have led to heavy casualties, whilst the fact that Napoleon did not have a battering train with him meant that it would be many weeks before formal siege operations could even be embarked upon, these being many weeks, of course, that Napoleon did not have at his disposal. All this placed the emperor in a most uncomfortable position. He could not take Antwerp, and was under great pressure to march in pursuit of the Prussians so as to maintain the momentum of the campaign, and yet to ignore Antwerp would have been to invite a reinvigorated Army of the Netherlands to retake Brussels and thereby at the very least cause him considerable political embarassment. What was needed, then, was to detach a force to mask the defenders, but so large was the garrison and so extensive the perimeter that the number of troops needed for such a project could not have been less than 40,000 men, this being a force so great that it would have left Napoleon with insufficient men to carry the war to the enemy elsewhere. And even were Antwerp to be blocked up in this fashion, there was still the problem of British control of the sea: what could have been done, for example, to prevent the dispatch of amphibious expeditions to raid the coasts of northern France or even conduct significant forays in the interior?[3]

What we see, then, is an exact replay of the situation that pertained in Andalucía in 1810. Having overrun Andalucía in a great blitzkrieg-style offensive, Marshal Soult had found himself baulked by the island city of Cadiz. Unable to storm the city, he had been forced to leave a third of his 60,000 troops to blockade it, thereby effectively neutralizing his forces for most of the next two and a half years: whilst columns could be put together for action elsewhere, usually in successive attempts to either take or, later, relieve, the fortress of Badajoz, it was only at the cost of stripping his dominions of their garrisons and thereby leaving them vulnerable to Allied forces operating in the interior or dispatched from Cádiz by sea.[4] How Napoleon would have dealt with the problem of Antwerp, we cannot know, though it may be assumed that, taking advantage of the Army of the Netherlands' need to rebuild its strength, he would have left the garrison to its own devices and marched on the Rhine in the hope of obtaining a victory over the Prussians, but it cannot be denied that the situation was at the very least very difficult. And would even victory against the Prussians have been forthcoming? In concentrating his forces and accepting battle at Ligny, Blücher had acted in defiance of the principles of the so-called Trachenberg Plan, the scheme agreed in 1813 which laid down that Allied commanders facing Napoleon should fall back, secure in the knowledge that other forces would move in against the emperor's lines of communications and force him to retreat.[5] In the wake of French success in the campaign of June 1815, however, it is at the very least probable that wiser counsels would have prevailed and that Napoleon would in consequence have been drawn ever deeper into northern Germany, leaving the armies of Austria, Russia and the south German states free to strike across the Rhine.[6]

Over and over again, then, one is brought back to the simple fact that Napoleon did not have enough troops for the task in hand. This being the case, we now need to consider the issue of France's mobilization in 1815 in more detail. When Napoleon returned to France, he was certainly greeted with acclaim by certain elements of the populace, but even he was not so self-deluded as to believe that he could place much faith in this phenomenon. Enthusiastic though it was, the army numbered only 175,000 men, this being a total that clearly had to be expanded in short order. To do this, the obvious way forward was to order a fresh levy of conscripts, and yet in the first instance this was ruled out as being politically dangerous. As Houssaye writes, 'Having just resumed the crown, [Napoleon] hesitated to resort to such an unpopular measure as the resumption of conscription, which Louis XVIII had recently abolished.'[7] All that was done, in consequence, was to recall the 33,000 men who were currently on leave or had been demobilized in 1814, and to issue an amnesty for the significantly larger number – some 85,000 – who were on the books as having deserted or failed to report for duty in the first place.[8] And even then the result was disappointing, only about two-thirds of the men concerned having rejoined the colours by the time the campaign began. To quote Houssaye:

> Numbers responded to the call merely to urge reasons for their exemption or disqualification … During the last year they had resumed their labours in the field and workshop; many of them had married, and these were all the less disposed to serve. In the departments where Royalist tendencies prevailed, the recalled men, feeling sure of public sympathy, behaved in a most disorderly way at the recruiting stations. They shouted, 'We will not go! Long live the King!'[9]

To the recalled soldiers were added perhaps 15,000 volunteers, whilst an extra 25,000 men were secured through an appeal to the 94,000 veterans who had been discharged from the service prior to 1814, though the men concerned were for the most part too unfit to serve in anything other than special garrison units.[10] However, these efforts were insufficient to meet the army's needs, and so recourse was had to mobilizing the National Guard. The response to the decrees concerned, however, was most revealing. In much of the north and the east – an area characterized by long traditions of military service which had coincidentally also had to run the gauntlet of the Austrians, Russians and Prussians during the invasion of 1814 – the men concerned for the most part came forward cheerfully enough, but elsewhere the picture was very different, Orne raising just 107 of the 2,160 men it was supposed to provide, Pas de Calais 437 out of 7,440 and Gers ninety out of 1,440. By the time that the campaign began, then, no more than three-fifths of the total strength of 238,000 had reported for duty.[11] Meanwhile, whether even these would be willing to fight was another matter. Ardent admirer of Napoleon though he was, even Hobhouse could not quite hide the issue. Thus, writing of a great review of the Paris National Guard which he witnessed shortly after his arrival in the capital, he noted that, whilst some units 'shouted loud and long and raised their caps on their bayonets', in general, 'all of them shopkeepers ... who have been great gainers by the short peace', the rank and file considered Napoleon's reappearance as 'the sign of war'. Had the situation been otherwise, Hobhouse continued, things might have been different, 'for they all cling to his palaces, his walks, his galleries, his columns, his triumphal arches, his bridges, [his] fountains and [his] quays, and all the imperial embellishments of the capital, and also they all lament, where they do not hate, the imprudence of the royal family and the advisers of the king'. However, the situation was not otherwise, and the bulk of the troops 'did not, therefore, hail him universally or very loudly'.[12]

Whatever doubts may be thrown up by the behaviour of the National Guard, Napoleon certainly had enough men to mount an initial strike. Yet beyond the 125,000 men of the Army of the North, French manpower was stretched very thin. Guarding the frontiers of the rest of France were no more than 73,000 troops. In theory, Rapp had 23,000 men at Strasbourg, Suchet 23,000 men at Lyons, Lecourbe 8,000 men at Belfort, Brune 6.000 men at Marseilles, Decaen 7,000 men at Toulouse and, finally, Clausel 6,000 men at Bayonne, but these figures included large numbers of national guards who were for the most part useless when it came to field actions: the total of regular troops may well have been no greater than 50,000.[13] In the Hundred Days as such, there was no fresh call-up, but, had the war gone on, things would have been very different. Thus, even victory was desperately dearly bought: at Ligny and Quatre Bras, the Army of the North suffered some 16,000 casualties, and it may be inferred that a subsequent triumph over Wellington would have cost at least 10,000 more. In short, in just four days, the chief French field army would have lost some 20 per cent of its strength. Heartened by victory, Napoleon would have responded by extending the draft to fresh age groups, but everything we know suggests that such measures would have been unlikely to obtain much in the way of success. To quote Gareth Glover, 'Perhaps the greatest myth of the entire Waterloo campaign is that France wholeheartedly followed the great man into war; the truth was far from it.'[14]

Nor was it just a matter of men. France's arsenals had been sufficiently well provided to ensure that the extra men who had reported for duty or volunteered for service had received the correct arms and equipment (though at least one of the famed regiments of *cuirassiers* rode to war without a single one of the sets of breast and backplates from which the units concerned derived their name). However, clothing them was a different matter. Many units went to the front dressed in little more than greatcoats and forage caps, then, while the battalions of the Middle Guard never got the famous bearskins to which they were entitled, but rather made the final attack at Waterloo wearing the headgear of their old regiments.[15] Even more problematic was the issue of horses: everyone agrees that the French cavalry at Waterloo was well-mounted, but what is recognized less often is that this was only achieved at the cost of virtually stripping France of horseflesh. In short, getting the Army of the North into the field was achieved by dint of scraping the bottom of the barrel, and this in turn begs the question of how the fresh troops needed to reinforce the army in the event of a prolonged campaign could have been equipped even had it been possible to levy them in the first place.[16]

Also at issue is the psychological ability of the army to withstand the pressures of a long war. Conventionally, the performance of the French army in 1815 is represented in the most laudatory of terms: the vast majority veterans of several campaigns, the soldiers are supposed to have hurled themselves on the Anglo-Dutch army with the utmost gallantry, and later to have resisted the advance of the Prussians quite literally to the death; deeply angered by the return of the Bourbons, they wanted revenge for the humiliations of the past year. Of their spirit of no better testimony can be found than the scenes that were witnessed by British officers in Brussels at the close of the campaign:

The French wounded are almost all quartered in the city hospitals, or in those houses whose owners may have shown a lukewarmness in the present contest. Their constant cry was, and still is, 'Vive l'empereur!' Some of them brought in from the field the other day, extremely weak from loss of blood and want of food... vented the same exclamation. Louis XVIII sent an officer ... to inquire if they were in want of anything and to afford assistance to those who required it. He visited every one of the hospitals, but I believe he could not prevail on one to accept of assistance from him in the name of his sovereign. They had no king but one.[17]

As might be expected, Hobhouse also waxed lyrical on the spirit evinced by Napoleon's army. To quote a description which he penned of a review which he witnessed in Paris in late May, 'Both on the present occasion and at other reviews I have remarked an enthusiasm, an affection, a delight apparent in the countenances of the troops at the sight of their general which no parent can command in the midst of their family.'[18] And, finally, a Frenchman who remarked on the enthusiasm of the soldiery was Lucien Bonaparte, the latter commenting how the wounded who made it back to Paris in the wake of the French defeat filled the air with shouts of 'Long live the emperor!' 'Our emperor has been betrayed! 'Arms! Give us arms!' and even 'I still have one arm with which to serve the emperor!'[19] To the very end, indeed, elements of the army wanted to fight on: in the course of Napoleon's flight to the sea, he was pressed by troops stationed in one of the towns he passed through to take the field again at the head of the army fighting the Vendéen rebels (see below).[20] Yet all was not quite as rosy as this might suggest. In the words of David Chandler, 'Indeed, it can be argued with considerable justice that Napoleon miscalculated the calibre of his army, regarding its quality with ... misplaced optimism.'[21] If the lower ranks were enthusiastic, their superiors were frequently gloomy and pessimistic, and in some cases downright disloyal. In so far as this last subject is concerned, we might cite the commander of the Fourteenth Division, General Bourmont, who fled to the Prussians with all his staff on the eve of the battle of Ligny, and, second, the unknown officer who galloped into Wellington's lines with the news of the impending attack of the Imperial Guard. Such cases, perhaps, were very much in the minority, but there is no doubt that they had a considerable impact. This made, as has often been observed, the army that marched across the Belgian frontier in 1815 a very brittle force. With the rank and file utterly devoted to Napoleon and deeply suspicious of their generals as those who had almost to the very last man rallied to Louis XVIII, the least reverse was likely to lead to shouts of treason, even downright panic. As Andrew Uffindell has written, then, 'As a consequence, the French soldier was a dangerous weapon.

He was capable of magnificent feats of arms, but also of failing his commander *in extremis.*'[22]

Such, at least, is the conventional explanation of the spirit of the French army in 1815. However, given that it is an argument originally taken from Houssaye, much more research is needed here. In particular, to try to explain the issue of the sudden collapse of the army in the final moments of the battle of Waterloo in terms of self-fulfilling fears of treason looks nothing short of disingenuous. In 1814 huge numbers of French soldiers had deserted, whilst, as we shall see, British sources frequently report that the soldiers who had fought Wellington at Bayonne, Orthez and Toulouse had been unanimous in welcoming the coming of peace. Given the experience of Bourbon rule, it may be that such war-weariness was set aside in the excitement of the return of Napoleon, but there yet remains another issue: in brief, with memories of 1814 fresh in their minds, the soldiers who fought in the campaign of the Hundred Days were ready enough to fight so long as there was a chance of victory, but take that chance away and demoralization was liable to become both instant and total. 'If Napoleon led [the Army of the North] to victory', wrote the American military historian, John Elting, 'it would shake down into a military machine like the one he had led to Austerlitz, Jena and Friedland. If defeated, it would be hard to rally.'[23] Whilst this claim is probably true enough, even this remark is open to challenge. As we shall see, the soldiers who rallied to Napoleon in 1815 had many grievances and were determined to secure what they saw as their just rewards – indeed, they might even be eager for a battle that would vindicate their reputation – but that did not mean they were enamoured of the idea of a fresh war of conquest. That this was the case is at least suggested by an incident that took place near Avesnes on 10 June at the headquarters of the division commanded by Jerome Bonaparte. In brief, according to Pierre Robinaux, having arrived to take up his command, Jerome reviewed the troops and then presided over an open-air repast to which all the officers were invited. Pleasant enough an occasion though this was, it had something of an edge in that the officer in charge of providing the musical entertainment slipped in a song which he had composed specially for the occasion whose refrain stated baldly that, if fate should eventually lead it to the frontiers of Germany, the army would not let itself be used for acts of aggression: 'This', remarked Robinaux, 'reflected the wishes of the whole army: had Bonaparte been successful and crossed the river, he would have demoralized it in its entirety.'[24]

To put it mildly, then, it is but necessary to scratch the surface to find that the view of the army was at best ambivalent, if not shot through with contradictions. A further problem is that in the hurry of mobilization, it had proved difficult to reconstitute the army in the exact state it was in 1814, the result being that many men ended up serving not with much-trusted old comrades, but with complete strangers.[25] And, as if this was not enough, the spirit of emulation and competition that had marked the old Grande Armée appears to have been fanned to a state of white heat by the frustrations of the previous year. To quote an anonymous veteran of the campaign of Waterloo:

> The interior of the army was torn to pieces by an anarchy similar to that which reigned without [a reference to the wholesale pillage in which the troops engaged in all the districts through which they passed]. It seemed as if an implacable hatred animated one corps against another, and that there existed an open war between them. No mutual sacrifices, no reciprocal confidence, no common feeling, but everywhere selfishness, arrogance and rapacity. When the commander of a column or regiment arrived at the post which he was to occupy, his first care was to seize everything within his reach with a total disregard of anyone who might succeed him. Guards were placed at the doors of houses which contained provisions, and, without any right than that of being the first occupant, they opposed themselves to every kind of division. These sentinels were frequently attacked by soldiers of other parties, and the matter proceeded to blows, in the course [of which] many were wounded, and some even killed, on both sides. The Imperial Guard, in its character of being the janissaries of the despot, were extremely arrogant towards the other troops: they repelled with disdain all commerce and contact with the other branches of the service and were justly detested by them. Their comrades submitted to this pretension only so far as the Imperial Guard were sufficiently numerous to endorse it, but, when they were in less number, they retaliated upon them. The different arms of cavalry were equally jealous and contentious of each other and of the infantry, whilst the latter, confident of its strength and numbers, threatened the cavalry with the bayonet, and insisted upon their own equality of rights and respect.[26]

The French army, then, was not a force that could be trusted, and certainly not one that was equipped, either mentally or physically, for a long campaign. To sustain it in such a case, what would have been required was a string of victories, and yet such a string of victories was scarcely a likely prospect. On many levels the French war machine was no longer the same threat as it had been, say, in the period 1805–7. First of all, there is the issue of Napoleon himself. Whilst there is no definite evidence that he was ill in the campaign of 1815, it is still possible to speculate upon his state of health. One thing that does emerge clearly enough in this respect is that he was increasingly prone to moments of introspection and self-doubt of a sort that he could ill afford. Here, for example, is Frank McLynn on the situation that developed in the wake of Ligny and Quatre Bras:

> Perhaps Napoleon knew in his heart that the game was up, for he went down with incapacitating illness ... Medical historians ... claim that he was suffering from acromegaly – a disease of the pituitary gland among whose symptoms are tiredness and over-optimism – but a more likely diagnosis is a psychogenic reaction to excessive stress and extreme frustration. Napoleon still expressed himself confident of total victory next day ... But on the 17th, still suffering from a heavy cold and bladder problems, he fell back into lethargy.[27]

Meanwhile, even if Napoleon was not ill, there is every reason to suppose that he was past his best, and that he had at the very least become physically sluggish. As even ardent Bonapartists admitted, indeed, the old dynamism had gone. To quote the staff officer, Paul Thiébault:

> His face ... had lost all expression and all its forcible character; his mouth, compressed, contained none of its ancient witchery; his very head no longer had the pose which used to characterise the conqueror of the world; and his gait was as perplexed as his demeanour and gestures were undecided. Everything about him seemed to have lost its nature and to be broken up; the ordinary pallor of his skin was replaced by a strongly-pronounced greenish tinge.[28]

Just as striking, meanwhile, is the description left by Auguste Petiet, a senior staff officer who served throughout the campaign at the emperor's headquarters. Thus:

> During his sojourn on Elba, Napoleon's stoutness had increased considerably. His head had acquired a great volume and had sunk into his shoulders, and he was fatter than normal for a man of forty-five. Also it was noticeable that during this campaign he did not remain mounted as long as on previous ones.[29]

Newly appointed as Minister of War, the erstwhile hard man of the Committee of Public Safety, Lazare Carnot, in after years told his son that he had been genuinely shocked by what he had seen:

> I no longer recognized him … The audacious escape from Elba appeared to have exhausted even his energetic sap. He drifted, he hesitated; in lieu of acting, this man of the promptest resolution, this man who had once been so imperious, this man to whom a word of counsel would have been regarded as an insult, procrastinated and asked the advice of all and sundry. Hitherto someone who had always not just given full attention to whatever needed it, but also never hesitated in taking on yet more work, he now constantly let himself be distracted, whilst he, the man who had always been able to fall asleep and wake up at will, had also become very somnolent. The decomposition of the man had followed on from the decomposition of the empire.[30]

Finally, someone who had occasion to observe Napoleon at unusually close quarters was the captain of HMS *Bellerophon*, Frederick Maitland. Whilst the emperor that he saw was a figure shattered by misfortune and exhausted by many weeks of stress and physical exertion and one who may well have been suffering from a severe bout of depression, the picture that he paints scarcely chimes with the image of the Napoleon of the heyday of *le grand empire*:

> Napoleon Bonaparte, when he came on board the Bellerophon on the 15th of July 1815, wanted exactly one month of completing his forty-sixth year … From his having become corpulent, he had lost much of his physical energy, and, if we are to give credit to those who attended him, a very considerable portion of his mental energy was also gone. It is certain his habits were very lethargic while he was aboard the *Bellerophon*, for, though he went to bed between eight and nine o'clock in the evening, he frequently fell asleep on his sofa in his cabin in the course of the day. His general appearance was that of a man rather older than he then was.[31]

Whether any of this mattered at Waterloo is obviously a matter of debate. For at least some Bonapartists, there has been a strong desire to emphasise physical infirmity as a causal factor in defeat, as this is an obvious means of deflecting criticisms of Napoleon's generalship as well as a way of connecting his downfall to the vagaries of destiny or fortune. Yet the emperor's admirers have never been united in taking this position. Flatly denying charges of lethargy, Houssaye, for example, is insistent that the emperor was on good form, even that 'Napoleon never exercised the commandership more efficiently and never was his action more direct'.[32] To take this line, of course, is immediately to be confronted with the issue of the responsibility for defeat: if Napoleon had his hand firmly on the tiller, it followed that it must ultimately be his fault that France was beaten. Like Napoleon himself, Houssaye evades this issue by throwing all the blame for defeat on Soult, Grouchy and a variety of other scapegoats. However, other observers are less forgiving. David Chandler, for example, both admired Napoleon generally and extolled his virtues as a military commander, and yet his judgement of the emperor's performance was deeply hostile:

> The chief responsibility for the outcome of the short campaign can only be laid at the door of the emperor himself. The original strategical conception was as brilliant as anything Napoleon ever devised ... but there were grave flaws undermining the entire effort ... In June 1815 Napoleon proved to be obstinate, arrogant and over-confident ... He tended to underestimate the courage and staying power of his opponents ... ignored Blücher's sense of loyalty, and ... discounted Wellington's ability as a general although there were plenty around him with personal experience of ... the Iron Duke's superb capabilities as a tactical leader. These errors led him to delay the opening of the battle on the eighteenth and then to deny Ney reinforcement at the vital moment ... Moreover, throughout the battle Napoleon failed to exercise sufficient control over his subordinates ... Jerome was permitted to turn a feint attack into a major effort, D'Erlon to adopt an outdated formation [and] Ney to throw away the cavalry.[33]

It seems, then, that, the question of whether Napoleon was ill at Waterloo matters little: much more serious was the fact that he was, at the very least, no longer quite the genius he had been. A weakened Napoleon might not have been so great a problem had he been supported by a team of able commanders. But many of his best marshals were either dead, not available or loyal to the Bourbons. His habitual chief of staff, Berthier, had fled into exile in Germany rather than take up arms with him again; Poniatowski, Bessières and Lannes were dead; Murat was in Naples; Moncey, Masséna, Periginon, Victor, Augereau, Saint-Cyr, Macdonald, Oudinot and Marmont had all either refused to abandon Louis XVIII altogether or not done so quickly enough for Napoleon's liking; and Kellermann, Sérurier and Lefebvre were too old for service. All that he had left were Davout, Soult, Ney, Mortier, Jourdan, Brune and Suchet, these being joined at the last minute by Emmanuel de Grouchy, a prominent cavalry commander promoted to the rank of marshal following a series of successes against Royalist rebels in the south of France in the weeks prior to the Waterloo campaign. As Andrew Roberts writes, 'Although fourteen marshals had fought in the Austerlitz campaign, seventeen in the Polish campaign, fifteen in the Iberian campaign, twelve in the Wagram campaign, thirteen in the Russian campaign, fourteen in the Leipzig campaign and eleven in the 1814 campaign only three were present in the Waterloo campaign.'[34]

This, however, was scarcely a winning team: when given a chance – and in 1815 it has to be said that Napoleon harried him unmercifully and on several occasions treated him so badly that he contemplated resignation[35] – Davout, certainly, was brilliant and Suchet very good, but that was about all that could be said, and even then it has to be said that Suchet had spent the entire period from 1809 to 1814 fighting in Spain and was therefore lacking in experience with respect to the campaigns that now threatened. Let us begin with Jean de Dieu Soult, the man to whom Napoleon gave the role of chief-of-staff. If Soult was a commander with a combat record that could at best be described as variable, he was much disliked by almost all his fellow generals on account of his arrogant manner. Certainly, the accounts of those who served with him in Spain are far from flattering. For a particularly mordant summation of his personality, we might turn to his chief *aide de camp*, Alfred de Saint-Chamans:

> I do not believe that it would be possible to meet a man who knew how to hide so much ability, perspicacity and finesse in the management of affairs beneath so gross an exterior ... In war he loved bold enterprises, and expressed himself with great force once he had settled on a course of action ... That said, it was well known that he did not risk his own person too much in that respect ... On the contrary, one could accuse him of ... being too careful in respect of keeping out of danger, this deficiency having grown in proportion with the great fortune that he had amassed (it is not, after all, uncommon to meet officers who do not worry about getting themselves killed when they are mere colonels ... but later hide behind a marshal's baton).[36]

This passage is, perhaps, a little unfair. In the words of another officer who served in Spain named Hyppolyte d'Espinchal, 'Attentive to the welfare of the soldier ... as well as careful to be sparing of his blood, he was just, fair and contemptuous of all intrigue. At the same time, meanwhile, appreciative of true merit, he never forgot any officer fortunate enough to have attracted his attention.'[37] Yet, even, so the general picture that emerges is one of a haughty and imperious satrap. Another veteran of the Spanish campaign was Antoine Fée:

> As commander of the Army of the South, the marshal appeared more as the King of Andalucía than as a simple lieutenant of the emperor. No monarch ever surrounded himself with as much majesty, nor was any court ever more servile than his. As Homer said of Jupiter, he could make Olympus tremble with a movement of his head ... The marshal was always accompanied by an imposing guard. On Sundays these élite troops formed a corridor leading to the door of the cathedral and presented arms at his passage, whilst he was followed by the civil authorities and a glittering general staff ... Formed in the school of the emperor, meanwhile, he echoed both his gestures and his style of address.[38]

Soult, then, was not the famously self-effacing Marshal Berthier who had served Napoleon so well as chief of staff ever since 1803, and his conduct of affairs has often been fiercely criticised. In the words of David Chandler, 'Soult was to be responsible for perpetrating several mistakes and misunderstandings in the written orders he issued and these, taken together, account for a great deal of Napoleon's ultimate difficulties.'[39] In this respect there is at least room for doubt – one cannot but admire the manner in which he got the battered forces that had been so badly defeated at the battle of Vitoria on 21 June 1813 back into action in the Pyrenees in little more than a month, whilst his record in Spain suggests that he was actually a better staff officer than he was a battlefield commander[40] – but even so some commentators insist that he should have been given the Ministry of War and Davout selected in his place.[41] Yet even had his talent equaled that of Berthier, there would still have been a problem in that he had served Louis XVIII as Minister of War and was therefore regarded by many soldiers as little more than a traitor. To quote Lamarque, 'Soult believed he could govern the army, but he failed to see that the rod of iron of the past had taken the arm of an emperor to wield: he tuned stomachs, excited hatred, provoked resistance, and he would surely have come to grief anyway even had not this fate not been accelerated by the great catastrophe that we are about to narrate.'[42]

So much for Soult. What, though, of his fellow marshals? Of Ney, Mortier and Jourdan – the three other figures of this rank who had joined Napoleon – none of them were much more than competent, while Ney in particular was very possibly suffering from some form of post-traumatic stress disorder on account of his harrowing experiences as commander of the rearguard during the retreat from Moscow.[43] As for Grouchy, whilst he had a very good record, he was completely lacking in experience of commanding formations made up of infantry, cavalry and artillery alike; still worse, the fact that he was promoted to the level, in effect, of an army commander, meant that the French cavalry in particular were deprived of a man who might very well have got a far better result out of them at Mont Saint Jean than was actually the case.[44]

At corps level, meanwhile, things were not much better: here, too, much talent had been lost, and this showed all too clearly. Mouton, Gérard and Reille were solid enough – Reille, indeed, had been the one French general to emerge with credit from Vitoria – but Vandamme had been the man responsible for the disaster at Kulm in September 1813, while Drouet was a nonentity who had repeatedly failed to distinguish himself in Spain.[45] Assuming that Napoleon himself was able to sustain the immense strain of the war which threatened, was this really the command element needed to steer the French army through what promised to be a greater trial than it had faced even in 1813 and 1814? 'Although the army was superb and full of ardour', wrote Jean-Baptiste Lemonnier-Delafosse, 'it was necessary to rejuvenate its leadership. However, more a slave to his memories and habits than might be imagined, the emperor made the mistake of putting it back under the leadership of its old commanders. Despite their decision to rally to the crown, the majority continued to desire the triumph of the imperial cause, but for the most part they nevertheless did not appear disposed to serve with the enthusiasm and devotion that the circumstances demanded. These were no longer the men who, full of youth and ambition, gave generously of their lives to achieve promotion and fame: they were men tired of war, who, having achieved the highest positions and been enriched by pillage of the enemy and the generosity of Napoleon alike, had no other desire than to enjoy their fortune peacefully in the shadow of their laurels.'[46] If this was so, however, it was not the only reason for the lack of enthusiasm that was so evident. Also an issue was the fact that, recognizing as they did the problems inherent in Napoleon's position, many of senior officers were openly defeatist. Returning to the subject of Jerome Bonaparte's open-air lunch with the officers of his division, we find that Pierre Robinaux came away deeply troubled. As he wrote:

In the whole course of the meal I did not once hear the prince say anything positive, whilst, pensive and worried as it was, his demeanour did not appear to me to augur particularly well. Such an attitude on the part of the brother of our emperor was not such as to electrify the heart of the soldier and gave courage to the army: indeed, I regarded his downcast air as the prelude to a ruin that seemed all too proximate.[47]

In 1815, then, Napoleon's war machine was anything but its old self: less likely to win battles than before, it was also less likely to be able to sustain defeat.[48] At the same time, it also has to be recognized that, if of variable quality, the armies that it would have had to face were not those of the days of Austerlitz, Jena and Friedland. Let us here assume that the bulk of the fighting would have been done by the armies of the eastern powers. Here the obvious place to begin is with that of Prussia. Assuming that Blücher and Gneisenau managed to disentangle themselves from the sort of Anglo-Dutch defeat on which this work is postulated, we can estimate that, not counting any reserves sent up from Prussia (potentially, the royal guard and two more corps), they would have had a force of at least 100,000 men available for immediate service, and possibly many more.[49] As to what these troops were capable of, one has only to look at the battles of Ligny and Waterloo. According to Hofschroer, the aspect which the Prussian forces presented in 1815 was scarcely encouraging. Thus: 'The armed forces fielded by the Kingdom of Prussia in 1815 were in terms of manpower, equipment and coherence of organization probably the worst Prussia employed in the entire Revolutionary and Napoleonic Wars.'[50] The problems, indeed, were manifold. In brief, war could hardly have come at a worse moment for Prussia in that the army was still in the process of incorporating all the new formations that had fallen to its lot as a result of the territorial gains authorized by the Congress of Vienna, namely the Grand Duchy of Berg, a large part of the Kingdom of Westphalia, strips of both Saxony and the Grand Duchy of Warsaw and the whole of the left bank of the Rhine. Excellent though all this was as far as Potsdam was concerned, capitalizing on the military resources which the new territories represented was not a simple matter, while further complications were caused by the need to absorb the more or less unruly *freikorps* raised in the war of 1813 into the regular army. Some of what this entailed was easy enough – the two infantry regiments possessed by the Grand Duchy of Berg, for example, were simply relabeled as Infantry Regiments Twenty-Eight and Twenty-Nine and those of the so-called Russo-German Legion (a force raised from German troops who had fallen into the hands of the Russian army in the campaign of 1812) as Infantry Regiments Thirty and Thirty-One – but other units had to be improvised from a variety of different sources including large numbers of more-or-less unwilling conscripts. Yet another issue was that the combined grenadier battalions that had previously been fielded by each infantry brigade had over the course of the winter been taken from their parent formations and sent off to Berlin for incorparation into an expanded royal guard. Many regiments, then, marched to war in a state of considerable disorganization with both coherence and experience in short supply. As if all this was not enough, there was considerable infighting among the Prussian generals – for example, the commander of the IV Corps, Bülow, was deeply jealous of the chief of staff, Gneisenau, and was so reluctant to obey his orders that his troops never arrived at Ligny and were extremely slow to get into action when they reached the battlefield of Waterloo – while even uniforms were in short supply, the two Berg regiments and the Russo-German Legion having mentioned having no option but to do battle in the distinctive uniforms they had worn prior to 1814. As Hofschroer concludes, then, 'The Army of the Lower Rhine was … a rag-tag force that presented a sorry picture.'[51]

This, however, is but half the story. The problems detailed by Hofschroer were serious enough, but the Prussian army could call on a number of strengths that had already been in evidence in the campaign of 1813–14. This is not the place to retail the history of the reform movement that had been set in train in the wake of the catastrophic defeats of Jena and Auerstädt, but, in brief, the army had been provided with a highly efficient general staff, a permanent system of higher formations and a new tactical doctrine marked by great flexibility and the use of large numbers of skirmishers, while, in theory at least, the officer corps had been rejuvenated, thrown open to the middle classes and subjected to a much improved system of training that stressed the need for individual initiative. In 1813, meanwhile, all this had been augmented by the introduction of the principle of universal military service. Henceforward, all unmarried men in good health aged from seventeen to twenty-four who were not otherwise engaged in the war effort – a provision that allowed young men of the middle classes to avoid serving with the masses provided they signed up for either a *freikorps* or one of the new volunteer *jäger* battalions raised as officer-training units – were to be balloted for service in the regular army, and all those from twenty-four to forty-five for service in a mobile militia entitled the *landwehr*. Finally, all those that were left over, together with boys aged from fifteen to seventeen, unmarried men aged from forty-five to sixty and all married men whatsoever were if necessary to serve in a home defence force entitled the *landsturm*.[52]

In institutional terms, then, the Prussian army of 1815 was a very sound organization. Meanwhile, something else that needs to be looked at is the question of its morale and fighting spirit. Starting at the top, there is the leadership provided by the exceptional team constituted by Blücher and Gneisenau. Driven by extreme hatred of the French – it was only with the greatest difficulty that Wellington succeeded in dissuading them from blowing up the Pont d'Iena in Paris – they instilled a spirit of the offensive into the forces under their command and refused pointblank even to think about the notion of failure. If the chief of staff was always a figure in the background supervising the movements of the army and dealing with a myriad of issues concerning planning and organization, Blücher was very much a soldier's soldier who was much given to charging into battle at the head of his troops: famously, of course, at Ligny he was thrown from his horse and then ridden over by Prussian and French cavalry alike while leading such a charge, but at the battle of Lützen, fought on 2 May 1813, he also distinguished himself in similar fashion, leading attack after attack on the French even after he had received a painful wound in the side from a spent musket ball. To fight the enemy, indeed, was at all times his first instinct, As Muffling remarked in his memoirs, 'His imperturbability in dangerous situations, his tenacity in misfortune and his courage which grew under difficulties were based on an awareness of his physical strength, which he had often used in hand-to-hand fighting during earlier campaigns. In this way he had gradually convinced himself that there was no military predicament from which one could not ultimately extricate oneself by fighting.'[53] Impulsive, warm-hearted and insanely brave, even on the march he was constantly to be seen riding among his troops and encouraging them onwards, the net result being that he was nicknamed 'Marschall Vorwarts' (an alternative nickname and one which in many ways was just as apposite was 'the hussar general'). An old family friend who encountered him for the first time in many years in 1813 has left a portrait that is affectionate, yet at the same time very telling:

> When I called on our old hussar general, he was cheerful as always and displayed that rare joviality with which he always knew how to win the hearts of those around him. He was … still the same man I had known before: rank, fame and years had not affected him in the slightest. He laughed, joked and also swore like any good hussar officer, and for everyone, high and low, general or corporal, he had a coarse joke, an apt jest, but also, if he thought it necessary a rebuke. This unaffected joviality, which nothing put off, was of inestimable value to the Army of Silesia and helped substantially to improve it and to fit it for great deeds.[54]

Sometimes, it has to be said, Blücher took enthusiasm to excess: if he fought too far forward at Ligny, he also came to within an ace of wrecking the entire campaign of 1814 by insisting on attacking alone in the wake of the Allied victory at La Rothière, the net result being the hammer blows of the battles of Champaubert, Vauchamps and Montmirail. Yet, if fighting at Ligny risked disaster, on the whole such was the superiority enjoyed by the Allies in the last campaigns of the war that what mattered more than anything else was the fact that the Prussian army could count on charismatic leadership of the first order: indeed, if ever there was a general who was capable of getting the best out of inexperienced troops, it was Gebhardt von Blücher.

However, morale is a quality that does not flow from the top, but is also something that is organic to the rank and file. Let us begin here with a somewhat stereotypical view in the form of the description of a regiment of Prussian troops which Archibald Alison observed in Brussels late in 1814:

We saw a body of 3000 Prussian *landwehr* enter Brussels, shortly before we left the city. The appearance of these men was very striking. They had just terminated a march of fourteen miles, under a burning sun, and were all covered with dust and sweat. Notwithstanding the military service in which they had been engaged, they still bore the appearance of their country occupations; their sun-burnt faces, their rugged features, and massy limbs, bespoke the life of laborious industry to which they had been habituated. They wore a uniform coat or frock, a military cap, and their arms and accoutrements were in the most admirable order; but in other respects, their dress was no other than what they had worn at home. The sight of these brave men told, in stronger language than words could convey, the grievous oppression to which Prussia had been subjected, and the unexampled valour with which her people had risen against the iron yoke of French dominion. They were not regular soldiers, raised for the ordinary service of the state, and arrayed in the costume of military life; they were not men of a separate profession, maintained by government for the purposes of defence; they were the *people of the country*, roused from their peaceful employments by the sense of public danger, and animated by the heroic determination to avenge the sufferings of their native land. The young were there, whose limbs were yet unequal to the weight of the arms which they had to bear; the aged were there, whose strength had been weakened by a life of labour and care; all, of whatever rank or station, marched alike in the ranks which their valour and their patriotism had formed. Their appearance suited the sacred cause in which they had been engaged, and marked the magnitude of the efforts which their country had made. They were still, in some measure, in the garb of rural life, but the determination of their step, the soldier-like regularity of their motions, and the enthusiastic expression of their countenances, indicated

the unconquerable spirit by which they had been animated, and told the
greatness of the sufferings which had at last awakened.[55]

The ideas that underpin this passage are, of course, a central part of the myth
of the *befreiungskrieg*: in brief, the people of Germany are seen nobly taking up
arms with one accord and striding out in search of justice and revenge. This is
a recurrent image that crops up time and again in accounts of the campaigns
of 1813 and 1814. 'What an inward transformation of the whole being this
crusade for freedom and Fatherland has effected in everyone', wrote Friedrich
Förster, a recent graduate of the University of Jena who enlisted in the famous
Lutzow *freikorps*. 'You would scarcely recognize those old braggarts from the
[Universities of] Jena and Halle, who based their reputations on having drunk
so many jugs of beer, on having fought so many [duels], or on having broken
the rector's windows. Now they stand in rank and file [and] obey the words of
command, and our whole existence has been inspired with a sense of dedication
which we never suspected.'[56] Meanwhile, Karl Friccius was the commander of
an East-Prussian *landwehr* battalion:

> I cannot praise adequately the men's willing acceptance of all the fatigues
> and deprivations, their obedient compliance with orders, their attentiveness
> and composure under arms, their increasing love of order, the skill with
> which individuals learned to behave in a natural warlike manner. Nor can
> I give high enough praise to the way in they lived peaceably together, how
> each man considered the good name of his company and of the entire
> battalion as his own, and, above all, how they were imbued with the sense
> of one for all and all for one in times of danger and difficulty, and of risking
> their lives for King and Fatherland.[57]

Such passages have, of course, to be read with caution. Even in 1813 large
numbers of Prussian conscripts deserted whilst such evidence as we have
suggests that those of the common people who enlisted voluntarily did so for
economic reasons only.[58] Thanks to the heavy losses suffered in the campaigns
of 1813–14 and the incorporation into the army of troops from such areas as the
Rhineland and Saxony, the crusading spirit that had been seen at Leipzig had to
a certain extent been dissipated, but even so it cannot be gainsaid that in 1815
the Prussian army fought with a savagery that was rarely equalled in the annals
of the Revolutionary and Napoleonic Wars. Here, for example is Hyppolyte de
Mauduit's account of the struggle that took place around the village of La Haye
during the battle of Ligny:

A regiment of Prussian infantry was sent against our left flank so as to support the one which was already attacking us from the front. It was already four o'clock. The attack was ferocious, but our troops contested it with so much courage and daring that it bogged down in the centre of the village. The defence was particularly desperate at the walled cemetery, and the Prussians were not able to take it despite receiving the support of a fresh infantry battalion. At length they were therefore forced to fall back with the aim of rallying their troops and reforming their columns of attack, but it was unfortunately in the midst of this carnage that the intrepid General Girard fell mortally wounded ... Notwithstanding these successive checks, the Prussian First Corps returned to the attack for a third time, and at the cost of losses as terrible as their efforts were unprecedented, at length made themselves masters of village and cemetery alike.[59]

Similar experiences were recorded in respect of Plancenoit, but to add yet another eyewitness account would simply be to pile up words for no good reason.[60] What is more interesting is what the British observed of the conduct of the Prussians both during and after the battle. Basil Jackson, for example, was an aide of Wellington's quartermaster-general, William de Lancey. Reaching La Belle Alliance at the climax of the battle as Zeithen's corps attacked the French from the vicinity of Papelotte, he found himself the witness of distressing scenes of cold-blooded murder:

Crossing to the left of the *chaussée*, I found myself involved with Prussian infantry streaming from the direction of Frischermont in no military order whatever as they swept onward bayoneting every wounded Frenchman they came upon. Seeing a knot of them standing close to a wall, I rode up and perceived a wounded light dragoon sitting against it, and there seemed to be some hesitation as to his fate, when I called 'Er ist ein Engländer' upon which the men raised their bayonets and the poor fellow was saved. The disorder of the Prussians ... was so great that I was glad to push on, and soon overtook our Fifty-Second Regiment and with it our glorious commander, but thinly attended.[61]

Similar scenes, meanwhile, were recorded by Mauduit. As he wrote, 'In this dreadful moment the Prussians' rage burst forth against anyone wearing the uniform of the Old Guard: they gave no quarter to any of our comrades unfortunate enough to fall into their hands either as prisoners or simply men who had fallen prey to shot or cold steel. God above! There never was such a butchery, never such a massacre as that of which Plancenoit was the theatre in that last hour.'[62]

In the days after Waterloo, the violence continued unabated, the Prussian forces engaging not just in acts of pillage, but also wholesale vandalism. For an eyewitness account, we have but to turn to the pages of Captain Mercer of the Royal Horse Artillery:

> The village of Loures, where we arrived about noon, presented a horrid picture of devastation. A corps of Prussians halted there last night, and, excepting the walls of the houses have utterly destroyed it. The doors and the windows [had been] torn out and consumed at the bivouac fire [while] a similar fate seems to have befallen furniture of every kind, except a few chairs and even sofas, which the soldiers had reserved for their own use and left standing about in the gardens and orchards, or in some places given a parting kick to, for many had fallen forward on the embers of bivouac fires and lay partially consumed. Clothes and household linen, beds, curtains and carpets, torn to rags or half-burned, lay scattered about in all directions. The very road was covered with rags, feathers, fragments of broken furniture, earthenware, glass, etc, large chests of drawers ... stood about broken or burned. The very floors had been pulled up and the walls disfigured in every possible way. It [is] needless to add that no human being was to be seen amidst the devastation.[63]

This behaviour, and especially the killing of wounded, was not normal in warfare in the more settled areas of Europe, and one is therefore led to conclude that the Prussian army was driven by a spirit that was quite exceptional and speaks to an anti-Napoleonic fervour that buttressed its morale and determination alike. Such were the numbers available to the Prussians, meanwhile, that it is difficult to believe that they would not have overwhelmed the 60,000 men who might have been available to Napoleon had active operations continued in Belgium. However, the Prussians were not on their own. Not counting the Spaniards and Piedmontese, both of whom were mobilizing their forces, Napoleon would also have to contend with a first wave of 150,000 Austrians and 168,000 Russians, and we must therefore think about the quality of these forces too.[64]

Beginning with the Austrians, the disaster represented by the campaign of Ulm had led to a major process of organizational reform that had seen the introduction of the corps system, and thereby greatly strengthened the Habsburg army's resilience and flexibility alike: hence the greatly improved performance which had confronted Napoleon in the campaign of 1809, the consequence being that it had been the Austrians who had gained the honour of being the first troops to inflict a defeat on the emperor in a field action (specifically at Aspern-Essling).[65] Other problems faced by the army had been tackled less effectively, but something had been done to address the issue of manpower by creating a reserve system that in theory allowed the rapid expansion of the infantry by some 40 per cent on the outbreak of war.[66] Meanwhile, when this came in August 1812, the Austrian commander-in-chief, Karl von Schwarzenburg, who, though by no means a brilliant tactician, was to prove an able strategist and highly successful coalition general, promulgated new instructions for the conduct of battles that stressed the use of columns covered by large numbers of skirmishers both in attack and defence: clearly, it was recognized that to expect the raw recruits which composed a large part of the Austrian forces to fight in line was simply unrealistic.[67] There remained, it is true, much to criticize, but the whitecoats who fought in the campaigns of 1813 and 1814 won a good opinion for themselves. 'Individual Austrian battalions and squadrons fought with great skill' wrote one Prussian officer, while the British ambassador, Sir Charles Stewart, was positively euphoric in his assessment: 'The composition of this army [i.e. Schwarzenburg's Army of Bohemia] was magnificent. Although I perceived a great many recruits ... the system that reigned throughout, and the military air that marked the soldier, especially the Hungarian, must ever fix it in my recollection as the finest army of the continent.'[68] As to the performance of these forces, these were mixed, but it was the Austrians who gained the day in the last major battle of the campaign at Arcis-sur-Aube on 20 March 1814.[69]

With such a record, there is no reason to suppose that the Austrians would not have been entirely capable of mopping up the scattered French forces that would have been facing them in 1815: admittedly, Rapp won a minor victory at La Souffel on 28 June, but sheer numbers forced the French to retire on Strasbourg nonetheless, whilst it is clear from Rapp's memoirs that he regarded his position as utterly hopeless.[70]

If the Austrians were solid, the Russians were still stronger. There is a tendency among Napoleonic military historians to see the Russian army of the Napoleonic as little more than an exercise in brute force, if not a veritable essay in military incompetence. However, recent research has suggested that this picture is greatly exaggerated. Whilst no-one could pretend that Alexander I's huge war-machine was without its problems, over the period from 1796 up until 1812 substantial military reforms under, first, Paul I, and then Alexander had vastly improved the army's training, efficiency and tactical abilities, while the terrible experiences of the campaigns of 1812–14 had honed its skills to a very high point indeed.[71] Even in 1813, indeed, foreign observers such as Sir Robert Wilson were impressed. Thus, whilst Wilson noted that the infantry were in a bad way on account of the terrible losses that had suffered, he did not hesitate to praise the other arms of service:

> The regular heavy cavalry are undoubtedly very fine, the men gigantic, horses, good, equipments superior and in perfect condition. The light cavalry are less striking in point of horses and general appearance, but some of the hussars and lancers are good. The artillery seems particularly fine and well appointed.[72]

In short, the Russian army was very tough and hard-hitting, whilst the general appointed to command the troops sent against France in 1815 was the very best commander that ever served Alexander I, namely Mikhail Barclay de Tolly, a progressive figure who had masterminded many of the most important reforms that had been undertaken since the Peace of Tilsit, planned the strategy that had brought Napoleon to grief in Russia and shown himself to be a skilled tactician in the campaigns of 1813–14. Against a failing Napoleon, he would have been a formidable foe, and there therefore seems even less doubt that the Russians could have accomplished their part in the campaign with gusto.[73]

The prognosis, then, does not look very good. Napoleon was outnumbered by a factor of at least three to one, unable to hope for much in the way of reinforcement, forced to rely on a set of generals who were scarcely the best that twenty-three years of near-incessant warfare had produced, and marching to war at the head of an army whose morale was distinctly questionable. Facing him, meanwhile, was a coalition that was unshakeable in its unity, free of the threat of revolt in its rear, possessed of resources that were near unlimited and determined to put an end to Napoleon once and for all. It was not a favourable combination, and in his heart of hearts the emperor knew it. No sooner, indeed, had the emperor's erstwhile private secretary, Méneval, returned from Vienna than his master was confessing to him that he already felt himself to be half-beaten. Thus:

> Generally speaking, the subjects of the emperor's conversation … were serious and seemed to affect him painfully … All his words were stamped with … a resignation which produced a great impression on me. I no longer found him animated with that certainty of success which had formerly rendered him confident and invincible. It seemed as if his faith in his fortune, which had induced him to attempt the very hardy enterprise

of his return from the island of Elba and … supported him during his miraculous march through France, had abandoned him … He felt that he was no longer seconded with the ardent and devoted zeal to which he was accustomed, and that, hampered as he was with the shackles which he had allowed to be placed upon him, he was no longer as free as formerly.[74]

Chapter 4

The Campaign of 1814

Given its physical separation from the rest of the Napoleonic Wars, there is a tendency for histories of the Waterloo campaign to treat it as an isolated, stand-alone episode with a context limited to nothing more than the experience of the restoration of the Bourbons. This, however, is clearly no way to proceed: whilst the return of Louis XVIII was certainly an episode of immense stress as far as the army was concerned, it was not the only issue in the recent past that weighed heavily on the situation. Just as important, if not more so, was the impact of the campaign of 1814. For the army this could act as a stimulus to further action: when Napoleon abdicated, in April 1815, many units could feel that they had never been defeated, that they were, indeed, better men than their opponents, while the endless narratives of treason and betrayal ensured that excuses for the triumph of the Allies were two a *centime*. Yet for civilian society – the very society to which Napoleon now appealed and whose support would be vital if the supposed miracle of 1793 was ever to be repeated – the campaign of 1814 represented something else entirely, namely the horrific culmination of many years of privation and sacrifice. At one and the same time, then, it was an experience that was both the launch pad for the flight of the eagle and the harbinger of its failure as well as a crucial factor in Napoleon's relations with France in 1815, and from this if follows that it must necessarily be investigated at some length.

Before going any further, however, let us examine some of the ways in which 1814 has been treated in the historiography. At one end of the scale, there is what might be called the school of Bonapartist assertion, namely the idea that, even in the wake of the retreat from Moscow and the battle of Leipzig, people and army alike stood four-square behind Napoleon, and, with the exception of some few cowards and traitors, remained loyal to him to the very end. The origins of this argument can be found in the memoirs and other writings of the emperor's many collaborators. In the history of the campaign published by his secretary, Agathon Fain, for instance, there is no mention of the difficulties that were encountered with respect to conscription, but considerable emphasis is placed on the popular resistance supposedly faced by the invaders from the moment they crossed the frontier. Thus:

The Allies ... began to fear the dangers of an uprising in France ... Prince Schwarzenburg found it was no less necessary to intimidate than to subdue. He threatened to hang every French peasant who should be taken with arms in his hands, and announced his intention of burning every village that should offer resistance to the invaders. That which the enemy feared and forbade was precisely what was necessary to be done. Napoleon issued orders for the levy in mass of the eastern departments. General Berkheim was appointed to command his countrymen the Alsatians. The people of Lorraine and the Franche-Comté evinced no less devotedness than the inhabitants of Alsace. Corps of partisans were organized in the Vosges and successfully opposed the enemy. On the banks of the Saône the people of Burgundy manifested as much courage and confidence as though they had been supported by armies in their rear. The inhabitants of Chalons cut their bridge, and the Austrians ... were compelled to halt.[1]

All but two centuries on, there are still patriotic Frenchmen determined to maintain the same position, come what may. In the preface, reference was already been made to Hourtoulle's *1814*. Alongside the romanticism represented by this work, however, there is an alternative argument that makes more of an effort to accommodate the very different reality. We come to the work of the already much-cited Henri Houssaye. The son of a leading novelist, Houssaye was originally a historian of ancient Greece, but service in the Franco-Prussian War, in which he greatly distinguished himself and won the Legion of Honour, kindled an interest in Napoleon, of whom he soon became a devoted admirer. Precisely because Houssaye had fought the Germans, the focus of his studies was always the events of 1814 and 1815, and between 1888 and 1905 he produced four substantial volumes on this last period of Napoleon's career, namely *1814: Histoire de la campagne de France* (Paris, 1888); *1815: la première abdication, le retour de l'ile d'Elbe, les cent jours* (1893); *1815: Waterloo* (Paris, 1899); *1815: la seconde abdication [et] la terreur blanche* (Paris, 1905). Based on detailed archival research, these remain a vital guide to the subject, and in fact have served as a de facto 'crib' for many of the popular writers who have followed in Houssaye's wake in the current era.[2]

In the current context, the key work is, of course, *1814*, and in so far as this is concerned, Houssaye's argument is as follows. In the wake of the campaign of 1813, we are told, France was prostrate. Industry and commerce were at a standstill; the fields untilled for want of hands; foodstuffs of all sorts extremely expensive; taxation crippling; the stock market in a state of collapse; the populace demoralized and war-weary; and the military utterly exhausted. Thus, 'In this state of ruin and desolation the whole population had but one desire, namely for peace, and this universal prayer rose to the steps of the imperial throne from city and from country, and even from the chiefs of the army themselves.'[3] In the circumstances, then, it was hardly surprising that there should be massive resistance to Napoleon's efforts to raise a new army, draft evasion spiralling and anti-conscription riots breaking out on all sides, the net result being that of the 650,000 men who were called up in the three separate levies of October 1813–January 1814, only about 175,000 ever reported for service. As for the National Guard, meanwhile, the situation was even worse, the number of men who were eventually got under arms coming to no more than 40,000. Given that there were insufficient arms, uniforms and equipment even for the much reduced forces that were still available, and that the cavalry and artillery alike were desperately short of horses, it may therefore be wondered how any sort of defence was achieved at all, but Houssaye found the answer in two separate developments. First of all, he perceived a sea-change in the attitude of the populace. This, he insisted, had never been quite as bad as the situation seemed to suggest – 'The people longed for peace, but they did not on that account blame the emperor'[4] – whilst invasion in any case lent an edge to the situation in that the Austrian, Russian, Prussian and German forces pouring across the Rhine inflicted unspeakable horrors on the population of the areas that they occupied. To quote Houssaye once again:

The invading army was fed and even clothed free of cost by means of requisitions, but that was not enough to satisfy the soldiers: as the Allies penetrated further into the country, and especially after their first reverses, their march was marked by fire, pillage and rape ... Sometimes the soldiers rushed upon their quarry with savage yells, sometimes they set to work calmly and methodically, and sometimes they deigned to laugh. One of their favourite occupations was to strip men and women naked and drive them with whips out into the snow-covered countryside. Another favourite pastime was to take the village mayor, priest or doctor, to grip his nose in pincers and drag him round and round the room, or again in a college the headmaster would be stripped naked and flogged in a courtyard before the assembled scholars ... At Nogent a cloth-merchant named Hubert was set upon by a dozen Prussians who pulled on his arms and legs till he was almost torn in pieces and a kindly bullet ended his sufferings, and at Provins a baby was thrown upon the fire to make its mother speak ... In the canton of Vandeuvre alone the number of people of both sexes who died as a result of violence was estimated at 550.[5]

The result of this behaviour, we are told, was to banish indifference: throughout the occupied regions, the populace leapt to arms and flung themselves on the invaders. However, it was not just that the people took up arms. On the contrary, within the army a combination of Napoleon's charisma, the desperate nature of the situation and the strength of its own internal bonding mechanisms worked wonders. We come here to the so-called *marie-louises*. Not quite the boy soldiers of legend – they were rather teenagers of nineteen called up a year ahead of time – and recruited in smaller numbers than is usually implied (Napoleon preferred fully-matured adults in their twenties and therefore gave instructions to place more weight on obtaining the services of the many men of earlier classes who had also now been called out), they yet became a symbol of heroism that ever afterwards loomed large in accounts of the campaign. In this exaltation of youth, needless to say, Houssaye was scarcely a reluctant participant. Thus:

In spite of all the deficiencies, of the 50,000 conscripts who passed through the depot of Courbevoie in the space of three months, only one per cent deserted. What a testimony to the honour of the soldiers of 1814! These poor youths, whose eyes filled with tears as they were dragged away from their desolate homes, were quickly transformed by the sight of the colours. From the bronzed veterans who had conquered Europe they learnt the noble self-denial and the cheerful fatalism which form the basis of the military spirit, and then, one day, at a review or before a battle, the emperor passed before them and they came under the spell of his fascination; from that moment they fought, not from patriotism, but solely for Napoleon. The nickname of '*marie-louises*' has been given to these poor little soldiers who had been torn away from their homes and formed into regiments and a fortnight later were hurled into the thick of battle, and this name of '*marie-louise*' they wrote large in their blood across the page of history. Those cuirassiers who could hardly sit their horses and whose furious charge crushed five hostile squadrons at Valjouan, they were *marie-louises* ... The conscripts of the Twenty-Eighth Regiment at the battle of Bar-sur-Aube [who held] the woods of Levigny with no weapon but their bayonets against four times their own number ... they were *marie-louises*. The Fourteenth Regiment of the Young Guard at the battle of Craonne who remained for three hours on the crest of a plateau within close range of the enemy's guns, while the grapeshot mowed down 650 men out of 950, they also were *marie-louises*. The *marie-louises* went coatless in bitter frost; ill-clad and ill-fed, they tramped bare-footed through the snow ... Yet through the whole campaign, they uttered no word of complaint, and in the ranks there was no murmur against the emperor. Truly France has the right to feel proud of her *marie-louises*.[6]

Clearly, there is a certain sleight of hand here: by Houssaye's own account, the class of 1815 was only expected to produce 150,000 men as opposed to the 600,000 men who were called up from previous classes, whilst we have, too, the admission already noted that priority was given to bringing in the older age groups: at best, then, underage recruits probably made up no more then one-fifth of the soldiers who fought in the campaign. Meanwhile, in so far as the conscripts who passed through the depot of Courbevoie are concerned, the suggestion seems to be that these men were all *marie-louises*, and yet no evidence is produced to substantiate such a claim, while elsewhere we learn that the general picture was very different. For example:

The forests filled with defaulters. In certain towns only a quarter of the numbers summoned reported themselves to the officials … There were numerous outbursts of feeling against the conscription, and in many departments each drawing of lots was the signal for a riot. At Toulouse a notice was posted up threatening to hang the first man who came forward to draw his number. On 20 January, at the request of the Prefect of Nantes, who expected a rising, the levy of 1815 was postponed for a fortnight … A detachment of conscripts from the Lower Seine started 177 strong, but only thirty-five arrived at their destination.[7]

However, let us set such passages aside, and accept, first, that the term *marie-louises* can be taken as comprehending all the conscripts swept into the army in 1814, and, second, that the appeal of Napoleon and the ethos of the army were together such as to banish all recalcitrance amongst those men who were actually inducted into the ranks. Such, at least, is the claim that appears to be at the heart of Houssaye's account of the campaign, whilst, to the end he insists that, whatever some of their commanders may have done in the course of the fighting, the rank and file and the subaltern officers remained loyal. Here, for example, is his account of the response of the army to the news of Napoleon's abdication:

The soldiers were less ready to forget their emperor and their colours than their generals. The announcement of the abdication filled the army with astonishment and anger … At Orléans the troops took possession of the town and forced the inhabitants to join them in cheering the emperor …

At Clermont-Ferrand the mayor proclaimed the Bourbons and marched through the town carrying the white flag, but the garrison broke out of the barracks, dispersed the procession and burned the flag on the main square … At Briare a division of infantry terrorised the whole countryside by its threats against the partisans of the Bourbons … In many towns the troops refused to take the oath of allegiance to the king.[8]

To conclude this review of *Napoleon and the Campaign of 1814*, then, what we have is a somewhat muddled work. Too honest a historian, perhaps, completely to deny the evidence of what he found in the archives in respect of popular opposition to the empire, Houssaye sought to elide this by the construction of a scenario in which, first, the atrocities of the Allied armies pushed the populace from indifference or even hostility to support for the campaign, and, second, the emperor and his army were able to assimilate large numbers of reluctant conscripts and persuade them to fight with great courage against overwhelming odds: if Napoleon was overthrown, then, the reasons are clearly to be sought elsewhere. This, however, is not good enough. Setting aside the fact that many of the claims in respect of popular resistance are buttressed by nothing more than assertion, the military narrative is entirely centred on events in the north and east of France – in other words the scene of Napoleon's own operations – and completely ignores the operations carried out by Wellington's Anglo-Portuguese army in the region of Bayonne and Toulouse, this being an area, as we shall see, whose reaction to foreign invasion does not fit in with Houssaye's postulations in the slightest. And at the same time, reading between the lines, it appears that all was not well even in Napoleon's own forces. In one of the quotes mentioned above, for example, we hear of the gallant stand of a light infantry regiment of the Young Guard at the battle of Craonne in the face of point-blank artillery fire, and yet it later turns out that the division to which it belonged was 'already much shaken and would have broken on the slightest provocation', its commander therefore deciding that to try to deploy from the columns into which his men were formed into line, let alone ordering a withdrawal, would be to risk disintegration. In short, what we see is not an act of heroic defiance at all, but rather a pragmatic confession of military inferiority.[9]

At many levels, then, there is much to question in Houssaye's account of the defence of France in 1814, and, by extension, much to question in the many works that have drawn so heavily upon him. A good example here is constituted by Ralph Ashby's *Napoleon against Great Odds* in which it is claimed that, if many men who were conscripted failed to report for duty, it was because the rapid disintegration of the postal service ensured that they never received their call-up letters, when in fact service was determined by lot via public ballots.[10] As even highly admiring biographies of Napoleon are now forced to admit, the issue of the public's faith in the emperor had become one that cannot be otherwise than admitted. 'Between 1800 and 1813', writes Andrew Roberts, 'draft evasion had dropped from twenty-seven percent to ten per cent, but by the end of 1813 it was over thirty per cent, and there were major anti-draft riots in the Vaucluse and the northern departments.'[11]

The implications of this situation were chilling. As the exiled emperor himself admitted on Saint Helena, the loss of his army at Waterloo left him with only one means of hanging on. As he told Barry O'Meara, 'My own opinion was that I could not have done so without shedding the blood of hundreds by the guillotine. I must have plunged my hands up to [the armpit] in blood.'[12] Nor is any of this surprising. Napoleon had come to power in France in 1799 as a man of peace, but in reality he had brought nothing but an endless war that had cost France very dear in almost every sense. In this respect the most obvious problem was that of conscription. Between, 1803 and 1814 some 2,200,000 men had been called to the colours. What, however, did such figures mean in human terms? Let us take as an example the tiny Breton fishing community of Plouider. A town of less than 3,000 inhabitants, between 1798 and 1813 it had provided the French army with no fewer than 475 conscripts of whom at least forty-two died in the course of Napoleon's campaigns.[13] Elsewhere, the situation was even worse: in the Department of the Isère, for example, losses among its 21,000 conscripts reached 47 per cent.[14] By 1815, then, France was a country in as great a state of grief as it was to be a century later. As a British visitor to Paris named William Fellowes wrote, 'This devoted country has bled at every pore and resembles one vast mourning family: three people out of five that one meets are habited in black, and it is impossible for a contemplative mind to banish from his recollections the sufferings which it has undergone even among the smiling scenes of luxury and voluptuousness which pervade the gay capital.'[15] Under the republic resistance to conscription had been widespread, large numbers of men fleeing or going into hiding rather than take their turn in the ranks, the brigandage that was in part the result of this situation being among the many reasons why the propertied classes welcomed the advent of Napoleonic rule in 1799. By dint of the imposition of extremely severe police measures, the emperor had got the problem under control, and it is clear that by 1810 most conscripts were reporting for duty as soon as they were called up.[16] Yet that does not mean that conscription was popular. On the contrary, more subtle forms of resistance, or, if not resistance, then at least more-or-less ingenious attempts to secure a cushy billet, continued under the surface: for example, the leading memoirist of the Peninsular War, Sebastian Blaze, opens his tale with an account of how, not wanting to risk the front line, he secured a position as a military pharmacist by affecting an interest in the natural sciences.[17] Elsewhere, such sleight of hand was replaced by downright fraud: from Gavin Daly, for example, we learn of a court case in the Department of Seine Inférieure which centred on the purchase of large numbers of fake medical certificates.[18] Meanwhile, if most conscripts set off to war, they generally did so in a spirit of melancholy resignation, even of mourning. Here, for example, is Pierre Robinaux's account of his departure from his home in December 1803:

> What a fatal day! I left a father and a mother in a state of the utmost desolation, and a sister who, though still very young, did not feel the pain any the less. Given over to agriculture … my dear parents had lost their every support and their only source of sustenance in their old age. As for me, only too aware of the significance of the moment, I was filled with a sadness of a nature that cannot be comprehended unless one feels it for oneself. Yet, despite our mutual affection, there was nothing for it but to consent to a separation that was inevitable.[19]

Doubtless there were happier young men than Robinaux. For example, a young boy from Issoudun named Antoine Fée admitted in his memoirs that, while he was saddened at leaving his parents and further grieved by the fact that friends and family alike regarded him as little better than a dead man walking, his vanity was flattered by the idea of being considered fit to take up arms, and that he in any case regarded the whole business as a great adventure.[20] Yet, even so, we are a long way from the legend. In consequence, the theme song of France's mobilization may be regarded as not the grandiloquent *Chanson du depart*, with its stress on enthusiasm and manly heroism, but rather the haunting *Conscrit de 1810* in which a young *provençal* bewails his fate and bids a sad farewell to his family (a counterpoint to this last, perhaps, is another song which Alison notes as having been very popular in the wake of Napoleon's downfall: entitled *Le retour de l'amant français*, it tells the story of a young soldier home from the wars who is reunited with his childhood sweetheart).[21] And, as more than one visitor to France pointed out, it had been this issue more than any other that had brought Napoleon to book. Morris Birkbeck, for example, was a Quaker landowner interested in agricultural reform who travelled to France in 1814 to investigate the state of French farming under the Republic and the Empire:

There was a magnificence about Bonaparte which carries you away in defiance of your sober judgement … Wherever you turn is some majestic monument of his taste. In fact, the grandeur of Paris was his creation, and you now see workmen busy in all parts, scratching out his name and defacing his eagles. This is very pitiful. The Bourbons, in their attempts to disgrace Napoleon by pulling down his statues and obliterating the ensigns of his power, are directing their attack against his least vulnerable part, and inviting a comparison greatly to their disadvantage. He executed many works of lasting utility and many of amazing splendour. Under his auspices the internal government of the country was wise and effectual: property was sacred, and crimes were rare because they could not be committed with impunity. It was through the madness of his external policy that his tyranny had become intolerable: for this he drained the best blood of his people, and sacrificed the commerce and manufactures of France, and to render the nation subservient to his ambition he laboured to enslave it. Let his successors pursue an opposite course; let them study peace, encourage commerce, and cherish liberty; then they will have no rival in Bonaparte. I think there is not in France any political party in his interest.[22]

Much the same opinion, meanwhile, was entertained by the Royalist champion François de Chateaubriand. As he later implied, conscription was the very essence of the experience of most citizens of the Napoleonic state and, with it, one that was deeply painful:

It is the style of the day to magnify Bonaparte's victories: the sufferers have disappeared; we no longer hear the imprecations, the cries of pain and distress of the victims; we no longer see France exhausted, with only women to till her soil; we no longer see parents arrested as a pledge for their sons, the inhabitants of villages made jointly and severally responsible for the penalties; we no longer see those conscription placards posted at the street corners, the passers-by gathered before those enormous lists of dead, seeking in consternation the names of their children, their brothers, their friends, their neighbours.[23]

However, it was not just conscription that afflicted France under Napoleon. Thus, in general, the emperor had not brought prosperity but rather ruin. Thanks to the long war with Britain, all France's ports had been blockaded with the result that the once immensely prosperous cities of Le Havre, Brest, Nantes, Bordeaux and Bayonne all saw themselves turned into veritable ghost towns, the various agricultural areas that had relied on their trade to absorb their products also suffering very badly. Also much affected were a number of internal *entrepôts*: in the Rhone valley sales at the great annual fair that had been held at the town of Beaucaire ever since the Middle Ages declined steadily from 31,900,000 *francs* in 1806 to a mere 17,000,000 in 1814.[24] Some places, true, had for a while done much better, the areas around Lille and Sedan acquiring substantial cotton industries, modern iron works opening in the region of Nevers, and the silk weavers of Lyons profiting enormously from the havoc wrought on their only real competitor – northern Italy – by the erection around France of tariff barriers designed to turn the wider Napoleonic empire into a captive market. Yet even this did not last: in 1810 Napoleon's attempts to undercut the Dutch and German smugglers who were currently turning the Continental Blockade into a mockery by sanctioning imports from Britain via French ports led to a deep economic depression that quickly spread from the *grand empire* back into France herself and was much exacerbated by a disastrous harvest in 1811. Whilst it is but fair to add that wages rose considerably in both town and countryside thanks to the shortage of labour consequent upon conscription, they did not keep pace with prices, and it did not help that the populace were assailed not just by ever-rising taxes, but also by a fiscal structure that privileged the propertied at the expense of the poor, the majority of whom had not been much benefited by the Revolution's abolition of feudalism and expropriation and sale of the lands of the Church (it might also be noted here that labourers both rural and urban were also assailed by savage combination laws as well as the need to carry a pass book that recorded their every move).[25] Finally, in so far as the peasantry are concerned, mention needs to be made of the so-called 'land-grab of 1813'. In brief, with Napoleon desperate for money in the wake of the Russian campaign, on 20 March of that year a law was promulgated allowing the state to expropriate and sell off all those plots of communal land which were currently being leased out for cultivation. How far this plan was actually put into operation is not entirely clear, but in parts of the north-east and south-east in particular its impact was extremely severe, many small peasants being thrown off holdings they had farmed for many years and being forced to bid for their re-acquisition in a market place in which they had little chance of competing.[26]

On the whole, then, France had benefited but little from her many sacrifices. The accounts of the British visitors who flocked to the country in the wake of the fall of Napoleon need to be taken with a pinch of salt, but they are at the very least suggestive. Having landed in Calais en route for Paris, for example, Archibald Alison was distinctly unimpressed by his first impressions:

We were much struck with the appearance of poverty and antiquity about Calais, which afforded a perfect contrast to the Kentish towns, and all the country towns through which we afterwards passed in France presented the same general character. The houses were larger than those of most English country towns, but they were all old, in few places out of repair, but nowhere newly built or even newly embellished. There were no newly painted houses, windows, carriages, carts or even signposts, the furniture and other interior arrangements of the inns were much inferior to those we had left … There were few carts and hardly any four-wheeled carriages to be seen in the streets, and it was obvious that the internal communications of this part of the country were very limited … All the lower ranks of people, besides being much worse looking than the English, were much more coarsely clothed, and they seemed utterly indifferent about the appearance of their dress … The peasants seem chiefly to live in villages … the cottages composing which … are very dirty and … have no gardens attached to them … A great part of the inhabitants seem oppressed with poverty to a degree unknown in any part of Britain. The old and infirm men and women who assembled round our carriage … to ask for alms appeared in the most abject condition, and, so far from observing, as one English traveller has done, that there are few beggars in France, it appeared to us that there are few inhabitants of many of these country villages who are ashamed to beg.[27]

A little way along the coast in Dieppe, the situation was not much better. Thomas Bowdler, for example, has this to say of what he saw when he landed at that town in August 1814:

Symptoms of long-stagnated trade and decayed population are evident. Many of the upper storeys (of which there are two to three in the roofs) are obviously untenanted and suffered to remain window-less and in dilapidation. Keels and ribs of vessels are to be seen along the beach and in the docks that seem to have been neglected by the builders till the timber is beginning to rot, and in fact the population, I am told, has declined from 26,000 to 20,000 … The conscriptions and military impositions of the late government during the last two years have, I understand, brought the whole of this neighbourhood to the brink of destruction.[28]

Meanwhile, the war continued unabated. Back in France Napoleon proceeded to try to rebuild his fortunes. Already a fiction, the French kingdom of Spain was now abandoned. Joseph Bonaparte had already been brusquely sacked in the wake of Vitoria, and, deciding that the moment was ripe to cut his losses, Napoleon now sent a message to Madrid offering to release the imprisoned Ferdinand VII on the understanding that the latter would make peace with France and expel the Anglo-Portuguese, only for his terms to be firmly rejected. Early in 1814 he decided to release Ferdinand anyway, but, whilst chaos ensued – in brief the result was a military coup that restored absolutism – it was much too late to make any difference. What was left of the Peninsular army was therefore going to have to keep fighting in the south-west, all that the emperor could do being to call up yet more levies. Nor was it of the slightest account that the emperor also released the Pope and directed him to make his way to Rome. Without the resources of the *grande empire* and with only 50,000 men left from the forces that had fought at Leipzig, the régime's demands therefore had to be exacting in the extreme. Taxes shot up dramatically: land tax rose by 95 per cent, and the salt and property taxes by 100 per cent, there also being steep rises in the sales taxes known as the *droits réunis*. As for manpower, in addition to the 350,000 men called up between January and April 1813, and another 30,000 men called up in August, October saw a demand for 120,000 men from the classes of 1809 to 1814 and 160,000 men from the class of 1815, this being followed a month later for a second for 300,000 from the classes of 1803 to 1814. And, as if this was not enough, another 180,000 men were mobilised for service as members of the National Guard. This was a *levée en masse* such as France had never seen since 1793 – alongside it, indeed, the 500,000 men raised under the Terror paled into insignificance – and, combined with the news of Leipzig, the impact was catastrophic.[29] Thus the war had already been unpopular in France, and the atmosphere produced by the news of Leipzig was one of growing panic. As Pasquier writes:

There was no longer any hope in anything: every illusion had been destroyed. There were certainly long columns in *Le Moniteur* full of patriotic addresses and expressions of devotion on the part of every corporation, every town council, but this official language had the appearance of a practical joke. It would have been much better by far for the government to have maintained a dignified silence.[30]

If confirmation was needed of the state to which France was reduced, it was the sights that accompanied the arrival of the survivors of the German campaign. 'The army returned in the most dreadful condition,' wrote Lavallette. 'The number of sick and wounded was immense; the hospitals and private houses were not enough to contain them, and that most deadly malady, typhus fever, attacked not only the army, but every village and town through which it passed.'[31] Conscripts, then, were hard to obtain whilst many of those that were netted were found to be unfit for service – no fewer than 600 out of a batch got together by the newly-appointed prefect of the Department of the Loire, Comte de Rambuteau[32] – a sure sign of widespread attempts to fake illness, if not to engage in self-mutilation (as cases of medical exemption were settled prior to the lists of those eligible for service being drawn up, the inference is that the men concerned had developed supposed physical handicaps, succumbed to wholly imaginary illnesses or inflicted the damage necessary to rule out enlistment – a favourite ploy was to amputate a trigger finger – only in the wake of drawing an unlucky number). As for recruits other than conscripts, there were scarcely any to be had: for example, an appeal made by the Prefect of Marne on 13 January for all discharged veterans to re-enlist immediately awoke almost no response while his efforts to get numerous workers who had lost their jobs to enlist in the Young Guard also proved a failure.[33] Finally, already high, the price of obtaining a substitute in the manner allowed by the conscription regulations became wholly unsustainable. To quote the wife of Marshal Oudinot:

> France had long since been exhausted, not so much of money … but of men. This last scarcity … threw whole families into despair and want. They really were bled to the uttermost. The poor man had to give his last son and in him lost his support, and in the fields it was often the women and girls who led the plough … And the same disasters occurred in the towns. Numbers of families condemned themselves perpetually to cripple their fortunes in order to save the young man whom other measures ended by reaching … . The crepe with which the Russian and Leipzig campaigns had covered France had not yet disappeared; bitter tears were still being shed.[34]

Despair, then, was widespread, and to this was added political disaffection. In few parts of the country was royalism much of a force – according to the Comte de Rochechouart, 'With the exception of the nobility, the clergy and a few wealthy members of the old bourgeoisie, the majority of the populace did not even know the name of Louis XVIII'[35] – but anger at the increased demands of the state in a number of places inflamed old political antagonisms. In 1810, then, a royalist secret society had been founded by an erstwhile *émigré* named Ferdinand de Berthier de Sauvigny whose father, the then intendant of Paris, had been murdered in the wake of the fall of the Bastille. Known as the Chevaliers de la Foi, this had initially remained a very small affair whose adherents were almost entirely limited to the old aristocracy, whilst its leadership recognized that any idea of it overthrowing Napoleon was laughable. Yet times changed, and in October 1813 Louis XVIII ordered Berthier de Sauvigny to intensify the movement's propaganda efforts and prepare for an insurrection. With the regime clearly tottering, it now began to gain recruits in greater numbers, and by the time of the final crisis was well established across western and south-western France as well as enjoying some support in Paris. Nor did it help, meanwhile, that many soldiers had been brutalised by long years' fighting in such theatres of war as Spain and Russia and came back across the Rhine resentful of civilian backsliding, this being something that sometimes led to serious trouble. 'The soldiers who were accustomed to live in conquered lands sometimes forgot that they had returned to their own country and behaved shamefully', complained one observer. 'I once saw a mounted Grenadier of the Guard knock an old man down into the mud, and, when the bystanders interfered, shout insolently at them and call them *tas de pékins* [literally, 'a bunch of Chinks']. A crowd quickly assembled and would have torn him to pieces but for the intervention of a couple of calmer spirits who managed to get him safely away.'[36]

On all sides, then, emerged signs of the populace's anger, the problem becoming so great that even the most toadying of the prefects had little option but to report it to Paris: as Munro Price has shown in *Napoleon: the End of Glory*, then, from all sides there came complaints of anti-government graffiti, threatening handbills and even death threats, while in both Pontarlier and Hazebrouck there were riots that in the latter case in particular all but amounted to wholesale revolts.[37] And even where there was no overt resistance, draft evasion once again became a serious problem, and with it a renewal of brigandage.[38] Almost everywhere, meanwhile, there was a mood of barely-suppressed fury. 'Observant minds saw plainly that the emperor had already lost his head, and that he would soon lose his crown. Consequently public opinion was violently opposed to him. His military and financial operations were loudly blamed. No longer dreaded, he became the butt of diatribes, satirical songs, lampoons, and all the other offensive weapons employed by French public opinion.'[39] Even attempts to play on fears of invasion had no effect: 'I was at the Vaudeville,' wrote the Duc de Broglie. 'The police had given orders for the performance there of an appropriate play, in which cossacks plundered a village, pursued young girls, and set fire to the barns: the piece was outrageously hissed from the very beginning, interrupted by the noise from the pit, and could not be terminated.'[40] Needless to say, the growing social instability could not but undermine the loyalty even of the régime's own personnel, who as *notables* inevitably had much to lose, as well as no desire to return to the days of Jacobinism and the *levée en masse* which a desperate emperor now seemed to be trying to revive (not only was the rhetoric of the régime increasingly echoing that of 1793, but Napoleon had sent out a number of extraordinary commissioners in the style of the old *deputés en mission*, introduced several measures intended to redistribute a certain amount of land to the peasantry, ordered the addition of independent companies who were supposed to function as guerrillas to every battalion of the National Guard and decreed the formation of a volunteer militia drawn from unemployed workers in Paris and other towns of northern France). 'The government,' wrote Fain, 'exerted every endeavour to rouse the public mind to noble resolution. "Surrounded by ruins, France raises her threatening head. She was less powerful, less rich and less fertile in resources in 1792 when her levies in mass delivered Champagne, in the year VII when the battle of Zurich stopped a new invasion by all Europe, in the year VIII when the battle of Marengo finally saved the country!"'[41]

These attempts somehow to revive the spirit of the so-called 'great crisis' of 1793 are generally agreed to have been utterly ineffectual. As even Fain admitted, 'Napoleon had in his hands the same springs, but they had lost the republican spirit which once tempered them.'[42] To quote an English internee who lived through the events of 1814 in Paris named Thomas Underwood:

Notwithstanding the exertions of government to 'nationalise' the war, the greatest indifference was evidently felt by the middle and lower classes now that their vanity was no longer gratified by conquest for themselves and insult to others. Every artifice was resorted to by the police to arouse the salves of its power from this apathy: one of these was the attempting to recall to the minds of the people (what they had been for fourteen years labouring to destroy) the energy they had manifested during the Republic. Towards effecting this object, verses in praise of the emperor adapted from the long-prescribed Marseillais hymn were performed on barrel organs, or sung in every street, but the revolutionary slang was ill adapted to the praise of imperial power and produced a truly ludicrous effect. During the twelve years of my residence in France, I never had listened to this piece of music, and only once (in 1803) heard *Ça ira* in passing an obscure wineshop on the Place du Grève. But all would not do: the whole class of young men had grown up imbued with the egotism of slaves, the true test of a despotic government.[43]

Just as scornful, meanwhile, was the contemporary chronicler Alphonse de Beauchamp, an erstwhile official of the Ministry of Police who had fallen out of favour with Napoleon in 1809 and after 1815 took service with the Bourbons:

> Entirely separated from the nation and deprived of any real assistance, Napoleon was now reduced to the usual resources of despotic government ... and, after having formed one furious resolution after another, he determined on applying desperate remedies as the only cure for the evils he had produced. He immediately dispatched commissaries to the military divisions of the empire for the purpose of presiding over the levies en masse and other measures of interior defence. Their number was twenty-seven, and they were selected from his Senate and Council of State. Did he wish to renew those sanguinary proconsulates which desolated the provinces during the horrors of the Revolution during the horrors of the Revolution? It was to be suspected and feared that he did, for these new commissaries were authorized to execute every measure of police, to make the decrees obligatory on every citizen, to arrest anyone they suspected of favouring the enemy, and bring him before a military commission of their own creation: in one word, they had the power of life and death ... But the arm of terror, so powerful under democratic anarchy, was feeble when raised by flexible courtiers, men devoid of energy, bending under the weight of ill-acquired wealth and alarmed at the responsibility of their appointments. In general, therefore, they confined themselves to pompous speeches or issued proclamations and addresses which breathed the spirit of flattery and servile devotion to their master.[44]

To the extent that the aim of the régime's rhetoric was to arm the people and persuade it to do battle with the invaders, it soon became clear that the whole scheme was futile. Starting with the National Guard, this in many cases was a mere sham. In the directly threatened city of Reims, for example, the local battalion turned out to have only 500 men instead of the regulation 600 and also to lack uniforms, whilst its independent guerrilla company never came into being; as for the rank and file, we learn that 'all of them very bourgeois, men of property or business, they were far more interested in policing the city than they were in fighting a war'.[45] At all events the National Guard put up no resistance whatsoever when a party of 150 cossacks appeared before the Porte de Mars on 6 February, the acting mayor, Andrieux, surrendering the city without a fight and employing the guard to maintain order.[46] As for the new volunteer militia, in the eyewitness account provided by Andrew Blayney, a British general captured in

Spain in 1814 and held in captivity in Verdun until evacuated in the direction of the River Loire, where this appeared at all, it was little more than a joke:

> The following day I remained at Orléans and was highly amused by the exhibition of ... the *levee en masse* which [was] now organizing ... To comply with this order, fowling pieces that had hung for centuries over chimneys were now brought forward, some without locks and others of which the locks were so rusty and out of repair as to be totally unserviceable. The number of these arms not being sufficient, different articles were given to different persons, one having a musket, a second the bayonet and a third the ramrod. The other two thirds of this motley group were armed with sticks, broken shovels or broken pitchforks, for their patriotism was not strong enough to bring forward any implement that was serviceable or useful in the farms. After their being mustered by their names with great ceremony, an old drunken drummer with a ragged coat, a cocked hat, wooden shoes and a broken drum was placed at their head, and they were marched off. What with their broad-brimmed hats and sabots, their ragged clothing and their own natural deformities, they presented so ludicrous a scene that, if Napoleon had studied to bring complete ridicule on the great nation, he could not have chosen a more suitable expedient.[47]

Useless in one sense, in another Napoleon's newfound Jacobinism was downright prejudicial, for it alienated the propertied classes. With a Royalist restoration no longer a serious threat in social and economic terms – on 1 February 1813 Louis XVIII issued a well-publicised declaration in which he promised to respect the status quo – the political establishment had no reason to support a fight to the finish. Already in December 1813 the *corps législatif* had effectively demanded that Napoleon make peace immediately, the growing lack of confidence being further manifested by the slow rate of purchase and discounted prices that pertained in respect of the bond issue of 200,000,000 *francs* that the regime had authorised to finance the war effort.[48] Also significant here was a run on the Bank of France that forced Napoleon to issue a decree limiting overall withdrawals to 500,000 *francs* per day, not to mention an ever-accelerating slowdown of economic activity that quickly produced a large number of bankruptcies.[49] Meanwhile, further signs of disaffection appeared in the administration, the prefects and their deputies now beginning to refuse to carry out their orders, to connive at draft evasion and the non-payment of taxes, and even to abscond altogether: on 26 January, for instance, the mayor of Reims, the Baron de Ponsardin, and the sub-prefect, Leroi, both fled the city on the pretext of orders that had been received that local authorities should remove themselves in event of invasion, an example which was quickly followed by the mayor of Soissons.[50] Even such exalted and well-paid figures as the prefects could no longer be counted on: in Marne, the Baron de Jessaint simply resigned, whilst others fled their posts or ceased to obey the orders sent them from Paris. Typical enough was the attitude of the erstwhile governor of the Grand Duchy of Berg, Jacques Beugnot, who was in the winter of 1813 appointed to the prefecture of the Department of the Nord. 'I gave up trying to levy conscripts. More than that, I sent home the young men from the leading families of the department who had been swept into the Gardes d'Honneur, and put an end to the persecution that had been directed against their parents ... And, finally, loudly proclaiming that, in the situation that the department might find itself invaded at any moment, all its people together would not be enough to defend it, I promised that no-one who was called up would be expected to serve outside its limits.'[51]

Beugnot's mention of the Gardes d'Honneur is particularly significant as it touches on an issue that rankled enormously with the propertied classes. Hitherto, despite the principle of universal military service, they had been able to safeguard their sons from conscription by means of the purchase of substitutes. Admittedly, this was something that had become harder by the year as the prices that could be commanded by access to this privilege had soared dramatically, while the freedom it obtained had ceased to be valid for a whole lifetime, but now covered a single levy only. In the wake of the retreat from Moscow, however, even this concession came to seem too costly to Napoleon, and on 3 April 1813 the formation was decreed of four new regiments of light cavalry that were to be raised by compulsion from among the wealthiest families of each department. As if this was not enough, meanwhile, insult was added to injury by the stipulation that the recruits were to provide their own mounts and meet the cost of their uniforms, which were, of course, suitably gorgeous, very much resembling those of the *Chasseurs à Cheval* of the Imperial Guard. This measure, which was in effect a punishment for doing no more than taking advantage of a concession that had been freely offered by the state, and at the same time negated investments that amounted in some instances to sums in excess of 100,000 *francs*, was a bitter pill indeed, while it was sweetened not at all by the promise that the troopers would automatically obtain a commission after a year's service: had they wished to become officers, they could have done so at any time without the extraordinary costs that were now heaped upon them. At all events the response was one of utter fury. Here, for example, is Archibald Alison:

No measure was omitted by Napoleon to secure the services, in the army, of all who could be of any use in it. The organization of the Garde d'Honneur was intended to include as large a number as possible of the young men whose circumstances had enabled them to avoid the conscription. No act of the imperial government seemed to have given more general offence in France than the formation of this corps, the number of which was stated to have amounted at one time to 10,000. They were, in the first instance, invited to volunteer, under the assurance that they were to be employed as a guard for Marie-Louise, and under no circumstances to be sent across the Rhine. A maximum and minimum number were fixed for each *arrondissement*, some number between which was to be made up by voluntary enrolments; but when any deficiency was discovered, as for example in Holland, where the young men were very little disposed to voluntary service in the French army, a balloting immediately took place, and a number greater than the maximum was compelled to come forward. Exemption from this service was impossible; immense sums were offered and refused. They were all mounted, armed, and clothed at their own expense; those who did not choose to march were sent off under an escort of *gensdarmes*; and ... brought up to join the army; and these young men, taken only a few weeks before from their families, where many of them had been accustomed to every luxury and indulgence, were compelled to go through all the duties and fatigues of common hussars. Some regiments of them, which were very early brought into action, having misconducted themselves, were immediately disbanded; their horses, arms, and uniforms, were taken from them for the use of the other troops, and they were dismissed, to find the best of their way to their homes. Those who remained were distributed among the different corps of cavalry, and suffered very severely in the campaign in France. We spoke to some of them at Paris, who said they had bivouacked, at one period of the campaign, *on snow*, fourteen nights successively, and described to us the action at Reims, one of the last that was fought, where half of their regiment were left on the field.[52]

With the 'masses of granite' on which Napoleon had always sought to base his regime in revolt, the new armies were not forthcoming: ordered to provide 5,000 men for the levy of 300,000 men on the classes of 1803–14, for example, Seine Inférieure managed only 1,457, whilst the country as a whole raised only 63,000.[53] Nor were things any better with regard to the two earlier decrees, these together producing only 95,000 men.[54] In Lyons, then, Marshal Augereau, was in despair; 'I am sent', he said, 'to command the army at Lyons: the emperor speaks of 20,000 men; I have not 4,000! And it is I, an old veteran of the Army of Italy, who is selected to surrender the second city of France to the enemy!'[55] Even had more men been secured, there were few arms: many of the National Guard, for example, were armed with no more than pikes and fowling pieces, at least 700,000 muskets having been lost in the campaigns of 1812–13.[56] Faced by disaster, the emperor displayed immense energy – 'He goes to bed at eleven o'clock,' his secretary, Baron Fain, told a concerned Lavallette, 'but he gets up at three in the morning and until evening there is not a moment when he is not working'[57] – but no amount of orders could change matters, whilst Fain admitted that his master was 'utterly tired out'.[58] Of peace, though, there was still no mention. 'Peace! Peace! It's easy enough to say the word,' Napoleon shouted at Beugnot, 'Am I to give up all that I possess in Germany? I have 100,000 men in the fortresses along the Elbe, in Hamburg and in Danzig. If the enemy are foolish enough to cross the Rhine, I will march to meet them … and have my garrisons fall on their rear, and then you will see the meaning of the word *débâcle*.'[59] Yet, in reality, Napoleon's power was on its last legs. In northern Italy, true, Eugène de Beauharnais, was still holding the line of the Adige, but, having first led his army northwards on the pretext of reinforcing the defenders, Murat suddenly declared against the emperor in a desperate bid to save his throne, whilst the British commander in Sicily, Lord William Bentinck, was preparing to set sail for Livorno with an Anglo-Sicilian expeditionary force. Of the Polish strongholds, all had fallen, and in Germany only Hamburg, Wittenburg and Torgau still held out; still worse, having all changed sides in the wake of the battle of Leipzig, the erstwhile members of the Confederation of the Rhine were all mobilising fresh armies against France. In Denmark and Norway Danish resistance was being crushed by Swedish troops. Yet another British expeditionary force was being readied for service in Holland. And in France there were only 85,000 men to defend the eastern frontier against an initial total of at least 350,000 Allies, whilst another 40,000 Frenchmen were facing 90,000 British, Portuguese and Spaniards in the south-west. With such few reinforcements as there were mostly invalids, customs guards, sailors and *gensdarmes*, many of even of the emperor's closest confidants were begging him to make peace on whatever terms he could get: 'With a blunt frankness only pardonable for its sincerity', wrote Lavallette, 'I told him that France was worn out, that the country could not bear much longer the intolerable burden under which it was crushed, and that the people would throw off the yoke in order to surrender … Particularly I spoke a good deal to him concerning the Bourbons, who would end by inheriting the spoils of his monarchy if ill-luck should overthrow him.'[60]

For the emperor, however, cheer was still to be found in the continued devotion of elements of the soldiery. Disaster notwithstanding, of this there was much evidence, not least in atmosphere that marked the ceremony in which Napoleon entrusted Marie-Louise and the King of Rome to the Paris National Guard prior to his departure for the front. As the emperor's valet, Marchand, remembered, for example, 'The enthusiasm generated by the emperor when he took the young king in his arms ... can never be forgotten by its witnesses. Frenetic and prolonged cries of "Vive l'empereur!" moved from the Hall of Marshals to the national guard assembled in the Carrousel ... These demonstrations of so true a love for his son moved the emperor: he kissed the young prince with a warmth that escaped none in the audience.'[61] In public, at least, Napoleon maintained a façade of confidence, telling the official of the Ministry of Police and member of the Council of State, Pierre Réal, for example, that, should the enemy make a dash on Paris, 'the inhabitants would rise and defend the capital'.[62] To this sally, Réal supposedly replied that the people would do so with their weapons not in their hands but rather at their feet – in other words that they would meet the invaders with their hands firmly in the air. At all events, the mood in Paris was one not of confidence, but of panic. As Underwood noted:

Towards the end of January 1814 the dreams of power, security and reliance on the omnipotence of their arms which the French had so long indulged, vanished before their increasing dangers. Apprehensions that the invading army would arrive at Paris were manifested by several of the inhabitants packing up their most valuable effects and sending them into those parts of France where it was least probable the enemy would penetrate, while at the same time many of the inhabitants of villages, farms and country-houses in the environs brought their furniture into the metropolis for greater security. Wagons and carts, thus laden, were daily seen on the boulevards and on all the roads approaching the capital. Even the Duke of Rovigo, minister of police, sent his daughters and the most valuable part of the furniture of his hotel in the Rue Cerruti to the neighbourhood of Toulouse. The Parisians of every class laid in, to the full extent of their circumstances, stores of flour, rice, vetches, white beans, potatoes, salt pork, herrings, etc.... . One day at the commencement of February the demand for potatoes was so great at the Marché des Innocents that a measure ... rose from the usual price of six *sols* to forty.[63]

The fears recorded by Underwood were only too well placed, for very soon France was gripped by the horrors of war, and, with them, concrete proof that the propaganda of the régime was in no way to be relied upon. Amongst the residents of Paris was the sister of Chateaubriand, Marie-Anne de Marigny. Herewith, for example, the entry in her diary for 17 February:

> Great alarm: some wounded have come in the night. The students of the Ecole Polytechnique and the prisoners of the Montaigu college [the chief military prison in Paris] have been sent off to reinforce ... the army. Cannons and caissons are rolling through the streets ... In the afternoon 4,000 prisoners appeared ... They were marched through the city and left by the Versailles gate. Many people came out ... to see them pass, and they were thrown gifts of bread and money. Someone who had gone out for a stroll told us that they had seen a convoy of wounded ... Their blankets were covered with blood, and the spectacle could not but call forth horror and pity.[64]

As the days passed, so the situation in Paris went from bad to worse. In this respect, Underwood's testimony is once again extremely graphic:

> All the disgusting imagery of war was now displayed within the walls of the capital. In consequence of the military hospitals being insufficient to receive the immense numbers of sick and wounded which continued to arrive, either from the armies or the evacuation of the military hospitals on the frontiers ... the city patients were driven from the hospitals and ... obliged to return to their crowded homes in the populous *faubourgs*, thus spreading contagion and misery in those abodes of wretchedness ... The Salpetrière was the asylum for indigent, infirm, aged and insane females ... From the middle of February to the end of March, 7,609 persons were brought into this hospital [alone] from the army, the great number of them labouring under typhus or chronic diarrhoea ... Such was the confusion in the administration ... that there was no wood for fuel, nor charcoal for heating the *tisanes*, which, from the severity of the weather, were frozen. The broken windows remained so: this, though it saved many of those attacked with fever, killed the pulmonary patients ... Contagion raged to such a degree ... that, out of six physicians and surgeons who attended there, three died ... All those who sorted the clothes of the dead soldiers died, as did also the man who fumigated the wards with chlorine ... During the whole of the month of February, the streets were filled with soldiers and raw conscripts whose route to join their regiments lay through Paris. Government not having made any provision for their subsistence, they

were under the necessity of begging in the streets. People fed and lodged them from mere compassion. On the 7th of February a court martial sat at Meaux to decimate those wretched beings (termed *traineurs*), who, sinking from inanition and sorrow at being torn from their families were unable to join their regiments with the required celerity. I saw the judgements, with the names of those who were shot, stuck up against the walls of the metropolis.[65]

At least those who experienced the war from inside the walls of Paris were safe. In those areas directly affected by the fighting, the situation was far more bleak. At the most simple level, there was the devastation wrought by battle. To quote Jean-Roche Coignet, for example, 'On the 27th January 1814 there took place the combat of Saint Dizier. No mere skirmish, it was a real battle, one of the very bloodiest sort indeed. The town was reduced to ruins by the fusillade, and one could count thousands of bullets in the doors and shutters; the trees in a small square were riddled with bullets; all the houses were pillaged, and not a single inhabitant dared remain in the town.'[66] By all accounts, meanwhile, devastation was widespread: 'For an extent of thirty miles in one direction towards the north of Champagne,' wrote Archibald Alison, 'every house near the great road had been burned or pillaged for the firewood it contained both by the French and the Allied armies, and the people were everywhere compelled to sleep in the open air.'[67] On top of this was the greater or lesser degree of brutality engaged in by the invading forces. In the south-west, as we shall see, Wellington did his best to keep his polyglot army under control, but in those areas occupied by the Austrians, Russians and Prussians the situation was very different. Pillage, then, was wholesale, while rape and murder were widespread, if not perhaps so general as was claimed by the propaganda of the regime. One eyewitness was the British representative at Allied headquarters, Sir Charles Stewart:

I witnessed here [La Fère-Champenoise] a very interesting, but, I fear, unfortunately too usual an occurrence that took place in the capture of the convoy and the enemy's baggage ... Being forward in the *mêlée*, I perceived not only that some of the cossacks ... had secured a general's *caliche* and baggage, but also that one of them had seized his wife, whose cries rent the air, and, with the aid of two other gallant tartars, was placing her behind him. I will not detail the frequent ... instances of barbarity which I fear have been too justly given of the progress of the Russian predatory hordes through France, but I reflect with satisfaction that it was my good fortune to rescue, even for a moment, a lovely ... Frenchwoman from the hands of these wild soldiers ... Not knowing in what manner better to place her in security, I ordered my own orderly hussar ... to place her *en croupe*, and carry her to my billet at headquarters ... But, alas ... my provisions were not so great as I flattered myself they were ... Sad to relate, either the same cossacks returned or others more savage and determined, and, perceiving my faithful orderly ... fell upon him, and, nearly annihilating him, reseized their victim ... Although the strictest enquiry was made through his whole army by the Emperor of Russia to whom I immediately repaired ... the beautiful ... Frenchwoman never reappeared again.[68]

Equally candid, meanwhile, was a lieutenant in the Russian Sumskii hussar regiment named Eduard von Löwenstern who experienced the campaign on the staff of Count Peter von der Pahlen:

The Count marched to ... Lhuitre, where he stayed at a country preacher's. The sour, dissatisfied face of this man of God and the bad treatment he gave us earned him, after Pahlen had left the house, a good flogging which I and Turnau could not keep ourselves from giving him to pay him back in full ... It rained continuously the whole night and the following day. Soaked to the bone and freezing, we came to Droupt-Saint Basle in the darkness. Every bivouac means the ruin of the nearby village. May God have mercy upon the unlucky place in which soldiers arrive in the night in a rainstorm. They all pour into the village to get in a dry place as soon as possible, and then there is no discipline, no power capable of protecting that village from plundering. This unfortunate fate also befell Droupt-Saint Basle ... We billeted in the palace and found the master of the house and his whole family hidden there. All of them were filled with fear and anxiety ... I had boundless pity for the unfortunate family who, without support in the middle of a battlefield ... were being subjected to all kinds of unpleasantness.[69]

Typical enough were the experiences of the family of the noted man of letters Charles de Pougens, their story being recorded by his niece, Louise de Saint Léon. Trapped in Soissons, they first experienced the terrors of siege and assault:

Taking refuge ... in a ground-level room whose firmly-sealed shutters kept us plunged in complete darkness, we listened with many shudders to the explosion of the bombs that rained around us; one shell fell with a terrifying crash in the garden barely a hundred paces from where we were, and reduced a very large tree to dust. Soon afterwards ... Soissons was taken by assault ... and the Russians hurled themselves on the ramparts emitting cries, or rather screams, that made us tremble. I won't go into any detail on the terrible events that followed: all that I will say is that the massacre of our poor soldiers and the pillage of the town lasted for a full hour.[70]

Soissons was liberated soon after, but Pougens and his family chose to flee to Louise's home in the nearby village of Vauxbuin. This, however, proved an unfortunate choice. On 2 March 6,000 cossacks descended on the village. Pougens managed at first to keep the group safe by persuading the commander that he had been a correspondent of the wife of Paul I, but no sooner had the cossacks departed than a large number of stragglers appeared and sacked Louise's house for a full seven hours. Utterly terrified, left almost without food and constantly threatened by further bands of marauders, Pougens and his family then made their way on foot to Nanteuil, where they managed to board a stage-coach bound for Paris. Even when the behaviour of the invaders was less violent, their presence was still a heavy burden. As one inhabitant of Reims complained, 'I have had eight of them in my house. Yesterday they got through thirty-six pounds of bread, ten pounds of meat ... forty-two bottles of wine and twelve bottles of brandy (which they complained was not strong enough). To all this was added a great deal of pepper and salt as well as some raw onion, and yet they still were not happy.'[71]

In the face of this danger, however, the response of the population was not to turn to guerrilla warfare. To quote Alphonse de Beauchamp:

It is true that government had ordered a general rising of the people in Alsace, the Vosges, the higher Saône, the Jura, the Doubs and Mont Blanc, a measure by which a third part of the population was expected to be armed. On the approach of danger, the prefect of the Vosges had made an appeal to the mountaineers, but these uncultivated men, not seeing themselves supported by any regular army ... and, moreover, dispirited by the despotism under which they had so long suffered, met the national stimulus with the *vis inertiae* which renders all the efforts of power unavailing.[72]

Here and there, there do seem to have been cases where national guards or other hastily-organized militias attempted to put up a fight – one such place appears to have been Bourg-en-Bresse[73] – but elsewhere the response was one of either torpor or, alternatively, downright hostility: sent to Dijon as one of the reborn *députés en mission*, for example, Philippe de Ségur was promptly run out of town whereupon the municipality opened the gates to the invaders.[74] Far more common as a reaction, indeed, was flight. As Blayney wrote:

> The advances of the Allied army produced scenes of a nature more extraordinary than we had yet seen at Verdun. For many days and nights there was a continual passage of families running away from Metz, Nancy and other places in the same direction, and their flight was so precipitate that, added to the extraordinary inclemency of the season, the situation of many of them was truly distressing, In one instance I saw a mother and several children in a little cart drawn by a cow and a goat, and another in which an ass and a large dog were yoked together.[75]

An important motive in all this, of course, was fear pure and simple, yet, even so, there is no reason to doubt the analysis of the British representative at Allied headquarters, Sir Charles Stewart. At bottom the inhabitants of France simply did not want to fight any more. Thus: 'The French nation appeared to me generally to favour the Allies; they seemed weary of the wars they were engaged in, and still more weary of their military ruler.'[76] That this was the case is suggested very clearly by the case of the south-west. In brief, in this region the invading forces behaved with far more restraint than they did in the north, and the result was that the tide of war swept across the country leaving scarcely a ripple in their place. That this was the case is very clear from the copious writings of Wellington's soldiers. Before going any further, however, it is important to state a number of qualifications. In the first place, of course, the inhabitants of any region that has been occupied by a foreign army have a strong interest in placating the new arrivals and avoiding retribution. As some of Wellington's soldiers recognized, then, protestations of devotion to the cause of the Bourbons and expressions of hatred of the emperor could not always be taken at face value. Thomas Playford, for example, was a sergeant-major in the Life Guards:

> After the termination of the war we reposed in quarters for a few weeks at the village of Astaffort. Here I met with a more kind and generous treatment from the French family where I was quartered than I had met

with since I left my father's house in Yorkshire. The people were civil and obliging generally, but the members of the family I was quartered upon were particularly so. There was some remnant of loyalty for the Bourbon family remaining in this part of France, and ... the people ... invited us to take part in a great public rejoicing for the restoration ... We went to church, took part in a public thanksgiving and shouted when the effigy of Bonaparte was burned in the market place, but there appeared to me something like political masquerade in the whole proceedings, for many of the people who shouted were Bonapartists at heart.[77]

Let us say that Playford is too cynical, and that the inhabitants of the areas occupied by Wellington's army were, if not genuinely devoted to the cause of Louis XVIII, then at the very least glad to be liberated. To move from here to an attempt to make use of the writings of the Duke's soldiers as part of a more general argument about the state of French public opinion in 1814 would be extremely foolhardy. Playford and his many fellows certainly have interesting things to say about the area in which they were operating, but this last scarcely equated to the whole of France. On the contrary, at its greatest extent the territory occupied by the Anglo-Portuguese army was the triangle defined by the Atlantic Ocean, the River Garonne and the Pyrenees. Roughly speaking, then we are talking about Gascony and Béarn, but these were provinces with little reason to love the regime. In the first place, the coastal towns – Saint Jean de Luz, Bayonne and, above all, Bordeaux – had all been badly hit by the British blockade.[78] In the second place, the barren pine forests of Les Landes had not been fertile terrain for the French Revolution, the result being that conscription had proved just as unpopular there as in better-known centres of resistance such as the Vendée. And, in the third place, as many of Wellington's soldiers noted, the southwestern-most extremity of the region was inhabited by the intensely Catholic Basques, a community that was repelled not only by the régime's anti-clericalism, but also its determination to, as it were, turn peasants into Frenchmen. In the 1790s, then, the whole area had been gripped by brigandage, whilst such was the resistance to conscription in the Pyrenean departments that in 1808 Napoleon was forced to give up the attempt to enforce it, and instead allow the region's manpower to serve in a number of volunteer police battalions that served only in their own localities.[79]

One other issue to consider here is the fact that the area round Bayonne was situated on the direct route to Spain. In 1794, 1801, 1807 and 1808, then, it had seen the passage of entire armies en route for service across the frontier. As the senior British commissary, Richard Henegan noted, to a lack of cultural affinity for Revolution and Empire was therefore added much hardship and disruption. Thus:

Again the natives of that remote part were passive spectators of the events that had sprung from the enthusiasm of the capital. The name of glory had not found its way to their mountains and their only acquaintance with the clash of arms was the passage of armed men through their peaceful valleys. On such occasions the supplies of the country were put in requisition to maintain them. Scarcity prevailed and the inhabitants suffered.[80]

Whatever the precise reason, the inhabitants of the south-west reacted with fury when Napoleon responded to the disaster at Leipzig by attempting to raise still more armies: efforts to organize an 'Army of Reserve of the Pyrenees' from the conscripts of the districts of Bordeaux and Toulouse produced no more than 17,000 men instead of the 30,000 that was planned, while the National Guard were invariably unwilling to turn out and almost impossible to keep together in those cases when battalions were actually mobilised.[81] To quote Henegan once more:

Adversity and failure are the tests of popularity, and the sanguine temperament of the French nation could ill brook the change from glorious conquest to ignoble defeat. The spell of invincibility attached to Napoleon's name was broken, and with it fell the enthusiasm that had sprung from it. For the first time it was discovered that the strength of the nation had been squandered in pursuit of the chimerical visions of ambition, that the blood of hundreds of thousands had been sacrificed to the aggrandizement of the few.[82]

In the south-west, then, the Allies were pushing at an open door, and all the more so as the ever-growing chaos ensured that Soult's forces were having in a most literal sense to live off the country. Of course, that door might yet have been slammed shut: wholesale plundering on the part of the Allied soldiery might well have produced an adverse reaction among the populace, and even, perhaps, a guerrilla war, but for most part, the scenes witnessed in those areas occupied by the Austrians, Russians and Prussians were not repeated. In the early days of the campaign there were, indeed, some problems: not least because they were desperately short of provisions, Wellington's Spanish units ravaged every village in sight when they crossed the frontier, while British soldiers also committed a variety of crimes.[83] This situation, however, was soon dealt with:

immediately after the battle of the River Nivelle (10–11 November 1813), the vast majority of the Spanish forces were sent back across the frontier so as to ensure that they caused no further trouble, whilst Wellington issued strict orders against pillage. As William Lawrence of the Fortieth Foot remembered: 'Lord Wellington had watched with hatred the many excesses committed by the enemy on the Portuguese and Spanish inhabitants during the late campaign, and had determined, now he had carried the war into France, to set them for the future a better example, and accordingly he issued a proclamation that no plundering was to be carried on on pain of death.'[84]

With this matter resolved, relations with the civilian populace soon became entirely tranquil. Faced with the threat of invasion, many inhabitants of the border areas had fled, but they now for the most part came back and settled down to life under occupation. 'The great road to Bayonne', wrote John Malcolm, 'was covered with crowds returning to their homes. It was a beautiful sight to behold the peasants, accompanied by their wives and children, passing unmolested through the very midst of a hostile army, and returning to their quiet occupations.'[85] For an interesting account of the situation we can turn to the commander of the Fifty-Third Foot, Sir George Bingham:

> On our entering France many of the inhabitants fled, having been ordered to do so by the Duke of Dalmatia. They have nearly all returned, and, being for the moment relieved both from conscription and contribution seem well pleased with the change. The venality and severity of Napoleon's government can hardly be conceived: no man could go from one village to another without a passport, and for this passport he was always obliged to pay. They were quite astonished when our generals granted passes to go beyond our lines without taking any remuneration: the great French generals so celebrated throughout Europe having in their own as well as in other countries been guilty of such dirty acts to raise their fortunes that a well-principled English country gentleman would be ashamed of.[86]

More important than the petty issue of passes, however, was the far more serious question of subsisting the forces of Marshal Soult. To quote Thomas Wildman of the Seventh Light Dragoons, for example, '[The local inhabitants] seemed happy to see the English. As they said, if the French had remained, they must have starved, for they took everything and paid for nothing.'[87] Much the same point, meanwhile, was made by George Bowles. Thus: 'Lord Wellington is quite as popular here as he ever was in Spain, and much more so than he is there at present ... Here the only thing the people fear is the return of their own army.'[88] Finally, here is the commissary Richard Henegan: 'After a very short residence among them we were looked at far more in the light of friends than of invaders of their country ... The presence of British troops became, through the proclamation of Lord Wellington, the guarantee of security to the inhabitants; the owners of the produce of the country received full value for it when purchased for the army, and confidence was maintained unbroken between the parties.'[89]

However, it was not just a matter of protection. For some weeks the headquarters of Wellington's army, Saint Jean de Luz experienced a positive bonanza. 'Saint Jean de Luz after a short time assumed all the appearance of a fashionable watering place', wrote the same observer. 'The breakwater that projected far into the sea was crowded daily as a morning lounge by Lord Wellington and his brilliant staff, by the gentlemen of the Guards, and, though last, not least, by many fair ladies, wives and maidens, some of whom had taken pity on the state of celibacy to which the sons of Mars are doomed, and had arrived from England to solace them by their presence.'[90] The advantages of such an influx can well be imagined, but it was not just the money to be made from supplying billets and other necessaries. On the contrary, there was also a revival of the commercial activity that had been so strangled by the blockade. As Bowles noted, 'Indeed, [the inhabitants] are all making their own fortunes as fast as possible. This [St Jean de Luz], being declared a free port, it is becoming a great *entrepôt* for colonial produce, which will be smuggled into the interior without much difficulty.'[91]

As the Anglo–Portuguese pushed ever deeper into France, so the sense of relief and renewed hope experienced at Saint Jean de Luz travelled with it. Everywhere the story was the same: the warmest of welcomes and adoring women by the score. As an example we might cite the account of an officer of the Forty-Third Foot of the scenes that took place in Toulouse following the battle of 10 April 1814:

As we trotted one after another under the gateway into the good city of Toulouse, nothing could exceed the joyful transports of its ... people. The authorities greeted the Marquis of Wellington officially, and the *canaille* knocked the bust of Napoleon from the front of the capitol and dashed it to fragments on the pavement! We may derive an excellent moral lesson from the popular frenzy which could thus treat the bust of a man who only a brief space of time before was the very idol of these same people. Young as I was at the time, I could not help laughing in my sleeve at the inconsistency of this brute violence. Groups of ladies promenaded the streets, and crowds of *grisettes*, in their lace caps and holiday suits, rushed from place to place crying, 'Vive notre bon roi! Vive Wellington! Vivent les anglais! Vivent les espagnols! Vivent les Portugais!'[92]

Moving on, almost every memoir, diary or collection of letters has stories to tell of good food, comfortable billets and the most marked attention to the author's creature comforts. To take just one example, Charles Crowe of the Twenty-Seventh Foot describes being warmly welcomed into French homes, first in a chateau near Hasparren, where he and his fellow officers enjoyed a pleasant musical evening with the owner and his three children, of whom the two daughters 'enthusiastically admired everything that was English'; second, at Saint Marie de Gosse, where a priest sold them a fine turkey and made him a present of a good map of France; and, third, at Sos, where the physician he was lodged with 'produced some excellent wine, pears, apples, walnuts and a variety of good things'.[93] Nor was it just individuals who took the invaders to their hearts: billeted for some weeks in the town of Castel Sarrazin, for example, the officers of the Ninety-Fifth later claimed that they were so popular in the town that, hearing that their erstwhile guests had suffered very heavily at Waterloo, the municipality wrote a letter in which it requested to be informed of the fate of every single officer.[94] As for the local women, they proved just as susceptible to the charms of British officers as had those of Spain and Portugal: to take just one example, Thomas Bunbury describes how he became infatuated with the sister of a French cavalry officer and was only narrowly dissuaded from eloping with her, whilst George Wood waxes positively lyrical on the subject of the women of Bayonne:

> The ladies, in particular, were exceedingly attentive and affable, so much so that they made a strong impression upon the hearts of our young sparks, and one of our officers was fortunate enough to make a lovely damsel … the partner of his life … So very engaging and agreeable are the charming young ladies of this town, that I may with truth assert [that] nearly the whole of the officers had in great measure lost their hearts. Even in the married ones, it required the greatest constancy and affection to retain their attachment for their affectionate wives at home, and so deeply were many of the bachelors in love that, had not a sudden order snatched them from this paradise of fascinating female society, many more would, I have no doubt, soon have sacrificed at the nuptial shrine.[95]

Meanwhile, once news had been received of Napoleon's abdication, joyful celebrations were everywhere the order of the day. For example:

Rejoining our regiment, [we] were soon on the march again for Bordeaux, which, being not more than a day's march distant, we reached the same night. We encamped at a place two miles off ... on the banks of the River Garonne ... Here we lay for five or six weeks, during which time the inhabitants made many excursions ... to inspect our army, swarms of costermongers likewise visiting us every day with wine, spirits, bread, meat, fish and fruit of every description for sale. Every Sunday afternoon the bands of all the regiments played while the French amused themselves with dancing, many of them, both male and female on stilts, which entertained us more than anything, and besides this there were all kinds of jollities in which our soldiers freely joined.[96]

This account of life at Bordeaux comes from after the close of hostilities. However, British soldiers also witnessed the revolt that took place in the city in late March that led to it becoming the first place in France openly to declare for the Bourbons. In brief, what happened was as follows. Very hard hit by the Continental Blockade, Bordeaux also happened to be one of the greatest strongholds of the Chevaliers de la Foi (a description, it has to be said applicable, in relative terms only) whilst the only garrison was a few hundred national guards. In February 1814, meanwhile, the final piece of the jigsaw fell into place in that the mayor of the city, Jean-Baptiste Lynch, got into contact with the Chevaliers and offered to help stage a revolt. In this, moreover, he was as good as his word. Having first secured assurances from Wellington that a force of troops would be sent to secure the city, on 12 March Lynch raised the white flag over the town hall in the presence of a cheering crowd.[97]

To conclude, then, what do we learn from this survey of the experiences of Wellington's soldiers in the campaign of 1814? First of all, it is abundantly clear that in the south-west of France there was almost nothing in the way of active support for Napoleon. This does not necessarily mean, of course, that the cause of Louis XVIII had triumphed: Jean-Baptiste Lynch was all too clearly a pragmatist who had come to the conclusion that a restoration was the only viable option, whilst someone else who supported the revolt was a prominent local liberal called Joseph Lainé who had played a leading part in events in the *corps législatif* in December 1813 and was committed above all to the cause of constitutionalism. As for the Chevaliers de la Foi, they would never have acted but for Wellington's dispatch of a large force of troops to the city under the command of William Beresford. That said, the whole of the south-west saw scarcely a hand raised in defence of the emperor. Rather than digging defences or helping to man the walls, the inhabitants of Bayonne rather happily carried on an illicit trade in luxuries with the forces blockading the city.[98] Conscription, as we have seen, was fiercely resisted; as John Fremantle wrote, the inhabitants of the district of Bayonne 'talk of nothing but insurrections at Bordeaux and its neighbourhood in consequence of their putting the conscription laws in force'.[99] And, finally, guerrilla resistance came there none: in the whole of the campaign only once did a force emerge that might have served as the makings of a partisan band, and it appears not only that this was little more than a band of brigands but also that it disappeared within a few days of its formation.[100] What is more, when the war finally came to an end, there was nothing but rejoicing: 'There was no end to gaiety,' wrote George Bell. 'We were out at balls, concerts and evening parties. We had the *entrée* into all the theatres ... for a *franc*. The people seemed happy and rejoiced over the new order of things.'[101]

To return to the impact of the campaign rather than the response of the populace, the south-west was comparatively lucky. Indeed, in much of southern, central and western France, the inhabitants escaped scot-free. Yet even in those areas which saw no fighting at all, insecurity and fear were widespread. Ever since the start of the war, for example, large numbers of prisoners of war had been incarcerated in a number of fortresses in the east and north-east of the country and the thousands of men involved were now put on the road in an attempt to keep them out of Allied hands. Through the bitter winter weather, then, from January onwards endless troops of ragged prisoners trudged south-westwards in the direction of such towns as Orléans. Under only minimal guard and in many instances bearing bitter grudges against all things French, the men concerned descended on town after town and at the very least demanded food and lodgings. One participant in these wanderings was the captive British general Andrew Blayney:

During our stay at Blois the town was constantly crowded by prisoners of war of all nations changing depots according to the movements of the Allied armies. Many of them were in a most miserable condition from fatigue, from the intense inclemency of the weather without clothing or shoes, and, above all from hunger, being often for many days together without receiving rations from the French government. Numbers sank on the march under their complicated calamities and perished miserably in the ditches, while others lost their fingers and toes by the frost and were rendered cripples for life. The numbers of English soldiers were so great that it was with much difficulty that I could procure sufficient money to relieve them, and I am with much concerned obliged to remark that in too many instances that relief was badly bestowed. The money, instead of being expended on necessaries, was instead squandered on drink which caused so many excesses that the commandant of the town declared that one hundred English prisoners caused him more trouble than a thousand of any other nation ... The prisoners, of whom there were about 70,000 in the neighbourhood were billeted on the inhabitants of villages who were forced to find [for] them in everything.[102]

To return to the main theatre of war, meanwhile, as has already been implied in the case of the south-western front, yet another danger was the behaviour of the French soldiers. With the supply situation worsening by the day and the weather unremittingly bitter, the hungry soldiers of the remnants of the Grande Armée turned upon their own countrymen with a vengeance. As the minor writer and composer, Pierre Giraud, remarked in his history of the campaign:

Napoleon ... saw the very heart of his empire ... exposed to all the calamities of war, and that his own troops augmented those calamities by their indiscriminate pillage and want of discipline. The evil was extreme and the consequences tremendous. The minds of the French were exasperated. They everywhere asked which was the most dangerous enemy of France. Frenchmen fled before their own countrymen ... Napoleon had suffered his troops to commit the greatest excesses when in an enemy's country to secure their attachment to his person, and to incline them to bear patiently all the fatigues ... to which he might expose them. The consequences of this detestable policy now recoiled on his own subjects.[103]

All this, of course, undermined confidence in the régime, the result being that the latter's propaganda became more and more risible. To quote Blayney once again:

Napoleon having gained some trifling advantage over the corps commanded by General Blücher, it was an object of consequence to make as much as possible of it, and accordingly it was pronounced throughout the streets [of Blois] by sound of trumpet and affixed in large characters on the walls of all the public buildings that the emperor had gained a complete victory and that the Russian army *étoit entièrement anéantie* ['had been entirely annihilated']. The same evening I was at the theatre, and between the pieces one of the actors appeared on the stage and read the ... account of this great victory ... The player ... entirely over-acted his part, and, by 'outstepping the modesty of nature', destroyed the impression he intended to make and rendered the whole account absurd. After running on with a string of unpronounceable Russian names and stating that the artillery, caissons, *fourgons*, baggage, equipage of the enemy had fallen into the power of the French, he concluded with 'Messieurs, l'armée russe est entièrement détruite, et ... sans nous avoir conté un seul homme de tué.' ['Gentlemen: the Russian army has been entirely destroyed, and ... that without us losing a single man.'] All the persons under government had been ordered to attend at the theatre on this occasion, the news was received with clapping of their hands and acclamations of 'Bravo! Vive Napoléon!' The eyes of the whole house were, as might be expected, turned on the English, and they seemed to be not a little surprised at John Bull louder in applauding than themselves and vociferating 'Bravo! Vive Napoléon! Encore! Encore!', which brought the actor forward again to repeat the news and he was even so stupid as to continue until the French at last perceived that we were turning them to ridicule, and from various parts of the house was heard, 'Bravo! Ce n'est pas vraie! Bravo! Qu'elle mensonge!' ['Bravo! It isn't true! Bravo! What nonsense!'] so that the authorities would have done much better in not permitting the mention of this pretended victory upon the stage. A few days proved the ridiculous exaggeration of the account, for this same totally annihilated Russian army resuscitated, as if by miracle, and gained some considerable advantages.[104]

Even in the army support for Napoleon was starting to dwindle. Sustained by the presence of the emperor, the troops fighting in Champagne displayed much devotion, not to say great heroism. Elsewhere, however, morale was low. In the course of his journey to the Loire valley, for example, Blayney found himself surrounded not just by prisoners, but also large numbers of stragglers and men who had for one reason or another been separated from their units:

Among the numerous groups of fugitive cavalry ... I observed several superior officers of hussars ... and one of them, an old colonel, seemed desirous to enter into conversation ... The old colonel observed that he and one of the other officers in company had now been in constant active service for twenty-four years, and that at present the successes or reverses of their arms were indifferent to them, as the former produced neither individual advantage nor national utility. 'Thus', concluded the veteran,

'I am heartily tired of it, and am now going to a depot for a remount, in which I shall endeavour to create as much delay as possible in order to avoid the rest of the winter's campaign.' Thus it appears a total change of sentiment has taken place in the French army, and those persons who at the beginning of the campaign were inflamed with military ardour and boasting of their exploits past and to come now think there is equal merit in escaping from 'the pomp, pride and circumstance of glorious war', or, more familiarly speaking, of evading their duty ... At Chalons ... I entered into conversation with some genteel and well informed officers of hussars and some *gardes d'honneur* ... They were all unreserved in their violent abuse of Napoleon, and it almost seemed as if they had ransacked the dictionary for abusive words to select those most forcibly expressive of their detestation.[105]

In the field the issue was particularly apparent in south-west France. In the latter part of the Peninsular War, it is possible to observe a certain deterioration in the fighting qualities of the French forces in Spain: at Vitoria, indeed, many of King Joseph's troops put up a relatively poor show. Further battered by months of defeat in the Pyrenees, particularly at the first and second battles of Sorauren and the battle of San Marcial, the defenders appear to have suffered a further slide in morale: at neither the crossing of the Bidasoa, nor the battle of the River Nivelle, was resistance particularly fierce, while on 14 December the last day of the battle of the River Nive saw a unit of French infantry actually mutiny rather than obey the orders that they had received to participate in yet another hopeless assault on the 'thin red line'. Of the opposition put up to the crossing of the River Adour, meanwhile, John Rous writes, 'The French officers were seen beating their men to get them on, but the unsteady behaviour of the conscripts was worse than anything I ever saw.'[106] That said, the rot was far from total. Of Orthez, for example, Harry Smith later wrote, 'I never saw the French fight so hard as this day', whilst the first historian of the campaign, a Guards officer named Robert Batty, remarked of the same battle that 'the enemy obstinately contested his ground, showing more than ordinary spirit in resisting the impetuous and well-combined attacks of the Allies'.[107] Equally, the night action brought on by the French sortie from Bayonne in the small hours of 14 April is generally agreed to have been as savage and costly as any of the many fights that preceded it.[108] Nevertheless, rot there was: when the fighting had come to an end, many British observers were agreed that, if the officers were often unhappy, the rank and file were overjoyed to have survived the war and be going home at last.[109]

In brief, then, Napoleonic France was in a state of complete disintegration. 'People realised,' wrote the wife of Marshal Oudinot, 'that, by yielding a certain number of his conquests in preceding years, the emperor might have saved France this invasion; that a little later, the line of the Rhine would at least have been left to him; that, even at the time we had reached, if he would only give the Duke of Vicenza (his representative at the congress of Châtillon), the latitude which that zealous functionary demanded, he would still obtain supportable conditions of peace. Peace! The cry was in every heart, for of glory, the everyday food of the country, France had had a sufficient share.'[110] According to the canon of the legend of Saint Helena, this was not so: rather, the emperor was betrayed in the course of the campaign by a succession of traitors – Talleyrand, Joseph, Marmont, Augereau – who at the moment of crisis sought to save their skins by throwing in their hands with the Allies. There is, of course, a certain kernel of truth here: such men had much to lose, and it is asking too much to believe that they were not at least in part activated by an instinct for self-preservation. Yet they were also reflecting a reality that could not be denied: there was neither the will nor the means to carry on the struggle, and therefore no point in carrying on to the bitter end.[111] Given the particular emphasis that is often placed on the failure of Joseph and Marmont to hold on to Paris, it is worth paying particular attention in this respect to the situation in the capital.

Here the fact was that the situation had been going from bad to worse. As the young Jacobin surgeon, Poumiès de Siboutie, remembered:

> Fighting was going on at the gates of Paris. The wounded were brought in in hundreds. We were soon overcrowded. Every available inch of space was filled: the ordinary sick had to be sent to their homes; the pensioners … and the incurables were turned out of their wards and herded together in dark corners and attics. Before long even that was not enough, and two casualties were assigned to every bed. Each day fresh means had to be devised to house the steadily increasing tide of sick and wounded. The unfortunate fellows dragged themselves to Paris, animated by a feverish desire to obtain shelter and succour. Some fell exhausted on the very steps of the hospital and expired as they reached the haven of a bed. Many had sores and wounds which had not been dressed for days, if ever. Every morning the hospital hearses bore thirty or forty corpses to their long rest. It was the same in all the other asylums and hospitals.[112]

Meanwhile, as even some of Napoleon's most loyal subordinates admitted, the propaganda of the régime was at best having little effect:

The *Moniteur* was filled with all the complaints, with all the lamentations, of the wretched inhabitants of Montmirail, of Montereau and of Nangis ... All the towns which had been afflicted with the scourge of war sent deputies to Paris to describe their misery and demand vengeance ... The great examples of antiquity were invoked; France was reminded of her achievements in 1792 ... But, it must be confessed, these measures produced at Paris and in all the great towns an effect quite contrary to that which was expected from them. The inhabitants were too civilised to adopt the decisive conduct of the Russians and the Spaniards. The imagination of the citizens was shocked at the violence of the measures suggested to them ... and peace was loudly demanded as the period of so many horrors.[113]

Meanwhile, between scenes of misery that became ever more dreadful, the arrival of swarms of desperate refugees and the collapse of normal economic life, conditions in the capital became daily more demoralising:

Fifteenth March: This evening between six and seven o'clock I saw about thirty sick or wounded soldiers lying in the street at the bottom of the Rue Rochechouart. They had been brought from Brie in carts, and, on arriving at the hospital at the top of the street, were refused admittance for want of room. The country people who had been put in requisition to convey them to Paris, brought them to this spot, turned them out of their carts, and there left them, hastening away lest they should be seized to carry bread to the army. Frequently those who had been pressed to convey the wounded for only five leagues, were detained fifteen or even twenty days from their homes in consequence of fresh requisitions ... The number of dead bodies seen either floating down the river or stranded on the banks, was immense and represented an appalling spectacle ... This was immediately after the battle of Montereau where the dead were thrown in to the river to avoid the labour and expense of interment. Many others were also committed to the stream from the hospitals at Nogent and other towns on the banks of the Seine. Hundreds of the wounded and diseased soldiers were packed together in large barges without awnings or other protection and exposed to severe frosts in consequence of which numbers perished and were thrown overboard ... During February the amount of taxes suffered little diminution in the mean daily receipt, which for the city of Paris is 70,000 *francs* ... In the month of March not more than two to three hundred *francs* could be obtained. All classes of persons showed the greatest reluctance to part with their money. Few workmen or artisans were employed, and those few could not obtain wages. So great was the stagnation of trade that shopkeepers were eager to sell their goods considerably under prime cost. Money became so scarce that many persons were obliged to send their forks and spoons to the mint to be coined … Before daybreak the terrified population of the country between Meaux and Paris came pouring into the capital with their aged, infirm, children, cats, dogs, livestock, corn, hay and goods of every description. The boulevards were crowded with wagons, carts and carriages thus laden, to which cattle were tied and the whole surrounded by women on foot. The distress of these poor refugees was augmented by being forced to pay the *octroi* at the gates of Paris, for which many were obliged to sell part of their stock at the barriers to obtain what they hoped would be security for the rest.[114]

Among the troops holding the city, meanwhile, morale was low. By dint of example and personal magnetism, Napoleon was to do wonders in respect of the increasingly desperate and hungry men he commanded in Champagne, but he could not be everywhere, whilst those he left in command elsewhere were but pale shadows of his imperial person. This, alas, could not be more true of anyone than his brother, Joseph, a decent and well-meaning individual, but also one who not only lacked serious military experience but was also notoriously weak-willed and possessed of little staying power. Left to hold the half-completed defences that ringed the capital with little more than 40,000 men, he was in a hopeless position, but he did not exactly inspire confidence either. 'I have just read in a newspaper', wrote the man of letters Edouard Mennechet, in a private letter to his mistress dated 22 March 1814, 'with respect to a review conducted by King Joseph in the [Place du Carrousel] a remark to the effect that if Paris is ever attacked, it will have as many defenders as it does inhabitants. Yes, without doubt: if it was a case of saving goods, family, honour, liberty, every citizen would indeed be a rampart … However, where the only choices is servitude, is it not the case that, master for master, they might choose the one they have the right to hate and overthrow rather than the one that they will be obliged to serve and defend? At that same review of which so much was made I observed that the old soldiers did not once join in with the cheers of the young soldiers. If the enthusiasm of such warriors is to be revived, if they are indeed to be led to victory, another voice – another sword – is needed other than that of Joseph Bonaparte. Resigned to death, for that is their duty, they are returning to the fight with no other hope than that of selling their lives dearly, and no expectation whatsoever that such an example will be set for them by a man who has never yet been seen on a field of battle.'[115]

As in 1870 and 1940, refugees were streaming west, thereby adding to the confusion. Amongst those who fled Paris as the enemy closed in was the imperial government:

> The Versailles road was free ... We let the empress, her suite and her escort set out, and at about four o'clock in the afternoon we ourselves departed ... It was almost dark when we arrived. We took possession of two adjacent rooms in an already crowded house in the Rue de l'Orangerie. During the whole night an incessant and confused noise told us of the passage of a large number of men, horses and carriages, and soon the daylight revealed the most astonishing sight that human eyes perhaps have ever looked upon. We stood motionless at our windows. What we saw passing ... was the empire, the empire ... with all its pomp and splendour, the ministers ... the entire council of state, the archives, the crown diamonds, the administrations. And instalments of power and magnificence were mingled on the road with humble households who had heaped up on a barrow on all they had been able to carry away from the houses which they were abandoning.[116]

On one level, fleeing the capital was the right move for Marie-Louise and the ministers as their capture by the Allies would in effect have left Napoleon without a state. Yet there is no doubt that the move did much to fuel the atmosphere of panic that reigned in the capital. To quote the prefect of the Tuileries, Louis de Bausset, 'What must have been the feelings of the inhabitants ... when they beheld the departure of ... the coaches of the members of the government and various ministerial chancelleries ... Certainly nothing could less resemble the movement of a court than this tumultuous retreat of persons and of luggage of all kinds.'[117]

The flight of the government took place on 29 March. Small wonder, then, that when the Allies attacked the city the next day, resistance was short-lived. Even counting the 6,000 national guards in the city, the defenders were outnumbered by some six to one, and it is very much to their credit that they managed to hold back the Allied attacks as well as they did. Here and there, indeed, Marmont's troops showed real heroism. 'Never did military France', wrote Chateaubriand, 'shine with a brighter glory: the last heroes were the 150 lads of the Polytechnic School, transformed into gunners in the redoubts on the Vincennes Road. Surrounded by the enemy, they refused to surrender: they had to be torn from their pieces.'[118] Impelled by a desire to defend their homes, even some of the National Guard seem to have done their best. Pierre Giraud was an eyewitness, and, withal, one by no means favourable to Napoleon: 'It would be a ridiculous vanity and a breach of truth to maintain that ... there were not many respectable citizens who now for the first time saw a battle, and who very soon rushed back, scarcely daring to look behind them, or knowing in what way they had effected their escape ... Justice, however, compels us to say to those who persist in accusing the Parisians ... that the National Guard ... left 500 men killed upon the field of battle beside a very considerable number of wounded.'[119] Heroism, however, was not enough, and at the end of the day the defenders evacuated the city, leaving the Allies to march into the city unopposed, and Napoleon with no option but to surrender.[120] An eyewitness to the relief and joy that followed the end of the fighting was Charles Stewart:

I feel it impossible to convey an accurate idea ... of the scene that presented itself on the 31st [March] in the capital of the French empire when the emperor of Russia, the King of Prussia and Prince Schwarzenberg made their entry at the head of the Allied troops. The enthusiasm and exultation generally exhibited must very much have exceeded what the most sanguine and devoted friend of the ancient dynasty of France could have ventured to hope, and those who were less personally interested ... could no longer hesitate in pronouncing that the restoration of their legitimate king, the downfall of Bonaparte and the desire of peace bad become the first and dearest wish of the Parisians ... The sovereigns, surrounded by all the princes and generals in the army ... entered the Faubourg Saint Martin about eleven o'clock ... The crowd was already so great, and the acclamations were so general, that it was difficult to move forward ... All Paris seemed to be assembled and concentrated on one spot; one mind and one spring evidently directed their movements. They thronged in such masses around the emperor and the king that, notwithstanding their condescending and gracious familiarity shown by extending their hands on all sides, it was in vain to attempt to satisfy the populace who made the air resound with the cries of 'Vive l'empereur Alexandre! Vive le roi de Prusse! Vivent nos liberateurs!' Nor were these cries alone heard, for, with louder acclamations if possible, they were mingled with those of 'Vive le roi! Vive Louis XVIII! Vivent les Bourbons! A bas le tyran!' The white cockade appeared very generally, and many of the national guards whom I saw wore them. This clamorous applause of the multitude was seconded by a similar demonstration from the higher classes, who occupied the windows and terraces of the houses along the line to the Champs Elysées. In short, to form an idea of such a manifestation of public feeling as the city of Paris displayed, it must have been witnessed, for no description can convey any description of it.[121]

To conclude, then, the campaign of 1814 had been an experience that was traumatic indeed. In addition to being exposed to demands for everything from men and money to horses and medical supplies, the people of France had been subjected to every form of the horrors of war, and all in the name of a cause in which they had for the most part long since ceased to believe and in the service of a regime which had on the one hand brought economic ruin and, on the other, failed to provide them with even a modicum of protection. The result was inevitable: if the populace had once voted Napoleon into power, it now voted to throw him out. To quote Chateaubriand once more, 'Nobody except the soldiers intoxicated with fire and glory wanted any more of Bonaparte, and, dreading lest they should keep him, the people hastened to open the gates.'[122]

Chapter 5

The Bourbon Restoration

At long last, then, France was at peace amidst a mood of rejoicing that saw the Bourbons greeted with wild excitement. Thomas Underwood, for example, has left us a graphic description of the scenes that accompanied the future Charles X's first visit to a theatre:

> After the first act, the Comte d'Artois came into the box of the sovereigns … The whole house rose, and there seemed to be a general competition who should be most vociferous in their applause … Among the most vociferous were many persons who for the past twenty years had been seen in the ante-chamber of every minister … dazzling and flattering *la grande nation* with pictures, poems and dramatic pieces in adulation of every demagogue and every revolutionary society and holding up the fallen emperor to the adulation of the universe and the adoration of their country. Those despicable sycophants having gained by this trade, pensions, ribands, snuff-boxes and portraits surrounded with diamonds, were now basely … giving the dying lions a kick in the hope of having new additions to their pensions and new orders to render their baseness more conspicuous.[1]

The delight witnessed by Underwood, however, is not entirely to be taken at face value, and all the more so as the audience at a Paris theatre is unlikely to have come from anything over than the propertied classes; indeed, as he himself stresses, there was a strong degree of opportunism afoot that was visible in the very persons of those who were now applauding the coming of the new regime most loudly. The whole of France had wanted peace, certainly; most of France had wanted rid of Napoleon, certainly again. But did anything more than a tiny minority of Frenchmen want the Bourbons back on the throne? This was a different question and one that could well be answered in the negative: when a few dozen young noblemen belonging to the Chevaliers de la Foi had ridden into Paris in the immediate wake of its evacuation in a forlorn attempt to give Louis XVIII some claim to the city other than by foreign bayonets, for example, they were greeted with indifference, even derision.[2] Placed on the throne though the

Napoleon in classic end-of-empire garb: the comparative simplicity of his grey coat and low black hat was designed to project an 'everyman image'. (*Napoleon I in 1814* by Jean-Louis-Ernest Meissonier)

1815 saw the revival of the guerrilla warfare known as the *chouannerie*. As in the period 1793–1800, bands of Breton peasants angered at threat of conscription took to the hills, in many instances managing to defy the troops and national guards sent against them and hold out to the end of hostilities. (*Chouan ambush*, Évariste Carpentier)

As the setting of this painting suggests, in the France of the Hundred Days peasant rebels enjoyed much popular support. (*Chouan band*, Charles Fortin)

French conscripts march off to glory through a gigantic triumphal arch watched by a crowd that is half-admiring, half-despairing. By 1814 such moments had been stripped of their last shred of illusion. (*Departure of the Conscripts in 1807* by Louis Léopold Boilly)

A far greater blow to French arms than failure in Russia, the Battle of Leipzig shattered the myth of Napoleon's invincibility and completely destabilized the French home front. (*The Battle of Leipzig, 1813, French Infantry Defend Against a Prussian Assault* by Paul-Émile Boutigny)

A somber picture replete with images of bleakness and exhaustion: by 1814 many of Napoleon's senior commanders had lost all faith in their master. (*Napoleon and His Staff, 1814*, by Jean-Louis-Ernest Meissonier)

A famous painting showing Marshal Marmont directing the defence of Paris in 1814. Note the touching details afforded by the exhausted refugee and the two wounded Pupilles de la Garde. Still more, interesting, perhaps, are the *grognards* in the foreground, their body language suggesting that they are none too certain of the marshal's loyalty. (*La Barrière de Clichy , 1814*, by Horace Vernet)

The myth of 1814 encapsulated: gallant French guerrillas attack Russian marauders who have just driven a helpless family from their home. (*Scene from the French Campaign, 1814*, by Horace Vernet)

Fought on the night of 14 May 1814 and therefore a full week after Napoleon's abdication, the Battle of Bayonne was the last combat of the campaign of 1814 and cost Wellington's army 838 casualties. (*The Sortie from Bayonne, 1814*, by Thomas Sutherland)

The Emperor Alexander and his staff look down on a crumbling French defence from the heights of Montmartre watched by a group of despondent French prisoners. (*The Battle of Paris, 1814*, by Gottfried Willewalde)

Protected by the Cossacks of the Guard, Alexander I and Frederick William III enter Paris to the cheers of a crowd delighted that the war is over. (*Russian army, Paris, 1814*, artist unknown)

The Imperial Guard weeps as it bids farewell to Napoleon at Fontainebleau in April 1814. For the majority of French soldiers the end of the war rather came as a great relief. (*Adieux de Napoléon à la Garde impériale* by Antoine Montfort)

In the wake of his fall from power, Napoleon was widely mocked. In this British cartoon, he is seen being drummed out of France and, delivering a gallows-style speech in which he warns his audience that 'he grasps at a shadow who grasps at all'. (*The Journey of a Modern Hero to the Island of Elba* by George Cruikshank)

A suitably portly Napoleon says goodbye to his miniscule island kingdom prior to embarking on the greatest gamble of his career. In the right foreground a rather more passionate farewell is taking place: one of the many ways in which French soldiers made themselves unpopular outside France was the way, as one observer put it, that they cuckolded a continent. (*Napoleon Bonaparte leaving Elba, 26 February 1815*, by Joseph Beaume)

Discontented and eager for revenge, the French army rushes to do homage to Napoleon on his return to France whilst the populace, accurately enough, are elbowed aside. (*Napoleon's Return from Elba* by Charles Steuben)

Napoleon as he was seen by most of Europe in 1815: a creature from a nightmare garlanded with death. (*Wahre Abbildung des Eroberers Napoleon Bonaparte, Kaiser der Franzosen. Anno 1815.* True picture of the conqueror Napoleon Bonaparte, Emperor of the French. 1815)

The Hundred Days saw thousands of Frenchmen fight against Napoleon. In the Battle of Thouars (20 June 1815) a force of Vendéen rebels were taken by surprise by 700 Imperial troops led by General Henri Delaage. (*The Battle of Thouars, 1815*, artist unknown)

One of the biggest battles to take place on French soil in 1815, the Battle of Rocheservière saw 8,000 Vendéen rebels commanded by Pierre de Suzannet heavily defeat 6,000 Imperial troops led by Jean Lamarque. In the wake of the battle, the rebel leadership sued for peace, but by then it was too late: Napoleon had already been defeated at Waterloo. (*The Battle of Rocheservière, 1815*, artist unknown)

Make several mistakes in the campaign of the Hundred Days though Wellington did, his leadership played a key role in gaining the decisive victory at Mont Saint Jean. (*The Duke of Wellington* after Sir Thomas Lawrence)

A tough and determined soldier who hated the French, Gebhard Leberecht von Blucher played a key role in the Waterloo campaign that has to a certain extent been downplayed by British historians. (*Gebhard Leberecht von Blücher*, artist unknown)

Whether arrayed in line or in square (as here) British infantry were near invincible on the battlefield. However, many of Wellington's infantry were not British, and particularly not in the crucial sector of

The German state of Brunswick was one of several to provide Wellington's Army of the Netherlands with troops. Deployed in the centre of the Allied line and worn down by heavy casualties, these troops recoiled even from the limited force of French troops that struck their sector of the line, and would almost beyond doubt have been swept away altogether if the attack had been delivered *en masse*. (*Brunswick Line Infantry at Quatre-Bras* by Richard Knötel)

the line occupied since the 1820's by the famous Lion Monument. (*The 28th Regiment at Quatre Bras* by Lady Butler)

Contrary to much British opinion, many of the Dutch troops who took part in the Waterloo campaign fought extremely well, whilst it was the fresh division shown here that played the crucial role in beating back the French attack in the sector closest to La Haye Sainte. (artist unknown)

The Imperial Guard sets off from La Belle Alliance to attack Wellington's crumbling line. Roped to the horse of the cuirassier in the right foreground is the unfortunate local farmer conscripted by Napoleon to serve as a guide. Rather than acknowledging the cheers of his men, meanwhile, the emperor would have been better employed ensuring that they attacked in a single mass. (*Napoleon's Last Grand Attack* by Ernest Crofts)

For several hours in the late afternoon and early evening of 18 June 1815, the village of Plancenoit was the site of the fiercest fighting on the battlefield. However, deep in the valley of the River Lasne, it was completely out of the line of vision of Wellington's soldiers: hence the belief later expressed by some of them that the Prussians had played no part in the battle. (*The Prussian Attack on Plancenoit* by Adolph Northen)

The French army streams away from Waterloo with a dejected emperor in its midst. In the wake of the battle, some soldiers continued to advocate resistance, and even to fight on, but in practice the Napoleonic adventure was at an end. (*Flight of French army from Waterloo*, artist unknown)

The hectic pace of the Hundred Days did not allow much time for official portraiture. However, dating from 1814, this study of a brooding, portly and whey-faced Napoleon foreshadows the still more unprepossessing figure that was to return from Elba in 1815. (*Napoleon at Fontainebleau*, workshop of Paul Delaroche)

Few of the Austrian and Russian troops deployed to invade France in 1815 saw action, but some fierce fighting did take place in Alsace. Had Napoleon triumphed at Waterloo and then managed decisively to defeat the Prussians as well, he would then have had to march south to deal with the Allied troops shown in this picture. (*The Siege of Strasbourg, 1815, Fighting at Oberhausbergen*, artist unknown)

Strasbourg was one of a number of French fortresses besieged in 1815. Undismayed by the news of Waterloo, the garrison held out till 4 September. (*The Battle for Grimma Gate* by Ernst Strassburger)

Bourbons may have been, they therefore had a great deal to do before they could count their hold on power as secure.

That said, it should not be thought that the Bourbons started with nothing. The Parisian surgeon, Poumiès de la Siboutie, was no royalist, but he was honest enough to admit that the Comte d'Artois (the first of the Bourbon princes to reach Paris) was greeted with real enthusiasm. Thus: 'The Count of Artois, who was said to have travelled in the train of the Allies, made his entry into Paris on the 12th of April. His entry had been cleverly headed by a proclamation in which, among other promises, he stated that there would be neither conscription nor taxation of necessities (*droits réunis*) in future. These magical words gained Louis XVIII a magnificent reception. He made his state entry on the 3rd of May in balmy spring weather. The city had made grand preparations. I saw the procession in the Rue Saint-Denis, and I must say that the cheers and applause of the crowd were thoroughly unanimous. The women were delirious with delight: they hung out of their windows, waved their handkerchiefs and screamed themselves hoarse.'[3] Equally Bonapartist, yet equally impressed, was Octave Levavasseur: 'All the way along our route, crowds filled … the streets and squares. Every window was a tableau of animated faces, of mouths crying, "Long live the king!" Never was there such a triumphal entry.'[4]

On almost every front, however, the Bourbons failed. What, then, had gone wrong? As the contemporary commentator, Pierre Giraud, put it, 'How was it that a group of princes who the previous April everyone had favoured, everybody rushed to second, who appeared to have called forth a complete revolution in situation and opinion alike, disappeared from the scene in fifteen days without any other opposition, any other resistance … than a vain representation of enthusiasm … an agitation without either end or resources, whose only result was a literary war, a war of pamphlets and newspapers in which one could be absolutely certain of never having to encounter the enemy face-to-face, and which yet, through the declamatory exaggerations of a disdain and self-confidence that were alike completely false, showed only too well alarm and self-doubt of the most absolute nullity?'[5]

What indeed? Giraud's answer is essentially that there was no enthusiasm in the first place; that the return of the Borbons had hinged upon events in two or three cities – Paris, Lyons, Bordeaux – that were either already in the hands of the invaders or on the brink of falling to them; that the crowds that filled the streets had in large part been composed of women (a section of society which he implies had neither a right to any voice on the matter, nor the sense to express itself in a rational way); that such moves in the direction of the overthrow of Napoleon that took place were the work of a handful of royalist conspirators only; that the army, the most truly representative institution in the whole of France, had been denied any voice in the matter. Indeed, he even goes so far as to claim that when peace came the vast expanses of the country which had yet to see an enemy soldier were on the brink of rising in a great *levée en masse* against the invaders.[6] In taking this line, he assuredly went too far, and yet it is for all that quite clear that massive problems faced the deeply unimpressive figure of Louis XVIII.

In this respect, given the importance of the issue, we should begin with the army. That this force should have presented the new regime with serious problems was all but inevitable. In the first place, much of the army had not shared the miseries of 1814, the many thousands of men tied up in isolated garrisons in Germany and elsewhere that had held out to the end having come home convinced that they were undefeated. Sharing their sense of betrayal, meanwhile, were the many prisoners of war who now returned from a captivity that had frequently been quite appalling. The outrage felt by these thousands of men knew no bounds. Taken by the Allies when the garrison of Dresden surrendered in 1813, for example, the Duc de Fézensac sat out the campaign of 1814 in captivity in Pressburg. According to his memoirs, he himself was resigned to the return of the Bourbons and, albeit without much in the way of enthusiasm, strove to hope for the best and to think of them in terms not so much of the figures they actually were, but rather the symbols of a glorious past and, indeed, the essence of France. Yet, if this was difficult for Fézensac, and that despite the fact that he was a member of the *ancien noblesse*, for officers – the vast majority, of course – who owed their all to the career open to talents of the Revolution and Napoleon, it was downright impossible. Rather the mood was one of impotent fury:

We learned successively of the passage of the Rhine, of the invasion of France, of the ever more impressive progress of the Allied armies. It is necessary to be a soldier to understand our irritation and sorrow. Only a few months ago we had been the masters of Europe and yet already our country was invaded. She was set to be conquered in her entirety and deprived of her independence, and the emperor to lose his crown, and we could do nothing to defend her most cherished interests. Disarmed, locked up far from France, we were reduced to reading of these events in the German press, the bombast and falsification of which could not but increase our affliction ... At length there arrived the news of the fall of Paris. For us this was a terrible day, and I immediately shut myself up in my room so as not to have to witness the odious triumphalism of the inhabitants ... After that news came thick and fast. We learned of the abdication of Napoleon, the exclusion of a regency and the re-establishment of the Bourbons. The irritation of the officers reached a peak: they had no idea who the various princes were, had never even heard them spoken of ... Having seen long-since what was likely to happen, I was strongly disposed to submit ... That said, there was a price: I wanted [the Bourbons] to conform freely and completely to the ideas of our century. No white cockade, then, no hint of the *ancien régime*. Those officers who had never known anything but the present state of affairs went much further, however ... They wanted nothing less than a regency, and regarded the government that had been set up in place of the son of their emperor as a usurper. I spoke with them a great deal and tried very hard to get them to be more reasonable, even more patriotic ... What mattered above all was to obtain a favourable peace and to deliver France of the presence of foreign armies, and this meant that the new government needed to be embarrassed as little as possible, that the whole of France needed to be united in its support. Such were my reasons, and I even managed to carry a few of them with me, but the impression did not last, the first acts of the new government scarcely being of a nature to win the support of the army.[7]

Whether they had been held in Allied prisons, manned the walls of such fortresses as Hamburg or Barcelona, or fought to defend France herself, meanwhile, many veterans of the campaign of 1814 now found themselves stripped of their posts and placed on half pay, the regime proceeding greatly to reduce the size of its swollen armed forces. To add insult to injury, meanwhile, those officers who were thus cast off were in effect sent into internal exile by being confined to their home towns. One man affected in this fashion was Jean-Roche Coignet. As he wrote, 'The government marched us off to plant cabbages in our home departments. We were on half-pay: seventy-three *francs* a month. There was nothing for it but resignation: keeping the grey for myself, I sold two of my horses, found a post for my servant ... and set out for Auxerre, the capital of my department, and there I proceeded to vegetate for the whole of 1814.'[8] For many veterans, indeed, war and the prospects that it brought was literally all they had. John Scott was an Edinburgh magazine editor who visited Paris in the summer of 1814. As he wrote, 'The air of the streets and public places of Paris is sufficient to impress this truth with melancholy force and to inspire fears of further disturbances. Walking one day in the Jardin de Plantes, I fell into conversation with a young Frenchman: his friends had destined him for the medical profession, but the conscription had seized him at an early age and dragged him from his studies, and now the peace left him, at twenty-five, ignorant and unprovided. He spoke of the Bourbons with bitterness and Bonaparte with zealous attachment.'[9] In all, some 13,000 officers found themselves placed on half pay.[10] Meanwhile, even those officers and men fortunate enough to have secured a place in the new army had to suffer the humiliation of watching hundreds of Bourbon favourites being promoted and decorated. Typical of the general feeling, perhaps, are the words of General Thiébault:

> Twenty-three years of terrible wars, begun with so much heroism, carried on so unflinchingly and gloriously, ended by blunders so great and disasters so appalling, had produced fatigue, exhaustion, disgust [and] anger. There had been a unanimous wish for peace, and peace had been obtained, but in the calm of repose the sentiment of honour resumed its rights. Having come to ourselves, we could fathom the depth of the abyss into which we had been hurled, and measure the distance from the giant we had lost to the man who took his place. Great errors, doubtless, had ... brought about the end of his mighty reign, but with him there had been great hopes and a future in view, whilst those who figured in his place offered neither security nor hope. No one could venture to expect anything from a family ... who, as Napoleon said, had in five-and-twenty years of deserved misfortune learned nothing and forgotten nothing. They insulted the army; they dismissed all the respectable officials; they snatched away all that could be snatched away from a nation that had already been despoiled. Less than this would have been the ruin of Napoleon at the height of his power and renown.[11]

Had it simply been a matter of reducing the size of the army, things would not have been so bad. Yet this was not the case. Whilst it was certainly not the case that the army was subjected to a wholesale purge in political terms – most of the senior commanders, including not least almost all the marshals and generals who went on to serve Napoleon in the Hundred Days, were kept on – particular irritation was caused by the fact that space was found for the numerous émigrés who now came back to France: within a year, then, 387 new generals had been appointed and another 6,000 nobles accommodated in a revived royal guard known, as in 1789, as the Maison du Roi consisting of expanded versions of the traditional Garde du Corps and Mousquetaires du Roi, the old guard of halberdiers known as the Cent Suisses, and several other formations such as the personal bodyguard allocated to the Comte d'Artois as heir to the throne.[12] Some of the men had at least been converted into competent professionals by years of service in states ranging from Portugal to Russia (not that that made them any more acceptable), but there were also plenty of figures who could not say even that much of themselves. As Poumiès de la Siboutie wrote, then:

> Laughter greeted the appearance of the old-fashioned colonels, major-generals and lieutenant-generals in their powdered hair [and] antediluvian uniforms … They bore themselves proudly and spoke imperiously, but the very name of those faithful old fossils – the Voltigeurs de Louis XVIII – excited ridicule … The ignorance of the newcomers of everything concerning soldiering … condemned them … in the estimation of the troops … They certainly acted as a drag on the Restoration and cooled the devotion of the army … The creation of the Gardes du Corps … completed the disaffection of the army. These companies of officers were a continual subject of derision to our veterans.[13]

From the Bourbon point of view, the re-establishment of the Maison du Roi is understandable enough: not to have done anything to assuage the feelings of the returning *émigrés* would have simply been to risk swelling the ranks of those who rejected Louis' efforts at reconciliation, whilst at the same time some of them genuinely deserved to be rewarded for their services in the wars against Napoleon. That said, however, it is quite clear that, even on a simple level, more could have been done to soften the blow. To quote Levavasseur, 'We did not take long to discover that our social position was much altered. In the course of the levees that took place every Sunday after Mass … when the name of one or other of our number was read out by the duty officer, it was received with barely a glance, let alone a gesture of common courtesy. However, if the next name on the list was that of some member of the petty nobility newly decked out in a hired uniform loaded down with epaulettes … he would be caressed, fêted, shaken by the hand, and all to remarks such as "This chap is one of ours!"'[14]

According to the same observer, the award of decorations and commissions to numerous Vendéen commanders caused particular bitterness: in so far as the army was concerned, such men were not just mere brigand chieftains, but also guilty of numerous atrocities against good Republicans. Further issues with the Maison du Roi, meanwhile, were its massive cost (20,000,000 *francs* a year in terms of salaries alone), its ostentatious uniforms and the fact that it put the collective noses of the Imperial Guard still further out of joint, not least because most of the latter's units were given stations outside Paris and its nomenclature altered in the most insulting of fashions (the notoriously proud and haughty Old Guard Grenadiers, for example, now became the Grenadiers du Roi).[15]

Yet another issue was the fact that the coveted Legion of Honour was given in large numbers to the returning *émigrés* and the pensions awarded to its holders halved. 'In this respect', complained the commentator, Lenormand, 'there was direct violation of the Charter [see below] as this promised that the army would retain its rank and pensions.'[16] And, last but by no means least, there was the linked issue of the cockade and the regimental flags. Throughout the Napoleonic Wars, the army had marched to war wearing the red, while and blue cockade of the Republic and carrying colours that were variants on the *tricolore*. Now, however, cockade and flag alike were to be white, this being something that was simply unacceptable to most soldiers, whilst the eagles that had topped the staffs were systematically confiscated and destroyed, the only survivors being a few that were hidden away by dedicated officers. To quote Octave Levavasseur once more, 'The fact is that at that time every possible means was made use of to tarnish our old glories, when it was these alone that sustained the honour of the nation.'[17] All this being the case, the Bourbons' efforts to flatter the army came to naught, and, indeed, added insult to injury. For example, the units of the First Division received their new colours in a great ceremony on the Champ de Mars that was a veritable carbon-copy of similar ceremonies that had been carried out under the emperor, but the pronounced religious character that they were given, and the fact that each colour in succession had a white cravat personally attached to it by the wife of the Duc d'Angoulême simply aggravated the soldiers and left them feeling angry and humiliated.[18]

From the very beginning, then, there was much unrest in the military. Here, for example, is Thomas Underwood:

Towards the middle of April the number of French officers and soldiers who had successively arrived in Paris having become considerable ... their natural insolence broke out ... This induced governor Sacken to order all officers of the Allied army who were not called to Paris on business to join their respective corps. Similar measures were taken by the French government and the National Guard received orders to take up all persons who broke the peace and the inhabitants of Paris were forbidden to interfere, but this was disregarded, and the French continued their aggressions and attempted to tear out the [sprigs of leaves] which the Allies wore in their caps. The quarrels continued to increase, the inhabitants taking part with the soldiers. On Friday 29th April there was much fighting in the gardens of the Palais Royale, and several persons were wounded on both sides ... When, after the 4th of May, the Allies were so foolish as to allow Louis XVIII to review the French troops in the courtyard of the Tuileries ... they not only tore the … verdure from the caps of the Allies, but tried to tear the silver medals of the Moscow campaign from the breast of the Russian military … This was followed … by a very serious affray … at a public house, where a party of the French attacked some Austrians. Several were killed on both sides; among them were some girls who had been dancing with the Allies.[19]

Present at a later review was the clergyman, Edward Stanley, the impression that he gives being one of an affair that was highly inauspicious. Too infirm to stand on his own two feet, let alone mount a house, Louis reviewed the troops from the security of an armchair that was still embroidered with imperial bees and was greeted with little in the way of enthusiasm: 'The shouts here were not what they ought to have been. Comparatively few cried "God bless him!" and I much fear the number who thought it was still less. The Duc de Berri, on horseback with Marshal Moncey on one side and Dupont on the other, reviewed the troops, who passed in companies and troops before them. As each company passed, the officer held up his sword and cried "Vive le Roi!" and some of the soldiers did the same, but not more than one out of ten.'[20] On another occasion Stanley witnessed an angry altercation between an officer and a group of Old-Guard grenadiers who were unwilling to serve the king and were threatening to desert unless they got their discharge papers immediately. 'A man standing by told me a short time ago a regiment of imperial Chasseurs when called upon to shout "Vive Louis XVIII.!" at Boulogne, to a man, officers included, cried "Vive Napoléon!", and I feel very certain that had the same thing been required today from the soldiers on the field, they would have acted in the same manner, and that the spectators would have cried "Amen."'[21] In September 1814 the Director of Police, the Comte d'Angles, complained that it was painful to see the gulf that existed between the joy, or so he claimed, that reigned among the bulk of the population and 'the truly alarming and possibly incurable tendencies of the military spirit', complaining that everywhere the soldiery displayed 'a countenance that was as aggressive as it was fretful'.[22] Another observer, meanwhile, was Archibald Alison, newly arrived in France in a bid to get to know a country that had had been inaccessible to British visitors for the past eleven years:

We had the good fortune to see the infantry of the Old Guard drawn up in line in the streets of Fontainebleau, and their appearance was fully such as justified the idea we had formed of that body of veteran soldiers … Their aspect was bold and martial; there was a keenness in their eyes which bespoke the characteristic intelligence of the French soldiers, and a ferocity in the expression of their countenances which seemed to have been unsubdued even by the unparalleled disasters in which their country had been involved. The people of the town ... complained in the bitterest terms of their licentious conduct, and repeatedly said that they dreaded them more as friends than the cossacks themselves as enemies. They seemed to harbour the most unbounded resentment against the people of this country, their countenances bore the expression of the strongest enmity as we walked along their line, and we frequently heard them mutter among themselves in the most emphatic manner, 'Sacré Dieu! Voila les anglais!'[23]

Away from Paris, there was also trouble in the south and south-west. At Clermont Ferrand 13 April saw a force of troops headed by a Major Vautrat of the Eighty-First Line break into the cathedral during mass and tear down the Bourbon flag that the mayor had caused to be raised on its bell tower two days before, the offending item than being torn to shreds and burned in the main square.[24] At Bayonne Charles Kinloch, a young officer who had been serving on the staff of Sir John Hope, reported that the garrison was openly disaffected. As he told his mother:

The officers (especially the juniors). are dreadfully sulky and angry. I don't think I ever saw such a number of dissatisfied countenances. Notwithstanding the governor's orders, few, if any, of them have hoisted the white cockade. One cannot be surprised at their attachment to the Napoleon dynasty when you recollect that almost all the seniors have been promoted from nothing, I may say, to the highest honours under his standard, and the young looked forward with eagerness to this same advancement. From the commencement of the blockade they had been kept ignorant of the great events which were taking place at their capital till at last the whole truth burst upon them at once without their minds being prepared for such an event, and the young men, in a manner now unfit for any profession, saw all their hopes of promotion and advancement dispersed in the course of a few hours, and the man they looked on as a demi-God humbled and dethroned.[25]

Hitherto relations between British and French officers had been reasonably friendly – there had, indeed, been much fraternization between the two in Spain and Portugal – but now the relationship came under increasing strain. As John

Rous wrote of the atmosphere that pertained in Bordeaux as the British army gathered there preparatory to taking ship for home:

> The French officers are very much inclined to quarrel; they cannot bear the sight of the English and take every opportunity of making themselves obnoxious. However, we have had so much the best of it, both with the broadsword and the pistol, that they begin to be more civil; they are the most blustering set of fellows I ever saw, but generally prove great dunghills when they find they cannot bully.[26]

'Great dunghills' or not, the officers also took refuge in a narrative of events that assuaged their wounded *amour propre*.[27] Here, for example, is Archibald Alison on a conversation that took place in Paris in May 1814:

> A French officer who introduced himself to us one night in a box at the opera, expressing his regard for the English, against whom, he said, he had had the honour to fight for six years in Spain, described the steadiness and the determination of the English infantry ... at Salamanca in terms of enthusiastic admiration. Another, who had been in the battle of Toulouse, extolled the conduct of the Highland regiments ... Of the military talents of the Duke of Wellington they spoke also with much respect, though generally with strong indications of jealousy. They were often very ingenious in deriving means of explaining his victories without compromising, as they called it, the honour of the French arms. At Salamanca ... in consequence of the wounds of Marmont and their generals, their army was two hours without a commander. At Vitoria ... it was commanded by Jourdan, and anybody could beat Jourdan ... Some of the Duke of Wellington's victories over Soult they stoutly denied, and others they ascribed to great superiority of numbers and to the large drafts of Soult's best troops [taken from him] for the purpose of forming skeleton battalions to receive the conscripts of 1813.[28]

Had the economy of France been able to accommodate the process of demobilization, the situation might not have been so bad, but this was very far from being the case, the result being that the problem was both exacerbated still further and rendered all the more dangerous. In brief, what was created was a ready-made crowd who could be expected in large part to rally to Napoleon. One of the first things that British visitors to France noticed, then, was the enormous number of ex-soldiers that filled the streets. As Scott wrote of Dieppe:

The most impressive aspect of the crowd before us … was its military aspect. Almost every man had some indication of the military profession about his person sufficient to denote that had been engaged in war. At the same time there was a self-willed variety in the dress of each which had a very unpleasant effect … We could scarcely imagine that the dark-visaged beings, some in long, loose greatcoats, some in jackets, some in cocked hats … some in caps, who darted us keen looks of a very over-clouded cast, had ever belonged to regiments, steady, controlled and lawful. They seemed, rather, the fragments of broken-up gangs, brave, dexterous and fierce, but unprincipled and unrestrained. Much of this irregularity and angriness of appearance was doubtless occasioned by the great disbandment of the army that had just taken place. The disbanded had no call to observe the niceties of military discipline although they still retained such parts of their military uniforms as they deemed convenient. They had not … either pursuits to occupy their time or … prospects to keep up their hopes; they still lounged about in idleness although their pay had been stopped, and disappointment and necessity threw into their faces expressions an expression deeper than that of irritation, approaching, in fact, to … indiscriminate and inveterate hatred. They carried about with them … the branded characteristics of forlorn men whose interests and habits opposed them to the peace of mankind.[29]

Whilst anger was at its hottest amongst the men who found themselves cast out from the military estate, by early 1815 it was clear that even those soldiers who were still in employment were not entirely to be trusted. Thus, it was bad enough that in January 1815, Rémi Exelmans, a distinguished officer who been appointed Inspector-General of the Cavalry and awarded the Order of Saint Louis, was discovered to have been engaging in treasonable correspondence with Marshal Murat, under whom he had served as an *aide-de-camp*, but still worse was the fact that, presided over by Marshal Mortier, the subsequent court martial proceeded to acquit Exelmans of all the charges against him.[30] Nor, it seems, was this the only evidence of partiality in the military estate. At about the same time a brawl erupted in a Paris street following an altercation between a shopkeeper and an officer who had urinated against the wall of the man's premises. This saw open defiance: when constables arrived to arrest the worst offenders, the many other officers in the vicinity rallied round them to shouts of 'No: you are not having them. If anyone dares touch even so much as one of us, things will really kick off, and then see where you'll be. We may not be nobles, but, if someone vexes us, we know how to defend ourselves.' Despite this, however, nothing was done, the men concerned being released without charge within a matter of hours.[31]

If the veterans of the Grande Armée were disaffected, this was something in which they were by no means alone. Setting aside issues of political preference, there was the issue of the behaviour of the occupying forces. 'The Prussian soldiers, indeed,' wrote Andrew Blayney, are so much complained of from their exhorbitant demands in their quarters that it has created dissatisfaction bordering on insurrection: they pay for nothing and are exceedingly nice in their palate, demanding delicacies in addition to their sustenance with a haughty and imperious tone.'[32] Arrogance was so much part of the Russian order of the day, meanwhile, that it gave a new addition to the French language in the form of the word '*bistro*', this being derived from the Russian for 'Quickly!'[33] To quote Poumiès de la Siboutie once more:

We were no longer masters in our own hospitals. We were forced, like everybody else, to give way to the enemy. We had to empty our wards, keeping only a few soldiers who were too ill to be moved and whom we had to put up as best we could in corridors and garrets. The enemy's sick and wounded had the best of everything. Linen-rooms, cellars, dispensary were raided and provisions of every description seized. They revelled in plenty while our own men could scarcely get bread. Such are the so-called rights of war: power triumphing over justice.[34]

Thanks to this behaviour, not to mention the atrocities engaged in the march on Paris, Allied officers were occasionally mobbed in the streets: Eduard von Löwenstern, for example, describes being accosted in the street by 'an old stinking woman smelling of brandy and garlic [who] put her fist under my nose and screeched in my face, "Qu'est-ce que tu veux, bougre de cosaque? Veux-tu casaquer?" [What do you want, you Cossack bugger? Are you on the pull?]'[35] However, such defiance does not seem to have been especially common. On the contrary, for many of the inhabitants, the priority was to placate the invaders, or even to profit from them. Nikolai Bronevskii, for example, was a staff officer serving at the headquarters of Blücher's Army of Silesia:

From the evening of 18 [30] March, our camps turned into bazaars. In an instant, anything one could desire was brought there: there was hardly any bargaining and sellers took whatever money was offered. Of course, everything seemed inexpensive to us. And where else can you find such an abundance of oranges, lemons, apples, fresh grapes … candles, wines in full and half bottles, porter, liqueurs … patties, oysters, cheese, rolls, in a word, you could have found anything you had ever desired. The following day we saw carriages with women arriving at our camp … Our officers then generously brought out scarves full of oranges, apples [and] sweets and gave them to the women. Acquaintances were made within the hour.[36]

There is little suggestion of sympathy for the Bourbons here, the women described by Bronevskii quite clearly being prostitutes. Other accounts, however, are more positive, Eduard von Lowenstern describing how he and his fellow officers were frequently invited to 'little gatherings' by the owners of a local chateau.[37] Such invitations, no doubt, had a political context, but other forms of fraternization were more personal. Thus, for thousands of French women, the presence of foreign soldiers became a source of pleasure, a means of escape, perhaps, from the drudgery and boredom of lives lived out at the whim of their husbands. Hardly had Archibald Alison reached Paris in the immediate wake of Napoleon's downfall, then, than he was remarking on a phenomenon that had in fact been common in almost every theatre of the Napoleonic Wars:

> We had very frequent opportunities of marking the truth of the observation that women have less bitterness against the enemies of their country than men. The Parisian ladies adopted fashions from almost all the allied troops … and those who were acquainted with officers of rank belonging to those armies appeared on all occasions to be highly flattered with the attentions they received from them. The same was observable in the conduct of the lower ranks. In the suburbs of Paris and in the neighbouring villages where many of the Allied troops were quartered they appeared always on the best terms with the female inhabitants, and were often to be seen assisting them in their work, playing with at battledore and shuttlecock in the streets, or strolling in their company along the banks of the Seine or in the woods of Saint Cloud, evidently to the satisfaction of both parties.[38]

That such scenes cut Napoleon's veterans to the quick cannot be doubted: indeed, mention has already been made of a fight occasioned by some soldiers catching a group of women *in flagrante delicto*. Yet the populace was scarcely to be blamed for doing what they could to ease their situation. In the first place, peace had not bring a return to prosperity. Prices, for example, remained very high, in which respect it did not help that for financial reasons it proved impossible to abolish the *droits réunis*. 'Tea, coffee, sugar and all colonial produce are all very dear', reported Thomas Bowdler.[39] Meanwhile, as witness the scenes witnessed by new arrivals in France at such ports as Calais, assailed by post-war depression and an influx of cheap British goods, the workers were suffering severe unemployment: 'A number of blackguard-looking men gathered round us, recommending their own services and different hotels with much vehemence and violent altercations amongst themselves, and troops of children followed, crying "Vivent les anglais! Give me one *sou*!"'[40] In Paris, meanwhile, the number of beggars was reported as being very numerous, the only saving grace that British visitors could report being that many of the children tried to earn the alms they received by turning somersaults or singing little catches.[41]

In 1789 one of the many factors that had brought Louis XVI and Marie-Antoinette to grief had been their indifference to the situation of the populace. Contrary to claims that the Bourbons, as well as forgetting nothing, had learned nothing, their latter-day representatives were keenly aware that their continued well-being was closely linked with that of the people. In January 1815, then, a circular letter sent out by the Ministry of the Interior to every single one of the prefects explicitly spelled out that popular discontent was closely linked to the availability of work and the price of food, and that, as well as keeping Paris closely informed of all information that bore upon these two points, they should do everything they could to stimulate employment and assure the supply of bread.[42] Conscious that the issue was one that was extremely pressing, moreover, the new regime did what it could to ameliorate the situation: here and there fresh public-works projects were embarked upon; foreigners who had come to France looking for work were deported; and migrants from the countryside were denied entry to Paris.[43] However, with money desperately short, these measures were at best patchy and in some cases downright counter-productive: barring migrants from Paris, for example, was simply to increase the pressure in the departments surrounding the capital. Privileged as an observer by his long stay in France, Alison recorded a country in thrall to poverty and economic stagnation:

The manifest signs of the decay of commerce in France cannot escape the observation of the traveller, more especially if he has been in the habit of travelling in England. The public diligences are few in number, and most miserably managed. It is difficult to say whether the carriage, the horses, or the harness, gives most the idea of meanness. Excepting in the neighbourhood of large towns, you meet with not a cart, or waggon, for twenty that the same distance would show in England ... The villages and towns throughout France are in a state of dilapidation ... No new houses, shops, and warehouses building, as we behold everywhere in England.

None of that hurry and bustle in the streets, and on the quays of the sea-port towns, which our blessed country can always boast. The dress of the people, their food, their style of living, their amusements, their houses, all bespeak extreme poverty and want of commerce ... In no country in the world is there found so great a number of beggars as in France ... These beggars are chiefly from among the manufacturing classes; the families of soldiers and labourers ... Another mark of the poverty of France at present occurs to me. In every town and particularly in the large cities, we are struck with the numbers of idle young men and women who are seen in the streets. Now that the army no longer carries away 'the surplus population of France' (to use the language of Bonaparte), the number of these idlers is greatly increased. The great manufacturing concerns have long ceased to employ them. France is too poor to continue the public works which Napoleon had everywhere begun. The French have no money for the improvement of their estates, the repair of their houses or the encouragement of the numerous trades and professions which thrive by the costly taste and ever varying fashion of a luxurious and rich community. The great meanness of their dress must particularly strike every English traveller ... In their amusements also is the poverty of the people manifested. A person residing in Paris, and who had travelled no further, would think this observation unjust, for in Paris there is no want of amusements: the theatres are numerous, and all other species of entertainment are to be found. But in the smaller towns, one little dirty theatre, ill-lighted, with ragged scenery, dresses and a beggarly company of players, is all that is to be found. The poverty of the people will not admit of the innumerable ... amusements which we find in every little town in England.[44]

Nor was it just a matter of the economy. Whereas in 1814 the Bourbons had not appeared so bad an option, perceptions quickly began to change. In fairness to Louis XVIII and his advisers, no attempt was made to turn the clock back to 1789. Feudalism was not restored, for example, while the Code Civil was retained unaltered along with all the structures of the Napoleonic state, including the council of state – now transformed into the king's privy council – the courts of law, the departments and the prefects. At the same time, virtually Louis' first act was the convocation of a constitutional convention composed of nine members of the Senate, nine members of the *corps législatif* and three erstwhile *émigrés*. As for Louis himself, while certainly aged and infirm, he was no fool, and saw quite clearly that he had no option but to come to some accommodation with the France of Napoleon. Indeed, he even received some plaudits. 'Generally speaking', wrote Giraud, 'public opinion pronounced itself in his favour. He was accorded plenty of natural spirit, a variety of talents and a solid education as well as a very good understanding of the situation in which he was placed. In his public demeanour, his treatment of all those who approached him, meanwhile, he manifested a graciousness, a kindness even, that awoke real interest.'[45] Dynamic, however, he was not. To quote François Guizot, 'Outwardly imposing, judicious, acute and circumspect, he could reconcile, restrain and defeat, but he could neither inspire, direct nor give the impulse … Persevering application to business was as little suited to him as active movement. He sufficiently maintained his rank, his rights and his power and seldom committed a glaring mistake, but, when once his dignity and prudence were vindicated, he allowed things to take their own course with too little energy or power to control men and force them to act in concert for the accomplishment of his wishes.'[46]

If only because he was too lacking in energy, then, Louis XVIII was no tyrant. That said, the document that resulted from the discussions of the commission – the Charter of 1814 – was scarcely the most progressive of works. Many basic freedoms – for example, of expression, religion, property and occupation – were guaranteed along with such principles as equality before the law and the right to due legal process, whilst France was granted an elected lower chamber as well as an appointed senate (in practice, the self-same body that had till 1814 formed a central part of the political apparatus of the Napoleonic state). Finally, conscription to the regular army was outlawed. Yet there was also much to complain about. Setting aside the facts, first, that its prologue stated that the Charter was accorded France as a measure of grace and favour by a Louis XVIII 'in the nineteenth year of his reign' (a statement that conveyed a complete refusal to recognize the legitimacy of the Republic and Empire) and, second, that Catholicism was made the official religion of the French state, the king was granted extensive powers in respect of legislation, including the right to issue ordinances relating to the catch-all categories of the security of the state and to implement the laws without reference to parliament at all. Able to choose his ministers freely, to dissolve the assembly and call fresh elections whenever he wished and to choose whomsoever he wanted as ministers, he also had unlimited powers of patronage with regard to the Senate, on whose membership there was no upper limit. Nor was the system of election to the second chamber much better in that both membership of the electorate and eligibility for election were subject to payment of a relatively high sum of money in terms of taxation, and the elections themselves conducted in an indirect fashion (in brief, the actual choice of deputies fell on departmental electoral colleges), the result of all this being that the electorate – no more than 100,000 – was tiny, and the number of potential deputies still tinier. If a constitutional king, Louis XVIII was therefore scarcely a parliamentary one, the result being that genuine liberals were unlikely to be satisfied (not that they could do very much about it: even if they by some miracle secured control of the chamber, it was specifically laid down that the Charter was not open to amendment).[47]

Out-and-out liberals, however, were in a minority, and it was therefore much to be hoped that the 'masses of granite' as a whole would rally to a system which appeared to guarantee many of its interests. Yet it soon appeared that the security on offer was illusory. In the first place, freedom of the press was restricted by a series of administrative measures; in the second, it became abundantly clear that the state machine was going to involve itself very heavily in the management of elections; and in the third the pretensions of the Church were widely encouraged: it was, for example, given control of secondary education, whilst strict ordinances were introduced enforcing respect for Sunday as a day of worship (in the event, such was the general outcry that these had to be abandoned almost immediately, but by then the damage had been done). Still worse, in contrast to the moderate views that Louis XVIII had been espousing in 1813, the *notables* found themselves threatened with loss of influence and land alike: not only were a quarter of the imperial bureaucracy dismissed, including just over 50 per cent of the prefects, but on 4 November 1814 a bill was passed stipulating that all landed estates and other properties that had originally been stripped from *émigré* noblemen and had not yet been sold should be restored to their original owners. With the regime clearly favouring the nobility, as witness Louis' reliance on such figures as the Comte de Blacas (his Minister of the Royal Household and de facto favourite), the principle of the career open to talent also seemed at risk. To quote an obscure pamphleteer's analysis of the causes of the collapse of the Bourbon monarchy in 1815:

One saw nothing any more other than chevaliers, viscounts, marquises and titles of every kind. It was a curious thing to hear the announcement in the salons of these personages, and then to witness their haughty entrance, claiming, as they very did, titles to which they had no real right ... Whilst it is beyond doubt right and proper to recognize the nobility of families who have rendered services to the state and left their descendents a good name, it is insulting to see men full of arrogance who have nothing more than an empty title pretending to constitute a privileged class.[48]

Indeed, in one or two places, there was a feeling that something even greater was at stake: round France there were plenty of *émigrés* who were at odds with the official line of reconciliation and wanted violent retribution. With tensions in the area particularly acute due to a long history of communal antagonism between Catholics – in the Revolutionary and Napoleonic era mostly ultra-royalist – and Protestants – mostly Republican, constitutional monarchist or Bonapartist – Nîmes saw the emergence of the so-called Societé Réal, an association headed by a number of erstwhile rebels that made it very clear that it was literally out for the blood of all those who had supported Napoleon.[49] In Paris, meanwhile, particularly lurid rumours surrounded the ostentatious memorial service that was organized to commemorate the twenty-second anniversary of the execution of Louis XVI: according to common report, gangs of hired thugs had been secreted in the capital with orders to sally out during the commemorations and attack anyone associated with the Revolution or Napoleon, Lazare Carnot being so convinced that these reports were true that he barricaded himself inside his apartment with a group of trusted friends and made ready to fight to the death.[50]

In this respect, many of the elements which surrounded Louis XVIII did his cause no favours. As we have seen, Louis himself was a genuinely pragmatic figure who was convinced of the need for compromise, but this was not the case with his brother, the Comte d'Artois. Thus, in his youth an irresponsible libertine who in many ways epitomised the worst excesses of the *ancien régime*, the future Charles X had responded to the Revolution by espousing a fervent Catholicism that could only be encouraged by the conviction of traditionalist thinkers such as Joseph de Maistre and Louis de Bonald that the turmoil that had engulfed France had been the work of a God determined to punish France for her sins. Utterly contemptuous of the Third Estate, he was only slightly less scornful in respect of Louis XVIII, not least on account of the latter's ill health. The initial hopes he entertained of acting as a power behind the throne and keeping the Restoration wedded to what Artois regarded as right and proper principles having been dashed by a display of determination on the part of the king that took him completely by surprise, he thereafter acted as a focus for all the many *émigrés* who had looked for a more hardline policy and made it quite clear that if he had his way France would enjoy a return to 1789 pure and simple under the leadership of such men as the Marquis de Villèle.[51] Nor was it just a matter of court politics: with the old nobility still possessed of 20 per cent of the land, the sort of men who flocked to Artois' standard were able to exercise considerable influence in small towns and villages across the country, this being something in which they were joined by many priests, men who had bought

Church lands often being denied the sacraments and subjected to sermons that threatened them with eternal damnation.[52]

Fear of counter-revolution, then, was very real. As the Comte d'Angles warned as early as April 1814:

> Amongst the upper classes, amongst men of the world possessed of the habit of reflection, one can perceive a general feeling of insecurity which in some instances has reached the level of fear of civil war. Such worries are every day reinforced by pamphlets and handbills ungarnished by the name of either author or printer whose style is designed to awaken old hatreds and provoke acts of vengeance, and is in general very much opposed to the clement and paternal views of the august members of the house of Bourbon.[53]

If all this shook the confidence of the 'masses of granite', it also had ripples further down the social scale. Thus, the peasantry, too, were concerned for such land as they had acquired during the Revolution, as well as being rife with rumours that the tithes and feudal dues were to be restored, the result being a number of displays of anti-royalist feeling, some of them quite serious.[54] In places, meanwhile, the trouble was augmented by such issues as the legacy of the turmoil of the 1790s: at Rennes, for example, pro-Republican peasants protested violently at the reappearance in the locality of a notorious *chouan* leader called Boisguy.[55] As for the *sans culottes* of Paris, support for Jacobinism remained strong enough for serious rioting to break out when a popular actress was denied a religious funeral by the Church in January 1815.[56] What made even the suggestion of wholesale counter-revolution all the more unwise was that, as even die-hard anti-Jacobins recognized, French society had undergone a profound change since 1789. To quote Alison once again:

> The general diffusion of a military spirit; the unprincipled manner in which war has been conducted, and the encouragement which has been given to martial qualities to the exclusion of all pacific virtues, have promoted the growth of the French military vices, particularly selfishness and licentiousness, among all ranks and descriptions of the people, and materially injured their general character, even in the remotest parts of the country. During the Revolution, and under the imperial government, men have owed their success in France almost exclusively to the influence of their intellectual abilities without any assistance from their moral character; in consequence, the contempt for religion is more generally diffused,

and more openly expressed than it was; and although loud protestations of inviolable honour are still necessary, integrity of conduct is much less respected. The abolition of the old, and the formation of a new nobility, composed chiefly of men who had risen from inferior military situations, has had a most pernicious effect on the general manners of the nation. The chief or sole use of a hereditary nobility in a free country, is to keep up a standard of dignity and elegance of manner, which serves as a model of imitation much more extensively than the middling and lower ranks are often willing to allow, and has a more beneficial effect on the national character than it is easy to explain on mere speculative principles. But the manners of the new French nobility being the very reverse of dignified or elegant, their constitution has hitherto tended only to confirm the changes in the general manners of a great proportion of the French nation which the revolutionary ideas had effected. There are very few men to be seen now in France, who (making all allowances for difference of previous habits) appear to Englishmen to possess either the manners or feelings of gentlemen. The best possible proof that this is not a mere national prejudice, in so far as the army is concerned, is that the French *ladies* are very generally of the same way of thinking. After the English officers left Toulouse in the summer of 1814, the ladies of that town found the manners of the French officers who succeeded them so much less agreeable that they could not be prevailed on, for a long time, to admit them into their society. This is a triumph over the arms of France which we apprehend our countrymen would have found it much more difficult to achieve in the days of the ancient monarchy.[57]

Albeit in a form that is much less jaundiced, precisely the same point is made by the agricultural reformer, Morris Birkbeck:

If we view France at large, apart from the busy politicians of the metropolis, nine-tenths of the people will be republicans when put to the test. To the Republic they owe all they possess of property and independence, but their only present prayer is for repose and security. Let the restored monarch look to this. There is a strong party in favour of tranquility, but very little love for monarchy out of the immediate circle of the court. Touch, or only threaten, the present arrangement of property, and such a fermentation will be excited in the republican mass as will shake Paris and 'discover its foundations'.[58]

Under the surface, meanwhile, there were other issues that threatened the stability of the new regime. Hatred of Britain, for example, was rife. As Thomas Bowdler noted:

The great body of the French nation is at present actuated towards our countrymen by a degree of hatred which I believe has seldom been equalled and is not easy to be expressed … There is not a man in France who does not feel (whatever he may say) that his country was prevented from giving [the] law to Europe by the persevering energy of Great Britain. To us he ascribes not only the destruction of his marine, the capture of his colonies and the loss of the Peninsula, but he considers us the principal authors of the defeats which he sustained in the north and the east, and … is continually saying in his own mind [that] the Allies never would have attempted the invasion of France had they not been encouraged by the victories of Wellington.[59]

Of rather less weight, but still worth mentioning is the question of the French national character. According to observers such as Alison, the French had always been a martial people, eager for glory, and this trait had been whipped to fresh heights by the events of the Revolutionary and Napoleonic Wars.[60] 'For others again, always restless, vain-glorious and fond of show, their faults had not only placed them in the power of Napoleon, but been increased ten-fold by his rule.'[61] This sort of remark, of course, is not to be taken at face value: all the evidence suggests that, with every battle, dissatisfaction with the regime increased, whilst claims such as those made by Alison and Scott arose from a discourse moulded by a conviction of innate British superiority. Yet, particularly among younger elements of the population, especially young men who had not experienced the horrors of war at first hand and had careers to make for themselves, it cannot but be denied that there was nostalgia for what was perceived as having been an age of opportunity. Buttressing such views, meanwhile, was the same refusal to accept the extent of France's defeat that was apparent in the army. To quote Alison yet again:

We never met with a Frenchman, of any rank, or of any political persuasion, who considered the French army as fairly overcome in the campaign of 1814; and the shifts and contrivances by which they explained all the events of the campaign, without having recourse to that supposition, were wonderfully ingenious. The best informed Frenchmen whom we met in Paris, even those who did not join in the popular cry of treason and corruption against Marmont, regarded the terms granted by Alexander to their city as a measure of policy rather than of magnanimity. They uniformly maintained, that the possession of the heights of Belleville and Montmartre did not secure the command of Paris: that if Marmont had chosen, he might have defended the town after he had lost these positions; and that, if the Russians had attempted to take the town by force, they might have succeeded, but would have lost half their army.[62]

The net result of all this was the emergence of the first signs of the nostalgia for the Napoleonic age which has continued to grip France down to the present day. As Alison wrote:

The patriotism of the French is certainly a very strong feeling, but it appears to be much tainted with … vanity and love of show … They assent to all that can be said of the miseries that [Napoleon] brought upon France, but add 'Mais il a battu tout le monde; il a fait des choses superbes a Paris; il a flatté notre orgueil national. Ah! C'est un grand homme. Notre pays a jamais été si grand, ni si puissant, que sous lui.' ['However, he has beaten everybody; he has done some superb things in Paris, he has flattered our national pride. What a great man: our country has never been so big nor so powerful as under him.'] The condition of the inhabitants of distant provinces was nowise improved by his public buildings and decorations at their capital, but every Frenchman considers a compliment to Paris … a personal compliment to himself.[63]

Whatever the truth of all this, France had beyond doubt acquired a vigorous public opinion, and no sooner had Napoleon fallen than this began to express itself in full force. To quote a report submitted by the Comte d'Angles on 22 April:

Inserted in the constitutional charter, the words 'liberty of the press' have turned the heads of authors, printers and, above all, journalists, and that in spite of the various restrictions which have been imposed in respect of this matter. In vain has the provisional government announced that the laws relating to the press and the printing industry should remain in force; in vain has the general police brought in a number of offenders: a torrent of writings of a more or less dangerous nature … of pamphlets motivated by a greater or lesser degree of ill will, have seen the light of day.[64]

Yet in the face of the growing turmoil, the regime remained almost entirely immobile, not to say complacent. On the one hand, the king was scarcely an energetic ruler and was therefore inclined to procrastinate rather than take any sort of radical action, while the *eminence grise* of the regime, the Comte de Blacas, was inclined to deal with problems by the simple means of denying their existence:

Never was the destiny of a state entrusted to more feeble and unskilful hands. M. de Blacas was, I confidently affirm, the most incompetent of ministers. To avert dangers, he thought it sufficient to despise them. In his sublime arrogance he readily imagined that revolutionists would never dare to conspire while he was minister. If any apprehensions were expressed respecting the future, he smiled; if it was insisted that there was good cause for alarm, he shrugged his shoulders; if the plots of the Bonapartists were denounced to him, he turned on his heel and went off, observing that 'no good royalist would repeat such nonsense, but that we might rest secure – 'dormir sur les deux oreilles' ['sleep with both ears shut']. This was his favourite phrase.[65]

The other ministers were not much better. As Foreign Minister, Talleyrand was superlative – his achievements at Vienna are undeniable – while the Minister of Finance, Joseph Louis, a secularised priest who had fled abroad in 1792 but returned in 1800 to serve Napoleon, proved surprisingly skilful in his own field, but Dupont was a poor choice as Minister of War (see Note 12); the Chancellor, Charles Dambray, a nonentity with no experience of government, who was only in the government at all because he was the son-in-law of a prominent official in the court of Louis XVI; the Minister of Marine, Pierre Malouet, a royalist member of the constituent assembly who, after nearly ten years as an *émigré*, had eventually rallied to Napoleon and served in various posts in the administration before falling out of favour in 1812 as a result of his opposition to the invasion of Russia; and the Minister of Marine, François de Montesquiou, a sometime abbot who had three times served as the president of the National Assembly in 1790, but defected from the Revolutionary cause over his opposition to the Civil Constitution of the Clergy, whose moderate talent was more than outweighed by a temperament and character so difficult that they repelled all who came into contact with him, not to mention a pronounced preference for the *ancien régime* that was out of step with the views of most of his fellows. Frequently inclined to clash with one another as they were and lacking any framework for joint discussion, to expect such men to take firm action even to defend Louis

XVIII against the mutinous mutterings of Artois and his supporters was utterly futile.[66]

With France clearly in the grip of both reaction and incompetence, it was not long before there were growing signs of political opposition. On the one hand Louis and the various bastions of his rule became the butt of endless satirical cartoons that circulated widely in Paris and other towns and cities, and on the other a variety of polemicists exploited a series of loopholes in the press regulations to publish numerous pamphlets in which they denounced the every action of the regime. And in the legislative assembly, a variety of speakers contested government policy and even secured a number of concessions. This hostile activity, of course, was far from being solely a Bonapartist phenomenon. On the contrary, many of the régime's critics were constitutional royalists, committed liberals who wanted nothing less than the return of Napoleon. Some, too, were diehard Jacobins who wanted the restoration of the Republic and saw the empire as the death-knell of the Revolution. Of this last tendency, perhaps, the chief representative was the some-time strong man of the Committee of Public Safety, Lazare Carnot, who, notwithstanding the position he had been given as Inspector-General of Engineers, answered the new regime's reactionary tendencies with a long manifesto entitled *Mémoire au Roi* in which he justified the principle of regicide and rehearsed grievance after grievance against the Bourbons.[67] Yet, for all the constitutional royalism of some and the crypto-republicanism of others, it was clear that among at least some sections of the populace Napoleon was already no longer the figure of hatred that he had been in 1814. Handbills, prints and graffiti kept the memory of the emperor alive; violets – a flower particularly associated with Napoleon on account of an incident after his abdication in which he was supposedly presented with a bunch by a little girl while walking in the gardens of the palace of Fontainebleau – were worn as buttonholes and carried as bouquets; and medallions of about the size of a one-*franc* piece began to circulate bearing the figure of Marie-Louise inscribed with the word 'hope' on the one side and 'courage' on the other.[68] As for the Royalist anthem, 'Vive Henri IV!', this was inevitably set to new words. Thus:

Vive l'empereur Napoléon! Vive ce grand monarque!
Plus vaillant qu'Henri IV et sa descendation.[69]

By early 1815, then, a mixture of nostalgia, anger and frustration was ensuring that popular Bonapartism, at least, was starting to recover from the nadir of twelve months previously: in late February, indeed, many of the leading citizens of Grenoble received anonymous letters that openly called for revolution and threatened all those who had collaborated with the Bourbons with dire punishment, whilst at the same time naming 1 March – the very day that Napoleon landed at Cannes – as the day that France should rise in revolt.[70] From the point of view of the exiled emperor, of course, all this was very encouraging, and there is no doubt that it was partly the news from France that decided him on a last-ditch attempt to regain his throne. That said, by the end of 1814 other issues had begun to push Napoleon in the direction of taking action. In the first place, the attitude of the Bourbon government was not helpful, the pension that it had guaranteed him never being paid in full. Still worse, Elba had essentially been the gift of an Alexander I eager to play the magnanimous prince, and there had always been those who regarded it as a place of exile that was not just generous but distinctly injudicious. Both Francis I and Metternich had been violently opposed to the arrangement, and all the more so the Treaty of Fontainebleau also gave Marie-Louise and her son the nearby Grand Duchy of Tuscany, a further source of worry being the proximity of Murat's Naples. Castlereagh, too, was very worried, whilst Sir Charles Stewart wondered 'whether Napoleon may not bring … powder to the iron mines which the island of Elba is so famous for'.[71] According to Bonapartist sources, from this dissatisfaction there emerged a settled determination to send Napoleon somewhere else, and there are, too, claims that a plot was afoot to have him murdered. Whether any of this was true, it is hard to say, though reputable historians such as Harold Nicolson have gone so far as to accept that the idea of moving him was certainly discussed in the winter of 1814, whilst a riot at Avignon during his journey into exile that almost saw him lynched by a mob may just have been the work of royalist agents. All that can be said for certain is that by the beginning of 1815 Napoleon's household was in the grip of something that amounted to panic. 'People feared for the emperor's person,' wrote Napoleon's valet, Marchand. 'News arriving from Vienna, via Livorno and Naples, was not reassuring … There was talk of Saint Helena … Navy commander Chautard was ordered to keep a vigilant watch on … ships cruising near Elba … Some defence measures were decided on for the outer gates.'[72] After Waterloo Napoleon claimed that it had been all this that determined him to act as he did, but the sceptic is compelled, first, to observe that Elba was a very small realm for a ruler of Napoleon's energy, and, second, that the optimism that had so sustained him in 1813 and 1814 was back with a vengeance. 'The emperor knew and stated that, outside of a few thousand schemers, the entire nation remained attached to him in spirit, opinion and heart, just as it was attached to the principles of national sovereignty and French honour; that it had only submitted to the necessity imposed by its enemy and the new Judas; [and] that out of 30,000,000 inhabitants, 29,500,000 … kept alive in their hearts the hope of overthrowing the princes.'[73] In the light of what had occurred in 1814, to cleave to such a belief seems extraordinarily blinkered, and yet by February 1815 Napoleon had resolved on escape, and all the more so as the unity of the erstwhile coalition still seemed decidedly shaky. Viewed in objective terms, the chances of success were slim – so much so, in fact, that it has been claimed that the whole adventure was provoked in an attempt to generate a pretext whereby 'the monster' could be chained up in some place of exile far from Europe – but on 26 February Napoleon sailed from Elba with his entire army of 750 men.

To what extent, however, was the emperor's gamble based on anything other than wishful thinking? Such a question is difficult to answer, and it is probable that it will never be susceptible of a final resolution. That said, even setting aside what came afterwards, it is difficult to accept the notion that the whole of France was panting for the return of the emperor. Certainly, here and there it is possible to come across references to an ardent desire for such a turn of events. In the early winter of 1814, for example, Alison was travelling south to embark on an extended stay in the pleasant climes of Provence:

For the first time, this day we had a very severe frost in the morning, but with the aid of the sun, which shone bright and warm, we enjoyed one of the finest days I ever saw. I sat and chatted with the coachman, or rather with Monsieur le Voiturier. I led the conversation to the past and present state of France, and the character of Napoleon, and immediately he, who till this moment appeared to be as meek and gentle as a lamb, became the most eloquent and energetic man I have seen. It is quite wonderful, how the feelings of the people, added to their habits of extolling their own efforts, and those of Bonaparte, supply them with language. They are on this subject all orators. He declared that Paris was sold by Marmont and others, but that we English do not understand what the Parisians mean when they say that Paris was sold. They do not mean that any one was paid for betraying his trust by receiving a bribe, but that, Marmont and others having become very rich under Bonaparte, desired to spend their fortunes in peace, and had, therefore, deserted their master. He said that Bonaparte erred only in having too many things to do at once; but that if he had either relinquished the Spanish war for a while, or not gone to Moscow, no human power would have been a match for him, and even we in England would have felt this. He seemed to think that it was an easy thing for Bonaparte to have equipped as good a navy as ours. He was quite insensible to the argument, that it was first necessary to have commerce, which nourishes our mariners from among whom we have our fighting seamen. He said, that, though this was a work of years for others, it would have been nothing for Napoleon: in short, he venerates the man, and says that, till the day when he left Paris, he was the greatest of men.[74]

That the coachman was not alone in his views, we need not doubt. However, as Alison goes on to point out, if the man was not quite the proverbial voice crying in the wilderness, his eloquence would certainly not have been welcomed by all of his fellows. That this was the case is suggested by the response of the populace to the news that France might soon find herself at war with Prussia and Russia thanks to the crisis over Saxony. Thus, in Valence a ostler in the inn that Alison stayed in told him that he had served for a year and was very anxious not to have to go to war again, whilst the wife of a common soldier gave him 'a most lamentable description of the horrors of the last campaign, and ended by praying for a continuation of the peace'.[75] Moving on to Orange, Alison stayed in another inn and here, too, heard not clamours for vengeance, but rather an analysis of the situation that was remarkably perceptive. As he wrote, 'The landlord, a respectable-looking man, gave us a good deal of news regarding the state of the country. He says, that the people in the south are all anxious for peace, and that those in France who wish for war are those who have nothing else to live on; that nobody with a house over his back, and a little money, desires to have war again.'[76] Finally reaching his destination in Aix-en-Provence, Alison was within a few weeks afforded yet another snapshot of public opinion in that the trial opened in the town of three men who had managed to escape the *gensdarmes* who were marching them away to the army following their conscription in the winter of 1813–14 and then helped spring another man who had remained in the clutches of the forces of law and order. Several of the *gensdarmes* having been killed in the subsequent affray, the perpetrators had been arrested and were now, despite the change of regime, on trial for murder. Eager to judge the state of public feeling, Alison attended the proceedings and was not disappointed: it quickly became obvious that the prisoners enjoyed universal support among the townsfolk, and the special tribunal dealing with the proceedings therefore evidently decided that discretion was the better part of valour, one of the defendants being acquitted altogether and the other two having their cases referred to the king with a recommendation for clemency after being found guilty of 'murder voluntary but without premeditation'.[77]

Alison's experiences are, of course, so many straws in the wind and it is by no means impossible that a traveller less hostile to Napoleon could have come to a rather different conclusion. Yet the reports of the Director of Police, D'Angles, suggest a picture that is much the same. Once again, one must be cautious: placed in the position that he was, D'Angles in some respects had every interest in assuring Louis XVIII that all was well. Yet, for all that, his writings have a ring of veracity that it is hard to deny. All the more conveniently for us, meanwhile, prompted by hints from Elba that something was afoot – in one case it was reported that Napoleon had recently told his personal guard that, whilst he knew that they were getting bored, 'the road is opening up before us, and still stretched far into the distance' and in another that he had said to a group of soldiers who asked to be relieved from his service, 'Have a bit of patience, my friends: we will all return together'[78] – in the week or so before Napoleon embarked for France, he wrote a series of reports in which he made a serious effort to summarise the state of public opinion. That all was not well, D'Angles was quite prepared to concede. 'I will not pretend that opinion is entirely sound', he wrote on 24 February 1815. 'Too many refractory elements are tormenting it.'[79] That said, however, evidently certain that nothing of any import was to be feared from Napoleon, he was reasonably confident that that the régime would be able to ride out the storm. 'I have done my best to enquire into the state of affairs, and have heard rumours and complaints, even observed discontent of various sorts. Yet what I see everywhere is a want of everything but words, an inability to effect anything, and the absence of any sort of plot, let alone one that is ready to be brought to fruition.'[80] The opposition, he maintained, was isolated, divided, leaderless and utterly lacking in any conception of how to achieve its aims, whilst it was, if anything, haemorrhaging support, most of those who might once have supported the return of the Republic – a group which he associated above all with those who had bought into the *biens nationaux* – having now come to accept the Charter. Indeed, in general, there was far more opportunism and personal ambition swirling around than ideological conviction: much of the ferment, he believed, was the product of struggles for power at the level of the locality that had nothing to do with party and everything to do with cupidity, whilst even in the more politicised atmosphere of Paris 'the parties … are chiefly based on personal calculation and individual fears and hopes'.[81] As he remarked, 'Egotism is the chief factor. So and so is for the king until the day when he is supplanted by a rival or forced to witness the collapse of some ambitious project; at that moment he throws himself into the ranks of the opposition.'[82] As for the Bonapartists, in a minority to start with, the vast majority did not want the return of Napoleon, but rather the politically-unattainable option of a regency headed by Marie-Louise, the idea of the emperor coming back being so awful that 'it terrifies even his most shameful henchmen out of their wits'.[83]

There is, of course, much misjudgement here: D'Angles appears unaware of the depth of resentment in the army and the swarms of half-pay officers and demobilized soldiers and also writes popular Jacobinism out of the script altogether. Yet, for all that, France in 1815 was scarcely a country on the brink of revolution: the wounds of 1814 were simply too raw and the memories of the realities of Napoleonic rule too stark. In the course of his trip to France, Edward Stanley made an extensive tour of the battlefields of the 1814 campaign. Here, for example, are his memories of Soissons:

The nearer we came to Soissons the nearer we perceived we were to the field of some terrible contest, and the suburbs, where the thickest of the fight took place, presented a frightful picture of war, not a house entire. It seems they were unroofed for the convenience of the attacking party, or set on fire, an operation which took up a very short space of time, thanks to the energetic labours of about 50 or 60,000 men. Indeed, fire and sword had done their utmost – burnt beams, battered doors, not a vestige of furniture or window frames. I cannot give you a better idea of the quantity of shot, and consequent number of beings who must have perished, than by assuring you that on one front of a house about the extent of our home, and which was not more favoured than its neighbours, I counted between 200 and 300 bullet marks. I was leaning against a bit of broken wall in a garden, which appeared to be the doorway to a sort of cellar, taking a sketch, when the gardener came up and gave me some particulars of the fight. He pointed to this cave or cellar as the place of shelter in which he and forty-four others had been concealed, every moment dreading a discovery which, whether by friend or foe, they looked upon as equally fatal. Fortunately the foe were the discoverers. Upon the termination of the battle, which had been favourable to the Allies, in came a parcel of Russians upon the trembling peasants. Conceiving it to be a hiding-place for French soldiers, they rushed upon them, but finding none, satisfied themselves with asking what business they had there, and turning them out to find their way through blood and slaughter to some more secure place of shelter. A small mill pool had been so completely choked with dead that they were obliged to let off the water and clean it out.[84]

The same point is made still more strongly by François Guizot. As he remarked, the military glory that surrounded Napoleon was, despite claims to the contrary, something that had long since ceased to touch civilian society, if, indeed, it had ever really done so. Thus, 'It was the remembrance of foreign intervention that constituted the wound and nightmare of France under the government of the Restoration. The feeling was legitimate in itself... . If it had pleased Heaven to throw me into the ranks of Napoleon's soldiers, in all probability that person would also have governed my soul. But, placed as I was ... other ideas and instincts ... taught me to look elsewhere than to predominance in war for the greatness and security of my country.'[85] In two or three generations more the horror of what had happened would have been softened, even buried, by the sands of time. However, the key phrase here is 'two or three generations'. Given that it is hard to imagine that memories of the realities of 1814 could be erased in a matter of months, memories, moreover, which were inseparable from that of Napoleon, it is difficult to find a more suitable conclusion for this chapter than that of Berthier de Sauvigny: 'Thus is confirmed ... that, in spite of all the blunders of the royal government, in spite of all the efforts of the opposition, the régime at first could have maintained itself no matter what happened and then could have consolidated itself, thanks to the experience acquired by its supporters and the discouragement of its opposition, if the audacious action of Napoleon had not compassed its fall.'[86]

Chapter 6

The Hundred Days

On 1 March 1815 Napoleon disembarked from the brig *Inconstant* at Golfe Juan on the Mediterranean coast of France. With him were no more than 1,000 men, most of them drawn from the single battalion of Old-Guard grenadiers and squadron of Polish lancers that had gone into exile with him in Elba. Within three weeks, however, to the horror of the whole of Europe, he was back in Paris as emperor and the unfortunate Louis XVIII fleeing into exile in Ghent. As friends and enemies alike observed, it was a remarkable event, possibly the most remarkable event, indeed, of a career already staggering in its immensity. Even the site of the landing seemed portentous. In the words of Sir Walter Scott, 'On the first of March … Napoleon, causing his followers once more to assume the three-coloured cockade, disembarked at Cannes … a small sea-port not far from Fréjus, which had seen him land, a single individual returned from Egypt, to conquer a mighty empire; had beheld him set sail, a terrified exile, for his place of banishment; and now again witnessed his return, a daring adventurer, to throw the dice once more for a throne or a grave.'[1] For a more immediate reaction, we may turn to Archibald Alison: 'On a sudden, that fallen Colossus is raised again, and its dark shadow has over-spread the brightening horizon. Could it be credited, that within one short month, that man whom we conceived detested in France, should have journeyed from one extremity of that kingdom to another, without meeting with the slightest resistance? I say journeyed, for he had but a handful of men, whom, at almost every town, he left behind him, and he proceeded on horseback, or in his carriage, with much less precaution than at any former period of his life.'[2]

What had happened? In brief, there are two explanations. For admirers of the emperor, people and army alike had no sooner heard that Napoleon had landed on the shores of France than they rushed to support him, followed with greater or lesser degrees of enthusiasm by at least some part of the élites, whereas, for those who are more sceptical, what took place is something far more mundane, namely a military coup in which popular participation was distinctly limited. A separate issue, meanwhile, is that of conspiracy versus spontaneity: whereas Scott and many others were keen to argue that the ground for Napoleon's restoration had been prepared by a series of plots and intrigues, François Guizot was inclined to give all the credit to Napoleon himself: 'There has been much discussion as to what ... brought back Napoleon on the 20th of March 1815. It is certain that ... there existed ... many plans and secret practices against the restoration ... But, if Napoleon had remained motionless at the island of Elba, these revolutionary projects would, in all probability, have successively failed ... It was Napoleon alone who dethroned the Bourbons in 1815 by calling up, in his own person, the fanatical devotion of the army and the revolutionary instincts of the popular masses. However tottering might be the monarchy lately restored, it required that great man ... to subvert it.'[3] In this chapter, we shall re-examine the so-called 'flight of the eagle' with a view to establishing a balanced view.

Let us begin, however, with the legend. Though the ideas concerned have a much longer provenance, a good place to begin here is once again the work of Henri Houssaye. In fairness, in his account of the so-called 'flight of the eagle' Houssaye does at least recognize the existence of a degree of suspicion amongst elements of the populace. In Cannes, for example, the surprised inhabitants are described as having questioned Napoleon's troops 'with more anxiety than sympathy', whilst at Grasse the emissary sent by the emperor to requisition supplies found himself confronted by a hostile crowd.[4] Once the emperor's little column had left Provence and entered Dauphiné, however, it was a different story. In brief, amidst scenes of wild celebration, large numbers of peasants are depicted as having sallied forth from their villages and joined Napoleon in his march on Grenoble, where a short-lived attempt to hold the town against him was thwarted by a popular rising which culminated in a gang of blacksmiths and wheelwrights literally ripping the gates of the city from their hinges and laying them at the emperor's feet.[5] And thereafter the story is one of an unbroken tide of insurrection sweeping across France: at Lyons, Villefranche, Mâcon, Tournus and Chalons, Napoleon was greeted by huge crowds which besieged the buildings in which he lodged and dogged his every movement, while the revolt became ever more widespread. 'Not only Lyons, but all of the towns of the Rhone, the Ain and Saône-et-Loire were in open insurrection', writes Houssaye. 'From this time onwards there was no stemming the tide of popular excitement. For forty leagues around, from the Doubs to the Loire it spread with overwhelming force ... The king could find defenders neither in the army, which continued hostile, nor among the people, which shared the sentiments of the army, nor among the bourgeoisie, which ... could offer no better pledge of devotion than pious wishes and protestations.'[6] With crowds on the streets, and regiment after regiment, not to mention general after general, defecting to Napoleon, Louis XVIII was left with no option but to flee, and on 20 March a triumphant emperor once more entered the Tuileries amidst scenes of the utmost jubilation.

As to the nature of what had happened in the days since Napoleon had landed, meanwhile, Houssaye was in no doubt whatsoever:

> Royalist writers ... have represented the restoration of the empire as the outcome of a purely military movement, akin to a Praetorian tumult or a Spanish *pronunciamiento*. Nothing can be further from the truth. The revolution of 1815 was a popular movement backed by the army. The soldiers, who adored their emperor, trembled at the very idea of finding themselves drawn up against him, and had made up their minds that nothing would make them fire upon him. On the other hand, habits of discipline had deprived them of independent initiative, so that they made no move until the wave of popular excitement carried them forward. It is certain that ... the defection of the troops throughout France came after, and not before, the movement among the peasants and working classes. It was the wheelwrights of the *faubourgs* [a term probably best rendered by the word 'slums'] who broke down the gates of Grenoble; it was the silk-workers of La Guillotière who demolished the barricades at the Lyons bridge; at Villefranche ... 60,000 peasants, and not a single soldier, were awaiting the emperor around their tree of liberty.[7]

We are in the presence, then, of a revival of the French Revolution, even of a second 1793, not to mention of a France that was solidly behind Napoleon, the experience of eleven months of Bourbon rule, or so it can be inferred, having eclipsed the war-weariness that had so hampered the emperor's efforts to defend France in 1814. Once given form by a writer as passionate and eloquent as Houssaye, meanwhile, this version of events became an established part of the Napoleonic creed. For a good example of its re-statement in relatively recent times, we have only to turn to David Hamilton Williams. Thus:

> By 6 March ... Napoleon had reached Gap, a day's march from Grenoble ... Already peasants who had heard of his landing were joining him, making of his march a cavalcade resembling a royal, or rather imperial, procession. At Gap the people erected a liberty tree, something not seen since the Revolution. The people sang revolutionary songs and shouted, 'Down with priests! Down with the aristos!', in scenes strongly reminiscent of the early, popular days of the Revolution. Seigneurial pews in its churches were ripped out and thrown on bonfires ... In Lyons crowds were roaming the

streets chanting the old slogans and singing the old songs of the Revolution
... as mobs attacked the homes of prominent royalists ... In the Isère four
royalist chateaux were attacked by National Guards and peasants. At La
Sône the royalist mayor attempted to prevent the rising of the *tricolore*
and was shot dead by his own guard. In Brittany, Dauphiné, Languedoc
and Lyonnais patriots formed federations of 'liberty and equality'; and
students, 'children of the empire', demonstrated and formed battalions
of *fédérés*, reviving the old volunteer units of the Revolution. Even in the
royalist strongholds of the Vendée ... the people ... erupted into violence
against the government, pillaging the homes of tax officials ... and burning
their record books. Napoleon himself was surprised by the extent to which
the spirit of the Revolution had entered into the minds of the French
people.[8]

In short, angered by eleven months of reaction under the Bourbons, the French
people burst forth to recover their lost liberty, Hamilton-Williams even going
so far as effectively to deny the army any agency in the process. What we have,
indeed, is a re-run of the French Revolution under the guidance of a Napoleon
become its very personification. One thinks here, too, of the 1970 feature-film,
Waterloo, in which, having entered Grenoble at the head of his growing army,
Napoleon is seen being cheered to the echo by the city's lower classes to the
accompaniment of choruses of the revolutionary anthem *Ça ira*.[9] Yet, like it or
not, it was the army that mattered.[10] Everywhere the story was the same. In this
respect the famous scene at Laffrey on the road to Grenoble in which Napoleon
supposedly braved the levelled muskets of the Fifth Line was but the tip of
the iceberg. All round the country bands of ex-soldiers filled the streets with
cries of 'Vive l'empereur!' and acclaimed Napoleon as the saviour of France,
while at Périgueux 300 half-pay officers donned tricolour cockades and held a
rally in support of his return.[11] Elsewhere, meanwhile, senior commanders who
attempted to obey the orders they received to march against Napoleon found
themselves facing mutiny. In the eastern city of Toul, for example, Marshal
Oudinot summoned his officers to see him:

Not long after, a treble row of officers was crammed in our room, forming
a circle with the marshal in the centre. He waited until they had all taken
their places in silence, and then expressed himself more-or-less in the
following terms. 'Gentlemen, in the circumstances in which we are placed
I wish to make an appeal for your loyalty. We are marching under the white
cockade. I am to review you tomorrow before our departure: with what cry

will you and your men reply to my "Long live the King!"?' These words were followed by absolute silence. Nothing so striking ever passed before my eyes ... I saw the storm was about to break; each second was a century. At last the marshal said, 'Well, gentlemen?' Then a young man of inferior rank stepped forward, and said 'Monsieur le Maréchal, I am bound to tell you, and no one here will contradict me: when you cry "Long live the king!", our men, and we, will answer, "Long live the emperor!"'[12]

Trying to rally the garrison of Lyons, Marshal Macdonald had a similar experience:

I was very excited. I finished my speech by saying that I had too good an opinion of their fidelity and patriotic feelings to think that they would refuse to do as I did, who had never deceived them, and that they would follow me along the path of honour and duty; the only guarantee that I asked of them was to join with me in crying, 'Long live the King!' I shouted this several times at the top of my voice. Not one single voice joined me. They all maintained a stony silence: I admit I was disconcerted.[13]

To pretend that Napoleon had no popular support at all in 1815 would be futile. Indeed, for French historians of many shades of opinion, it is possible to go much further. Here, for example, is the *doyenne* of Napoleonic studies, Jean Tulard, 'The movement ... was primarily a peasant and working-class one; the army was to rally to the emperor later, and, in the case of the higher cadres, only partially.'[14] In an important article on what he refers to as 'the revolution of 1815', the more more left-wing Pierre Levêque is particularly insistent on this point. 'In general, what is most striking about "the flight of the eagle" is its essentially popular character. The role played by the adhesion of the officers and rank-and-file was capital, true enough, but it is necessary to take care not to exaggerate it.'[15] The emperor, we learn, was greeted with delight on his triumphal progress through the Alpes Maritimes and Burgundy – the peasants, we are told, flocked to see his cavalcade pass by amidst loud cheers of 'You are the Angel of the Lord: they wanted to tie us to the land, but you have come to save us!'[16] – acclaimed in Lyons, and positively mobbed when he got to Paris, whilst, according to Hobhouse at least, 'All the young men, with the exception of the debauched representatives of the noble houses whose hopes were revived during the restoration, are in favour of Napoleon, at least of the new order of things in opposition to the re-establishment of the ancient régime.'[17] None of this, however, should surprise us. Thus, the Alpes Maritimes was a Protestant area much afflicted by fears that the local Catholics were bent on a purge; Burgundy a region that had been devastated by the Austrians, Russians and Prussians in 1814 and therefore one in which a war of revenge may have held fewer terrors than the rest of the country; Lyons a centre of the silk industry that had benefited enormously from the deliberate strangulation of silk production in northern Italy under the aegis of the *grand empire*; and finally Paris, a city where old-style Jacobinism was still rampant and, in addition, somewhere that had benefited tremendously from an extensive programme of public works embarked upon with the express purpose not just of giving France a capital fit for an emperor, but of putting bread on the tables of the Parisian poor, a further benefit that it enjoyed being that it was but lightly affected by the scourge of conscription: given that the population of Paris in the Napoleonic Wars was around 500,000, its total of 15,976 conscripts (roughly 3 per cent of the population) does not seem particularly excessive.[18] As for the young men of the class to which Hobhouse may be assumed to be referring (a few lines earlier he eulogises the enthusiasm displayed by the pupils of the Lycée Imperiale in the course of a great review), loss of empire was accompanied by loss of advancement. Hence, or so one assumes, the despair evinced by an encounter which Alison had in Nevers in the winter of 1814. Thus, 'At the inn here I met with a young officer, who although only (to appearance) seventeen or eighteen, had been in the Spanish war, at Moscow, and half over the world. He struck his forehead, when he said, "Nous n'avons plus la guerre."'[19] Meanwhile, to return to the schoolboys of the Lycée Imperiale, there is plenty of evidence to suggest that few groups in society are so avid for military adventure as boys who have just missed out on taking part in some great struggle: indeed, Hobhouse specifically tells us that 'these youths had wished to fight the last year at the defence of Paris'.[20]

Yet we must needs be cautious in reading such accounts. That there was genuine excitement in Paris, there seems no doubt, Hobhouse, for example, providing us with a lengthy description of the rapture with which Napoleon was received when he visited the Théâtre Français to attend a performance of a play about the Greek hero, Achilles.[21] Here, meanwhile, is the account of William Ireland, a notorious literary forger who had foisted several fake Shakespeare plays upon the London art world, and was currently in Paris carrying out some research:

From the moment that the departure of the Bourbons was made public, the arrival of the emperor was anxiously expected and, consequently, on the 20th of March at an early hour no inconsiderable bustle was manifested throughout Paris. Numerous reports were in circulation as to the barrier by which he would enter as well as the precise hour when he might be expected. Thus, being misled by contrary statements, I proceeded in various directions, and about midday was attracted with multitudes to the Boulevard Montmartre where I arrived in time to see a body of about 2,000 troops, covered in dirt and dust, who were accompanying several pieces of heavy artillery, every man wearing the tricolour cockade, while, at stated intervals of five minutes as they advanced, shouts of 'Vive l'empereur!' rent the air, in which they were joined by the vociferations of the populace who accompanied them, every soldier having a citizen linked to either arm, demanding tidings of the march of Napoleon and the period of his arrival at the capital ... In this manner they continued along the boulevards, and, turning down the Rue de la Paix, halted in the Place Vendôme where it appears they were to remain until further orders. I repaired to the Tuileries, when, taking my station as near as possible to the Pavillon de Flore, after waiting hour after hour, during which period the expectant but wearied crowds were many times replaced with fresh comers, at past eight o'clock when, on a sudden, a distant shout was heard which continued rapidly increasing, and, after a lapse of some minutes, a small escort galloped into the square, and immediately afterwards a small carriage rattled along at full speed containing the object so long and ardently expected by the accompanying multitude ... On gaining the portal it was with infinite difficulty that Napoleon could alight from the dreadful pressure, and no sooner had he gained the bottom of the grand staircase than he was raised from the ground and borne up the flight of stairs upon the shoulders of the officers.[22]

However, in another passage, it should be noted that Hobhouse seems to suggest that the excitement in Paris was not co-terminus with the arrival of Napoleon, but rather grew in proportion to the emperor's assurances that he wanted nothing more than peace.[23] Thus:

Paris, on the entry of Napoleon, presented but a mournful spectacle. The crowd which went out to meet the emperor remained in the outskirts of the city; the shops were shut; no-one appeared at the windows ... There was no noise nor any acclamations: a few low murmurs and whispers were alone heard ... at the string of six or eight carriages which preceded the troops. The regiments then passed along: 'Vive l'empereur!' Not a word from anyone. They tried the more popular and ancient explanation, 'Vive

Bonaparte!' All still silent. The patience of the dragoons was exhausted: some brandished their swords, others drew their pistols … exclaiming, 'Criez, donc, "Vive l'empereur!"', but the crowd only gave way, retreating without uttering a word … It is his moderation, that is to say, the repeated offers he has made to the Allies to maintain the Treaty of Paris, that has rallied the pride and self-love of France round his person.[24]

Rather similar, meanwhile, is the equivalent passage in the memoirs of Lavallette, it being claimed that the capital responded to the fall of the king with a display of apathy that was distinctly disconcerting:

The hours passed. Paris was quiet: the inhabitants who lived at a distance from the Tuileries did not come near it; everyone remained at home. The departure of the king and the emperor's arrival was a tremendous event so unparalleled that fourteen centuries of monarchical government had presented nothing so extraordinary. Nevertheless in every mind indifference seemed to be the feeling which predominated. Was the occurrence beyond the grip of average intelligence? Or did the common sense of the people tell them that these two sovereigns were not fighting for the welfare of their subjects, and that for the people the only result would be suffering and sacrifice?[25]

Obviously, such accounts are immediately confronted by the problem of the wild scenes described to have taken place at the Tuileries when Napoleon finally entered its precincts, but these, it seems, were the work, not of the people, but of a large number of half-pay officers who had congregated at the palace in the hope of receiving the imperial favour, and can therefore be discounted.[26]

The fact is, then, that Parisian opinion was split. To quote Guizot:

The army identified itself with him with an enthusiastic and blind devotion. Amongst the popular masses a revolutionary and warlike spirit, hatred of the old system and national pride, rose up at his appearance and rushed madly to his aid … But by the side of this overwhelming power there appeared almost simultaneously a proportionate weakness. He who had traversed Paris in triumph … re-entered Paris at night exactly as Louis XVIII had quitted that capital, his carriage surrounded by dragoons and only encountering on his passage a scanty and moody populace. Enthusiasm had accompanied him throughout his journey, but at its termination he found coldness, doubt, widely disseminated mistrust and cautious reserve.[27]

This is, of course, the verdict of a confirmed royalist who had never compromised with the Napoleonic régime and immediately resigned his newly-obtained post as Secretary-General of the Ministry of the Interior rather than serve the emperor in 1815. Yet his opinion is shared even by such an observer as the militant Bonapartist Lavalette. As the latter noted, if there was little positive enthusiasm for the cause of Louis XVIII, the propertied classes were opposed to the emperor while even the *sans culottes* were not inclined to rally to Napoleon unaided. Thus:

> I used to go for walks in the suburbs: everywhere was the appearance of absolute indifference; the work and usual habits of the people remained the same. But every evening the police were carefully investigating the tendencies in the wine-shops and the places where the people used to meet, and they were alarmed by the fierce talk and dreadful schemes to which whispered utterance was given. No arrest among the lowest classes of the people was risked for fear of causing riots of which the consequences might be terrible. But it must be admitted that the state of feeling was not the same among the middle classes, which includes the people engaged in trade and those connected with law and finance. No interest was taken by them in the position of the court, at whose expense any smart saying secured immediate popularity, but the too recent memory of the presence of the foreign enemy gave rise to deep anxiety and a sort of stupor at the emperor's arrival. However, with the exception of some young men who enlisted at Vincennes in the royalist cause, no-one made any application to enrol themselves for fighting.[28]

Even in Paris the régime clearly felt a need to flatter the crowd: on Sunday 4 June, then, a great *fête* was held marked by the distribution of free bread and sausage, the conversion of numerous fountains so that they ran with wine instead of water, concerts, illuminations and a dramatic fireworks display whose centrepiece was a representation of the ship that had brought the emperor from Elba.[29] Away from such special cases, the situation was very different. Alison, for example, was caught by the news at the holiday residence he had taken at Aix-en-Provence. As he wrote in his diary on 6 March, 'We have now something worth mentioning in our journals, and are likely to have enough of news for some time to come. The usurper of France is again landed, and close in our neighbourhood

... The commotion excited in Aix by this news is not to be conceived. The hatred and detestation in which Bonaparte is held here, becomes very evident ... With a very few exceptions, all ranks of people express these sentiments. The national guard were immediately under arms, and entreated their commanding officer and the civil authorities, to permit them to go in pursuit of the ex-Emperor.'[30] As Napoleon's cause went from strength to strength, meanwhile, so the initially reasonably sanguine mood became ever darker and more fearful. Deciding that he and his party would have to make a run for the safety of Bordeaux, which he understood to be holding out against the rebellion, Alison found time to write one more entry in his diary:

> This unfortunate town is now a melancholy spectacle; for all the thinking part believe that the cause of the Bourbons is lost. Our poor landlord, a violent royalist, has just been with us. He affirms that he could have predicted all this; for when he sold the white cockades to the military, they often said, 'Eh bien; c'est bon pour le moment, mais cela ne durera pas long temps.' ['Not to worry: it is only for the time being: all this isn't going to last for very long.'] Poor man, he is in perfect agony, and his wife weeps all day long. If all the people of France thought as well as those at Aix, Napoleon would have little chance of success; but alas, I am much afraid he will find more friends than enemies.[31]

Based as this assessment was in large part on little more than prejudice, Alison was way out in his calculations. Whilst those places that had welcomed Napoleon continued to show much fervour for his cause – confronted by the handful of loyal troops commanded by the Duc d'Angoulême, for example, the inhabitants of Lyons rushed to arm themselves and barricade the streets[32] – it was not just Aix-en-Provence that rejected Napoleon. In the strongly Catholic Nord the fleeing Louis XVIII was greeted along the road and in such towns as Lille by crowds of inhabitants begging him not to abandon them – 'In Picardy, Artois and Flanders', claimed Rillier, 'the king was sincerely loved ... "Bring him back", shouted the peasants, "and we will join you."'[33] – whilst riots, protests and disturbances were reported from an extraordinary range of towns and villages, the places mentioned including Aix-en-Provence, Abbeville, Alençon, Amiens, Armentières, Avignon, Bayonne, Beauvais, Boulogne, Calais, Dunkerque, Lisieux, Marseilles, Montpellier, Poitiers, Saint Omer, Sète and Versailles.[34] Typical, perhaps, were the scenes that took place in Moulins on 20 March. Thus, ordered to march to Lyons to assist in the suppression of Royalist resistance in the south, the National Guard mutinied and made common cause with a large crowd of peasants who had invaded the town.[35] As in 1814, meanwhile, encouraged by the presence in the city of Artois' daughter-in-law, the Duchesse d'Angoulême, the authorities in Bordeaux overtly declared for Louis XVIII.[36] Such feelings penetrated not just major centres of population, but also remote country villages. 'Even in our peaceful valley of the Saulx,' wrote Madame Oudinot, 'the population were … both suspicious and hostile … The emperor cannot have long retained his illusions on the chances of power which remained to him, because in 1815 it was much less the wish of the nation than of the army that had brought him back from Elba.'[37]

All areas of the country were equally threatened by the return of Napoleon. As we have seen, there was as yet no conscription, but it was not just conscription that Frenchmen had to worry about. Alone against the world, indeed, France would very soon have found herself being bled dry and not just of its young men. Under the empire, although taxation had been high enough, it had been palliated by the fact that the Napoleonic régime was being heavily subsidised by its many annexed territories and client states. All that burden, however, was now to fall on the unfortunate people of France. Just keeping the army that fought at Waterloo in action required 5,000,000 *francs* per month, and that in turn meant raising the budget that had been agreed by Louis XVIII's government for 1815 from 298,000,000 *francs* to a minimum of 400,000,000. But it was not just the army that fought at Waterloo. Appointed Minister of the Interior, for example, on 15 April the hero of 1793, Lazare Carnot, informed Napoleon that mobilizing the élite companies alone of the National Guard was going to cost 40,649,493 *francs*.[38] Yet hardly had Napoleon arrived in Paris than it became all to clear that there was scarcely enough money even for the ordinary business of Louis XVIII's government, let alone anything more grandiose. In the words of the newly re-appointed Minister of Public Treasure, Nicholas Mollien, 'The money that remained to the treasury barely exceeded the amount needed to meet the last commitments of the royal government … The transfers which the receivers-general had been accustomed to make … had been suspended ever since the departure from Elba; the collection of the sums owing from the public had everywhere diminished; and the confidence which gives access to credit was non-existent.'[39] There were, to be sure, other ways of raising the money required than taxation – it was planned, for example, to raise enormous sums from the sale of the properties of all those who had fled abroad – but even so the country was somehow going to have to be forced to pay more. To quote Alan Schom, however, this could not but make 'onerous demands on the people of France whose economy had been practically destroyed as a result of ten years of Napoleon's nearly incessant warfare'.[40] As he continued, the implications were bleak indeed. Thus: 'It could only be done at bayonet point, whereas the emperor could not afford to alienate further a people who would now have to yield up their sons and husbands, as well as their last penny, yet again.'[41] At the same time, it should be remembered that this huge effort would have been asked of a France afflicted by one of the greatest natural disasters that the world has ever seen. In brief, on 6 April 1815 the East Indian volcano known as Tambora erupted in an explosion that pumped so much smoke and ash into the atmosphere that the whole world was plunged into metereological chaos. With sunlight obscured by the ash, temperatures fell dramatically with the result that 1816 became known as 'the year without a summer'. Of course, the effects of this crisis would have affected all the combatants of 1815 more or less equally, but such were the demands that were to be imposed on France that popular resistance could not but have been much inflamed.[42]

Whether popular resistance amounted to anything very much is another matter. The return of Napoleon was not popular, certainly, but nor was taking on the army. Having fled Aix-en-Provence, Alison made his way to Bordeaux to take ship for England via Narbonne and Carcassonne, only to discover that it was a depressing experience. Thus, in so far as actual fighting was concerned, the will to resist was non-existent. Here and there, true, he came across groups of young *chevaliers* who were seemingly ready to take on Napoleon's forces, but the common people were at best apathetic. On 23 March, for example, he passed through the village of Moux: 'One of the police officers read out a number of proclamations sent by the prefect of the department, exciting the people to exertions in repelling the usurper. The cries of "Vive le Roi" were so faint, that the officer harangued the multitude on their want of proper feeling. He did not, however, gain anything. One of the mob cried out that they were not to be forced to cry out "Vive le Roi!"'[43] Nor were things any better when Alison reached his destination:

Things look very ill … The town of Bordeaux is in a dead calm; the sounds of loyalty have ceased, and a mysterious silence reigns throughout the streets, but I am sure all is not well. The cries of 'Vive le roi' are not heard today … Every individual in this city … hates and detests the tyrant as cordially as he detests them. They expect immediate destruction if he takes the town. Their commerce must be ruined; yet there is no exertion, nothing but noise. 'Vive le Roi' is in every mouth, [but] it costs nothing. Subscriptions … for arming the militia, go on slowly … although, as far as shouting and bellowing is required, they are willing to levy any contribution on their lungs. The French are indeed miserably poor, but they are also miserably avaricious: no national spirit.[44]

So feeble was the revolt in Bordeaux that no attempt was made to disarm the troops stationed in the city or the nearby fort at Blaye, while the arrival of a mere 300 men a day or two after Alison took ship for England was all that was required to restore order.[45] As he concluded, then, 'The idea so current in France, that this event [i.e. the return of Napoleon] will only occasion a civil war, is unworthy of a moment's attention. Every inhabitant in every town he passed was said to be against him. We heard of nothing but the devoted loyalty of the national guards; but at Grenoble, at Lyons, and at Paris, was there found a man to discharge his musket? No! Against a small number of regular and veteran troops, no French militia, no volunteers will ever fight, or if they do, it will be but for a moment; each city will yield in its turn.'[46]

Elsewhere, too, the cause of armed resistance proved a failure. If Bordeaux presented a depressing picture, so, too, did Provence. Here the chief focus of insurrection was the Duc d'Angoulême. Sent out from Paris to raise the standard of revolt in the south, he first called in at Bordeaux, to whose safekeeping he entrusted his wife, and then established his headquarters at Nîmes where he hoped to be joined by up to 10,000 volunteers. In the event, however, scarcely half that number appeared, whilst Angoulême – a singularly unprepossessing figure who was utterly lacking in charisma – proved extremely ineffective as a cheerleader for the royalist cause and was also very slow to get his campaign off the ground. Bolstered by a handful of regular troops who had initially backed the Bourbons, Angoulême's forces eventually got into action at the end of March. By this time, however, it was much too late: with Napoleon firmly established in Paris and the vast majority of the regular army now firmly in his camp, popular enthusiasm drained away, while those units which had declared for Angoulême in many cases mutinied and changed sides. Hopes of seizing Lyons were therefore dashed, while it became ever more apparent that fear of counter-revolution was driving the *lyonnais* and their neighbours further north ever deeper into the camp of Napoleon. Paralysed by indecision, Angoulême fell back to the town of La Palud, and on 8 April gave up the struggle altogether, signing a convention with the forces hemming him in and going into exile in Spain, and leaving his peasant volunteers to make their way to their homes as best they could, though not before some of them had been murdered by vengeful *fédérés*.[47]

Only in Brittany and the Vendée was the picture any different. Even here resistance was slow to get off the ground, an initial attempt on the part of the Duc de Bourbon-Condé to raise the peasantry in revolt proving a complete failure, thereby providing added fuel to the now generally-accepted argument that the counter-revolutionary risings in the west in the course of the 1790s had little to do with loyalty to the monarchy per se.[48] So dispirited was the unfortunate duke that he fled into exile in Spain, but within a matter of days Napoleon solved the difficulty for him by issuing the decrees ordering the mobilization of the National Guard and the recall of all those men who had been demobilized following the close of hostilities in 1814. As we have seen, conscription itself was not restored, but so sensitive was the region to the issue that such niceties went by the board, the result being that within a matter of days it was once again in flames. In Brittany, then, as many as 20,000 peasants were organized into fresh bands of the irregulars known as *chouans* by such leaders of the resistance movement of the 1790s as Henri du Boishamon, Guy de Trégomain and Louis de Sol de Grisors, while in the Vendée another 25,000 peasants took arms in improvised armies commanded by noblemen such as Louis and Auguste de la Rochejacquelin, whose brother, Henri, had been one of the great heroes of the *grande guerre du Vendée* of 1793. Also involved in the Vendée were other leaders of the 1793 insurrection such as the Comte d'Autichamps and Charles Sapinaud de la Rairie and, by a strange chance, an erstwhile general in Napoleon's army named Simon Canuel who had fought against the rebels in the 1790s but gone over to the Bourbons in 1814 and then refused to rally to Napoleon.[49]

What followed should not be exaggerated. As in 1793 the response of the region was anything but united: whilst the countryside was solidly rebel, the urban populace declared for Napoleon, such massacres as the one that had taken place at Machecoul never having been forgotten; hence the strong support that was seen for the *fédéré* movement (see below). At the same time military success was limited. Whilst a number of towns were occupied and some small columns of national guards and *gensdarmes* overcome, most notably at Echaubrognes, augmented by a number of reinforcements, Napoleon's forces were soon on the offensive once more. Desperately short of arms and supplies, the insurgents were defeated in engagements at Aizenay, Saint Gilles-sur-Vie and Mathes, whilst they also suffered the loss of Louis de la Rochejacquelin and Pierre Constant de Suzannet, a particularly daring leader whose personal history during the Revolutionary and Napoleonic period is a veritable odyssey of adventure, and soon fell prey to squabbling among themselves (amongst the dead at Aizenay was also to be found Ludovic de Charette, a nephew of the Marquis de Charette who had been perhaps the greatest leader of the rebels of 1793). Yet fighting continued throughout the Hundred Days, and it was not until 20 June that the last insurgent forces still in the field were defeated at the twin battles of La Rocheservières and Thouars.[50]

North of the Loire matters were more serious. Here insurrection had never taken the form of the 'crowd armies' seen in the Vendée in 1793 and once again in 1815, but rather low-level guerrilla warfare waged by small bands of insurgents that were both far harder to target and far easier to subsist. Matters were a little more grandiose in the Hundred Days – on occasion, columns of several thousand men took the field – but for the most part matters remained much the same, and the departments of Morbihan, Finistere and Côtes du Nord continued to witness much rebel activity until the final cessation of hostilities: on 1 July, for example, 1,000 *chouans* attacked the town of Châteauneuf-du-Faou whilst a week later another force launched a similar action against the little port of Guérande. Yet in the end, as in the Vendée, there was a limit to what could be achieved by bands of armed civilians: at Redon, for example, a mere twenty-three national guards and *fédérés* succeeded in holding out in a church for several days when the town was occupied by a large force of rebels.[51]

It seems, then, that the people were not much to be feared in a military sense: as Hobhouse claimed, indeed, the hopeful visions that were entertained of popular counter-revolution outside France were wildly exaggerated.[52] However, the *notables* were another matter as, without their help, France simply could not be governed. From the very beginning, then, the emperor sought to reach out to them. As he told the archivist of Grenoble, Jacques Champollion-Figeac, for example, 'Without me you would have had a republican revolution. The Bourbons do not know France and I am now persuaded that her destiny can only be accomplished by the efforts of a liberal government.'[53] No sooner had Napoleon arrived in Paris, meanwhile, than he issued a series of decrees that were designed to win these forces over, a key move here being the abolition of censorship on 24 March. Even before reaching the capital, meanwhile, he had taken a key decision, namely to return to a more parliamentary form of government. On 13 March, then, a proclamation issued in the course of his brief stay in Lyons announced the convocation of a special meeting of the electoral colleges that elected the lists from which Napoleon had hand-picked the deputies of successive imperial parliaments, the proclamation comparing this assembly with the so-called *champs de mai* of Charlemagne (in itself, an ominous turn of phrase: although the gatherings to which it referred sometimes featured the presentation of petitions of grievance, the term had rather referred to the mustering of Charlemagne's nobles and the feudal levy on the eve of war). and announcing that the deputies would be given the task of drawing up a new constitution.[54]

Whatever may have been in Napoleon's mind in drafting the proclamation of 13 March, the centrepiece of his programme was the document known as the *Acte Additionnel aux Constitutions de l'Empire*. A title insisted on by an emperor unwilling entirely to turn his back on the political structures which he had created, was bad enough, but still worse was the fact that Napoleon never had the slightest intention of letting control of the process slip out of his hands. Instead, on reaching Paris he immediately established a special committee charged with the same task that he had but a few days previously accorded the electoral colleges, the *champ de mai*, like all Napoleon's parliaments being left with no other role than the ratification of projects emanating from the executive power. Admittedly, one of the members of the committee was Lazare Carnot, but the truth is that the old revolutionary was always likely to be in a permanent minority, all of the other members – Antoine Boulay (usually referred to by his title of Comte Boulay de la Meurthe), Jean de Cambacéres, Jacques Defermon des Chapelières and Michel Regnault de Saint Jean d'Angély – were all not just moderates who had opposed Robespierre and his *montagnards*, but also men who were closely associated with Napoleon. One may conclude, then, that Carnot was included as a mere figleaf designed to buy off the more radical of Napoleon's supporters, whilst by his own account he does not appear to have been much listened to. As he later told his son, Hyppolyte, for example:

One day our conversation touched on the new direction which it was necessary to impart to the administration. I told him that in my view governance could almost be allowed to go its own way, that all that was necessary, indeed, was to listen to public opinion … To this I added that I believed that it was infinitely easier to govern in a constitutional fashion than in a despotic one, for in such a case the body of the nation would lend its support, whereas it would otherwise be a matter of having to dominate it by a series of acts of authority, even of living in a constant state of hostility. However, this argument did not accord with the character of Bonaparte at all: whilst he wanted to be popular, he believed that, if he were to relax his grip on the reins by even a little, all power would escape him.[55]

Accompanying the elaboration of the *acte additional*, meanwhile, was a petty drama that underlines both the frailty of human nature and the continued capacity of Napoleon to exert enormous personal charm. The man most associated with the new constitution, then, was not one of the original commission at all but Henri Benjamin Constant de Rebecque, a Swiss Protestant who was cousin to the Jean Victor Constant de Rebecque who served as the Prince of Orange's chief of staff at Waterloo. Between 1795 and 1811 the lover of Napoleon's bitter opponent, Madame de Stäel, ever a convinced liberal and with it a ferocious critic of the emperor, he had lived out the whole of the Napoleonic Wars in various cities in Germany, but, following the restoration of the Bourbons, he had settled in Paris and been rewarded with a seat on the council of state. Much alarmed at the return of Napoleon, he had initially fled to the security of the Vendée, but was encouraged to return to Paris by some judicious wheedling on the part of Napoleon and, in the course of a single interview in the Tuileries, persuaded not only to change sides but even to draft the final version of the *acte additionnel*. In the account that he left us in his diary Constant was laconic, but nonetheless very telling: 'I saw him. He made me very welcome and after a long conversation charged me with the task of drafting an outline constitution. I cannot but agree that he is an astonishing man.'[56]

Winning over Constant, whose position on the council of state was promptly confirmed, was a considerable coup for Napoleon. Yet, in effect, the attempt to gain the support of the *notables* as a whole was so much wasted effort. Initially the aim was to conserve in their positions anyone who would serve the new régime, the only officials who were actually replaced being those who abandoned their posts or actively opposed the emperor. Indeed, following a show of repentance, even some refractories were found posts in the administration. Yet plenty of officials stepped down nonetheless: in the Department of the Allier alone, the prefect fled whilst the sub-prefects of Moulins, Montluçon and Lapalisse were all seized by mysterious illnesses that required them to request leaves of absence.[57] Still others acceded to the coup, but made it only too clear that their allegiance was at best conditional: Prefect of the Ain in 1814, Léonard Rivet tried to excuse his decision to serve Louis XVIII as Prefect of the Dordogne with a grovelling letter in which he claimed that he would not have been able to provide for the education of his children had he been deprived of his salary and, still worse, that his sole motive in remaining in office now was the hope of receiving the bounty of the emperor.[58] Enthusiasm, meanwhile, ranged from limited to non-existent: in the Allier again, the commission set up to mobilize the National Guard did absolutely nothing beyond drawing up a list of those who were eligible for service, whilst in the Pas de Calais the departmental administration made only the most token of gestures in respect of the confiscation of the properties of noblemen who had fled abroad.[59]

With war brewing, however, it became increasingly apparent to the new Minister of the Interior, Lazare Carnot (see below) that this situation could not be tolerated and on 20 April a list of special commissioners was charged with the task of rooting out royalism from the administration.[60] The resultant purge, however, was a failure. Not only was there little enthusiasm for stepping into the shoes of the men who were thus dismissed, but the move was actually counter-productive. As Lavallette complained:

> As was clearly necessary, there were many changes in the prefects' appointments, but favouritism combined many mistaken selections with some good ones. There were appointed many young men who were zealous, but who could not inspire much confidence. On all sides it was proclaimed that the law should prevail, and yet the majority of the emperor's special commissioners who were sent to the departments everywhere dismissed underlings in order to find room for men who had formerly held the appointments or for those who in past days had given proof of patriotism. Not only did that procedure hinder the transaction of official business … but it added a further increase to the number of the discontented.[61]

Nor was the discontent limited to the victims of Carnot's emissaries. For example, within a matter of days of having fled his post as Prefect of the Department of Isère in the face of Napoleon's troops, Joseph Fourier was not only received back into the fold, but appointed to the key prefecture of Lyons. However, confronted by demands that he dismiss the commander of the National Guard and the whole of the city council with the exception of the mayor, Fourier took umbrage and tried to refer the matter to Paris, eventually resigning from his post when it became clear that Carnot would not back him.[62] In general, meanwhile, the administration slid into complete chaos: 'Only eight departments kept the same prefect throughout the period; thirty had three or more incumbents, and some as many as five or six. Some departments were without a prefect for weeks on end … About sixty of the sub-prefects and forty of the secretaries-general were replaced.'[63] To make matters worse, talent was desperately short, for many of Napoleon's most experienced administrators were as reluctant to have anything to do with the new regime as the majority of the high command: sometime governor of the Grand Duchy of Berg, Beugnot joined Louis XVIII in Ghent, while, despite being offered first the Ministry of Foreign Affairs and then the Ministry of the Interior, the erstwhile Minister of Justice, Mathieu Molé, fled into exile in Switzerland rather than serve the restored regime.[64] Meanwhile, even among those men who did accept appointment, at best, morale was low, Mollien, for example, confessing that the only reason that he resumed his old post as Minister of Public Treasure was a desire to save something from the wreckage.[65] As Napoleon's architect-in-chief, Pierre Fontaine, wrote, 'We were certain it was all over, and yet we had to carry out the orders we were given.'[66] What is surprising, then, is that Napoleon's correspondence for 1815 does not contain more complaints of the nature of the one that follows: 'Make it known to the prefect of Calvados that note has been taken of the facts that he is idle, that he is too much of a socialite, that there is no sign of urgency in his department, [and] that nothing is being printed there to enlighten and stir up public opinion.'[67]

As for the new constitution, this was generally scorned, not the least of the problems being, first, that it was simply given to France by the emperor rather than being the product of a constitutional convention, and, second, that it was not a new document per se, but rather simply an amendment of what had gone before. Indeed, there were even stories that the document published in *Le Moniteur* on 23 April was not the genuine article, but rather a less generous substitute hastily cobbled together by the emperor and put forward in lieu of the original. In the words of Hortense de Beauharnais. 'Nobody saw in this association of an old régime with a new one anything other than a concession extracted by the force of circumstance and a means of restoring absolute power in the future. At the same time the ... venomous criticisms of a number of impassioned writers whipped up violent opposition.'[68] Meanwhile, wrote Hobhouse, 'I never recollect in my life to have experienced such a change in that which a man is apt to call public opinion ... as took place at Paris at the appearance of the *acte additionnel* ... Both royalists and republicans, as well as some of those who are supposed more attached to the emperor flew upon it at once.'[69] And, finally, here is the Savoyard academic Champollion-Figeac: 'A nationwide wave of revulsion overwhelmed Napoleon's sad invention ... In spite of the positive spin given to the document in so skilful a fashion by the learned Sismondi [i.e. Jean de Sismondi, a progressive Swiss economist and historian resident in Paris who had become a great admirer of Napoleon] and a Benjamin Constant newly appointed to the Council of State, the entire country was as upset as it was alienated.'[70]

In line with proceedings in the period 1793–1804, the new document was subjected to a plebiscite, but, despite recent attempts to argue otherwise, the result was this was at best unconvincing. Thus, whereas in 1793, 1795 and 1800, participation in such concourses had been relatively limited, amounting to a maximum of 33 per cent in 1793 to a minimum of 22 per cent in 1795, the growth in the power of the French state under Napoleon had achieved levels of participation that were significantly higher, namely 58 per cent in 1802 and 50 per cent in 1804 (in reality, the turnout was probably somewhat lower as the local authorities had a strong interest in making as strong a showing as possible). In 1815, however, this expansion in political participation was wiped away, the 1,300,000 electors who returned ballots representing precisely the same level of participation as that achieved by the Thermidorian Reaction in 1795. However, this was not the end of the matter. In the first place, the ballot was not secret: rather, those entitled to vote had to sign their names on lists held in open sight in the *mairie* of their local commune, the fact that opinion had to be expressed in this fashion giving mayors, first, the chance to intimidate the electorate and, second, to manipulate the result, either by excluding all those who were illiterate – a useful way of eliminating lower-class protest in cities such as Paris – or writing in the names of the same group and claiming that they had all voted in favour. True enough, there were only 5,000 negative votes, and, true enough again, failure to vote cannot necessarily be equated with abstention, let alone opposition: in some areas dissident mayors appear to have refused to organize ballots, thereby preventing electors having any say one way or another, or to have doctored the lists so as to exclude known Bonapartists. However, such qualification notwithstanding, it is hard to regard the plebiscite as a success for the regime. Still worse, France was shown to be deeply divided on geographical grounds with the whole of the Nord, Normandy, Brittany and Provence solidly unenthusiastic – in some places in Brittany, fewer than 5 per cent of the electorate showed up – and participation at its highest in central and eastern France (in other words precisely those areas of the country that had been most favoured by the Revolution as well as those in which the ravages of war had been at their worst in 1814: in such places, it seems, desire for revenge may have outweighed fear of further sacrifice).[71]

With the constitutional process hijacked by Napoleon, the proposed *champ de mai* was redundant as originally envisaged. However, always fond of great public festivities which served at one and the same time to laud the successes of his regime, call attention to its grandeur, gratify the common people and associate populace and *notables* alike with its structures, Napoleon decided to continue as planned, but to turn it into an immense public ceremony that would announce the result of the plebiscite – that this would be favourable was simply taken as read – formally ratify the *acte additionnel* and emphasise the union of army, nation and new régime. Eventually scheduled for 31 May, the event was soon devouring immense sums of public money, not least because it required the construction of a huge amphitheatre that could seat 20,000 people. Yet when the great day came, such was the furore caused by the *acte additionnel* that it proved something of a flop. As a military event, it worked well enough: presented with a new set of eagles to replace its Bourbon flags, the army for the most part responded with enthusiasm (these flags are worthy of comment: partly out of a view for economy and partly out of a desire to adopt a more popular style, the flags were stripped of most of the heavy gold embroidery that had characterised them under the empire, though the effect was somewhat spoilt by the fact that they continued to proclaim the emperor to be the pinnacle of the military estate rather than the nation).[72] However, with their role restricted to witnessing Napoleon's signature of the new constitution, the representatives of the political classes were at best lukewarm in their response, not the least of the problems being that hardly anybody could hear what was going on. Perhaps the most heartening aspect of the affair was the manner in which spare tickets were snapped up by the people of Paris, but, if public interest in reform was apparent, it was difficult to avoid the general air of cynicism and disillusion. To quote Poumiès de la Siboutie, 'I formed the opinion that the assembly was not favourably disposed towards the emperor. He was very late in coming. When at last he appeared, the vast throng rose shouting, "Vive la France! Vive la nation!" The few feeble cries of "Vive l'empereur!" could barely be distinguished.'[73]

In fairness, Napoleon did not delay in giving life to the new parliamentary institutions which he envisaged. In order to create a legislative assembly as quickly as possible, as an interim measure on 30 April the electoral colleges were ordered to convene on 4 May to choose not lists of potential deputies as had been the case hitherto but rather actual deputies who could represent them in Paris. The result, however, was not very encouraging. In general, participation ran at about one-third of the membership of the various colleges and in many places in the south, in particular, was ludicrously small. As for the deputies, whilst many came from the structures of the regime, the fact that plenty of them were either men who had played no part in public life since Brumaire or had been repeatedly passed over when it came to selecting deputies for seats in parliament suggests that there was the makings of a strong oppositional block.[74]

Nor were things much better when the new legislative assembly opened its sessions in the first week of June. Of this body, indeed, it is enough to know that it ever afterwards attracted the scorn of die-hard Bonapartists. 'It is painful to have to say', writes the devoted Méneval, 'that never was the nation represented by a political assembly more ignorant of its true interests, more below its mission, in presence of circumstances of such extraordinary gravity. While numerous foreign armies were pressing in upon us on every side, [the majority] gave voice to none but vain tirades and untimely discussions on abstract constitutional theories. It was unable either to inspire the hearts of Frenchmen with a hatred for foreign domination and to proclaim the danger which was menacing the fatherland, or to rally itself to Napoleon's dictatorship, the only means which remained to triumph, perhaps, over a formidable league.'[75] Drawn entirely from the propertied classes, the deputies of the lower chamber from the start proved as combative as they were obstructive, challenging the emperor on a variety of procedural issues, proclaiming their determination to revise the *acte additionnel* and electing as their president Jean Lanjuinais, a veteran Breton politician who had played a leading role in the debates on the abolition of feudalism and the civil constitution of the clergy in the period 1789–92 and gone on to vote against the establishment of the empire in 1804. To quote the naturalist and sometime soldier, Jean-Baptise Bory de Saint Vincent, who was elected to the assembly by his home town of Agen, whilst the deputies were prepared to co-operate in the defence of *la patrie*, they believed it was their task, first, 'to oppose by all the means at our disposal any project of conquest, any foreign war', and, second, 'to deny the head of state the blood of the *enfants de la patrie* and the treasure of the citizens for any other purpose than the repulse of unjust aggressions'.[76] As for a proposal that the chamber should vote Napoleon the title of 'Saviour of the Country', this was indignantly shouted down. When, resplendent in his coronation robes and flanked by his brothers, Joseph and Lucien, the emperor attended the state opening on 7 June, he was received civilly enough, but once again shouts of 'Vive la France! Vive la Nation!' predominated over those of 'Vive l'empereur!'[77] In short, the writing was on the wall: in the France of 1815, even more than in the France of 1814, patriotism was not synonymous with loyalty to the throne. As Hobhouse remarked in a letter written on 11 June, 'Should Napoleon meet with any signal disaster, it is an opinion of some (and I heard it publically delivered a day or two ago) that the representatives will think that the state is to be saved by other hands.'[78]

In the end, however, the problem was not the constitution: with its 'chamber of peers', limited electorate and indirect system of elections, the *acte additionnel* was conservative enough to reassure the interests of the propertied classes, whilst yet offering the people of France as a whole a de facto declaration of rights that was not dissimilar from that of 1795.[79] At the same time its much greater electorate than the one offered by the Charter meant that, with a certain amount of amendment, it might have eventually served as the basis for a regime that was genuinely parliamentary.[80] Rather, the trouble was the context. As Collins notes, 'It was anybody's guess whether Napoleon had in mind a constitutional monarchy run by the propertied classes or a popular dictatorship like that of the Jacobins.'[81] Such is the judgement of a later historian of admirable objectivity, but across France many *notables* could not go even so far in giving Napoleon the benefit of the doubt. In his memoirs Guizot insists that there is plenty of evidence that the emperor would never have honoured his promises, and repeatedly quotes him to this effect. Thus: 'They drive me into a path that is not my own; they enfeeble and enchain me. France will seek me, but find me no longer … France demands what has become of the old arm of the emperor, the arm which she requires to control Europe … When peace is made, we shall see.'[82] Whether anything of the sort was actually said is another matter, whilst one also has to wonder how far Napoleon's table-talk was common knowledge. Yet in the end the matter is of little account. As in the rest of Europe, the reality of the emperor's rule had been such as to destroy all the faith the propertied classes had once placed in him. To quote Guizot again, 'His character and his history deprived his word of all credit.'[83]

Setting aside the fact that the 'masses of granite' he was effectively seeking to win over had little reason to trust Napoleon, the moderation of his new political settlement was belied in the first instance by the tone of his speeches and declarations – 'Napoleon's own proclamations', notes Robert Toombs, 'used unmistakeably revolutionary language'[84] – in the second by the appointment of Lazare Carnot as Minister of the Interior and the equally notorious Joseph Fouché as Minister of General Police, and, in the third, by the emergence of a Jacobin movement known as the *fédérés*, recruited to a very large extent from among the *sans culottes* that attempted to keep alive the traditions of 1793 and, with official patronage, set about establishing an armed militia of its own.[85] About the *fédérés* we shall hear more very shortly, but by the time of the *champ de mai*, there was one other factor to be taken into account. In brief, by now there was no possible doubt: Napoleon meant war. To quote Guizot yet again: 'The unsettled feeling of the middle classes in 1815 was a legitimate and patriotic disquietude. What they wanted, and what they had a right to demand, for the advantage of the entire nation, was that peace and liberty should be secured to them, but they had good reason to question the power of Napoleon to accomplish these objects.'[86]

Napoleon, then, faced the armies of Europe without the support of the 'masses of granite'. However, perhaps property could be substituted by the populace. According to the legend – a legend that persists to this day – in 1793 the Revolution had been saved by the *enfants de la patrie* springing to arms and overwhelming the armies of the *ancien régime*. As nothing of the sort actually happened in 1793, it is doubtful whether it could have done so in 1815. Thus, there is good reason to doubt whether the *fédérés* – the obvious fount for any such movement – could ever have fulfilled such a role. For the time being, however, let us take the movement at face value and quote the words of an interested eyewitness to the first stirrings of this movement in Paris:

On Sunday last, 14 May, a body of the workmen of Saint Antoine and Saint Marceau, representing a federation which had two days before formed itself in those suburbs to the number of 30,000 [members], marched before the emperor at the Tuileries. The express purpose of this union is to form a body of sharpshooters to operate in advance of the National Guard in case the enemy shall present itself before the capital. They demand arms with which they promise to guarantee Paris against the reappearance of the Allies. The number ... amounted to 12,000 ... the greater part being in their labouring dresses ... This movement of the suburbs glances at the National Guard of Paris, most of whom are reputed to be peacefully inclined, and to think more of the preservation of their shops than of the glory and integrity of France ... The example of Paris has been followed in other departments, particularly in Burgundy and Brittany, where the federation is meant as a counterpoise to the royalism of a portion of the province ... The government is under some embarrassment in the regulation of its conduct respecting these movements, which it cannot wholly encourage, although the least suspicion that they are looked upon with distrust would leave the emperor no support but the sword of his Guard. Accordingly, the utmost care has been taken to give a military form and organization to these voluntary levies.[87]

Amongst all this there was in some instances much martial ardour. One recruit to the movement was Poumiès de la Siboutie. As he later wrote, 'Public opinion had indeed changed since 1814. We were eager to join the newly formed companies of artillery, and attended drill twice a day in the gardens of the Luxembourg. We were filled with a fervent desire to blot out all recollection of our pusillanimous conduct in 1814. It was not merely blind passion for Napoleon that animated us. Our susceptibilities had been hurt in every conceivable way under the Restoration, and we really looked upon him as our avenger.'[88] Meanwhile, all over the country from the middle of May onwards the authorities were instructed to enrol the *fédérés* in a new militia that was envisaged as an adjunct to the National Guard. Yet were even the most ardent *fédérés* really prepared to do battle against the legions of Europe? One suspects not. Even in the capital there was much backsliding. According to Waresquiel, for example, 'In some districts of Paris the workers who had been enrolled did not attend musters, whilst in others they had to be enrolled by force, sometimes by the influence of proprietors who were more progressive than they were. The archives of the prefecture of police ... show that the beautiful vision of the working classes uniting in favour of an emperor who had suddenly become the standard bearer of popular welfare did not exist except in the imagination of a few republican pamphleteers.'[89]

As Mollien points out, then, in the end the appeal to the principles of 1793 proved a failure: 'These unfortunate proclamations ... had no effect other than to cause agitation in some quarters and discontent in others.'[90] At most, in fact, all that could be expected was that the *fédérés* would take on gangs of *chouans* and not always even then: in Nantes, for example, only 300 of the city's 1,000 militiamen proved willing to sally beyond the city's gates.[91] As for the idea of using them on campaign, this was out of the question; as the Prefect of Ile et Vilaine wrote to the commander of the National Guard from his capital of Rennes in a letter dated 9 May:

> The zeal of our *fédérés* is limited to the sort of actions in which they have taken part, and is very far from preparing them to suffer the obligations which it is proposed to impose on them. A large number of them are composed of men devoted to useful trades who are indispensable for the support of their families. If it is a question of marching to the support of some spot in the department that is under threat ... they are ready enough, but it is impossible to think in terms of forming them into battalions that could be sent off to garrison some distant point for any length of time.[92]

If there was popular support for Napoleon, then, there can be little confidence that it could somehow have been translated into a people's war. Even in the midst of the excitement that greeted Napoleon in the course of his march on Paris there are signs that the issue of compulsory military service was likely to prove a problem. Thus, in Grenoble – the first major town to fall to him – we are told that that the erstwhile emperor entered the town to a tumultuous welcome.[93] An eyewitness was Jacques Champollion-Figeac, who, as we have already seen, occupied the position of the city's archivist:

> Village by village, the population of the countryside flocked to join the escort of Napoleon ... and the noise of the crowd was so great that it served him as a veritable courier. A little after nine o'clock in the evening [of 7 March], garnished by a few Polish lancers, the resultant mass finally reached the walls of the city where they were greeted by the cheers of the inhabitants and the garrison alike. However, the gates remained shut. Mounted on horseback, Napoleon rode forward almost alone, and, knocking on them with his snuff-box, cried out 'Open up! Come on, open up!' The answer came back that the keys had been taken by General Marchand [i.e. the governor], but in no time at all the gates had succumbed to a rain of blows from within and without alike. Born on a torrent of popular enthusiasm,

Napoleon then slowly made his way on foot to the hotel of the Three Dauphins, where lodgings had been prepared for him in advance by its owner, an erstwhile member of the Consular Guard.[94]

Yet in Stendhal's *Life of Napoleon*, a work that can hardly be described as being hostile to the emperor (Stendhal, a distinguished novelist whose real name was Marie-Henri Beyle, was a devoted admirer of Napoleon who had taken part in the Russian campaign and fled into exile in 1814), we read the following:

> The next day Napoleon reviewed his troops on the parade ground. There again he was surrounded by the townsfolk. Enthusiasm was at its height, yet it inspired none of the obsequiousness with which people are wont to approach kings. They shouted incessantly beneath his windows and to his face, 'No more conscription: we won't have it any longer and we want a constitution!'[95]

This rather ambivalent attitude on the part of the citizens of Grenoble is confirmed by a letter from Joseph Fourier that was written just days before the emperor's arrival: 'Amongst the inhabitants of the town and the surrounding countryside can be found men imbued with sentiments that are lacking in reason in political terms, but, for all that, they are not partisans of Bonaparte.'[96] From Bas-Rhin came much the same message: 'The inhabitants of this department regard the Bourbons with neither affection nor enthusiasm. That said, they don't want Bonaparte either: cold and reserved, they are simply waiting to see what happens.'[97] As even the enthusiastic Bonapartist Lavallette put it, then, 'The wish to have Napoleon was less insistent than the desire to get rid of the Bourbons.'[98] Indeed, one may go still further, and suggest that the reality was that for many of the inhabitants the question of who was in charge made not the slightest difference. To quote the Maison du Roi officer, Frédéric Rillier:

> [Dijon] offered a singular aspect: white cockades alternated with tricolour ones without the slightest tension or resentment, and the people looked on with indifference, waiting quietly until such time as bayonets gave them a master. One sensed a nation accustomed to revolutions, such limited interest as it displayed in the events that were currently in train being explained by the fact that they generated a bit of excitement without at the same time shedding any blood.[99]

For those who wish to argue that Napoleon could somehow have prosecuted a lengthy campaign on the back of victory at Waterloo, all this is scarcely encouraging. Nor does it help when one considers what is known of events on the home front once the fighting had actually broken out. Sufficient popular support existed for the impression to be created that France was indeed a nation-in-arms. According to Sir Walter Scott, for example, support for the war effort was very strong in those areas of the country that were directly threatened by invasion:

> The ... departments which bordered on Germany met the wishes of Bonaparte to their utmost extent. They remembered the invasions of the previous year with all the feelings of irritation which such recollections naturally produce. Accordingly, they formed free corps of volunteers, laboured at fortifying towns and passes, constructed *têtes du pont* and multiplied all means of defence which the country offered.[100]

Based as it is on a journey to France undertaken after Waterloo, this account must needs be regarded as hearsay. Yet it is not entirely unsubstantiated. With regard to Burgundy in particular, the nineteenth-century historian Develay claims that there was so much clamour to secure places in the National Guard, that the local authorities had to create a number of supplementary companies.[101] More up-to-date and far better substantiated, meanwhile, the work of Paul Leuilliot has shown that in Alsace mobilization went relatively smoothly, the two departments which made it up (Bas-Rhin and Haut-Rhin) managing to raise 19,860 men for the field battalions of the National Guard as well as as many as ten officially-authorized bands of partisans.[102] Neighbouring Franche-Conté, too, appears to have done well: fleeing Paris when war finally broke out for fear that he would otherwise risk internment, Hobhouse made for Switzerland, and later claimed that en route he saw a country ready to do battle with the invaders. Herewith, for example, the letter that he wrote just prior to hearing the news that Napoleon had been defeated:

> The people here look upon a drawn battle as impossible, and, judging from the spirit of all the neighbouring departments, are confident of present and final success. I must inform you that from Fontainebleau to the frontiers, through all the country we have traversed, there appears but one sentiment, that of defending the national cause to the last. In the Jura and the long line of the frontier we have pursued, the whole population is in arms. Posts and beacons are established at every turn of the road and

guarded by peasants of all ages with pikes and fowling pieces. In Franche-Comté the schoolchildren have enrolled themselves, and a body of them actually passed in review before a general at Dôle ... I do not say that the emperor ... is the object of universal regard, but I do assert that the Bourbons are much less so ... The predominant wish, I may say passion, of the people and soldiers in every part of the country I have seen is peace, which the ignorant, sanguinary statesmen of [the] congress will not see or allow because they are in want of war themselves. Nothing but the general recognition of the necessity of defending their independence could have prompted the noble exertions which, whatever may be their issue, must give them claim to an admiration that no belligerents since the struggles of the Swiss and Dutch republics can extort from an unprejudiced observer.[103]

Finally, according to Lucien Bonaparte, at least, news of Waterloo led to dramatic scenes in the capital, thousands of men, women and children massing in the gardens of the Tuileries and literally begging for arms on their knees, whilst Scott tells us that the inhabitants of Paris sallied out in large numbers and laboured long and hard to improve the defences that the Allies had pierced so easily in 1814.[104]

The desire to stave off the horrors that had been seen in 1814, however, is scarcely the same as enthusiasm for war: one wonders, for example, what the feelings of the citizens of Strasbourg were when on 10 May the mayor declared the city to be in a state of siege and ordered the inhabitants to undertake the in most cases quite impossible task of laying in a whole year's supply of food?[105] Elsewhere, meanwhile, the picture could not have been more different. Sent to Moulins as one of Carnot's special commissioners, for example, Jean Colchen encountered a situation that could only be described as dismal:

In the towns as much as in the countryside, the people are not displaying the slightest energy, while they are under the influence of the enemies of the current state of affairs ... As for the recall of men who have served as soldiers in the past, this has either produced no result whatsoever or evoked the most limited of responses ... In short, on entering this department, one could believe oneself back under the regime of Louis XVIII.[106]

For a detailed picture of the situation that pertained in much of France, one may turn to the Pas de Calais. Subjected to the same mobilization orders as the rest of the country, from the beginning the populace showed itself reluctant to comply – of the 7,400 men the department was supposed to provide for the mobile element of the National Guard, for example, only 2,923 had been secured by 21 April, for example – while there was a growing number of desertions, matters not being helped by the fact that many mayors showed little energy in their response to the problem, large numbers of them therefore having to be either removed or suspended. Desperate to remedy the situation, the new prefect, Dumont, issued a stream of orders, appeals and threats, but to no avail, and the result was that he was left with no option but to use some of the men he had managed to get together to form a 'mobile column' with which to raid the towns and villages of the department. Deeply angered by this behaviour, and all the more so as the men concerned proceeded to engage in wholesale extortion, the populace drifted ever further into the camp of outright opposition, the situation reaching such a state that there was talk of the area being in open insurrection. According to the Prussian ambassador, Von der Goltz, for example, 'No obedience, no activity, much uncertainty … The soldiers are singing royalist songs in their guardrooms and we may well see them swelling the ranks of your Majesty … All the young men have taken to the woods to escape conscription and are awaiting the arrival of the allied armies with impatience. Many of them would like to enlist in the royal army, but they are frightened of getting their parents into trouble. The National Guard is generally favourable to the king … and will never be redoubtable to anyone other than the partisans of Bonaparte.'[107]

Under Napoleon, of course, until very late in the day open disaffection had received short shrift at the hands of the *gendarmerie*, but this force could no more be counted upon than the 'masses of granite': on the contrary, whilst for the most part loyal to the emperor, its ability to function was undermined by the transfer of many men, and, still worse, horses, to the army, as well as the need to organize mobile columns to fight such insurrections as those of the Vendée.[108] Also in chaos were the agents of the secret police. In 1815, then, the manipulation of public opinion that had played so crucial a role in the governance of the *grand empire* collapsed. As Guizot wrote, 'Everywhere, and particularly in Paris, people … uttered their thoughts without reserve: in public places as well as in private drawing rooms, they went to and fro, expressing hopes and engaging in hostile plots as if they were lawful and certain of success; journals and pamphlets increased daily in number and virulence and were circulated almost without opposition or restraint.'[109] Sent to Ghent to report on the domestic situation to Louis XVIII, meanwhile, Guizot encountered many police controls, but little desire to hamper his movements. 'More than one official face appeared to say to the unknown traveller, "Pass on quickly" as if they dreaded making a mistake or damaging a useful work by interfering with its supposed design.'[110]

The greatest test of the regime, of course, came at the actual moment of invasion, and here it was found gravely wanting. Thus, when the Allies finally entered France, such enthusiasm as there was evaporated like smoke. Indeed, the situation described by Wellington's soldiers is completely different. As we have already noted, the arrival of Napoleon in France had given rise to considerable unrest, and the march on Paris that followed the French defeat provided a host of evidence that, in reality, support for the emperor was at best limited. 'Here an assemblage of rustics awaited us,' wrote the Royal-Horse-Artillery officer, Alexander Mercer, of his battery's arrival at the French frontier:

> Their principal object, no doubt, was to gaze at the strangers, but they gave themselves infinite trouble to make us comprehend that we were about to cross the frontier and enter the soil of France. Drawing a long line in the mud right across the road and vociferating altogether, [they cried,] 'Ici, monsieur! Voila, monsieur! Regardez, monsieur! C'est ici, monsieur, que vous entrez en la France!' And when we crossed their line, they grinned and jumped about like so many monkeys ... From what I have seen of these people it appears very doubtful whether they care a farthing who reigns over them. Be that as it may, we undoubtedly entered France amidst the cheers and greetings of the populace.[111]

Pressing on, Mercer and his men encountered similar scenes wherever they went. 'They seem a very ignorant, simple people, the peasantry of this country ... Since passing the frontier, we have found them everywhere pursuing their rural labours with as much tranquillity as in the most profound state of peace, quite undisturbed by, and exhibiting little interest in, the continued passage of foreign troops ... through their villages. The arrival of strangers attracted a concourse of villagers to our bivouac, many old women and young girls bringing quantities of very fine cherries for sale ... Nor have we seen any trace of [an enemy], having found the peasantry everywhere as peaceably occupied as if no war existed.'[112] Similarly, travelling from Boulogne to Paris at about the same time, William Fellowes describes a countryside that was in anything but a state of agitation. Thus: 'In all the towns and villages the inhabitants were just as tranquil as at any former period, and except [for] their frequent exclamations of loyalty and pleasure at seeing us, they appeared as indifferent as if no current affairs of moment were in agitation in their capital.'[113] Attacked by Wellington's forces, meanwhile, Cambrai, Peronne and Valenciennes put up almost no resistance – at Cambrai, indeed, a group of the inhabitants even assisted the assault by letting some of the attackers through a postern gate – and then celebrated their deliverance. To quote Sir Walter Scott:

> In all these towns, so far as I could discover, the feeling of the people was decidedly in favour of the legitimate monarch, and I cannot doubt that this impression is correct, because elsewhere, and in similar circumstances, those who favoured Bonaparte were at no pains to suppress their inclinations. In one or two towns they were preparing little *fêtes* to celebrate the king's restoration. The accompaniments did not appear to us very splendid, but when a town has been so lately taken by storm, and is still garrisoned by foreign troops and subjected to military requisitions, we could not expect that the rejoicing of its inhabitants should be attended with any superfluity of splendour.[114]

Even in the capital, where the *fédéré* movement had been at its strongest, the invaders were welcomed. In the immediate aftermath of Waterloo, there had been much bravado. In the words of Sir Walter Scott, 'The populace ... confided in what had been repeatedly and carefully impressed upon their minds – that Paris could only fall by treachery – and boasted that they had now ... Soult and Davout ... to direct the defence of the capital instead of Marmont, by whom ... they were taught to believe it had been basely betrayed.'[115] Indeed, as the last actions of the campaign raged outside the walls, so the excitement mounted to fresh heights. To quote the same observer, 'The temper of the ... soldiers had risen to frenzy, and the mob of the *faubourgs*, animated by the same feelings of rage, vomited threats and execrations both against the Allies and against the citizens of Paris who favoured the cause of peace and legitimacy.'[116] Having returned to Paris from a brief exile in Switzerland, Molé even claimed that he saw the beaten emperor mixing with an excited crowd desperate to persuade him to renew the fight:

> In the vicinity of the Elysée, the Chambers and the quays, horrible groups could be seen in which popular orators thundered against the aristocracy and the Bourbons ... Fearless as ever ... [Napoleon] sometimes went unguarded into the streets and let a crowd collect round him ... One evening ... in the Avenue de Marigny, I found myself drawn along by the crowd and witnessed the saddest sight imaginable. He was on the terrace in uniform ... Some charcoal-burners and porters were talking familiarly with him, begging ... him to sieze the crown again. He was replying to them in word and gesture, pointing to his heart and bending down to shake

hands, while his chamberlains and equerries threw money to the crowd … Perhaps I alone at that moment had any idea of the effort it cost him to fawn upon the plebs I had seen him treat with so much authority and disdain.[117]

Yet no sooner had the Allied forces arrived than, some mutterings aside (see below), it was a different story. As William Wheeler of the Fifty-First Foot wrote, 'The good people of Paris began to pour out of the city and mix among us as if nothing had been the matter … Refreshments of all sorts came in to our camp: it was truly astonishing to see what confidence the inhabitants placed in us.'[118] In so far as Wellington's soldiers were concerned, meanwhile, the friendly relations established in the course of the campaign continued into the peace that followed. As one veteran later remembered, 'The French people were greatly attached to the British and I assure you I never spent so pleasant a time during my soldiering. I have seen the old and young shed tears in abundance at our leaving them, and numbers of men, being discharged, went back and got married, and are there to this day.'[119]

Inherent in all this is beyond doubt a reaction to the experiences of the campaign. British soldiers were far from being saints, but, as in 1814, the combination of ruthless discipline and a commissariat that paid for all the produce it requisitioned signified protection to a population traumatised by war.[120] Angered by what they saw as their betrayal by the home front in 1814, Napoleon's soldiers were by no means well disposed towards civilians, whilst the departments crossed by the Allied armies in 1815 – areas that had for most part not been directly affected by the campaigns of the previous year – had necessarily had to bear a heavy burden in the run-up to the campaign. On this, at least, Scott could speak with some authority:

The … advance into Belgium had the … advantage of relieving the people of France from the presence of an army which, even upon its native soil, was a scourge of no ordinary severity … In the public walks, in the coffee houses and theatres of Paris, the conduct of the officers towards a *pékin* (a cant word by which, in their arrogance, they distinguished any citizen of a peaceful persuasion), was, in the highest degree, insolent and over-bearing. The late events had greatly contributed to inflame the self-importance of the soldiery … They had … deposed one monarch and re-elected another to the throne from which he had abdicated. This gave them a consciousness of power and importance, neither favourable to moderation of conduct nor to military discipline. Even while yet in France they did not hesitate to inflict upon their fellow subjects many of those severities which soldiers in general confine to the country of an enemy, and, to judge from the accounts of the peasantry, the subsequent march of the Allies inflicted on them fewer, or, at least, much less wilful evils on them than those which they had experienced at the hands of their own countrymen.[121]

This is not to say that there had been no popular agitation at all when the news arrived of Waterloo. To return to Hobhouse, for example, he gives us a vivid description of the consternation that reigned in parts of pro-Napoleonic Burgundy:

We had passed Mâcon and had arrived at the little town of Saint Albin, the next stage ... when a man on horseback begged to say a word to us, and asked in a whisper whether we had heard the news? 'What news?' 'Why, bad news, the worst.' The emperor had returned to Paris – had abdicated. Two merchants passing through Tournus on their way to Lyons had been shown a Paris journal stating the fact. What journal? 'The *Journal Général.*' It was natural that we should add 'You must not believe that journal; it is a suspected paper.' Our informant replied that he thought so too, and that the merchants had been followed by a gendarme and taken to the prefect, who, however, upon examining their paper, had suffered them to depart. The fact was the more unaccountable as the telegraph at Lyons had that morning announced a second victory gained over the allies in which their cavalry had been nearly annihilated. Our informant ... did not believe the story but was evidently much disturbed and accompanied us to the next stage to meet the courier from Paris. At Tournus we ... found everyone in extreme anxiety. The post-house was surrounded with crowds who ... wished to know our opinion on the subject and were not a little pleased at hearing our arguments on the improbability of the fact ... At Sennecy, the next stage ... the truth burst upon us. We paused but still did not altogether resign our incredulity, for we could only see a paper called the *Journal des Campagnes* in a small tavern where some country fellows and people of the town were dining and joined with us in still wishing to wait for the *Moniteur* itself, of which, however, an extract was given in this journal. The fatal intelligence was read aloud; Napoleon had gained victories on the 16th and 17th, attacked the English on the 18th and beat them up to half past eight in the evening when, a desperate charge being made on some English batteries by four battalions of the Middle Guard, and these battalions being thrown into confusion, a rout took place ... The whole army began to run ... and a complete defeat ensued ... At the close of the recital the persons present said it was not, could not, be true. One added, 'If so, the Bourbons will come back ... but they shall reign over stones: the men will die or depart to some happier country.'[122]

To consternation was added fear: terrified of renewed atrocities in the style of those that had occurred in 1814, in many places in the path of the oncoming Allied armies the populace fled their homes and buried their valuables.[123] All this tumoil, however, came to nothing. In Paris, for example, the popular quarters refused point-blank to recognize the authority of the provisional government – representatives of the assembly who were dispatched to harangue the crowds were met with loud cries of 'Vive Napoléon!', for example[124] – while a few *fédérés* had essayed resistance. Yet, as an eyewitness noted in a record of events that he jotted down as events moved from one hour to the next, such was the weight of opinion against them that they were quickly swamped:

Thursday, 22nd ... three o'clock in the afternoon. The abdication of Bonaparte is announced by a proclamation. The stocks open at fifty-nine *francs* with great applauses and some cries of 'Vive le roi!' They continue to rise notwithstanding the alarm now occasioned by a perceptible movement among the *fédérés*, whose threats and violence commence from this time. These men cry 'Vive l'empereur!' There is no emperor is replied to them by thousands. Many of the *fédérés* are apprehended by the National Guard. Others of them, in bodies, go to the Palais Elysée, and there demand Bonaparte to head them. Marshal [*sic*] Bertrand appears: he tells them it is not by cries of 'Vive l'empereur!' that they can serve the emperor: they must serve him *les armes a la main*; they loudly call for arms. Disturbances take place in the Palais Royale caused by decorated officers attempting to make the passers-by cry 'Vive l'empereur!' The National Guard in its usual excellent spirit apprehends all disturbers [of the peace] whatever side they may take ... A vague consternation prevails everywhere in the consequence of the apprehension that an explosion of some sort will take place tonight. But the surprising number, good spirit and firm countenance of the National Guard are tranquilizing.[125]

Elsewhere the picture was much the same. In brief, popular support for Napoleon was not entirely absent. Mercer, for example, has an interesting anecdote of how he tricked admissions of continued devotion to the emperor from various members of the populace by feigning personal admiration for him, whilst at the western town of Niort the fleeing emperor was greeted with cheers and acclamations by the inhabitants, the latter having for weeks been terrified out of their wits by the menacing attitude of the *chouans* of the surrounding countryside.[126] Equally, travelling to Paris a month or two after Waterloo, Sir Walter Scott witnessed an amusing scene in which some carters first managed to so encumber a road with their vehicles as to bring a Prussian supply column to a complete standstill and then accompanied their deliberately bumbling attempts to clear the obstruction with a stream of smiling explanation and apology that was in fact composed of the grossest personal insults.[127] Very striking too, in Scott's opinion, was the fact that the frequent parades, grand reviews and mock battles organized in and around Paris for the benefit of the Allied monarchs attracted few spectators, this being something that he found quite astonishing in a city with such a reputation for being addicted to public spectacle.[128] Finally, in Lyons the arrival of the Austrian commissioners sent to take the surrender of the city provoked a furious outbreak of rioting, whilst in Arras a handful of *fédérés* barricaded themselves in the citadel and opened fire on the joyous crowds that took over the city in the wake of the arrival of a detachment of royalist troops.[129] Yet, for all that the all-but universal appearance of white cockades or ribbons meant, as Scott inferred, less than nothing – as he remarked, 'There was a degree of suspicion, arising from this very unanimity, concerning the motives for which these emblems were assumed.'[130] – such residual loyalty to the emperor as still existed was incapable of sustaining popular resistance, let alone a guerrilla war, whilst the emperor's cause was not helped by the fact that the retreating French troops were ruthless in their pillage of the countryside through which they passed.[131]

Even if we accept, then, that popular support for Napoleon was far from non-existent, that there were, indeed, areas of the country, or, at least, towns and cities, in which it was positively rampant, it is therefore clear that the *fédéré* movement was not a substitute for a powerful regular army. It could, perhaps, assist the National Guard and the regulars in the suppression of equally poorly-armed Breton peasants, not to mention bully and intimidate popular officials, but it could no more withstand the oncoming Allies than Angoulême's royalist volunteers could hold Bordeaux. If limited, the services that it could offer the régime were not inconsiderable, and yet one cannot but feel that they did not make up for the absence of the 20,000 troops who had to be deployed in the interior to fight the *chouans* and their allies. Meanwhile, the possibility of popular unrest did not stay the hands of the structures of government one whit in the wake of Waterloo. Thus, when an exhausted and dispirited Napoleon arrived back in Paris on 21 June, he was confronted by a legislative assembly and house of peers (a body which had been hastily brought into existence shortly after the former opened its sessions) that were determined to put an end to his rule. Terrified that the emperor would overthrow them by means of a military coup, the lower house, led by none other than the hero of 1789, Lafayette, declared itself in permanent session and, further, that any attempt to act against it would be deemed to be an act of treason. Meeting with his ministers and council of state, the emperor at first attempted to insist that the vast majority of the deputies and peers alike were sound, and that they could yet be persuaded to back him were he to call a joint session and ask for dictatorial powers. This plan, however, received no support, whilst an even crazier scheme put forward by Lucien Bonaparte to the effect that Napoleon should overthrow the assembly by force was also rejected. Instead, a delegation consisting of Carnot and Regnault de Saint Jean d'Angély were dispatched to win the deputies over. This attempt failing, a second delegation consisting of Lucien Bonaparte and all six ministers of the government appeared before the lower house and attempted to put the case for fighting on, only to be overwhelmed by a storm of criticism and angry questions, not to mention demands for Napoleon's immediate abdication. At length agreement was secured in respect of the establishment of a special commission consisting of the ministers of the government plus five members from each chamber of the assembly that would deliberate as to the course of action that should now be followed. For Napoleon, however, there was clearly no longer either space or tolerance, and, persuaded that if he did not abdicate, he would be deposed, on 22 June he sent a note to the chamber of deputies informing them that he was stepping down for the good of the nation in favour of his infant son.[132]

The sequel to these events – the last-ditch offer on the part of Napoleon to serve his country as commander-in-chief rather than head of state; the determined efforts of the assembly to turn the *acte additionnel* into something more acceptable; the attempts of the new government to obtain a favourable peace; the armistice of 3 July; and, finally, the flight of Napoleon and his eventual surrender to the Royal Navy – for the most part need not detain us here: the story, after all, is one that has been told many times over.[133] What is of interest, however, is the almost unanimous refusal of the deputies to sanction any continuation of the fighting beyond what was necessary to secure an armistice. When Carnot and Marshal Davout attempted to argue that France was not in quite so hopeless a position in military terms as had been painted, they were simply shouted down. In the end, then, Napoleon was proved to be quite right. On coming to power in 1800, he had argued that he could not govern France without the support of the 'masses of granite' – essentially, the interests of landed property – but now those 'masses of granite' had become millstones that were relentlessly grinding the last shreds of his power to dust. Some of the army might yet have been willing to fight on – a few garrisons, indeed, insisted on holding out and continued to defy the invaders until well into the autumn – whilst, always given that it proved possible to find arms for them, the *fédérés* could possibly have constituted a useful auxiliary force. Yet, concerned by the threat of revolution, angered by the failure to move far enough in the direction of a truly parliamentary régime, not to mention Napoleon's all too evident duplicity, alienated by ham-fisted political intervention and, above all opposed to further military adventures, the *notables* would not back the emperor, and, so long as that was the case, the enormous number of ordinary people who had shown themselves to be indifferent to the cause of Napoleon, let alone downright hostile to him, could not possibly be coerced into either paying their taxes or sending their sons to the army. Nor can they be blamed for taking such a line. As we have seen, even victory at Waterloo would have been a blind alley in strategic terms that would have left the Army of the North in a very difficult position whilst at the same time in all probability galvanising resistance to the emperor from one end of Europe to the other, a position, in short, in which France was already beaten. As Marshal Ney, already angry at the manner in which he was being scapegoated for the defeat, put it in a speech to the house of peers, 'It is simply not the case, as has been claimed, that 60,000 men can be got together. This is quite impossible: there is not a single man on the northern frontier: the enemy can enter at any time he chooses. It will be a very great deal if Marshal Grouchy or Marshal Soult will be able to muster 20 to 25,000 men. I was in command throughout the retreat … and I am absolutely certain of what I am saying … As for what has been said about the Guard, it is quite untrue: I was the man giving the orders, and not a single man could be rallied. There is nothing else to be done for the well-being of the country other than to open negotiations with the enemy. If they so wish, they can be in Paris in six or seven days.'[134]

In military terms at least, then, Waterloo was indeed a 'glorious irrelevance' (or, perhaps, if it is so preferred, an 'irrelevant glory'). Even so late as 18 June Napoleon could still have won the campaign, but there was no way that he could have secured anything more than a stay of execution. Sooner or later, even had there not been wholesale revolt in France, there would have been a decisive victory somewhere else, the only difference being that the 30,000 dead who fell at Quatre Bras, Ligny, Waterloo and Wavre would beyond doubt have been multiplied many times over: such was the discontent engendered by the new war that it cancelled out much of such popular support as the emperor initially received, left the *fédérés* isolated and powerless and rendered a badly disrupted administration utterly incapable of mobilizing France for a prolonged war. In that sense, at least, Waterloo did matter, while it mattered too that, thanks to the prominent role played by the Duke of Wellington in the decisive battle of the campaign, the British were able to ensure that the eventual peace settlement was far more moderate than the Prussians at least would have liked it to be, and that a balance of power was restored that kept Europe from the horrors of another general war for the next ninety-nine years. In so far as the events of the campaign are concerned, then, let us close with what Waterloo, and. specifically, the climactic attack of the Imperial Guard, says about Napoleon, in which respect one can do no better than turn to the words of Stephen Coote:

> The tactical dispositions which Napoleon had insisted on were catastrophic, suicidal ... Five battalions of the Middle Guard – some 4,000 men – were to form the first wave of the attack. They were to march in columns that made up a crude arrowhead ... Nothing could have been more disastrous. The outnumbered men were being obliged to march uphill without the momentum a brigade formation would have given them ... without cavalry protection and with their own firepower reduced by the formation imposed on them by the emperor whose praises they were shouting and who had lied to them [by telling them that Marshal Grouchy had come]. Nothing showed more clearly how fatigue, inertia [and] cynical and unthinking arrogance ... had corroded Napoleon's military genius. Once the fiery young officer had been transformed into an eagle by the discovery of his ability. For years he had hovered in the skies above Europe, darkening it with his wings. Now those wings were feeble, broken even.[135]

There is, however, one area that still needs coverage. In brief, if the eagle was rejected so massively in 1815, how does one account for the fact that within a very few years France had embraced the Napoleonic legend? Here one can only say that human memory is extremely fickle. From the beginning, of course, the exiled emperor had a band of loyal supporters – grizzled veterans of the Grande Armée and erstwhile *fédérés* – deeply embittered by a defeat which they universally ascribed to betrayal, and these men undoubtedly strove to keep the image of the emperor brightly polished even if it was initially only within the confines of village or backstreet taverns (after 1830, of course, political change in France brought with it opportunities denied them in the immediate aftermath of Waterloo, whether it was involvement in radical journalism or the publication of memoirs singing the praises of their sometime leader). However, this handful of enthusiasts was quickly joined by ever greater numbers of new recruits as Napoleon began to benefit from, first, the pathos generated by his exile on the distant rock of Saint Helena and, with it, the prolific writings of his personal suite, and, second, the blunders of a régime purged of the desire for reconciliation for which Louis XVIII, at least, had stood in 1814: while 'White Terror' swept the south, Marshal Ney and General de la Bédoyère (the villain, in Bourbon eyes, of the dramatic confrontation at Laffrey) were executed by firing squad and some 6,000 individuals brought to trial. As time went by, meanwhile, so still other factors began to come into play, namely the capacity of the human mind to move on from past horror – a process that caused the miseries of Napoleon's wars to be all but eclipsed within a generation – the desire of the French bourgeoisie for a return to an age of grandeur whose cost even to themselves they had forgotten, the survival of a republicanism imbued with the concept of the emperor as a fallen hero and the determination of a July Monarchy aware of its growing unpopularity to cloak itself in the glories of the *grand empire*: hence, of course, the return of Napoleon's body to Paris in 1841 and the construction of the grandiloquent tomb that remains a place of pilgrimage to this day.[136]

Under the Second Empire, of course, the process of deification was pushed still further, whilst the traumas of the Franco-Prussian War, 1914–18, 1940, the loss of the French colonies and, finally, the gradual loss of France's one-time cultural pre-eminence in a world that is ever more anglophone, ensured that for successive generations of Frenchmen and, indeed, French women, Napoleon remained a symbol of good times and national greatness. To this, meanwhile, must be added the pull of personal ambition: while many French historians have striven over the years to present the case against Napoleon, or, at least to offer a balanced view, over the years far too many have clearly seen praise of the emperor as the path to recognition (where, that is, the pull of the Napoleonic legend has been insufficient to work its fatal attraction anyway).[137] Given all this, it is hardly surprising that the wheel has turned in France so far that in certain quarters the bicentennial of 2015 was marked by claims that in the end it was Napoleon who had won the battle of Waterloo as it was his ideas that are triumphant in the Europe of today. This is, of course, utterly untrue – the European Community of today has nothing whatsoever in common with the *grand empire* – but such is the strength of the Napoleonic legend that there can be no doubt that Waterloo is a battle that will never cease having to be refought.[138]

Notes

Preface

1. D. Hamilton-Williams, *The Fall of Napoleon: the Final Betrayal* (London, 1994), pp. 294–5.
2. Whilst Hourtoulle admits that 'out of the 900,000 men taken into the armies, less than half were able … to take up their places beneath the eagles', the reader is left with the impression that the problem lay in nothing more than want of time on the one hand and want of weapons and equipment on the other. 'Some did not [report] to the army in time, before the end of the fighting. Raising troops was one thing, equipping, arming and training them was quite another.' Cf. F.G. Hourtoulle's *1814: the Campaign for France – the Wounded Eagle* (Paris, 2005), p. 4.
3. *Ibid*, p. 175. Marmont had been given the title 'Duke of Ragusa', and such was the notoriety of his behaviour in 1814, that the French language acquired a new verb for betrayal in the shape of *raguser*.
4. *Ibid*.
5. Hamilton-Williams, *Fall of Napoleon*, p. 293.
6. D. Hamilton-Williams, *Waterloo, New Perspectives: the Great Battle Reappraised* (Chichester, 1993), pp. 170–1. Unfortunately, more balanced writers have also sometimes fallen prey to this line of thinking, albeit usually in rather less extreme forms. Here, for example, is Andrew Field: 'There is no doubt that if Napoleon had been successful in destroying these two armies, the morale of the allies would have been seriously affected … It could certainly be argued that the determination of the allies would have been shaken to the point where they were prepared to make an accommodation with France, but, at worst, it would still buy the emperor considerable time, the time he needed to secure his position. And it is certainly true to say that a great victory would have galvanised the majority of France behind him.' Cf. A.W. Field, *Prelude to Waterloo: Quatre Bras – the French Perspective* (Barnsley, 2014), p. 11.
7. H. Houssaye, 1815: *Waterloo, 1815* (London, 1900), pp. 1–3.
8. Cf. G. Dallas, *The Final Act: the Roads to Waterloo* (New York, 1996); A. Schom, *One Hundred Days: Napoleon's Road to Waterloo* (London, 1992); S. Coote, *Napoleon and the Hundred Days* (New York, 2004).
9. Cf. M. Crook, '"Ma volonté est celle du people": voting in the plebiscite and parliamentary elections during Napoleon's Hundred Days, May-June 1815', *French Historical Studies*, XXXII, No. 4 (Fall, 1989), pp. 619–45; M. Crook, 'Uses of democracy: elections and plebiscites in Napoleonic France' in M. Grosse and D. Williams (eds.), *The French Experience from Republic to Monarchy, 1792–1824: New Dawns in Politics, Knowledge and Culture* (Basingstoke, 2000), pp. 58–71.
10. Cf. M.C. Thoral, *From Valmy to Waterloo: France at War, 1792–1815* (Houndmills, 2011); G. Daly, *Inside Napoleonic France: State and Society in Rouen, 1800–1815* (Aldershot, 2001); D. Sutherland, *The French Revolution and Empire: the Quest for a Civic Order* (Oxford, 2003).
11. The relevant volume here is P. Dwyer, *Citizen Emperor: Napoleon in Power, 1799–1815* (London, 2013).

Chapter 1

1. History does not relate how or why the French *pas de-charge* acquired this nickname in the British army, but so it did.

2. The account of the climax of the battle of Waterloo that follows is entirely fictional. In fact, the Guard did not attack for a further one-and-one-half hours, by which time the Prussian IV Corps was on the verge of breaking into the vital village of Plancenoit in the French right rear, and the Prussian I Corps just about to advance from Papelotte directly on Napoleon's headquarters at La Belle Alliance. Still worse, two battalions were left behind as a reserve, while the ten battalions that did make the final charge fanned out into three separate echelons and struck Wellington's line at different points in a manner that rendered defeat a virtual certainty. That said, in the sector immediately to the west of the famous crossroads, the situation was still bad enough, and that despite the fact that it was only hit by five battalions. Thus, the brigades of Vincke, Kielmansegg and Ompteda were routed, that of Halkett thrown into considerable disorder and the Nassauers and Brunswickers driven back pretty much in the manner described, the fact being that the only force to which real injustice has been done is Chassé's Dutch (though it is, of course, admitted that the exploits of Maitland's Guards and Adam's light infantry have necessarily had to be omitted, these having taken place in the vicinity of Hougoumont). At the same time, of course, it was not Wellington who lost his leg, but rather Uxbridge. For a recent analysis, cf. G. Glover, *Waterloo: the Defeat of Napoleon's Imperial Guard: Henry Clinton, the Second Division and the End of a 200-Year-Old Controversy* (Barnsley, 2015). As to what actually happened, the repulse of the Guard caused the whole of the French left wing to dissolve in panic, whereupon Wellington ordered the whole of his centre-right forward in a great counter-attack that in a few minutes had reached La Belle Alliance. However, the triumph was shared by the Prussians: at precisely the same moment, IV Corps finally drove the French from Plancenoit while I Corps struck diagonally into the heart of the French centre-right, it being these movements that ensured that the rout of the French became general.

3. P. Beslay (ed.), *Un officier d'état-major sous le premier empire: souvenirs militaires d'Octave Levavasseur, officier d'artillerie, aide de camp du Maréchal Ney, 1802–1815* (Paris, 1914), p. 304. The reference to forming square is almost certainly erroneous: one can only assume that, amidst the noise of battle, Levavasseur misheard what was being shouted. According to a story gleaned by Sir Walter Scott after the battle, meanwhile, the emperor rode along the main road to a spot only a few yards short of La Haye Sainte, and having made a speech in which he claimed that Wellington's infantry and cavalry had been completely destroyed, concluded by pointing straight up the highway and shouting, 'There, gentlemen, is the road to Brussels!' Cf. W. Scott, *Paul's Letters to his Kinsfolk* (Edinburgh, 1816), p. 106.

4. P. Fleury du Chaboulon, *Memoirs of the Private Life, Return and Reign of Napoleon in 1815* (London, 1820), II, p. 190.

5. H. de Mauduit, *Les derniers jours de la grande armée ou souvenirs, correspondance et documents inédites de Napoléon en 1814 et 1815* (Paris, 1848), II, pp. 418–19. It is worth offering a word of explanation here about the organization of the Imperial Guard in 1815. Some 19,000 strong in the campaign of Waterloo, this consisted of infantry, artillery and cavalry and was split into three sections – the so-called Young, Middle and Old Guards, of which the first and second consisted of infantry only, the second of infantry and cavalry, and the third of all three. Of these troops, however, only some of the infantry and artillery were involved in the final attack, including, specifically, the First Regiment of Grenadiers à Pied, the First Regiment of Chasseurs à Pied and one battery of the Horse Artillery of the Guard (all Old Guard) and the Second and Third Regiments of Grenadiers à Pied and the Second Regiment of Chasseurs à Pied (all Middle Guard). For a sumptuously illustrated analysis, cf. P. Juhel, *De l'île d'Elbe à Waterloo: la garde impériale pendant les cent-jours, 1815* (Paris,

2008). According to the account presented by General Drouot to the House of Peers on 22 June, the attack was to be seconded by the whole of such cavalry as remained to the Guard, but, like the rest of the French horse, the Guard's four regiments had been used up in the earlier mounted attacks, and it is difficult to know how much they could actually have achieved at this stage. Cf. address of General Drouot to the House of Peers, 23 June 1813, *cit*. L. Bonaparte, *La verité sur les cent jours* (Paris, 1835), p. 140.

6. That the intention was a general assault is confirmed by Philippe le Doulcet de Pontécoulant, an officer of the Foot Artillery of the Guard who was very close to Napoleon at the crucial moment and later wrote a detailed account of the campaign. Thus: 'He [i.e. Napoleon] ordered all the troops of the First Corps ... to resume their positions ... while on our left General Reille was instructed to form his entire corps in column of attack ... and overcome the extreme right of the [Anglo–Dutch] line with the bayonet.' P.G. le Doulcet de Pontécoulant, *Napoléon à Waterloo, 1815, ou précis rectifié de la campagne de 1815 avec des documents nouveaux et des pièces inédites*, ed. C. Bourachot (Paris, 2004), pp. 252–3.

7. Mauduit, *Derniers jours de la grande armée*, II, p. 417. The officer who remembered seeing Marshal Ney was Captain Pierre Robinaux of the Second Line, who had spent the entire day fighting in the vicinity of Hougoumont. Cf. G. Schlumberger (ed.), *Journal du route du Capitaine Robinaux, 1803–1832* (Paris, 2009), p. 180. Meanwhile, much confusion surrounds the name of General Drouet, who in many accounts appears either as 'Drouet d'Erlon' or 'D'Erlon'. The muddle arises from the fact that the then Jean-Baptiste Drouet was ennobled by Napoleon as Comte d'Erlon in January 1809. It being the practice of the author to refer to Napoleon's commanders not by their titles but rather their surnames (so Marshal Ney rather than Prince de la Moskowa and Marshal Soult rather than the Duc de Dalmacie), the form used in this work will be Drouet. However, care should be taken to avoid confusion with the General Antoine Drouot who commanded the Imperial Guard.

8. K. Leslie to W. Siborne, n.d, *cit*. H.T. Siborne (ed.), *Waterloo Letters: a Selection from Original and Hitherto Unpublished Letters Bearing on the Operations of the Sixteenth, Seventeenth and Eighteenth June 1815* (London, 1891), p. 356.

9. Cf. J. Kincaid to W. Siborne, 2 May 1839, *ibid*, p. 266.

10. The presence of this watershed often surprises visitors to the Waterloo battlefield. At its highest point actually higher than the ridge held by Wellington, it completely blocks the line of sight between Hougoumont and La Haye Sainte, whilst it also means that the field of fire possessed by the Anglo–Dutch artillery was in some places much reduced: stationed at precisely the point where the watershed bifurcated from Wellington's line in the direction of La Belle Alliance, Mercer tell us that enemy cavalry falling back from his position were soon covered by a 'swell in the ground'. Cf. A.C. Mercer, *Journal of the Waterloo Campaign kept throughout the Campaign of 1815* (London, 1870), I, p. 316; A. Barbero, *The Battle: a History of the Battle of Waterloo* (London, 2005), pp. 247–8.

11. Much controversy has been generated by the question of the performance of Wellington's artillery during the battle. After the battle Wellington seems to have been convinced that he had been let down by his gunners and famously made scant reference to them in the Waterloo dispatch. How far this was justified is unclear, but what does seem to be the case is that at some time between five and six o'clock two batteries posted overlooking the dell immediately west of La Haye Sainte were pulled out of the line on the pretext, genuine or otherwise, of replenishing their ammunition. Still worse, at around the same time two other batteries stationed in the immediate vicinity of La Haye Sainte were moved to reinforce the slopes above Hougoumont. All that was left to defend the sector now attacked by the Guard, then, were the batteries of Ross, Gardiner, Cleeves and Lloyd, all of which had been more-or-less shot up: Ross's battery, for example, had lost three of its six guns and Gardiner at

least one other. Cf. N. Lipscombe, *Wellington's Guns: the Untold Story of Wellington and his Artillery in the Peninsula and at Waterloo* (Oxford, 2013), pp. 372–82.

12. Mercer, *Journal of the Waterloo Campaign*, pp. 325–30 *passim*.

13. J. Kincaid, *Adventures in the Rifle Brigade in the Peninsula, France and the Netherlands from 1809 to 1815* (London, 1830), pp. 341–2. For an even more dramatic account of the situation in the Anglo-Dutch centre, we might turn to the chief of staff of the Second Netherlands Division, Pieter van Zuijlen van Nyevelt: 'The enemy started attacking again. Its artillery was advanced and hurled death and terror into our ranks. Our losses rapidly increased: already no reserve existed, all [having] been pushed ahead … The attack was most violent: entire battalions were destroyed and replaced by others. Regiment after regiment confronted each other and soon they were so reduced that others were called who in their turn had to give place to other victims. The slightest advantages of terrain were defended, and the smallest obstacles, which in other circumstances would not even have been noticed, were the object of fights upon which was expended the courage of a lion.' P. van Zuijlen van Nyevelt to J.V. Constant de Rebecque, 25 October 1815, *cit.* J. Franklin (ed.), *Waterloo: Netherlands Correspondence* (Ulverston, 2010), pp. 56–7.

14. G. Caldwell and R. Cooper, *Rifle Green at Waterloo* (revised edition; Leicester, 2015), p. 57.

15. M. Ney to J. Fouché, 26 June 1815, *cit.* L.R.B. Maizeau, *Vie du Maréchale Ney, Duc d'Elchingen, Prince de la Moskowa* (Paris, 1816), p. 180. Cf. also address of General Drouot to the House of Peers, 23 June 1815, *cit.* Bonaparte, *La verité sur les cent jours*, p. 140: from this we learn that the Guard were to 'march upon the enemy and overcome all those who resisted with the bayonet'. That Napoleon should have attempted precisely the sort of manoeuvre depicted here was very much the opinion of contemporary French analysts. Here, for example, is the view of General Frédéric Guillaume de Vaudoncourt, the editor of the prestigious *Journal des Sciences Militaires*: 'The Second Corps had been checked in front of the chateau of Goumont [i.e. Hougoumont], around which it had become somewhat bogged down. Meanwhile, although Marshal Ney was holding out at La Haye Sainte, he had not been able to advance a single pace from the position which he was occupying: all he had had been able to do, indeed, was to secure his gains with those troops that he had at his disposal. In this situation, the course of action that Napoleon ought to have adopted was to capitalise on the suspension of Bülow's attack [on Plancenoit] by launching a massive blow on the [Anglo-Dutch] centre. To achieve success in this respect, what was needed was to have the Second Corps and the whole disposable force of the Guard move on the plateau beyond La Haye Sainte with the utmost rapidity. To succeed, however, this attack would have had to be concluded before seven o'clock … Despite the losses that had suffered by Second Corps in the course of the day, Napoleon could by these means have concentrated 18,000 men to the left of La Haye Sainte. Given that the Duke of Wellington had no more reserves to send into the line, when the Prussian corps of General Zeithen arrived on the battlefield at half past seven, it would have been confronted, even swept away by a mass of fugitives.' F. Guillaume de Vaudoncourt, *Histoire des campagnes de 1814 et 1815 en France* (Paris, 1826), IV, pp. 74–5.

16. For the travails that befell Ompteda's brigade, see G. Glover, *Waterloo: Myth and Reality* (Barnsley, 2014), pp. 161–3. Over the fate of the Eighth Line, there appears to be some mystery: according to one account, its attack never got off the ground at all, the men rather being cut down by a sudden charge whist still changing formation from square to line. Cf. Barbero, *The Battle*, p. 242.

17. For a discussion of this episode, see P. de Wit, 'Hanoverian issues', accessed at <http://www.waterloo-campaign.nl/bestanden/files/notes/june18/note.14.pdf>, 29 May 2015.

18. Cf. 'Report of the First Hanoverian Infantry Brigade on its participation in the battle of La Belle Alliance', *cit.* G. Glover (ed.), *The Waterloo Archive, II: German Sources* (Barnsley, 2014), pp. 96–7.

19. T. Morris, *Recollections of Military Service in 1813, 1814 and 1815 through Germany, Holland and France including some Details of the Battles of Quatre Bras and Waterloo* (London, 1845), p. 149.

20. *Cit.* C. Divall, *Redcoats against Napoleon: the Thirtieth Regiment during the Revolutionary and Napoleonic Wars* (Barnsley, 2009), pp. 171–2.

21. *Ibid*, pp. 176–7.

22. For example T. Clayton, *Waterloo: Four Days that Changed Europe's Destiny* (London, 2014), p. 491.

23. The Hanoverian reports and other documents that are the best sources for this episode are confused and in many instances distinctly self-serving, but it is clear that the two brigades collapsed and took no further part in the battle. Cf. Glover (ed.), *The Waterloo Archive, II: German Sources*, pp. 103–14.

24. E. Macready to Lieutenant-Colonel Gawler, 30 November 1836, *cit.* Siborne (ed.), *Waterloo Letters*, p. 330.

25. *Cit.* Clayton, *Waterloo*, pp. 508–9. For the vicissitudes experienced by this battalion, cf. G. Fremont-Barnes, *Waterloo, 1815: the British Army's Day of Destiny* (Stroud, 2014), pp. 223–6; B. Cornwell, *Waterloo: the History of Four Days, Three Armies and Three Battles* (London, 2014), pp. 292–6.

26. E. Macready to Lieutenant-Colonel Gawler, 30 November 1836, *cit.* Siborne (ed.), *Waterloo Letters*, p. 331. As will be appreciated, Macready's account throws all the blame on the unnamed unit that 'rushed in' upon the battalion (presumably, the composite battalion made up of the Thirtieth and Thirty-Third Foot commanded by Elphinstone: see below). However, though other letters sent to Siborne by officers in the two battalions deny that any disorder took place, there is a strong sense that he is protesting a little too much: however orderly, the retreat to the hedge was clearly undertaken in a moment of panic. Also interesting is the fact that the battalion was deployed in square, this being a formation that was little suited to the task of fighting off an infantry attack.

27. Morris, *Recollections*, p. 153.

28. Why this unit was present in the centre is unclear, but one of its three battalions had been fighting at Hougoumont and the other two over on the extreme left wing at Papelotte and the need to reinforce the centre may have been seized upon as a good opportunity to bring the regiment back together again.

29. Barbero, *The Battle*, p. 230.

30. J.V. Constant de Rebecque, 'Account of the Waterloo campaign' (n.d.), *cit.* Franklin (ed.), *Waterloo: Netherlands Correspondence*, p. 19

31. *Ibid.*

32. *Cit.* P. Hofschroer, *1815, the Waterloo Campaign, the German Victory, II: from Waterloo to the Fall of Napoleon* (London, 1999), p. 137. Whilst the main points of this account are fair enough, to a certain extent Von Kruse was clearly writing for effect. Thus, the violent firefight of which he speaks at the beginning of the passage is pure invention, while the last sentence is a study in ambiguity and half-truth: rather than joining 'the small bodies of brave men on the plateau', the units mentioned all too clearly themselves turned and ran at the sight of the first battalion giving way. As for the reference to the French square, given that it is quite clear that the Guard at scarcely any point checked in its advance, Von Kruse must simply have been mistaken in what he remembered. That the attack was mounted at all was extremely creditable to the troops concerned. The first troops to arrive on the scene after the First Regiment was ordered to the centre was its first battalion, and this immediately came under terrible artillery fire that killed or wounded so many men that its commander, a Major von Weyhers, decided to try to capture the battery that was inflicting all the damage, the French guns being only 200 yards away. Arrayed in close column of

companies, the battalion charged forward bravely enough, but it was first hit by a blast of canister that badly wounded Von Weyhers, and then charged by some French cuirassiers who cut off two of its companies and put many of them to the sword. See Clayton, *Waterloo*, pp. 488–91.

33. For a description of the situation in this sector at this point, cf. J. Leach, *Rough Sketches in the Life of an Old Soldier during a Service in the East Indies, at the Siege of Copenhagen in 1807, in the Peninsula and the South of France in the Campaigns from 1808 to 1814 with the Light Division, in the Netherlands in 1815, including the Battles of Quatre Bras and Waterloo, with a Slight Sketch of the Three Years passed by the Army of Occupation in France* (London, 1831), pp. 390–2. Though under severe pressure, the riflemen never wavered, but held their ground admirably. However, their inability to intervene in what was going on the other side of the crossroads is illustrated by an incident in which a number of officers stationed on the battalion's right flank warned Leach that the French were showing signs of pushing up the main road through the cutting by which it crossed the summit of Mont Saint Jean and therefore asked permission to wheel their men to the right so that they could take the road in flank, only to be told by Leach that he had no men to spare for such a task and that any breakthrough would have to be dealt with by the much-tried Twenty-Seventh. Cf. Caldwell and Cooper, *Rifle Green at Waterloo*, p. 59.

34. Cf. N. Sale, *The Lie at the Heart of Waterloo: the Battle's Hidden Last Half Hour* (Stroud, 2014), pp. 73–6.

35. The issue of Wellington's generalship is possibly more open to question than might be imagined. From the beginning, Wellington had shown an exaggerated concern for his right flank and had placed the bulk of his forces, including most of his British infantry in echelon behind the chateau of Hougoumont; evidently enough, he feared a French attack there would turn his army's right flank. Yet, whilst the open ground west of Hougoumont was indeed inviting, it was never likely that the emperor would have attacked there, not least because, in the event of success, the Anglo–Dutch would have been driven back into the arms of the Prussians. Always far more likely, then, was a thrust against Wellington's centre designed to cut it in two, and it was, in fact, precisely such a plan that Napoleon set in motion, the object of the long battle round Hougoumont essentially being to pull troops away from Wellington's centre. Cf. Barbero, *The Battle*, pp. 80–1.

36. Mercer, *Journal*, p. 312.

37. W. Siborne, *The Waterloo Campaign, 1815* (fourth edition; Birmingham, 1894), p. 514. Discussing the battle with Lord Palmerston in the course of a visit to Paris by the latter in September 1815, Wellington gives a still more discreditable account of this incident, claiming that the troops concerned fired at him when he rode up to rally them. Cf. Viscount Palmerston, *Selections from Private Journals of Tours in France in 1815 and 1818* (London, 1871), p. 14. According to Wellington, the culprits were Nassauers rather than Brunswickers, but this appears to be the product of a lapse of memory on his part as no evidence has been found that the Duke was in the vicinity at the time of Kruse's counter-attack.

38. W. van Heerdt to E. van Löben Sels, 19 September 1841, *cit.* Franklin (ed.), *Waterloo: Netherlands Correspondence*, p. 159. As a sergeant in the Eighth Hussars later remembered, by the time that the Guard attacked, the regiment had lost all capacity to take part in the fighting. Thus: 'Towards the end of the affair we stood in battle order behind the Fourth Light Dragoon Regiment and were galled by severe cannon fire which inflicted severe losses on both men and horses. Soon the remnants of the regiments became intermixed. Colonel Duvivier and Brevet Major de Quaita were dismounted: to the last, being my company commander, I offered my horse, and I mounted a trooper's horse. We reassembled close to the Forêt de Soignies. At this time I saw the Prince of Orange being carried away wounded. His Royal Highness addressed us in a gracious way, saying "Forward Hussars!".

Cit. ibid, p. 164. Reading between the lines of these accounts, it is quite clear that what happened was nothing less than a panic-stricken rout that carried the Eighth to Waterloo and beyond. Meanwhile, the worst example among the German cavalry is the unit of well-heeled Hanoverian volunteers known as the Cumberland Hussars, this simply riding off the field en masse at about five o'clock in the afternoon under the lead of its colonel, Georg von Hake. Cf. P. de Wit, 'Hanoverian issues (1).: the retreat of the Cumberland Hussars at the battle of Waterloo', accessed at <http://www.waterloo-campaign.nl/bestanden/files/notes/june18/note.14.pdf>, 30 July 2015. In fairness, earlier in the afternoon the brigade of Dutch-Belgian heavy cavalry commanded by General Albert Trip van Zoudtlandt had lauched a successful counter-charge against some French cuirassiers but it had suffered heavy casualties and does not appear to have been fit for service thereafter. Cf. Barbero, *The Battle*, p. 222.

39. Cf. G. Glover (ed.), *Eyewitness to the Peninsular War and the Battle of Waterloo: the Letters and Journals of Lieutenant-Colonel the Honourable James Stanhope, 1803 to 1825* (Barnsley, 2010), pp. 177–92 *passim*. After the French were repulsed, the brigades of Vivian and Vandeleur did charge the enemy, but to believe that the situation here described could have been restored by a repeat of the attack of the Household and Union Brigades is clearly optimistic in the extreme: indeed, even with the whole of the French left wing falling apart in rout, the Twenty-Third Light Dragoons contrived to be driven back by some French cavalry that had ridden up to support the Guard. Cf. Glover, *Waterloo: the Defeat of Napoleon's Imperial Guard*, pp. 151–2.

40. W. Scott, *Paul's Letters*, pp. 91–2.

41. *Cit.* Barbero, *The Battle*, p. 258. One of the many creditable things about the forward wheel of Colborne's brigade that broke the second wave of the Guard in the real battle was the fact that, in charging forward in the manner that they did, the Fifty-Second were risking disaster from the same sort of flank attack that the same Sir John Colborne had been forced to endure at Albuera in 1811.

42. J. Shaw-Kennedy, *Notes on the Battle of Waterloo* (London, 1865), pp. 126–7.

43. D.H. Chassé to C. Nepveu, 27 April 1836, *cit.* Franklin (ed.), *Waterloo: Netherlands Correspondence*, p. 116. The reference to the horse artillery battery being commanded by Major van der Smissen is somewhat confusing. Technically speaking, Chassé is correct in that that officer commanded to the two batteries that formed the artillery component of the Third Netherlands Division. However, the horse artillery unit that took part in the attack was under the direct command of Carel Krahmer.

44. *Cit.* Clayton, *Waterloo*, p. 534.

45. L. van Delen to J.V. Constant de Rebecque, 11 November 1815, *cit.* Franklin (ed.), *Waterloo: Netherlands Correspondence*, p. 125.

46. A. Munter to his family, 22 July 1815, *cit. ibid*, p. 141.

47. Constant de Rebecque, 'Account of the Waterloo campaign', *cit. ibid*, p. 20.

48. In fairness to Detmer's troops, it is but justice to observe here that in reality their courageous counter-attack saved the day in the sector we are discussing. The way having been prepared by Krahmer's guns, they charged home and broke the three grenadier battalions facing them, later being reinforced by the troops of both Kielmansegg and Kruse, all of which returned to the fray. Such was the courage that the Dutch troops displayed, that it would be an injustice not to cite at least one account of their triumph. Hendrik Holle, then, was a lieutenant in the Sixth Militia: 'Now we were deployed in battle order. General Chassé came before our front … and had the muskets shouldered. He said, "In a few moments you will leave the second line and go over to the first. Keep calm, depend upon my command and especially your brave officers. The battle is not yet decided, but how great will it be for you to have taken part in its outcome." The repeated shouts of '"We would rather die for king

and country!" forced him to stop his speech. Within moments we formed close columns and … advanced. Our brave colonel was killed with some twenty others … When we had closed to within thirty paces of the enemy we … began to pour a heavy fire into them, which made them turn and run in the greatest confusion.' H. Holle to his sister, 10 July, 1815, *cit. ibid*, pp. 138–9. As for Wellington's loss of his leg, the victim was, of course, not the Duke, but Uxbridge. It should be observed, however, that the two were riding literally side by side when the latter was hit: a foot to the left and Waterloo might well have become an echo of Trafalgar.

49. It scarcely needs to be said that, in reality, this is a British account. Cf. Anon, *Some Particulars of the Battle at Waterloo in a Letter from a Sergeant in the Guards* (London, 1816), p. 6. However, had Detmers' men really been defeated, then it can be assumed that the scene would had have been very much as described here, whilst the reference to the French being in line is perfectly compatible with the use of *l'ordre mixte* referred to above. Even as it was, there appears to have been some confusion that endangered the advance, a captain in the Nineteenth Militia named Gerard Rochell later remembering that, as they closed with the enemy, the Dutch columns were badly disordered by an encounter with some fleeing British and Brunswick troops. Had the Guard responded with even a little more steel, then, the charge could well have been repulsed. Cf. G. Rochell, 'Account of military service and the Waterloo campaign', *cit.* Franklin (ed.), *Waterloo: Netherlands Correspondence*, p. 149.

50. This is something of a moot point: Uxbridge had done well in the campaign of La Coruña under Sir John Moore, been responsible for the charge that had overthrown Drouet's grand attack on Wellington's centre-left and in general shown great courage, while he was also well connected in Britain. That said, as he candidly admitted, it was in large part his fault that the Household and Union Brigades had got so out of control, whilst, having very publically eloped with the wife of his brother, Henry, he could expect little support from Wellington. At the same time, there was an obvious successor in the person of the highly popular and extremely competent commander of II Corps, Rowland Hill.

51. Connoisseurs of the battle of Waterloo will know well enough when this account slides into complete fantasy. It will be noted, however, that the changes that have been made to the narrative of the actual battle are actually very few. Thus, it is assumed, first, that Napoleon met Marshal Ney's request for reinforcements in the wake of the fall of La Haye Sainte, not with a snarling 'Troops? Troops? Do you expect me to make troops?', but rather with a recognition that the situation demanded that he threw in every single man that remained to him; second, that the attack of the Guard was handled in such a fashion that its troops hit the wavering defenders simultaneously and at one point only; and, third, that Ney chose not to follow the watershed leading from La Belle Alliance to the Anglo-Dutch position as he actually did, but rather to use it to cover his left flank from enfilading fire, the result being, of course, that his troops necessarily struck the very weakest point in Wellington's line. Underpinning the whole, meanwhile, is the firm belief that that the Guard advanced not in square, as is often claimed, albeit on grounds that have always seemed to the current author to be somewhat dubious, but rather in column: good troops could certainly manoeuvre in square, but to have attempted to attack in this formation would have been a recipe for disaster. For a French account that is quite specific that the Guards advanced in column, cf. Le Doulcet de Pontécoulant, *Napoléon à Waterloo*, p. 252.

52. For this incident, see Houssaye, *1815: Waterloo*, p. 177.

53. See B. O'Meara, *Napoleon in Exile or a Voice from Saint Helena: the Opinions and Reflections of Napoleon on the Most Important Events of his Life and Government in his own Words* (London, 1822), I, pp. 174–5.

54. C. Bourachot (ed.), *Souvenirs militaires du Captaine Jean-Baptiste Lemonnier-Delafosse* (Paris, n.d.), p. 224. For a highly amusing analysis of 200 years of French attempts to claim

Waterloo as a victory, cf. S. Clarke, *How the French won Waterloo (or think they did)* (London, 2015).

55. For a convincing exposition of such an argument, see A. Uffindell, 'Napoleon and Waterloo' in J. North (ed.), *The Napoleon Options: Alternate Decisions of the Napoleonic Wars* (London, 2000), pp. 187–202. It is interesting to note that, to allow Napoleon to secure even such success as he is permitted to obtain in this chapter, Uffindell felt it necessary to augment his forces with one of the corps that in reality he sent to pursue Grouchy. A weakness in the case the author makes, meanwhile, is that that commander is assumed simply to have sat passively on his hard-won gains of the day before at Limale throughout 19 June. Whilst Grouchy was clearly out of his depth in the position which he had been given in the wake of Ligny, this is stretching the imagination more than somewhat: by crossing the River Dyle and forcing back Thielmann's right flank, Grouchy had opened the way for his men to attack Blücher in the rear, and it is difficult to believe that he would not have exploited this opportunity.

56. Anon, *The Journal of the Three Days of the Battle of Waterloo, being my own Personal Journal of what I saw and of the Events in which I played a Part in the Battle of Waterloo and Retreat to Paris* (London, 1816), pp. 43–4.

57. *Ibid*, p. 25.

58. D.G. Chandler, *The Campaigns of Napoleon: the Mind and Method of History's Greatest Soldier* (London, 1966), p. 1092.

59. *Ibid*, p. 1067. The idea that the attack was postponed till late in the morning to allow the ground to dry out enough for the French artillery to be able to manoeuvre effectively, and, more particularly, make the best proper use of its firepower, is clearly preposterous: by the time the rain stopped at dawn on 18 June, it had been coming down in torrents for the best part of twenty-four hours and it is clear that such was the weather that there was no chance of the ground hardening to any significant degree. If the Army of the North did not attack, then, it was rather because, delayed by the rain, a large part of its forces were still coming up from Quatre Bras. However, one technical issue that may have been of genuine significance is that of the infantry's muskets. As Drouet says, 'The troops had passed the whole night in the open without the slightest shelter. Not a musket could be fired.' J.B. Drouet, *Le Maréchal Drouet, Comte d'Erlon: vie militaire écrit pour lui-même* (Paris, 1844), p. 96. Indeed, according to the same observer, having come up to the front line to view the situation, the emperor made specific reference to the issue in the orders that he gave him for the morning. Thus, 'Have the men prepare some food and get their arms in order, and then we will see towards midday.' *Cit. ibid*, p. 97.

60. Bülow's recalcitrance is admitted even by pro-Prussian historians. For a good example, see Hofschroer, *Waterloo to the Fall of Napoleon*, p. 98.

61. The extent to which this criticism is fair is open to much doubt. In brief, it is the opinion of Gareth Glover, one of the most careful and thorough of the numerous authors who published books on Waterloo in the course of the 2015 bicentenary, that, given that he had been specifically ordered to pursue the Prussians, it is unreasonable to argue that Grouchy should have, as is often argued, marched to the sound of the guns, not the least of the problems being that, had he attempted to do so, he would probably not have arrived in time to have much of an effect. That said, the marshal does not get off the hook entirely, it being Glover's view that he should have pressed home his advance on Wavre with much more determination and vigour than was actually the case, and, further, that, had he done so, he could well have restricted the relief column dispatched by Blücher to the single corps of General Bülow. Numbering 30,000 men, as it did, this would still have been a great help, but as Glover says, 'whether this would … have been sufficient to destroy Napoleon is difficult to answer'. Cf. Glover, *Waterloo; Myth and Reality*, p. 215.

62. Chandler, *Campaigns of Napoleon*, p. 1018.
63. With some justice, Drouet points out that Napoleon never intended to fight a battle at Quatre Bras, Ney's role rather being entirely defensive. As he said, 'The occupation of Quatre Bras had no other goal than to occupy the English army with the aim of stopping it from sending any detachments in aid of the Prussians.' Drouet, *Le Maréchal Drouet*, p. 95.
64. *Cit.* Chandler, *Campaigns of Napoleon*, p. 1056. For Drouet's view of the affair, meanwhile, cf. Drouet, *Le Maréchal Drouet*, pp. 95–6. As might be expected, this exonerates Drouet of any guilt and throws the whole blame on Ney.
65. A. Uffindell, *The Eagle's Last Triumph: Napoleon's Victory at Ligny, June 1815* (London, 1994), p. 200.
66. For an excellent summary of this affair, cf. Glover, *Waterloo: Myth and Reality*, p. 77. The chaos produced by the order sent to Ney was even worse than is outlined here. In brief, when Drouet's corps appeared at Ligny, it did not do so where Napoleon anticipated that Ney's troops would appear – i.e. beyond and in the rear of the Prussian right wing – but rather directly behind the French troops attacking that sector of the line. Scared that the new arrivals represented not reinforcements but rather Allied troops marching to attack their rear, the men concerned broke off their attack in confusion, the result being that the Prussians were given a much-needed breathing space. As to who the fault was for all this, it is Glover's contention that it was the *aide de camp* charged with carrying that sparked the whole incident off. In brief, issued at 3.15 p.m., the order that he was carrying said nothing at all about Drouet's troops in particular, but rather directed Ney to manoeuvre with his whole force against the Prussian right flank and rear. However, the *aide de camp*, unsurprisingly enough, was eager to ingratiate himself with the emperor, and, having apparently come across Drouet by pure chance, deliberately ignored protocol and persuaded him to march directly on Ligny without first informing Ney. As if all this was not bad enough, a by-blow of this excess of zeal was that Drouet's corps turned east much too far to the south, the result being its arrival on the battlefield in the wrong place and with the effects we have just outlined. Of course, the very fact that Napoleon had to summon Ney at all is suggestive of just how little aware he had been that what he was facing at Ligny was nothing less than the entire Prussian army.
67. C. Chesney, *Waterloo Lectures: a Study of the Campaign of 1815* (second edition, enlarged; London, 1869), p. 131.
68. V. Cronin, *Napoleon* (London, 1971), p. 503.
69. Field, *Prelude to Waterloo*, p. 194.
70. Glover, *Waterloo, Myth and Reality*, p. 91.
71. Uffindell, 'Napoleon and Waterloo', p. 202.

Chapter 2

1. N. Bonaparte, *The Waterloo Campaign edited and translated by Somerset de Chair* (London, 1957), p. 154.
2. Hamilton-Williams, *Waterloo, New Perspectives*, pp. 170–1.
3. Field, *Prelude to Waterloo*, p. 11.
4. R. Muir, *Britain and the Defeat of Napoleon* (London, 1996), p. 374.
5. O. Connelly, *Blundering to Glory: Napoleon's Military Campaigns* (Wilmington, Delaware, 1987), p 201.
6. *Ibid.*
7. D. Gates, *The Napoleonic Wars, 1803–1815* (London, 1996), p. 269.
8. M. Price, *Napoleon: the End of Glory* (Oxford, 2014), p. 257.
9. H.A.L. Fisher, *Napoleon* (London, 1912), pp. 225–6.
10. D. Dufour de Pradt, *The Congress of Vienna* (London, 1816), p. xi.

11. R. Metternich (ed.), *Memoirs of Prince Metternich* (New York, 1881), III, pp. 254–5.

12. P. Dwyer, *Citizen Emperor: Napoleon in Power, 1799–1815* (London, 2013), p. 526. For Talleyrand's view of the situation, cf. Dallas, *The Final Act*, p. 298.

13. A.L.C. La Garde-Chambonnas, *Anecdotal Recollections of the Congress of Vienna*, ed. A.D.V.M. Fleury (London, 1902), pp. 415–17.

14. C.F. de Méneval, *Memoirs to Serve for the History of Napoleon I from 1802 to 1815*, ed. R.H. Sherard (London, 1895), III, pp. 349–50.

15. J.C. Hobhouse, *The Substance of Some Letters written by an Englishman Resident in Paris during the Last Reign of the Emperor Napoleon* (London, 1816), I, p. 14. Eager to witness what he conceived of as a triumph of liberty in the face of the *ancien régime*, Hobhouse had responded to the news of Napoleon's escape from Elba by hastening to Paris from which he proceeded to dispatch a long series of letters to Byron and other contacts, alternately providing a running commentary on events in France and penning eloquent pleas for Napoleon to be left in peace.

16. A.W. Neithardt von Gneisenau, *The Life and Campaigns of Field-Marshal Prince Blücher of Wahlstatt from the Period of his Birth and First Appointment in the Prussian Service down to his Second Entry into Paris in 1815* (London, 1815), pp. 395–6.

17. Price, *Napoleon: the End of Glory*, p. 256.

18. H. Nicholson, *The Congress of Vienna: a Study in Allied Unity, 1812–1822* (London, 1948), pp. 229–30.

19. *Ibid*, p. 230.

20. C. Stewart to G. Jackson, 4 April 1815, *cit*. Lady Jackson (ed.), *A Further Selection from the Diaries and Letters of Sir George Jackson, K.C.H, from 1809 to 1816* (London, 1873), II, p. 485. Cf. also R. Muir, *Wellington: Waterloo and the Fortunes of Peace, 1814–1852* (London, 1815), pp. 23–4.

21. Dallas, *The Final Act*, p. 315.

22. *Cit*. W.E. Channing, *Memoirs of Napoleon Bonaparte* (London, 1840), pp. 363–4. Of course, the fact that Napoleon embarked on so sustained an attempt to stave off war cannot but beg the question of his sincerity. In the short term, at least, the French ruler should be afforded the benefit of the doubt as he not only had an army to rebuild but was also confronted by massive internal unrest, and many of his apologists have therefore implied that Waterloo was a battle that need never have been fought. Cf. A. Roberts, *Napoleon the Great* (London, 2014), p. 746. Amongst the emperor's entourage, however, there was much gloomy speculation. Hortense de Beauharnais, for example, had privately urged Napoleon to appoint Caulaincourt as Foreign Minister on the grounds that this might serve as a guarantee of his good faith, and thereby gain France the peace she needed, but, while the emperor had acted on her suggestion, he had otherwise been totally dismissive: Caulaincourt was 'too much inclined to favour foreigners' and Hortense herself a mere woman who should not concern herself with politics. Encountering Caulaincourt shortly afterwards, Hortense told him of her fears and begged him to act. '"Everyone knows that you are the only one who has always taken the side of peace before the emperor. Your advice is now more necessary than ever. You must oppose ideas of fresh conquests with all your strength." "I am sure you are right," replied Caulaincourt, "but what can I do if the emperor has not changed and decides that he wants to regain Belgium." "My God! He isn't talking of this already?" "No, but I am concerned that he was received with so much enthusiasm. A little resistance would have been better. How can a man not feel that anything is possible to him after such a welcome? And would he not wish to attempt anything and everything?"' J. Hanoteau (ed.), *Mémoires de la Reine Hortense* (Paris, 1927), II, p. 338.

23. Price, *Napoleon: the End of Glory*, pp. 250–6.

24. For a strong statement of this position, cf. C.J. Esdaile, *Napoleon's Wars: an International History, 1803–1815* (London, 2007). On the period 1813–14 in particular, cf. Price, *Napoleon the End of Glory*, pp. 71–250 *passim*.

25. P. Schroeder, *The Transformation of European Politics, 1763–1848* (Oxford, 1994), pp. 549–50. Meanwhile, it is worth noting that Schroeder's position is supported by the equally eminent Jeremy Black. Thus: 'For Napoleon and his supporters in France, the international situation in 1815 was a baleful consequence of his earlier quest for glory and his destructiveness towards others. Napoleon's attempt … to overturn this … ran up against not only the superior resources of his opponents, but also the weight of recent history.' J. Black, *The Battle of Waterloo: a New History* (New York, 2010), p. 36. According to Méneval, indeed, even Napoleon thought war was inevitable: 'He told me that all that was happening could not surprise him, and that it as in the nature of things that, in making his attempt, he had understood that he could appeal only to the courage and patriotism of the nation and to his sword.' Cf. Méneval, *Memoirs*, III, p. 445.

26. Fleury de Chaboulon, *Memoirs*, II, pp. 12–19.

27. Roberts, *Napoleon the Great*, p. 742; R. M. Johnston (ed.), *In the Words of Napoleon: the Emperor Day by Day* (London, 2002), p. 308.

28. Dwyer, *Citizen Emperor*, p. 523.

29. J. Rapp, *Memoirs of General Count Rapp, first Aide-de-Camp to the Emperor* (London, 1823), p. 343.

30. Cf. Bonaparte, *La verité sur les cent jours*, p. 34.

31. For all this, cf. Nicholson, *Congress of Vienna*, pp. 148–81; Schroeder, *Transformation of European Politics*, pp. 523–38; A. Zamoyski, *Rites of Peace: the Fall of Napoleon and the Congress of Vienna* (London, 2007), pp. 365–411; M. Jarrett, *The Congress of Vienna and its Legacy: War and Great-Power Diplomacy* (London, 2013), pp. 96–131.

32. *Cit.* Fleury de Chaboulon, *Memoirs*, II, p. 20.

33. *Ibid*, pp. 31–2. The Basel talks are particularly interesting in that they originated in an attempt by Metternich to resolve the crisis by seeking to persuade Napoleon's Minister of Police, Fouché, to launch a coup against the emperor. Though scarcely friendly in its intent, this scheme does suggest that war was not the be-all-and-end-all of at the very least the Austrian chancellor's policy. The French ruler would have to go, certainly, but if this could be done without recourse to all-out hostilities, then so much the better.

34. Nicholson, *Congress of Vienna*, p. 232. According to the leading proponent of German unification, Heinrich vom Stein, who was an eyewitness, whilst certainly very angry, Alexander even affected a façade of magnanimity when he summoned Metternich to his presence to explain the matter. Thus: 'Metternich, so long as we live, no word must pass between us again on this affair. We have other things to do now. Napoleon is returned and therefore our alliance must be firmer than ever.' *Cit.* J.R. Seeley, *Life and Times of Stein or Germany and Prussia in the Napoleonic Age* (Cambridge, 1878), III, pp. 328–9.

35. Méneval, *Memoirs*, III, p. 433.

36. *Cit.* Gneisenau, *Life and Campaigns of Field-Marshal Prince Blücher*, pp. 397–8.

37. F. Maitland, *Narrative of the Surrender of Buonaparte and of his Residence on Board HMS Bellerophon with a Detail of the Principal Events that occurred in that Ship between the 24th of May and the 8th of August 1815* (London, 1826), pp. 116–17.

38. Cf. Hamilton-Williams, *Waterloo, New Persepctives*, pp. 68–9.

39. Jarrett, *Congress of Vienna*, pp. 160–1.

40. That this was the chief hope of Napoleon, there is at least a strong possibility. To quote a passage from one of the many monologues he delivered on Saint Helena, 'My intentions were to attack and to destroy the English. This, I knew, would produce a change of Ministry. The indignation against them [i.e. the Ministers] for having caused the loss of 40,000 of

the English army would have excited such a popular commotion that they would have been turned out. The people would have said, "What is it to us who is on the throne of France, Louis or Napoleon? Are we to sacrifice all our blood in endeavours to place on the throne a detested family? No: we have suffered enough. Let them settle it among themselves." They would have made peace. The Saxons, Bavarians, Belgians, Wurtemburgers, would have joined me. The coalition was nothing without England. The Russians would have made peace, and I should have been quietly seated on the throne.' *Cit.* O'Meara, *Napoleon in Exile*, I, pp. 175–6.

41. For two accounts of political reaction to the return of Napoleon, see R. Muir, *Wellington: Waterloo and the Fortunes of Peace* (London, 2015), pp. 25–7; Black, *Battle of Waterloo*, pp. 66–9.

42. For a brief discussion, see A. Bryant, *The Age of Elegance, 1812–1822* (London, 1950), pp. 352–3.

43. H.T. Dickinson, 'Popular conservatism and militant loyalism, 1789–1815', in H.T. Dickinson (ed.), *Britain and the French Revolution, 1789–1815* (London, 1989), p. 124.

44. A. Alison, *Travels in France during the Years 1814 and 1815 comprising a Residence at Paris during the Stay of the Allied Armies and at Aix during the Landing of Bonaparte* (Edinburgh, 1815), I, pp. 204–6.

45. Cf. T. Chapman, *The Congress of Vienna: Origins, Processes and Results* (London, 1998), p. 50.

46. *Cit.* E.F. Henderson, *Blücher and the Uprising of Prussia against Napoleon, 1806–1815* (London, 1911), p. 269. So angry had Blücher been at the terms of the Treaty of Paris, that he had actually resigned his commission.

47. *Cit.* Fleury de Chaboulon, *Memoirs*, II, p. 30.

48. Zamoyski, *Rites of Peace*, p. 445.

49. Hanoteau (ed.), *Mémoires de la Reine Hortense*, II, p. 355. Napoleon was still insisting on Saint Helena that the peoples of Europe would have joined him. See O'Meara, *Napoleon in Exile*, pp. 424–5.

50. Thanks especially to Michael Rowe, we have a considerable corpus of material on the Rhineland in the Napoleonic epoch. Cf. M. Rowe, 'Between empire and home town: Napoleonic rule on the Rhine, 1799–1814', *Historical Journal*, XLII, No. 3 (September 1999), pp. 643–74; M. Rowe, 'France, Prussia or Germany? The Napoleonic Wars and shifting allegiances in the Rhineland', *Central European History*, XXXIX, No. 4 (December 2006), pp. 611–40; M. Rowe, 'Resistance, collaboration or third way? Responses to Napoleonic rule in Germany', in C.J. Esdaile (ed.), *Popular Resistance in the French Wars: Patriots, Partisans and Land-Pirates* (London, 2005), pp. 67–90.

51. P. von Muffling, *Passages from my Life, together with Memoirs of the Campaign of 1813 and 1814* (London, 1853), pp. 204–5.

52. Zamoyski, for example, tells us that a number of guards officers drank the health of Napoleon at a gathering at Hesse-Darmstädt, but, without further details, it is impossible to say what this represented: whilst the men concerned may have been sincere in toasting the emperor, and, by extension, desirous of his success, the gesture could just as easily been an ironic manifestation of pleasure that war had returned and, with it, the opportunities which they had been denied by the coming of peace. Cf. Zamoyski, *Rites of Peace*, p. 445.

53. D. Lardner, *Poland* (London, 1831), p. 258. For a brief discussion of Poland in the Hundred Days, cf. J. Czubaty, *The Grand Duchy of Warsaw, 1807–1815: a Napoleonic Outpost in Central Europe* (London, 2015), pp. 193–4.

54. F. Rillier, 'Les cent jours en Belgique et la France', in A. Jullien (ed.), *Soldats suisses au service étranger* (Geneva, 1910), I, p. 244.

55. S. Coote, *Napoleon and the Hundred Days* (London, 2004), p 172.

56. *Cit.* Seeley, *Life and Times of Stein*, III, p. 327.

57. Cf. C. Clark, *Iron Kingdom: the Rise and Downfall of Prussia, 1600–1947* (London, 2006), pp. 374–5.

58. G. Jackson to Lady Jackson (?), 27 March 1815, *cit.* Jackson (ed.), *Further Selection from the Diaries and Letters of Sir George Jackson*, II, p. 480.

59. F. Guizot, *Memoirs to Illustrate the History of my Time* (London, 1858), I, pp. 63–4.

60. Cf. Zamoyski, *Rites of Peace*, p. 445.

61. Diary of G. Jackson, 26 February 1815, Jackson (ed.), *Further Selection from the Diaries and Letters of Sir George Jackson*, p. 474; P. Hofschroer, *1815, the Waterloo Campaign, I: Wellington, his German Allies and the Battles of Ligny and Quatre Bras* (London, 1998), pp. 50–2.

62. For the views of Muffling on the Saxon mutiny, cf. Muffling, *Passages from my Life*, pp. 208–9.

63. Hobhouse, *Substance of Some Letters*, I, pp. 14–17. In the wake of the fall of Napoleon, some support was expressed in Belgium for the idea of union with France, but it is very clear that those concerned were not remotely nostalgic for *le grand empire*. Cf. Anon, *Lettre d'un belge a Sa Majesté Louis XVIII, Roi de France* (Brussels, 1814).

64. Material on the experiences of Belgium in the Revolutionary and Napoleonic period is not extensive. However, for the initial years, see J. Polasky, 'The French Revolution exported: a Belgian perspective', *Consortium on Revolutionary Europe Proceedings*, XVI (1986), pp. 203–12; J. Polasky, 'Traditionalists, democrats and Jacobins in Revolutionary Brussels', *Journal of Modern History*, LVI, No. 2 (June 1984), pp. 227–62; J. Polasky, *Revolution in Brussels, 1787–1793* (Hanover, New Hampshire, 1987).; M. Rapport, 'Belgium under French occupation: between collaboration and resistance, July 1794–October 1795', *French History*, XV, No. 1 (March 2002), pp. 53–82.

65. M. de Marbot, *The Memoirs of Baron de Marbot* (London, 1892), II, pp. 441–2.

66. J.H. Adeane and M. Grenfell (eds.), *Before and after Waterloo: Letters from Edward Stanley, sometime Bishop of Norwich* (London, 1907), p. 196. One may, indeed, go still further here. Thus: 'It was in vain that General Maison, an active, brave and experienced officer, commanded a French corps in the north. He had too small a body of troops and found himself under the necessity of abandoning Brabant to its fate … Besides, the attitude of the Belgians seemed absolutely hostile towards the French, for at Malines, Brussels and almost all the towns of Brabant, the inhabitants received the Allies with every demonstration of joy.' Cf. M. de Beauchamp, *An Authentic Narrative of the Invasion of France in 1814* (London, 1815), I, p. 297.

67. For a discussion of a different case, cf. J. Dhondt, 'The cotton industry at Ghent during the French Revolution' in F. Crouzet, W. Chaloner and W. Stern (eds.), *Essays in European Economic History* (London, 1969), pp. 15–52.

68. Alison, *Travels in France*, I, pp. 286–7.

69. *Ibid*, p. 287.

70. *Ibid*, p. 279.

71. Beauchamp, *Authentic Narrative*, I, p. 96.

72. Anon, *Journal of the Three Days of the Battle of Waterloo*, p. 23. One issue that needs to be considered here is the impact that feeding the substantial Allied forces cantoned on their soil had on the Belgian population. Not least because they were fed from Britain, relations with the British appear to have been reasonable, but the Prussians, who rather aimed to live off the country, behaved in a much harsher manner. Whose fault this was is unclear and it may be that the Dutch government should bear a share of the blame – Gneisenau, indeed, attempted to throw the whole of it upon them – but the brutality with which many Prussian troops behaved after Waterloo cannot but lead one to suspect that he was protesting too much: Belgium had, after all, been a part of France under the empire,

while the inhabitants of the area which the Prussians were Walloons rather than Flemings. Whether the resentment, or, indeed, the problem, was significant enough to create the risk of an uprising is another matter. For all this, cf. Hofschroer, *1815, the Waterloo Campaign, I:*, I, pp. 118–21.

73. W. Scott, *Paul's Letters*, pp. 59–60.
74. E. Lecky (ed.), *Un général hollandais sous le premier empire: mémoires du Général Baron de Dedem de Gelder, 1774–1825* (Paris, 1900), p. 339.
75. Alison, *Travels in France*, I, pp. 237–8.
76. Adeane and Grenfell (eds.), *Before and after Waterloo*, p. 221.
77. For all this, cf. S. Schama, *Patriots and Liberators: Revolution in the Netherlands, 1780–1813* (London, 1977), pp. 622–35. The issue of conscription, in particular, is covered by J. Joor, 'A very rebellious disposition: Dutch experience and popular protest under the Napoleonic regime, 1806–1813' in A. Forrest *et al* (eds.), *Soldiers, Citizens and Civilians: Experiences and Perceptions of the Revolutionary and Napoleonic Wars, 1790–1820* (Basingstoke, 2009), pp. 181–204.
78. For a recent study of the contribution of the Dutch-Belgians, cf. V. Baker-Smith, *Wellington's Hidden Heroes: the Dutch and Belgians at Waterloo* (Oxford, 2015).
79. *Cit.* Houssaye, *Waterloo*, p. 45. It is worth noting that looting was a problem even before the French army crossed the frontier. Here, for example, is an anonymous account penned by a French veteran of the campaign: 'With a total disregard for their unhappy countrymen … the French soldiers treated the farmers and peasantry with the most extreme rigour, and, considering pillage as one of their indisputable rights, almost made a merit of practising it in every excess. Everywhere they went, they sacked the houses, and, under the pretext of seeking for provisions, broke open the doors, committed outrages upon the inhabitants, and seized whatever suited their purposes and thus, at one and the same moment, rendered themselves unfit for war and indisposed the country against them. It is truly afflicting to acknowledge that the greater part of the officers opposed only a feeble resistance to this infamous pillage … Nor was it, perhaps, possible to repress those disorders in an army which had been formed to them by the habit and example of twenty years. It was, in fact, by this system of brigandage that the Emperor Napoleon had succeeded in so firmly attaching the soldiers to his name and cause.' Cf. Anon, *Journal of the Three Days of the Battle of Waterloo*, pp. 13–15.
80. Anon, *Journal of the Three Days of the Battle of Waterloo*, pp. 23–4.
81. A.H. Atteridge, *Joachim Murat: Marshal of France and King of Naples* (London, 1911), pp. 278–83. Murat's adventure is held to have played a considerable role stiffening the resistance of the Allies to Napoleon in that it seemed to offer convincing proof that Napoleon was planning war on Europe right from the very start. In fact, however, it is all but totally irrelevant: the great powers had decided on war well before Murat made his move, the most that can be said being that the Tolentino campaign provided them with useful propaganda material.
82. One may in fact take this point still further. Not only were Italian nationalists few and far between, but the majority of the handful that existed were erstwhile Jacobins who were bitterly hostile to Napoleonic rule on the grounds that it was a betrayal of the republican spirit of the 1790s. Cf. R. Johnston, *The Napoleonic Empire in Southern Italy and the Rise of the Secret Societies* (London, 1904).
83. Lord Burghersh to Lord Castlereagh, 31 January 1815, *cit.* R. Weigall (ed.), *Correspondence of Lord Burghersh, afterwards Eleventh Earl of Westmorland, 1808–1840* (London, 1912), p. 93.
84. *Ibid*, pp. 93–4.
85. Atteridge, *Joachim Murat*, pp. 289–94.

86. The reference is to a chapter title in Best's *War and Society in Revolutionary Europe, 1770–1870* (London, 1982).
87. Guizot, *Memoirs*, I, pp. 64–5.

Chapter 3

1. Hindsight is, of course, a wonderful thing. For contemporaries of Waterloo, it was difficult to feel such confidence. Jorgen Jurgensen was a Danish seafarer who witnessed the battle from close at hand: 'Whatever different opinions may exist respecting that remarkable event itself, there can only be one as to the benefits resulting from it. Had the English been totally defeated, the Prussians must have retreated. In addition to the numerous and formidable army which Bonaparte had already collected, there were 300,000 men in France ready to take up arms, who only waited the issue of a first battle before they declared themselves. All the countries to the south [*sic*] of the Rhine would shortly have been occupied.' J. Jurgensen, *Travels through France and Germany in 1815, 1816 and 1817 comprising a View of the Moral, Political and Social State of those Countries* (London, 1817), I, pp. 12–13.
2. C.B. von Sachsen-Weimar to E. van Löben Sels, 29 August 1841, *cit.* Franklin (ed.), *Waterloo: Netherlands Correspondence*, p. 77. The reference to the camp at Bayen is a mystery, alas.
3. For details of the siege of Antwerp in 1584–5, cf. C. Duffy, *Siege Warfare: the Fortress in the Early-Modern World, 1494–1660* (London, 1979), pp. 76–80. It might here be asked whether the Anglo-Dutch army would have been capable of resuming the offensive in the wake of a defeat at Waterloo. However, whilst it is likely that subsequent commanders would have exercised great caution, they would almost certainly have been in receipt of substantial reinforcements, many of them of much better quality than the troops that made up the original British contingent: at the time of the battle, indeed, at least sixteen infantry battalions that had fought in the Peninsula were still in transit from America, while others could have been called back from stations such as Gibraltar. Deeply frustrated at having missed out on the first chance British troops had ever had to do battle with Napoleon, the men involved would beyond doubt have arrived in Antwerp eager for the fray. For example, according to Sir George Bell, his battalion was most disappointed when it was not sent to Belgium immediately. Cf. B. Stuart (ed.), *Soldier's Glory, being* Rough Notes of an Old Soldier *by Sir George Bell Arranged and Edited by his Kinsman, Brian Stuart* (London, 1956), p. 148.
4. For the strategic situation that pertained in respect of Cádiz in the wake of the fall of Andalucía in 1810, cf. C.J. Esdaile, *Outpost of Empire: the Napoleonic Occupation of Andalucía, 1810–1812* (Norman, Oklahoma, 2012), pp. 338–98 *passim.*
5. That this was the case is implicitly acknowledged even by Blücher's chief of staff, Auguste von Gneisenau. Thus: 'Prince Blücher … resolved to give battle in his position at Sombreffe, although his Fourth Corps was not yet in line and his army, in point of numbers … much inferior to that of the French'. Cf. Gneisenau, *Life and Campaigns of Field-Marshal Prince Blücher*, p. 403.
6. For a discussion of the Trachenberg plan, cf. J.P. Riley, *Napoleon and the World War of 1813: Lessons in Coalition Warfighting* (London, 2000), pp. 118–20. That it was very likely that the same scheme would be followed once again is suggested by the fact that its progenitor, Schwarzenburg's chief of staff, Josef Radetzky, continued to serve in the same capacity in 1815.
7. Houssaye, *Waterloo*, p. 6.
8. Implicit in these orders was a clear attempt to remobilise the whole of the class of 1815, i.e. the so-called *marie-louises*, who, as we shall see, played so prominent a role in the historiography of the campaign of 1814. However, it should be noted that these men were

expected to fight because, if only in theory, they were already 'on the books': there was no attempt to call men up afresh.

9. Houssaye, *Waterloo*, p. 5. Also worth quoting is Hobhouse; 'There is … in the army such a spirit of independence, and so weary are the superior officers of the perpetual labours of the last war, so anxious are the new men to assure what they have obtained, that no-one here thinks that, under any supposition, Napoleon would be able to persuade … his troops … to carry a war beyond the Rhine.' Hobhouse, *Substance of Some Letters*, I, p. 205. Napoleon himself tacitly admitted that there were many problems, suggesting to Davout that it might be easier to get the men concerned back if they were promised that they could serve in the Guard, and ordering the formation of mobile columns composed of twenty-five gensdarmes and 100 infantrymen in each department to round up the most recalcitrant. H. Plon and J. Dumaine (eds.), *Correspondance de Napoléon I publiée par ordre del'Empereur Napoléon III* (Paris, 1858–69), XXVIII, p. 205.

10. With regard to the volunteers, some accounts reduce their numbers to a mere 6,000, whilst it should be noted here that many were not Frenchmen, but rather mere flotsam and jetsam: there were, for example, survivors of some of the many foreign contingents that had still been fighting for Napoleon in 1814 and also even a battalion of erstwhile slaves who had gravitated to the port of Bayonne. Also interesting, meanwhile, is the fact that Napoleon was forced to curtail the activities of the recruiting parties sent to bring in men on the grounds that their activities might antagonize the public and even provoke disorder. Cf. Houssaye, *Waterloo*, p. 5; Schom, *One Hundred Days*, p. 200. For the attempt to reach out to men discharged from the service prior to 1814, cf. Houssaye, *Waterloo*, p. 9.

11. Houssaye, *Waterloo*, pp. 7–8. According to Alan Schom, the number was even smaller, a mere 90,000 in fact. Cf. Schom, *One Hundred Days*, p. 200. It need hardly be said that admirers of Napoleon take a different view: 'In communes which furnished only eight to the conscription (Malmaison, for instance), sixty have marched, and in a neighbouring commune forty have gone instead of the former five. Three of the gardeners of the imperial chateau of Malmaison … marched at an hour's warning. No reluctance is manifested in the recruits: if there were any, these means of recruiting an army would be impracticable.' Hobhouse, *Substance of Some Letters*, I, p. 213.

12. Hobhouse, *Substance of Some Letters*, I, pp. 41–2. It is particularly worthy of note here that, although the matter is dressed up with talk of providing it with elite companies of grenadiers and *voltigeurs*, no fewer than 25,000 regular troops had to be diverted to the National Guard to stiffen its battalions even to the extent that they could be relied on for garrison duty. If this is so, the inference can only be that Napoleon regarded the National Guard as being militarily useless, and, very probably, politically unreliable. Cf. M. Lamarque, *Mémoires et souvenirs du Général Lamarque* (Paris, 1835), I, p. 71.

13. Not counting the National Guard, there were another 25,000 troops engaged in internal security operations, particularly in the Vendée.

14. Glover, *Waterloo: Myth and Reality*, p. 14.

15. According to Elting, a Prussian cavalry unit got a nasty shock at Ligny when it charged a ragged-looking battalion that it assumed to be National Guard only to discover that it was a veteran formation of the Middle Guard. Cf. J.R. Elting, *Swords Around a Throne: Napoleon's Grande Armée* (London, 1988), p. 651. The most complete guide to the uniforms worn in the Waterloo campaign is constituted by P. Haythornthwaite *et al, Uniforms of Waterloo in Colour* (Poole, 1974). Meanwhile, such was the degree to which the army was unprepared for war in 1815 that it has to be recognized that taking the field as early as the middle of June was by no means the least achievement of Napoleon's career. As Drouet remarked in his memoirs, 'It would be difficult to describe the activity that one saw on all sides and in every branch of the service.' Drouet, *Le maréchal Drouet*, p. 94.

16. The strongly pro-Napoleonic Maximien Lamarque claims that by the time that the campaign began, no fewer than ten manufactures employing 6,000 workers had been set up in Paris alone for the repair and fabrication of muskets, and that the end of the year would have seen production reach at least 300,000, but whether such figures could have been sustained without a restoration of the measures employed by Carnot in 1793 is a moot point. Cf. Lamarque, *Mémoires et souvenirs*, I, p. 40.

17. S. Monick (ed.), *The Iberian and Waterloo Campaigns: the Letters of Lieutenant James Hope, 92nd (Highland). Regiment, 1811–1815* (Heathfield, 2000), p. 272. Cf. also Leach, *Rough Sketches*, pp. 393–4: 'Fighting under the eye of Napoleon, and feeling what a great and important stake they contested for, will account for their extraordinary perseverance and valour, and for the vast efforts which they made for victory.'

18. Hobhouse, *Substance of Some Letters*, I, p. 395.

19. Cf. Bonaparte, *La verité sur les cent jours*, p. 36.

20. J. Thiry, *Les débuts de la seconde restauration* (Paris, 1947), p. 121.

21. Chandler, *Campaigns of Napoleon*, p. 1023.

22. Uffindell, *The Eagle's Last Triumph*, p. 40.

23. Elting, *Swords Around a Throne*, p. 654.

24. Schlumberger (ed.), *Journal de route de Capitaine Robinaux*, pp. 176–7.

25. Cf. Barbero, *The Battle*, pp. 35–6.

26. Anon, *Journal of the Three Days of the Battle of Waterloo*, pp. 15–16.

27. F. McLynn, *Napoleon: a Biography* (London, 1997), p. 617. Setting aside the pressures of the campaign, one issue that was certainly weighing heavily on Napoleon's spirit was the question of his wife and son: not only had Francis I refused to allow the pair to travel to Paris to be reunited with him, but in early April Marie-Louise herself had sent him a message requesting a separation. Meanwhile, McLynn's point in respect of Napoleon's feelings in the wake of Quatre Bras and Ligny is corroborated by Drouet. Thus: 'Wanting to do battle with the English, the emperor made up a force of around 40,000 men under General [*sic*] Grouchy and ordered him to follow closely on the heels of the Prussian army and make sure of the point on which it was directing its retreat. That done, he immediately marched with the rest of his army to rejoin Marshal Ney at Quatre Bras. However, this place had just been evacuated by the English. Coming across me some way short of the position that they had occupied, the emperor said to me in a tone of profound chagrin, "France is lost."' Drouet, *Le maréchal Drouet*, p. 96.

28. A.J. Butler (ed.), *The Memoirs of Baron Thiébault, late Lieutenant-General in the French Army* (London, 1896), II, p. 421. In fairness, it has to be said that this image is challenged by Hobhouse whose descriptions of various reviews he witnessed during his sojourn in Paris paint a picture of a Napoleon much energised by once more being in the presence of his soldiers, and, what is more, a Napoleon who was adept as ever into charming them into a state of the utmost excitement and adulation, accepting petitions here, handing out a cross of the *legion d'honneur* there, and tweaking a nose or pinching a cheek somewhere else. E.g. Hobhouse, *Substance of Some Letters*, I, pp. 394–5. At a grand review that was held in the Tuileries on 4 June in which the eagles of every regiment in the army were paraded before him, for example, he is supposed to have spoken to almost every single one of the 10,000 men there, and in general to have affected an extremely jovial and kindly manner. *Ibid*, pp. 448–9.

29. *Cit.* Field, *Prelude to Waterloo*, p. 28.

30. H.L. Carnot (ed.), *Mémoires sur Carnot par son fils* (Paris, 1863), II, p. 423.

31. Maitland, *Narrative of the Surrender of Buonaparte*, pp. 208–10.

32. Houssaye, *Waterloo*, p. 293. Also worth noting here is the view of François Guizot: 'It has been pretended even by some of his warmest advisers that at this period the genius

and energy of Napoleon had declined, and they sought in his tendency to corpulence, in his attacks of languor, in his long slumbers, the explanation of his ill fortune. I believe this approach to be unfounded and the pretext frivolous. I can discover in the mind and actions of Napoleon during the Hundred Days, no symptoms of infirmity. I find in both his accustomed superiority. The causes of his ultimate failure were of a deeper cast: he was not, as he had long been, upheld and backed by general opinion and the necessity of security and order felt throughout a great nation; he attempted, on the contrary, a mischievous work, a work inspired only by his own passions and personal wants, rejected by the morality and good sense, as well as by the true interests of France. He engaged in this utterly egotistical enterprise with contradictory means, and in an impossible position. From thence came the reverses he suffered and the evil he produced.' Guizot, *Memoirs*, I, pp. 65–6. Meanwhile, someone who had a close view of the emperor, albeit of a somewhat brief nature, and was much impressed, was the municipal archivist of the city of Grenoble, Jacques Champollion-Figeac. What we see, indeed, is a whirlwind of activity. 'That self-same day – 8 March – the emperor worked all morning ... At one and the same time the most pressing orders were sent out, the most urgent problems set on the road to solution and decrees emitted in the imperial name sent out to every place that acknowledged his rule ... At every instant papers were brought to him: he took them from their bearers and either scanned through them or read them in detail. Almost all of them were immediately torn up and thrown under the table where the petitions thus thrown aside lay heaped on top of one another like bones in some devastated cemetery ... The freedom of his spirit was visible ... in the calm that marked his countenance, in the attention that he paid to every detail.' J.J. Champollion-Figeac (ed.), *Fourier et Napoléon: Egypte et les cent jours – mémoires et documents inédits* (Paris, 1844), pp. 225–31 *passim*.

33. Chandler, *Campaigns of Napoleon*, pp. 1091–2. If Chandler berates Napoleon for his failings in the course of the campaign, Lamarque goes even further. While regarding Napoleon as infinitely preferable to the Bourbons and willing at every step to give him the benefit of every possible doubt in political terms, he was at root a republican, and was bitterly critical not so much of the manner in which Napoleon conducted the campaign, but rather of the very thinking that underpinned it. In his eyes, rather than attacking, Napoleon should rather have adopted a defensive strategy while at the same time proclaiming a republic – something that he claimed would have elicited pro-French risings across Europe – and making every effort to arm the people and prepare the way for guerrilla warfare, whereas, in fact, 'whether driven by his unquiet spirit, or irritated by the petty *contretemps* that he faced at home, the emperor decided to essay a grand coup, to play a game of *trente et quarante* [a form of blackjack], in short to consign both his existence as a sovereign and that of France as a nation to the throw of a dice.' Lamarque, *Mémoires et souvenirs*, I, pp. 32–4, 77. However, whilst the suggestion that Napoleon was no longer capable of rational thought in 1815 is interesting, it can be argued that his conduct was very much part and parcel of a wider picture that is visible throughout his career. Cf. C.J. Esdaile, 'De-constructing the French Wars: Napoleon as anti-strategist', *Journal of Strategic Studies*, XXXI, No. 4 (August 2008), pp. 515–52.

34. Roberts, *Napoleon the Great*, p. 744.

35. Cf. Schom, *One Hundred Days*, pp. 195–9.

36. A. de Saint-Chamans, *Mémoires du Général Comte de Saint-Chamans, ancien aide de camp du Maréchal Soult, 1802–1832* (Paris, 1896). pp. 34–5. In accusing Soult of cowardice, Saint Chamans, an embittered individual who seems to have been convinced that the marshal could have done more to further his career, may have gone too far, but it is clear that in battle Soult had a habit of producing ambitious plans and then failing to see that they were executed effectively

37. H. d'Espinchal, *Souvenirs militaires, 1792–1814*, ed. F. Masson and E. Boyer (Paris, 1901), pp. 46–8. Note that even D'Espinchal has to admit that Soult could be 'severe, brusque and, on occasion, greedy'. *Ibid*, p. 46. Meanwhile, according to several veterans of the Spanish war, one unfortunate divisional commander was subjected to so brutal a dressing-down by him that the unfortunate man immediately committed suicide. Cf. L.F. Lejeune, *Memoirs of Baron Lejeune, Aide de Camp to Marshals Berthier, Davout and Oudinot*, ed. A. Bell (London, 1997), p. 74; S. Blaze, *Mémoires d'un apothicaire sur la guerre d'Espagne pendant les années 1808 à 1814* (Paris, 1828). II, p. 216.

38. A.L.A. Fée, *Souvenirs de la guerre d'Espagne, dite de l'independance, 1809–1813* (Paris, 1856), pp. 135–6.

39. Chandler, *Campaigns of Napoleon*, p. 1021. According to Elting, who provides a considerable list of the evidence of his carelessness, Soult 'was accused (possibly with some exaggeration) of having made more mistakes in four days than Berthier had in nineteen years'. Elting, *Swords Around a Throne*, p. 655.

40. To this end, it is worth noting that even the hostile Saint-Chamans was forced to admit that Soult 'forgot nothing, and was as much abreast of the smallest details as he was of the greatest military operations'. Saint-Chamans, *Mémoires*, p. 34.

41. Predictably enough, Soult's most recent English-language biographer, Peter Hayman, is vigorous in his refutation of such remarks, pointing out that, in contrast to his diatribes in respect of Ney and Grouchy, Napoleon is not recorded as having uttered any criticism of Soult on Saint Helena. Cf. P. Hayman, *Soult: Napoleon's Maligned Marshal* (London, 1990), p. 232.

42. Lamarque, *Mémoires et souvenirs*, I, p. 11.

43. Ney's behaviour in 1815 has come in for much comment. According to an admiring chronicler writing in the very wake of his execution, the problem was rather guilt. Thus: 'Though still without fear, he was no longer without reproach: the memory of just one action had poisoned his entire life. He marched ahead of the man who had cost him so many sacrifices, but he did so without joy, without energy, in the style of a man who was attempting to expunge a deep stain with which his conduct had besmirched him.' Maizeau, *Vie du Maréchal Ney*, p. 152.

44. One commander whose absence Napoleon particularly lamented was Marshal Murat. Indeed, on Saint Helena, he went so far as to claim that, had Murat been present at Waterloo, the day would have been won. Thus: 'I informed him that … it was asserted that Murat had imputed the loss of the battle of Waterloo to the cavalry not being properly employed, and that he had said that if he (Murat). had commanded then the French would have gained the victory. "It is very probable", replied Napoleon. "I could not be everywhere, and Murat was the best cavalry officer in the world. He would have given more impetuosity to the charge. There wanted but very little, I assure you, to gain the day for me. Break two or three battalions, and in all probability Murat would have effected this." O'Meara, *Napoleon in Exile*, II, pp. 60–1. Finally, another commander who was under par in 1815 was Mortier: appointed to the command of the Imperial Guard, on the very eve of the campaign he fell ill and had to be replaced by Drouot.

45. The only English-language biography of Vandamme takes a favourable view of him as a commander and implies that he was treated as a scapegoat in the wake of Kulm, but it scarcely makes a strong claim for him as a general. Thus: 'A dedicated career soldier and an excellent division and corps commander, he was a thorn in the side of … Napoleon and most every officer under whom he served. Like Patton, he was the man any king would want to lead troops into battle, but he was outspoken to a fault. His exalted opinion of his own military talents and his low esteem of his contemporaries resulted in numerous problems with those above him in the hierarchy.' Cf. J.G. Gallagher, *Napoleon's Enfant Terrible:*

General Dominique Vandamme (Norman, Oklahoma, 2008), p. 3. Meanwhile, Drouet's memoirs suggest a man constantly ready to shift the burden of guilt to other shoulders and unfailingly keen to portray himself as an over-looked military genius, as witness, for example, his account of Vitoria. Cf. Drouet, *Le maréchal Drouet*, pp. 76–9.

46. Bourachot (ed.), *Souvenirs militaires du Capitaine Jean-Baptiste Lemonnier-Delafosse*, p. 201; this translation owes something to the one offered by Andrew Field; cf. Field, *Prelude to Waterloo*, p. 18. Much the same point is made by Méneval, who claims that 'certain of the principal leaders of the army, demoralised by the recollection of the events of 1814, had lost that energy and confidence which often forces the hand of success'. Méneval, *Memoirs*, III, p. 452. For a recent discussion of the marshals, see D.G. Chandler (ed.), *Napoleon's Marshals* (London, 1986). Meanwhile, for details on officers such as Vandamme and Drouet, cf. J. Tulard, *Dictonnaire Napoléon* (Paris, 1989) and A. Pigeard, *Les Etoiles de Napoléon* (Paris, 1996).

47. Schlumberger (ed.), *Journal de route de Capitaine Robinaux*, p. 177.

48. In fairness, the French army recovered from Waterloo surprisingly well. Grouchy's troops returned to France undefeated – indeed, they even inflicted a number of reverses on the Prussians – and showed real spirit in their response to the Allied attacks on Paris, while considerable defiance was also visible elsewhere, a few fortresses even hanging on into the autumn. However, it is important to note that none of the men concerned had gone through the experience of Waterloo and that awareness of just how crushing the defeat had been was limited: writing in his journal at some point after the battle Stanhope noted that the French would barely admit they had been beaten, let alone decisively crushed. *Cit.* Glover (ed.), *Eyewitness to the Peninsular War and the Battle of Waterloo*, p. 179.

49. Blücher had gone into the campaign of Waterloo with 117,000 men. Of these 20,000 had been lost in one way or another at Ligny whilst it may be assumed that at least another 10,000 could have gone the same way in the fighting at Wavre and Plancenoit, to which should be added a considerable number of deserters. Let us say, then, that 80,000 men were still with the colours when the army fell back across the Rhine, but this figure takes no account of the 26,000 troops from the armies of those German states that had been assigned to the command of the Prussians who had been deployed to watch the valley of the river Moselle under General Freidrich von Kleist, and could easily have been marched to join Blücher. Of the quality of these last troops we need say no more than that, like many of the foreign auxiliaries in Wellington's army at Waterloo, they were schooled in the tactics of the *Grande Armée*, but capable of little more than second-line duties. As in 1814, then, they were to spend the campaign of 1815 blockading French fortresses, but, for all that, they would still have come as a useful reinforcement.

50. Hofschroer, *1815: the Waterloo Campaign I*, I, p. 59.

51. *Ibid*, p. 69. Ever determined to maximise Prussian glory, it has to be said that Hofschroer has something of an axe to grind here: in brief, the more that the problems faced by the Prussian army in 1815 are emphasized, the greater appear Blücher's achievements at Waterloo, and the easier it is to explain away defeat at Ligny. At all events, Muffling provides us with a much more positive picture. Thus: 'The troops of the Army of the [Lower] Rhine turned out in good state from their winter quarters, the recruits well drilled … well fed, healthy, well clothed, in the best state of discipline and eager for war. The troops recently placed on the Prussian footing were all in the same condition, i.e. the free corps transformed into battalions of the line, the Russo-German Legion, the regiments of the Grand Duchy of Berg and the still unapportioned Saxons.' Muffling, *Passages from my Life*, p. 224. On the other hand, he does agree that there was considerable jealousy of Gneisenau: 'The more it became known that Gneisenau really commanded the army and that Blücher merely acted as an example as the bravest in battle and the most indefatigable in exertion, understanding

only to stimulate others by fiery speeches, the louder became the discontent of the four generals who had commanded armies in 1814 and were senior in commission to Gneisenau.' *Ibid*, p. 225. Meanwhile, other observers were genuinely impressed with what they saw. Here, for example, is Lord Palmerston's account of a review which he attended outside Paris on 4 September 1815: 'I went at eight to a sham fight of the Prussians in the plain of Grenelle about two miles out of Paris. There appeared to be about 20,000 men of all arms. They were drawn up in two bodies, and, after some evolutions of cavalry, one line advanced and the other retired ... The manoeuvres were said to represent the later attack of the Prussians upon Paris ... The troops manoeuvred with great quickness and accuracy and the Duke of Wellington was marched pleased with their manner of deploying from column.' Palmerston, *Selections from Private Journals of Tours in France*, p. 12.

52. Despite its age, the most detailed guide to the reform of the Prussian army in the wake of Jena and Auerstädt remains W. Shanahan, *Prussian Military Reforms, 1786–1813* (New York, 1945), but this can usefully be supplemented by G.A. Craig, *The Politics of the Prussian Army, 1640–1945* (Oxford, 1955), pp. 37–62, and W.M. Simon, *The Failure of the Prussian Reform Movement, 1807–1819* (New York, 1971), pp. 145–80. On the subject of conscription, in particular, meanwhile, cf. D. Walter, 'Meeting the French challenge: conscription in Prussia, 1807–1815', in D. Stoker *et al* (eds.), *Conscription in the Napoleonic Era: a Revolution in Military Affairs?* (Abingdon, 2009), pp. 24–45. Finally, for a detailed discussion of the Prussian tactical system, cf. P. Hofschroer, *Prussian Napoleonic Tactics* (Oxford, 2011).

53. *Cit*. A. Brett-James (ed.), *Europe against Napoleon: the Leipzig Campaign, 1813, from Eyewitness Accounts* (London, 1970), p. 45.

54. *Cit. ibid*, p. 47. For a modern biography, cf. M. Leggiere, *Blücher: Scourge of Napoleon* (Norman, Oklahoma, 2014).

55. Alison, *Travels in France*, I, pp. 280–1.

56. *Cit*. Brett-James (ed.), *Europe against Napoleon*, pp. 21–2.

57. *Cit. ibid*, p. 41.

58. Cf. Clark, *Iron Kingdom*, p. 366.

59. Mauduit, *Derniers jours de la grande armée*, II, p. 66. For a detailed account of the battle of Ligny, cf. Uffindell, *The Eagle's Last Triumph*, pp. 91–115.

60. For a description of the fighting, cf. Hofschroer, *1815*, II, pp. 116–24.

61. R.C. Seaton (ed.), *Notes and Reminiscences of a Staff Officer chiefly relating to the Waterloo Campaign and to Saint-Helena Matters during the Captivity of Napoleon* (London, 1903), p. 56.

62. Mauduit, *Derniers jours de la grande armée*, II, pp. 436–7.

63. Mercer, *Journal of the Waterloo Campaign*, II, pp. 57–8. Moving closer to Paris, the same author came across similar devastation at a place called Garges; *ibid*, pp. 71–2. Another British observer was an ensign of the Guards named Rhys Gronow: 'We perceived, on entering France, that our allies the Prussians had committed fearful atrocities on the defenceless inhabitants of the villages and farms which lay in their line of march. Before we left La Belle Alliance, I had already seen the brutality of some of the Prussian infantry, who hacked and cut up all the cows and pigs which were in the farmyards ... On our line of march, whenever we arrived at towns or villages through which the Prussians had passed, we found that every article of furniture in the houses had been destroyed in the most wanton manner: looking glasses, mahogany bedsteads, pictures ... and mattresses had been hacked, cut, half-burned and scattered about in every direction, and, on the slightest remonstrance of the wretched inhabitants, they were beaten in the most shameful manner and sometimes shot.' N. Bentley (ed.), *Selections from the Reminiscences of Captain Gronow* (London, 1977), p. 53.

64. For reasons of space, attention will here be confined to the Austrians and Russians. However, like their counterparts who served with Prussians on the Rhine, the troops from Bavaria, Wurttemburg and Baden were efficient enough and certainly capable of taking on such tasks as the blockade of fortresses.
65. Cf. G. Rothenberg, *Napoleon's Great Adversaries: the Archduke Charles and the Austrian Army, 1792–1814* (London, 1982), pp. 103–22.
66. This feat was achieved by the addition of reserve battalions to infantry regiments that were only mobilised on the outbreak of war. In 1809 a *landwehr* had also been formed, but this experiment had been only partially successful, and no attempt was made to repeat it in 1813.
67. Appointed Allied commander-in-chief in September 1813, Schwarzenburg earned many plaudits as an Eisenhower *avant la lettre*. As the highly-respected military reformer Herman von Boyen noted, 'I would call the selection of Prince Schwarzenburg to be commander-in-chief not only of the Army of Bohemia, but of all the military forces, a special favour of destiny. As a commander he appeared to lack decision and wide vision, and he may well have depended more than was desirable upon the views of his associates, but his incalculable merit in the particular situation was not only to have borne with composure the presence of the three sovereigns and the numerous plans put forward by their staffs, and to have set them diplomatically aside, but also to have striven constantly to reconcile the most contradictory views.' *Cit.* Brett-James (ed.), *Europe against Napoleon*, pp. 82–3.
68. *Cit. ibid*, p. 83.
69. Cf. Rothenberg, *Napoleon's Great Adversaries*, pp. 187–90.
70. Rapp, *Memoirs*, pp. 357–74. It should also be noted that the Austrians very easily saw off Murat at the battle of Tolentino.
71. Not the least of the improvements was the formation of a modern general staff on the Prussian model. For the reforms of the period prior to 1812, cf. D. Lieven, *Russia against Napoleon: the Battle for Europe, 1807 to 1814* (London, 2009), pp. 102–20. Useful as an overview, meanwhile, is A. Mikaberidze, 'The Russian army', in G. Fremont-Barnes (ed.), *Armies of the Napoleonic Wars* (Barnsley, 2011), pp. 36–56.
72. *Cit.* Brett-James (ed.), *Europe against Napoleon*, p. 66.
73. For a detailed biography of Barclay, cf. M. and D. Josselson, *The Commander: a Life of Barclay de Tolly* (Oxford, 1980).
74. Ménéval, *Memoirs*, III, pp. 443–6.

Chapter 4
1. A. Fain, *The Manuscript of 1814: a History of Events which led to the Abdication of Napoleon written at the Command of the Emperor* (London, 1823), pp. 42–4.
2. For a sharp critique of Houssaye's work, cf. P. Geyl, *Napoleon For and Against* (London, 1949), pp. 150–7. For example, '*1814* gives a very detailed account of events of that year, the campaign in France, the abdication at Fontainebleau. The writer does not enter into discussions as to intentions and responsibilities. With all the greater assurance does he distribute blows and favours. The previous events which had landed Napoleon and France in that tragic situation, he brushes aside in his introduction, with a remark supposed to have been made by a peasant: "It is no longer a question of Bonaparte. Our soil is invaded: let us go and fight." From this reasoning – or refusal to reason – follows naturally the thesis of complete solidarity between France and Napoleon. It leads the writer to take up a position of fierce hatred against all those who thought that in this crisis France could be saved at the cost of Napoleon. When finally, after miracles of leadership and energy, Napoleon's resistance against the Allied armies is beginning to collapse, he appears at Fontainebleau … as the true hero of tragedy, abandoned by cowards.' *Ibid*, p. 150.
3. H. Houssaye, *Napoleon and the Campaign of 1814* (London, 1914), p. 3.

4. *Ibid*, p. 5.
5. *Ibid*, pp. 38–43 *passim*.
6. *Ibid*, pp. 24–6.
7. *Ibid*, pp. 7, 19.
8. *Ibid*, pp. 508–9.
9. *Ibid*, p. 150. A similar ambiguity may be observed with respect to the already-mentioned stand by Pacthod's two National Guard divisions in the face of overwhelming numbers of enemy at La Fère-Champenoise. Compelled to form square by their opponents who were composed entirely of cavalry, Pacthod's men stood their ground for some time and then managed to pull off the difficult feat of retiring some distance in the very midst of the enemy. On one level this might be seen as courage, yet in square troops clinging together in this fashion was as much a response to terror as it was to appeals to defy the enemy: quite simply, even though it might be being subjected to heavy fire, a square offered the illusion of safety. For a good account, cf. A. Mikhailofsky-Danilevsky, *History of the Campaign in France in 1814* (London, 1839), pp. 312–16.
10. R. Ashby, *Napoleon against Great Odds: the Emperor and the Defenders of France, 1814* (Santa Barbara, California, 2010), pp. 6–7.
11. Roberts, *Napoleon the Great*, p. 690.
12. *Cit.* O'Meara, *Napoleon in Exile*, II, p. 68.
13. Y. Gac, 'Plouider et les guerres napoléoniennes', <http://memoire.plouider.infini.fr/spip.php?article28&lang=fr>, accessed 22 April 2015.
14. A. Pigeard, 'La conscription sous le premier empire', <http://www.napoleon.org/fr/salle_lecture/articles/files/conscription_le_Premier_Empire1.asp>, accessed 22 April 2015.
15. W.D. Fellowes, *Paris during the Interesting Month of July 1815: a Series of Letters addressed to a Friend in London* (London, 1815), p. 22.
16. Cf. I. Woloch, 'Napoleonic conscription: state power and civil society', *Past and Present*, No. 111 (May 1986), pp. 101–29.
17. Blaze, *Mémoires d'un apothicaire*, I, p. 2.
18. Daly, *Inside Napoleonic France*, pp. 240–1.
19. Schlumberger (ed.), *Journal de route du Capitaine Robinaux*, p. 13. Utterly miserable, Robinaux deserted, within a few weeks of his enlistment, only to be recaptured within a few hours; *ibid*, pp. 17–21. What is particularly notable is the absence of any sense that the army represented an opportunity, a gateway, indeed, to a career open to talent. For young men of property and education, by contrast, service in the army was a very different matter. Whilst some continued to hang back, others never gave the matter a second thought. 'I joined the service in 1804 at the age of twenty', recalled the Duc de Fézensac. 'I had wanted to embrace a military career for a long time, but various circumstances had prevented my parents for giving their consent any sooner.' Duc de Fézensac, *Souvenirs militaires de 1804 à 1814* (Paris, 1863), p. 7.
20. Fée, *Souvenirs de la Guerre d'Espagne*, pp. 1–2.
21. Cf. <http://cahiersdelachanson.free.fr/textes%20de%20chanson/1810_Le_conscrit.htm>, accessed 22 April 2015; for the lyrics of *Le retour de l'amant français*, cf. Alison, *Travels in France*, I, pp. 141–2.
22. M. Birkbeck, *Notes on a Journey through France from Dieppe through Paris and Lyons to the Pyrenees and back through Toulouse in July, August and September, 1814* (London, 1815), pp. 83–4.
23. F.R. de Chateaubriand, *The Memoirs of François René, Vicomte de Chateaubriand, sometime Ambassador to England* (London, 1902), III, p. 66. An erstwhile *émigré* who had fought in the army of Condé in 1792, Chateaubriand was, of course, a bitter critic of Napoleon, indeed,

perhaps the most bitter and outspoken critic of his day. Yet his remarks here cannot be gainsaid, supported as they are by the very similar views espoused by François Poumiès de la Siboutie, a young surgeon from Périgord of Jacobinical tendencies who had recently finished his studies in Paris. Thus: 'Napoleon's name was reviled everywhere ... There was hardly a family ... that had not to weep for one or more of its members. "As long as Napoleon is at the head of affairs", they grumbled, "we shall never have anything but war: no peace is possible while his insatiable ambition survives." Herein lies the true explanation for our lack of patriotism at the crucial moment.' F.L. Poumiès de la Siboutie, *Recollections of a Parisian (Docteur Poumiès de la Siboutie) under Six Sovereigns, two Revolutions and a Republic, 1789–1863*, ed. A. Branche and A. Dagoury (London, 1911), p. 126.

24. B. Fitzpatrick, *Catholic Royalism in the Department of the Gard* (Cambridge, 1983), p. 7.

25. For general discussions of the French economy under Napoleon, cf. Sutherland, *French Revolution and Empire*, pp. 339–46; G. Ellis, *The Napoleonic Empire* (second edition; Houndmills, 2003), pp. 107–19; Thoral, *From Valmy to Waterloo*, pp. 147–74.

26. N. Plack, 'Napoleon's land-grab', *History Today*, LXIII, No. 3 (March 2013), pp. 6–7.

27. Alison, *Travels in France*, I, pp. 4–5, 12.

28. T. Bowdler, *Diary of an Excursion to France in the Months of August and September 1814* (Edinburgh, 1814), pp. 10–14.

29. Cf. Price, *Napoleon: the End of Glory* (Oxford, 2014), pp. 171–2.

30. Duc d'Audiffret-Pasquier (ed.), *Mémoires du Chancelier Pasquier* (Paris, 1895–1914), II, pp. 100–1.

31. A.M. Chamand, *The Adventurous Life of Count Lavallette, Bonaparte's Aide-de-Camp and Postmaster-General, by Himself*, ed. L. Aldersey White (London, 1936), II, p. 25.

32. G. Lequin (ed.), *Memoirs of the Comte de Rambuteau* (London, 1904), p. 105.

33. A. Dry, *Reims en 1814 pendant l'invasion* (Paris, 1902), p. 57.

34. G. Stiegler (ed.), *Memoirs of Marshal Oudinot, Duc de Reggio compiled from the Hitherto Unpublished Souvenirs of the Duchesse de Reggio* (New York, 1897), pp. 252–3.

35. L.V.L. Rochechouart, *Souvenirs sur la révolution, l'empire et la restauration* (Paris, 1892), p. 328.

36. Poumiès de la Siboutie, *Recollections of a Parisian*, p. 126.

37. Price, *Napoleon: the End of Glory*, pp. 173–4.

38. In Seine Inférieure, for example, ever more efficient policing ensured that banditry completely disappeared from the region from late 1806 to late 1813. However, the months following Leipzig saw a number of attacks on the roads together with many reports of armed gangs. Cf. Daly, *Inside Napoleonic France*, p. 79.

39. B. Barère, *Memoirs of Bertrand Barère, Chairman of the Committee of Public Safety during the Revolution* (London, 1896), III, p. 168.

40. R. Ledos de Beaufort (ed.), *Personal Recollections of the late Duc de Broglie, 1785–1820* (London, 1887), I, pp. 241–2.

41. Fain, *Manuscript of 1814*, p. 19. The quote is from a speech of Regnault de Saint Jean d'Angely in the legislative assembly.

42. *Ibid.*

43. T.R. Underwood, *A Narrative of Memorable Events in Paris preceding the Capitulation and during the Occupancy of that City by the Allied Armies in the Year 184, being Extracts from the Journal of a Detenu who continued a prisoner on parole in the French Capital from the Year 1803 to 1814, also Anecdotes of Bonaparte's Journey to Elba* (London, 1828), pp. 2–3.

44. Beauchamp, *Authentic Narrative*, I, pp. 64–5.

45. Dry, *Reims en 1814*, pp. 58–9.

46. *Ibid*, pp. 74–82.

47. A. Blayney, *Narrative of a Forced Journey through Spain and France as a Prisoner of War in the Years 1810 to 1814* (London, 1814), II, pp. 330–1.

48. The revolt of the *corps législatif* was a seminal event that deserves a little more attention than it has been given here. In brief, the root of this affair was a piece of monumental mismanagement on the part of Napoleon. In brief, hoping to manage any subsequent debate so as to engineer a vote in his favour, and, in particular, a declaration that he had done everything he could to obtain a peace settlement, he offered to allow the chamber to examine all the documents relating to his negotiations with the Allies. Unfortunately for him, however, due to a variety of factors, including, not least, his own provocative behaviour, he lost control of the proceedings, and the documents eventually went before a commission composed of men who were notoriously critical of the regime. The result being a report that did not just demand peace but also effectively threatened Napoleon with being overthrown if he did not proceed to the immediate establishment of a genuinely parliamentary regime, the emperor responded by dissolving the assembly post-haste and then publically excoriating a number of deputies who had appeared at a New Year reception at the Tuileries as traitors and rebels. Cf. Price, *Napoleon: the End of Glory*, pp. 176–83.

49. Cf. Thoral, *From Valmy to Waterloo*, p. 200.

50. Dry, *Reims en 1814*, pp. 60–6.

51. J.C. Beugnot, *Mémoires du Comte Beugnot, ancien ministre, 1783–1815*, ed. A. Beugnot (Paris, 1868), II, p. 68.

52. Alison, *Travels in France*, I, pp. 229–31. Edward Stanley retails a story in respect of this topic that is all too typical: 'A friend of our landlord's paid at various times 18,000 *francs* (about £900). He thought himself safe, but Bonaparte wanted a volunteer Guard of Honour. He was told it would be prudent to enroll himself, which in consideration of the great sums he had paid would be merely a nominal business, and that he would never be called upon. He did put his name down; was called out in a trice and shot in the next campaign.' Adeane and Grenfell (eds), *Before and After Waterloo*, p. 119.

53. Daly, *Inside Napoleonic France*, p. 246; Sutherland, *French Revolution and Empire*, p. 371.

54. M.V. Leggiere, *The Fall of Napoleon: the Allied Invasion of France, 1813–1814* (Cambridge, 2007), p. 69.

55. *Cit.* Lequin (ed.), *Memoirs of the Comte de Rambuteau*, pp. 103–4; Leggiere, *Fall of Napoleon*, p. 73.

56. In the Department of the Loire, for example, the newly-appointed prefect, the Comte de Rambuteau, only succeeded in arming the 8,000 National Guards he eventually managed to get together by dint of purchasing every weapon he could from private gunsmiths and the civilian populace. Cf. Lequin (ed.), *Memoirs of the Comte de Rambuteau*, pp. 108–9.

57. *Cit.* Chamand, *The Adventurous Life of Count Lavallette*, II, p. 26.

58. *Cit. ibid.*

59. *Cit.* Beugnot, *Mémoires*, II, p. 57.

60. Chamand, *The Adventurous Life of Count Lavallette*, II, pp. 26–7.

61. P. Jones (ed.), *In Napoleon's Shadow: being the First English-Language Edition of the Complete Memoirs of Louis-Joseph Marchand, Valet and Friend of the Emperor, 1811–1821* (San Francisco, 1998), pp. 34–5. Napoleon may have been moved, but other observers were more cynical. Here, for example, is Thomas Underwood: 'This [ceremony] produced the wished-for effect: several of the officers stepped from their places and approached nearer to him; a considerable number were in tears and among that number were many who were far from being admirers or willing supporters of the imperial government, but who were impressed by the scene. The next day the whole was considered as a theatrical display got up by Bonaparte.' Underwood, *Narrative of Memorable Events in Paris*, pp. 9–10. Meanwhile, as Beauchamp points out, like so much else done by the regime to whip up

support at this time, the ceremony was at best clumsy, on the one hand giving the public the impression that Paris was in imminent danger and on the other focusing attention on Napoleon's determination to fight on in a situation which even he seemed to be confessing was absolutely desperate. Cf. Beauchamp, *Authentic Narrative*, I, pp. 134–6.

62. Underwood, *Narrative of Memorable Events in Paris*, p. 10.
63. *Ibid*, pp. 1–2.
64. J. Ladreit de la Lacharrière (ed.), *Journal inédit de Madame de Marigny, augmenté du journal de T.R. Underwood* (Paris, 1907), pp. 15–16. The prisoners were men taken at the battle of Champaubert. But, as Underwood notes, their display proved completely counter-productive. 'The National Guard was under arms at the barrier of Pantin before eight o'clock in the morning to receive the prisoners taken at Champaubert. The boulevards were thronged by two o'clock. At four a column of about 5,000 Russians and Germans were paraded along the boulevards ... The papers had boasted that there would be 15,000. This show ... was received by the people in a very different manner from that which the government intended or expected. The multitude assembled to see them pass evinced the greatest pity, and money and whatever eatables could at the instant be procured were freely bestowed even by the poorest persons. Those who passed on the 18th were still better treated as the people had time to provide for them. On both days a considerable quantity of bread was thrown from the windows. Mademoiselle Bourgoin, the celebrated actress of the Théâtre Français, manifested her gratitude for the liberality which she had received in Russia ... by attending ... with her carriage full of provisions, which she distributed. Mademoiselle Regnault of the Théâtre de la Opéra Comique did the same, as did also her friend, Boyeldieu, the musical composer, who had likewise been greatly patronized in Russia.... It was said that many of these prisoners had been taken long anterior to the battle of Champaubert. It certainly manifested to the government that the people of Paris had no animosity against the Allies, notwithstanding the crafty means employed to excite it. Indeed, much of the humanity of the better classes was systematic and intended to evince their attachment to the cause of the Allies.' Underwood, *Narrative of Memorable Events in Paris*, pp. 29–31.
65. Underwood, *Narrative of Memorable Events in Paris*, pp. 24–6. For a grim account of conditions in Paris' hospitals, we can do no better than turn to the memoirs of the surgeon, Poumiès de la Siboutie: 'Typhus fever broke out and took heavy toll of the troops ... The Hôpital de la Pitié was quickly overfilled. The beds were partially stripped, only one mattress being left for each, the remainder were placed on the floor; straw was strewn in the corridors, in the halls, even in the church. The sick lay in long rows side-by-side; gaps left by death were filled at once.' Poumiès de la Siboutie, *Recollections of a Parisian*, pp. 12–13.
66. L. Larchey (ed.), *Les cahiers du Capitaine Coignet* (Paris, 1883), pp. 370–1.
67. Alison, *Travels in France*, I, p. 86.
68. Viscount Londonderry, *Narrative of the War in Germany and France in 1813 and 1814* (London, 1830), pp. 288–9. It is not known how common rape actually was, but it would be naïve to think that it did not occur on a fairly widespread basis. Certainly stories of such behaviour were commonplace. Travelling from Dieppe to Paris in July 1815, William Fellowes was told by the postillion of his coach that the cossacks had been raping women on every street corner ('a tout coin'). Fellowes, *Paris in the Interesting Month of July 1815*, p. 66.
69. *Cit.* A. Mikaberidze, *Russian Eyewitness Accounts of the Campaign of 1814* (London, 2013), pp. 108–9. In fairness, Russian commanders issued repeated orders against plundering, but, as was tacitly admitted, there was no checking the cossacks in particular. 'It is a curious fact related to me by an officer of distinguished rank in the Russian service that the cossacks were not informed of their being out of the territory of the emperor of Russia until they were nearly crossing the Rhine, otherwise they would have immediately commenced their usual

system of plunder even in the country of their allies.' Fellowes, *Paris during the Interesting Month of July 1815*, p. 65. On the other hand, there are some voices that put forward a more favourable view. 'Troops do not walk up and down the earth like lambs, but rather like roaring lions, seeking whom they may devour', wrote Edward Stanley. 'However, here let us insert once for all the account I have invariably received from sufferers throughout the whole theatre of war—that the conduct of the Russians and French was widely different; the former generally behaving as well as could possibly be expected, and pillaging only from necessity; the latter seem to have made havoc and devastation their delight. They might perhaps act on principle, conceiving that it was better for the treasure and good things of the land to fall into their hands than the enemy's. One poor woman, wife of a postmaster, a very well-behaved, gentlewoman-like sort of person, told me that when 80,000 Russians came to their town she escaped into the woods (you will remember the snow was then deep on the ground and the cold excessive) where for two days she and her family had nothing to eat. The cossacks then found her, but did no harm, only asking for food.' Adeane and Grenfell (eds), *Before and After Waterloo*, pp. 153–9.

70. L.B. de Saint-Léon, *Mémoires et souveniers de Charles de Pougens* (Paris, 1834), pp. 261–2.

71. Cit. Dry, *Reims en 1814*, p. 89.

72. Beauchamp, *Authentic Narrative*, I, p. 80. It is now generally accepted that popular resistance in those areas of France invaded by the Austrians, Prussians and Russians was almost non-existent. For a detailed discussion of this subject, cf. A. Uffindell, *Napoleon, 1814: the Defence of France* (Barnsley, 2009), pp. 177–87. On the other hand at least one contemporary narrative of an anti-Napoleonic nature can be found that makes rather more of the matter than Uffindell. Thus, according to the author and composer, Pierre Giraud, 'The inhabitants of the invaded provinces, irritated by the pillage and outrage to which they had been exposed, took up arms in many places and, without rising *en masse*, killed many scattered soldiers.' Extraordinarily, the observer concerned stated that as many as 15,000 Allied troops had perished in this manner, but this figure is impossible to believe: only 34,000 French troops were killed in action in the whole of the Peninsular War, whilst he himself is forced to go on to admit that the phenomenon 'did not produce any general or spontaneous resolution and had little effect on the operations of the belligerent powers'. P.F.F.J. Giraud, *The Campaigns of Paris in 1814 and 1815 with a Sketch of the Campaign of 1813, or a Brief and Impartial Relation of Events from the Invasion of France by the Foreign Armies in 1814 to the Capitulation of Paris and the First Dethronement and Abdication of Bonaparte with a Concise History of the Events of the 15th, 16th, 17th and 18th of June 1815 or the Termination of his Political Life* (London, 1815), p. 78.

73. Beauchamp, *Authentic Narrative*, I, pp. 84–5.

74. *Ibid*, pp. 123–5.

75. Blayney, *Narrative of a Forced Journey*, II, p. 282.

76. Londonderry, *Narrative of the War in Germany and France in 1813 and 1814*, p. 269.

77. G. Glover (ed.), *A Lifeguardsman in Spain, France and at Waterloo: the Memoirs of Sergeant-Major Thomas Playford, Second Lifeguards, 1810–1830* (Godmanchester, 2006), pp. 29–30.

78. For some discussion of the economic impact of the Napoleonic era in Bordeaux, see L. Bergeron, *France under Napoleon* (Princeton, New Jersey, 1981), pp. 167–8; M. Broers, *Europe under Napoleon* (London, 1996), p. 181.

79. For all this, see <http://www.1789-1815.com/arfr3_ch_montagnes_1808.htm>, accessed 12 December 2014. Redesignated as *chasseurs de montagne*, at least some of these auxiliaries were dispatched to Spain in 1809, but so great were the numbers of men who deserted in protest that they eventually had to be withdrawn from the struggle.

80. R. Henegan, *Seven Years' Campaigning in the Peninsula and the Netherlands from 1808 to 1815* (London, 1846), II, p. 138. That the proximity of the war in Spain was an issue was

also recognized by Beauchamp. Thus: 'Public opinion was the more opposed to his [i.e. Napoleon's] cause in this part of France from the violent requisitions which were made to support the Army of Spain.' Beauchamp, *Authentic Narrative*, II, p. 5.

81. C. Oman, *A History of the Peninsular War* (Oxford, 1902–1930), VII, pp. 289–93.

82. Henegan, *Seven Years' Campaigning*, p. 196. To anger, perhaps, was added genuine shock. To quote William Lawrence of the Fortieth Foot: 'After nearly six years of deadly fighting, we had got clear of Spain and Portugal and carried the war into our enemy's very kingdom. Portugal and Spain had long had to contain the deadly destroyers, but now the tide was changed, and it was the inhabitants of the south of France who were … to be subjected to the hateful inconveniences of war. They had little expected this turn in their fortunes: Napoleon had … at one time had the ambitious idea of driving us out of the Peninsula, but he now found us forcing his own army into its own country.' G.N. Bankes (ed.), *The Autobiography of Sergeant William Lawrence, a Hero of the Peninsular and Waterloo Campaigns* (London, 1886), pp. 175–6.

83. Henegan, *Seven Years' Campaigning*, II, pp. 129–31, 186–7; Anon., *Personal Narrative of a Private Soldier who served in the Forty-Second Highlanders for Twelve Years during the Late War* (London, 1821), pp. 218–20; I. Robertson (ed.), *The Subaltern: the Diaries of George Gleig during the Peninsular War* (Barnsley, 2013), p. 109.

84. Bankes (ed.), *Autobiography of Sergeant William Lawrence*, p. 176. More importantly, perhaps, these orders were strictly enforced. In the wake of the battle of Orthez, for example, Joseph Donaldson of the Ninety-Fourth Foot recalled seeing the corpse of a British soldier who had been executed for theft hanging from a roadside tree; J. Donaldson, *Recollections in the Eventful Life of a Soldier* (Edinburgh, 1852). p. 226.

85. J. Malcolm, 'Reminiscences of a campaign in the Pyrenees and south of France in 1814', in Anon. (ed.), *Memorials of the Late War* (Edinburgh, 1831), p. 270.

86. *Cit.* G. Glover (ed.), *Wellington's Lieutenant, Napoleon's Gaoler: the Peninsula and St Helena Diaries and Letters of Sir George Rideout Bingham, 1809–21* (Barnsley, 2005), p. 229.

87. *Cit.* M. Birks (ed.), *The Young Hussar: the Peninsular-War Journal of Colonel Thomas Wildman of Newstead Abbey* (Brighton, 2007), p. 77.

88. *Cit.* G. Glover (ed.), *A Guards Officer in the Peninsula and at Waterloo: the Letters of Captain George Bowles 1807–1819* (Cambridge, 2008), p. 86.

89. Henegan, *Seven Years' Campaigning*, II, pp. 137–9

90. *Ibid*, II, pp. 141–2.

91. *Cit.* Glover (ed.), *Guards Officer in the Peninsula and at Waterloo*, p. 86. It should also be noted that much money could be made from assisting in the transport of food for Wellington's forces, many small vessels from Saint Jean de Luz soon becoming engaged in bringing up shipments of supplies from the Spanish port of Pasajes; see Oman, *Peninsular War*, VII, p. 219.

92. J.H. Cooke, *A Narrative of Events in the South of France and of the Attack on New Orleans in 1814 and 1815* (London, 1835), p. 5. For a French account of Wellington's entry into Toulouse, cf. Beauchamp, *Authentic Narrative*, II, pp. 295–7. Herewith an extract: 'About ten o'clock the British commander appeared with his staff and entered the city by the bridge of the Saint Cyprien suburb. Forty thousand persons of both sexes ran to meet him, not knowing how to express their joy and the sincerity of their enthusiasm … Loud shouts of "Long live the king! Long live Wellington!" resounded on every side.' *Ibid*, p. 295.

93. G. Glover (ed.), *An Eloquent Soldier: the Peninsular War Journals of Lieutenant Charles Crowe of the Inniskillings, 1812–1814* (Barnsley, 2011), pp. 227–8, 237–8, 277.

94. Kincaid, *Adventures in the Rifle Brigade*, pp. 296–300; Leach, *Rough Sketches in the Life of an Old Soldier*, p. 368.

95. T. Bunbury, *Reminiscences of a Veteran, being Personal and Military Adventures in Portugal, Spain, France, Malta, New South Wales, Norfolk Island, New Zealand, Andaman Islands and India* (London, 1861), I, pp. 257–61; G. Wood, *The Subaltern Officer: a Memoir* (London, 1825), pp. 237–8.

96. Bankes (ed.), *Autobiography of Sergeant William Lawrence*, pp. 191–2.

97. Price, *Napoleon: the End of Glory*, pp. 208–11; Oman, *Peninsular War*, VII, pp. 391–7.

98. Stuart (ed.), *Soldier's Glory*, p. 114.

99. *Cit.* G. Glover (ed.), *Wellington's Voice: the Candid Letters of Lieutenant-Colonel John Fremantle* (Barnsley, 2012), p. 170.

100. Oman, *Peninsular War*, VII, pp. 439–40.

101. Stuart (ed.), *Soldier's Glory*, p. 139.

102. Blayney, *Narrative of a Forced Journey*, II, pp. 336–7, 409.

103. Giraud, *Campaigns of Paris in 1814 and 1815*, pp. 61–2.

104. Blayney, *Narrative of a Forced Journey*, II, pp. 342–6.

105. *Ibid*, pp. 291–6.

106. I. Fletcher (ed.), *A Guards Officer in the Peninsula: the Peninsular-War Letters of John Rous, 1812–1814* (Staplehurst, 1997), p. 96. At about the same time, meanwhile, another Guards officer was writing that 'the French army … are badly fed and not paid [and] consequently desert pretty fast, and, unless Bonaparte can contrive to raise a little hard cash, I suspect the discontented will soon form the majority'. *Cit.* Glover (ed.), *Guards Officer in the Peninsula and at Waterloo*, p. 87.

107. G.C. Moore-Smith (ed.), *The Autobiography of Sir Harry Smith, 1787–1819* (London, 1910), p. 163; R. Batty, *Campaign of the Left Wing of the Allied Army in the Western Pyrenees and the South of France in the Years 1813–1814 under Field-Marshal the Marquess of Wellington* (London, 1823), p. 131.

108. For some excellent accounts of this action, see Henegan, *Seven Years' Campaigning*, II, pp. 215–19; J. Dobbs, *Recollections of an Old Fifty-Second Man* (Waterford, 1863), p. 59; Glover (ed.), *Guards Officer in the Peninsula and at Waterloo*, p. 91.

109. E.g. Glover (ed.), *Guards Officer in the Peninsula and at Waterloo*, p. 92.

110. Stiegler (ed.), *Memoirs of Marshal Oudinot*, p. 253.

111. This conflation of cold-blooded self-interest and hard-headed military analysis is perfectly expressed by Thiébault. Thus; 'I cannot refrain from the admission that since the collapse of Leipzig my ideas had undergone a change. The army which the emperor had succeeded in remaking had been split up, beaten and cut to pieces till it no longer had a fifth of the number with which to face enemies elated by victory. Could France, in spite of her exhaustion and with all the confidence and dash gone out of her, still undertake a national war? Such a war could have no result unless protracted, and of this the strength and fury of our enemies allowed no hope. Lastly, considering that Napoleon could not have any more losses or commit another mistake, while the allies could still commit plenty with impunity, I despaired for the first time of the success of our arms and the safety of our country, while the possible interests of my family took, for the first time in my life, the first place in my thoughts. At the moment of shipwreck the individual separates himself from the crowd until nothing remains which he is not ready to sacrifice to his own interests.', Butler (ed.), *Memoirs of Baron Thiébault*, II, p. 397.

112. Poumiès de la Siboutie, *Recollections of a Parisian*, pp. 122–3.

113. A.J.F. Fain, *Memoirs of the Invasion of France by the Allied Armies and of the last Six Months of the Reign of Napoleon* (London, 1834), pp. 161–2. For some very similar remarks, cf. Underwood, *Narrative of Memorable Events in Paris*, pp. 32–3. In brief, this last author argues that, rather than persuading the inhabitants of the need to fight to the death, the constant stress on the atrocities being perpetrated by the cossacks rather had the effect of

causing them to demand an immediate end to the war as the only means of saving their lives and property.

114. Underwood, *Narrative of Memorable Events in Paris*, pp. 36–43 *passim*.

115. E. Mennechet, *Lettres sur la restauration: seize ans sous les Bourbons, 1814–1830* (Paris, 1832), I, pp. 3–4.

116. Stiegler (ed.), *Memoirs of Marshal Oudinot*, pp. 254–5.

117. L. de Bausset, *Private Memoirs of the Court of Napoleon and some Public Events of the Imperial Reign from 1805 to the First of May 1814* (Philadelphia, 1828), pp. 403–4.

118. Chateaubriand, *Memoirs*, III, p. 54.

119. Giraud, *Campaigns of Paris in 1814 and 1815*, pp. 96–7.

120. By the end of the day, it was clear to all that the battle was lost. As Underwood recorded in his journal, 'The fortunes of the day were now decided: the national guards who were without the walls returned in disorder. One of them told us that the … troops of the line were running from all their posts and that the road on the other side of the wall was strewed with the muskets they had thrown away. In this they had been imitated by the national guard, as I saw several without arms though in uniform. The Allied cavalry were now advancing by the fields from Clichy; a squadron of French went to meet them. We were in expectation of seeing a charge, but when they were within about 200 yards of each other the French coolly wheeled about and came leisurely back, the allied cavalry continuing as slowly to advance … At twenty minutes after four the artillery abandoned by the French on the summit of Montmartre was turned upon Paris which the enemy began to cannonade. One ball passed just above our heads and ploughed up the earth just behind us.' Underwood, *Narrative of Memorable Events in Paris*, p. 73.

121. Londonderry, *Narrative*, pp. 301–2. Cf. also Underwood, *Narrative of Memorable Events in Paris*, pp. 104–16. Amongst the scenes witnessed by Underwood was an unsuccessful attempt to pull down the Vendôme Column with its statue of Napoleon and triumphal frieze representing his victories.

122. Chateaubriand, *Memoirs*, III, p. 57.

Chapter 5

1. Underwood, *Narrative of Memorable Events in Paris*, pp. 179–80.

2. *Ibid*, pp. 103–4.

3. Poumiès de la Siboutie, *Recollections of a Parisian*, p. 138.

4. Beslay (ed.), *Un officier d'état-major sous le premier empire*, p. 250.

5. P. Giraud, *Des Bourbons et des puissances étrangeres le 20 mars 1815* (Paris, 1815), pp. 6–7.

6. *Ibid*, pp. 8–20.

7. Fézensac, *Souvenirs militaires*, pp. 480–4.

8. Larchey (ed.), *Cahiers du Capitaine Coignet*, p. 381.

9. J. Scott, *A Visit to Paris in 1814, being a Review of the Moral, Political, Intellectual and Social Condition of the French Capital* (London, 1816), pp. 176–7.

10. J.P.T. Bury, *France, 1814–1940* (sixth edition; London, 2003), p. 5.

11. Butler (ed.), *Memoirs of Baron Thiébault*, II, pp. 408–10.

12. G. de Berthier de Sauvigny, *The Bourbon Restoration* (Philadelphia, 1966), p. 76. In respect to the personnel policy followed by the new administration, one should also mention here one or two figures who had served the regime but had been discredited or been sidelined, the most prominent of these being the commander of the army that had been forced to surrender at Bailén, Pierre Dupont, who now found himself elevated to the post of Minister of War. As Berthier de Sauvigny points out, Dupont was a particularly unfortunate choice. Appointed for no better reason than the fact that he was clearly not Napoleon's man, he

had never commanded a formation higher than a division, and soon showed himself to be completely out of his depth. Cf. *ibid*, p. 61.

13. Poumiès de la Siboutie, *Recollections of a Parisian*, pp. 138–9, 143. The good doctor appears to have been a little confused here: as no 'Voltigeurs of Louis XVIII' ever existed, the terms must have been a nickname only, albeit a very witty one.

14. Beslay (ed.), *Un officier d'état-major sous le premier empire*, p. 253. For a concrete example of such a complaint involving a group of officers from the Fifty-Eighth Line, cf. G. Firmin-Didot (ed.), *Royauté ou empire? La France en 1814 d'apres les rapports inédits du Comte Angles* (Paris, n.d.), p. 19.

15. Cf. A. Ward *et al* (eds.), *Cambridge Modern History, IX: Napoleon* (London, 1902–10), p. 567. According to Octave Levasseur, Marshal Ney sought to reassure Louis as to the Guard's reliability by leading a large delegation consisting of some of the best men of each regiment to wait upon Louis at Compiègne in the course of his journey to Paris: this gesture, it seems, was acknowledged graciously enough, but the king ignored the advice given him by Ney to the effect that he should give the Imperial Guard the place that rather went to the Maison du Roi. To have taken such a decision, of course, would have been a risk, but it would nonetheless have been a move that was extremely politic, Levavasseur going so far as to claim that in 1815 Napoleon told Ney that, if Louis had followed his advice, the 'flight of the eagle' could never have been rendered a success. Cf. Beslay (ed.), *Un officier d'état-major sous le premier empire*, p. 247.

16. M. Lenormand, *Réflexions impartiales sur le gouvernement de Louis XVIII et sur les fautes qui en ont entrainé le décadence* (Paris, 1815), pp. 12–13.

17. Beslay (ed.), *Un officier d'état-major sous le premier empire*, p. 253.

18. For a graphic description of this ceremony, cf. Mennechet, *Lettres sur la restauration*, I, pp. 172–3.

19. Underwood, *Narrative of Memorable Events in Paris*, pp. 187–8, 191–2. If a more specific example is required, a young officer in the Russian Guards named Nikifor Kovalskii not only admits to engaging in such an action in the Bois de Boulogne, but reports that in his regiment clashes between French and Russian officers were so frequent that the latter had to be ordered never to appear in the streets in uniform when they were off duty. Cf. Mikaberidze (ed.), *Russian Eyewitness Accounts of the Campaign of 1814*, p. 251.

20. E. Stanley to M. Stanley, 11 July 1814, *cit*. Adeane and Grenfell (eds.), *Before and After Waterloo*, pp. 139–40.

21. E. Stanley to M. Stanley, 28 June 1814, *cit. ibid*, p 107.

22. Firmin-Didot (ed.), *Royauté ou empire?*, p. 134

23. Alison, *Travels in France*, I, p. 81. The anger current in the Imperial Guard at this point is confirmed by a report submitted by Louis XVIII's new Director of Police, the Comte d'Angles, on 22 April. Thus: 'The reports arriving at the Ministry of General Police state that the Imperial Guard, which currently occupies an area stretching from Nevers to Fontainebleau is displaying an attitude of a most menacing character and continuing to show itself to be devoted to Napoleon. The division of that force into a number of smaller corps and its distribution amongst a number of different garrisons a good way from the capital is one of the most important points that should occupy the attention of the Minister of War.' *Cit*. Firmin-Didot (ed.), *Royauté ou empire?*, pp. 2–3. Levavasseur, meanwhile, offers many details of the anger that gripped the Guard in consequence of Louis XVIII's decision to confide his personal security during the march on Paris not to the Imperial Guard, but rather those Swiss troops serving in the French army who had survived Napoleon's last campaigns. Cf. Beslay (ed.), *Un officier d'état-major sous le premier empire*, p. 249.

24. Cf. Firmin-Didot (ed.), *Royauté ou empire?*, p. 7.

25. G. Glover (ed.), *A Hellish Business: the Letters of Captain Kinloch, 32nd Light Infantry, 1806–16* (Godmanchester, 2007), p. 198.

26. *Cit.* Fletcher (ed.), *Guards Officer in the Peninsula*, pp. 123–4. See also Stuart (ed.), *Soldier's Glory*, pp. 142–3; Robertson (ed.), *The Subaltern*, pp. 183–4.

27. How far the views discussed in this section extended to the rank and file, it is difficult to say. In the course of the campaign of 1814, as we have seen, evidence of a split between the officers and the men they commanded had been plentiful, and it is not unreasonable to suppose that such feelings persisted into the peace. Such at least was the experience of Archibald Alison when he travelled from Paris to Provence in November 1814: 'At the inns the valets and the ostlers were for the most part old soldiers who had marched under Napoleon. They seemed happy, or at least always expressed themselves happy, at being allowed to return to their homes: one of them was particularly eloquent in describing the horrors of the last few months; he concluded by saying that, had things gone on in this way for much longer, Napoleon must have made the women march.' Alison, *Travels in France*, II, p. 8. One force that was certainly absolutely delighted to be demobilised was the National Guard, one of the very few positive contributions made by the Comte d'Artois to the situation being the manner in which, having been appointed as its commander, he went out of his way not just to stand it to down at the earliest possible moment, but also to flatter its sensibilities.

28. *Ibid*, I, pp. 214–15. At least the officers concerned were prepared to concede that the Anglo-Portuguese army was a worthy opponent. With regard to the Austrians, Prussians and Russians, however, it was a different matter. Thus, the two last were 'veritable brutes without the slightest intelligence' whilst the Austrian infantry, in particular, were 'worthless'. *Ibid*, I, pp. 212–13.

29. J. Scott, *Visit to Paris in 1814*, pp. 17–19. In all some 200,000 men were demobilised, this being a figure that was far too large to be accommodated by France's battered economy. Cf. Bury, *France, 1814–1940*, p. 5.

30. E.L. Lamothe-Langon, *Private Memoirs of the Court of Louis XVIII* (London, 1830), II, p. 55.

31. Firmin-Didot (ed.), *Royauté ou empire?*, pp. 241–3.

32. Blayney, *Narrative of a Forced Journey*, II, p. 469.

33. To speak of bullying being the order of the day in the Allied armies is, perhaps, to go too far: in fact, the Allied commanders issued frequent directives reminding their troops that the war had not been waged against the French people but rather Napoleon, and that they were therefore to behave with the utmost moderation. For example, the proclamation of General Barclay de Tolly, 2 April 1814. cit. Mikaberidze (ed.), *Russian Eyewitness Accounts of the Campaign of 1814*, p. 261. To return to the eponymous shouts of *bistro*, meanwhile, D'Angles was amused to note that the shopkeepers and taverners of the capital were quick enough to complain at the loss of custom that resulted from the departure of the occupying forces in the course of the summer. Cf. Firmin-Didot (ed.), *Royauté ou empire?*, p. 37.

34. Poumiès de la Siboutie, *Recollections of a Parisian*, pp. 138–9.

35. Mikaberidze (ed.), *Russian Eyewitness Accounts of the Campaign of 1814*, p. 257.

36. *Cit. ibid.* p. 248.

37. *Cit. ibid.* p. 260.

38. Alison, *Travels in France*, I, pp. 16–17.

39. T. Bowdler, *A Postscript to the Letters written in France in 1814* (London, 1815), p. 19.

40. Alison, *Travels in France*, I, p. 3.

41. J. Scott, *Visit to Paris in 1814*, pp. 110–11.

42. Circular letter of F. de Montesquieu. 26 January 1815, cit. Champollion-Figeac (ed.), *Fourier et Napoléon*, pp. 173–82.

43. Firmin-Didot (ed.), *Royauté ou empire?*, p. 14.
44. Alison, *Travels in France*, II, pp. 169–82 *passim*.
45. Giraud, *Des Bourbons et des puissances étrangères le 20 mars 1815*, pp. 45–6.
46. Guizot, *Memoirs*, I, p. 41.
47. Cf. P. Pilbeam, *The Constitutional Monarchy in France, 1815–1848* (Abingdon, 2000), pp. 2–4; Berthier de Sauvigny, *Bourbon Restoration*, pp. 65–70. A contemporary critique from a liberal perspective is provided by François Guizot: 'Timid and obstinate ... [the Charter] replied to the pretensions of the revolutionary system by the pretensions of the ancient form, and presented itself purely as a royal concession instead of presenting itself, such as it truly was, a treaty of peace after a protracted war, a series of new articles added by common accord to the old compact of union between the nation and the king.' Guizot, *Memoirs*, I, pp. 33–4.
48. Lenormand, *Réflexions impartiales sur le gouvernement de Louis XVIII*, pp. 8–9. For the policy of the régime with respect to social, educational and religious matters, cf. Pilbeam, *Constitutional Monarchy in France*, pp. 4–5; Berthier de Sauvigny, *Bourbon Restoration*, pp. 77–9.
49. Fitzpatrick, *Catholic Royalism in the Department of the Gard*, p. 31. Interestingly, Giraud alleges that a plot was afoot at the very highest level to launch a bloody purge of all erstwhile supporters of the Revolution and Napoleon alike in a latter-day replay of the massacre of Saint Bartholemew's day in 1572. Cf. Giraud, *Des Bourbons et des puissances étrangeres le 20 mars 1815*, pp. 41–2. This is utterly unfounded, but the fact remains that political tension was on the increase and that at least some elements of the 'masses of granite' had come to believe that they were in real danger.
50. Carnot (ed.), *Mémoires sur Carnot*, II, pp. 397–9.
51. Cf. V.W. Beach, *Charles X of France: his Life and Times* (Boulder, Colorado, 1971), pp. 125–43 *passim*.
52. F. Artz, *France under the Bourbon Restoration, 1814–1830* (New York, 1963), pp. 13–14, 127–9.
53. *Cit.* Firmin-Didot (ed.), *Royauté ou empire?*, p. 2.
54. Cf. *ibid*, p. 103; Sutherland, *French Revolution and Empire*, p. 376.
55. Firmin-Didot (ed.), *Royauté ou empire?*, p. 235.
56. Lamothe-Langon, *Private Memoirs of the Court of Louis XVIII*, II, pp. 49–52; Firmin-Didot (ed.), *Royauté ou empire?*, pp. 210–17. Curiously enough, the epicentre of the disturbances was the self-same church of Saint Roch which had been the chief bulwark of the Vendémiaire revolt of 1795.
57. Alison, *Travels in France*, I, pp. 149–51. One issue that particularly struck Alison was the extent to which the French had turned their back on religion. Thus: 'The most striking and formidable part of their general character is the contempt for religion which is so frequently and openly expressed. In all countries there are men of a selfish and abstracted turn of mind who are more disposed than others to religious argument and doubt, and in all there are a greater number whose worldly passions lead them to the neglect ... of religious precepts, but a great nation among whom a cool selfish regard to personal comfort and enjoyment has been deliberately substituted for religious feeling, and where it is esteemed reasonable and wise to oppose and wrestle down by metaphysical arguments the natural and becoming sentiments of piety is hitherto ... an anomaly in the history of mankind. We heard it estimated at Paris that 40,000 out of 600,000 inhabitants of that town attend church, one half of which number, they say, are actuated by real sentiments of devotion, but to judge from the very small numbers we have ever seen attending the regular services in any of the churches, we should think this proportion greatly over-rated. Of those whom we have seen

there, at least two thirds have been women above fifty, or girls under fifteen years of age.'
Ibid, I, pp. 124–5.

58. Birkbeck, *Notes on a Journey through France*, p. 85.

59. Bowdler, *Postscript to the Letters written in France in 1814*, pp. 31–2. In a performance of *Hamlet* that was staged in Paris in May 1814, D'Angles reported that a particularly hostile reference to England was greeted by loud cheers. Cf. Firmin-Didot (ed.), *Royauté ou Empire?*, p. 17.

60. For Alison's views in respect of this issue, cf. Alison, *Travels in France*, I, pp. 204–6.

61. J. Scott, *Visit to Paris in 1814*, p. 177.

62. Alison, *Travels in France*, I, pp. 208–9. Similar views are recorded by Edward Stanley: 'The people may or may not like their emancipation from tyranny, but their vanity … has been tarnished by the surrender of Paris, and they declare on all hands that if Marmont had held out for a day Bonaparte would have arrived, and in an instant settled the business by defeating the Allies. In vain may you hint that he was inferior in point of numbers (to say anything of the skill and merit of the Russians perhaps would not have been very prudent), and that he could not have succeeded. A doubting shake of the head, significant shrug of the shoulders, and expressive "Ba, Ba," explain well enough their opinions on the subject … I will allow you – I would allow myself perhaps, when I look back to the circumstances connected with the war – to wish that all the country, Paris included, had been sacked and pillaged as a just punishment, or rather as the sole mode of convincing these infatuated people that they are the conquered and not the conqueror of the Allies. Wherever I go, whatever field of battle I see – be it Craonne, Laon, Soissons, or elsewhere – victory is never accorded to the Russians. "Oh non, les Russes étaient toujours vaincus." One fellow who had been one of Buonaparte's guides at Craonne had the impudence to assure me that the moment he appeared the Allies ran away. "Aye, but," said I, "how came the French to retreat and leave them alone?" "Oh, because just then the *trahison* which had been all arranged 19 months before began to appear." Again, at Laon I was assured that the French drove all before them, and gained the heights. "Then," said I, "why did not they stay there?" "Oh, then reappeared *la petite trahison*". And so they go on, and well do they deserve, and heartily do I wish, to have their pride and impudence lowered.' E. Stanley to M. Stanley, 28 June and 19 July 1814, *cit.* Adeane and Grenfell (eds.), *Before and After Waterloo*, pp. 106, 156.

63. *Ibid*, I, pp. 129–30.

64. *Cit.* Firmin-Didot (ed.), *Royauté ou empire?*, p. 5. By no means all the material concerned was pro-Napoleonic. On the contrary, D'Angles also found himself having to take action against cartoons portraying Napoleon in one instance as a composite of human remains, and in another as a tiger. *Ibid*, p. 13.

65. Lamothe-Langon, *Private Memoirs of the Court of Louis XVIII*, II, pp. 32–3.

66. For all this, cf. Berthier de Sauvigny, *The Bourbon Restoration*, pp. 60–2. A particularly devastating analysis is found in the memoirs of François Guizot. Thus: 'M. de Talleyrand … had neither the inclination nor habit of sustained, systematic labour … He was at once ambitious and indolent, a flatterer and a scoffer … The Abbé de Montesquiou was a thoroughly honourable man … but volatile, inconsiderate … little suited for long and bitter contentions … and incapable of leading his party or himself in the direction which reason directed they should follow … M. de Blacas … remained at the Tuileries what he had been at Hartnell, a country gentleman, an emigrant, a courtier … with no political genius, no ambition, no statesmanlike activity.' Guizot, *Memoirs*, I, pp. 37–40. In fairness to Louis XVIII, it should be pointed out that his choice of ministers provides further evidence of his conciliatory attitude. Thus, only Blacas and Dambray had no connections with the Revolution at all, Talleyrand, Louis, Montesquiou, Dupont and Malouet having all been implicated in it to one extent or another before (in the case of three of the four, at least)

ending up in the service of Napoleon. Recognition, then, was paid to the simple fact that Louis could not survive without the co-option of the Napoleonic state. That said, in so far as the Comte d'Artois and his supporters were concerned, so far as possible the pill was sweetened by the selection of figures who had eventually broken with the emperor.

67. Cf. Carnot (ed.), *Mémoires sur Carnot*, II, pp. 366–88.

68. Firmin-Didot (ed.), *Royauté ou empire?*, p. 102. For a reproduction of one particularly clever image, cf. <http://www.napoleonprisonnier.com/napoleon/violette.html>, accessed 14 August 2015.

69. Cf. Firmin-Didot (ed.), *Royauté ou empire?*, p. 21. As D'Angles remarked, 'The rhyme is scarcely rich, and the style still worse.'

70. Cf. Champollion-Figeac (ed.), *Fourier et Napoléon*, pp. 182–4.

71. *Cit.* C. Webster, *The Foreign Policy of Castlereagh, 1812–1815* (London, 1931), p. 249.

72. Jones, *In Napoleon's Shadow*, pp. 126–30.

73. *Ibid*, p. 138.

74. Alison, *Travels in France*, II, pp. 12–13.

75. *Ibid*, pp. 40–1.

76. *Ibid*, pp. 43–4. The landlord's point was reinforced by the fact that those who were enthused by the prospect of a new war in Alison's experience invariably consisted of demobilized soldiers down on their luck. For example: 'One man (a shopkeeper to appearance) said, that his son, a trumpeter, when he heard the drum, leapt from his seat, and, dancing about the room, exclaimed, "La guerre! La guerre!" On the route this morning, we met with a small party of five or six soldiers returning to their homes; two of them had lost their right arms, and two others were lamed for life. They all agreed that they would never have wished for peace; and that even in their present miserable state they would fight. They were very fine stout fellows, about 40 years of age; but they had the looks of ruffians when narrowly examined.' *Ibid*, p. 40.

77. *Ibid*, pp. 59–60.

78. Cf. Firmin-Didot (ed.), *Royauté ou empire?*, pp. 260–1.

79. *Cit. ibid*, p. 262.

80. *Cit. ibid*, p. 263.

81. *Cit. ibid*, p. 269.

82. *Ibid*.

83. *Ibid*.

84. E. Stanley to M. Stanley, 22 July 1814, *cit.* Adeane and Grenfell (eds.), *Before and After Waterloo*, p. 159.

85. Guizot, *Memoirs*, I, p. 29.

86. Berthier de Sauvigny, *Bourbon Restoration*, p. 84.

Chapter 6

1. W. Scott, *The Life of Napoleon Buonaparte, Emperor of the French with a Preliminary View of the French Revolution* (London, 1827), III, p. 201.

2. Alison, *Travels in France*, II, pp. 79–80.

3. Guizot, *Memoirs*, I, p. 40.

4. H. Houssaye, *The Return of Napoleon* (London, 1934), pp. 52, 54.

5. *Ibid*, pp. 86–9.

6. *Ibid*, pp. 104, 113, 118.

7. *Ibid*, p. 144.

8. Hamilton-Williams, *Waterloo, New Perspectives*, pp. 56–61 *passim*. Hamilton-Williams not being the most reliable of sources, how far this passage can be taken at face value, it is difficult to say. At all events, if there was excitement amongst the rural populace, in particular, it was

not much remarked upon, one of the few exceptions being Lavallette, who tells us that as, Napoleon neared Paris in the last stage of his journey from the Mediterranean coast to the capital, his way was thronged by such folk. Thus: 'Officers arriving at Fontainebleau in advance of the emperor told us it was very difficult to make headway along the road. Dense crowds of peasants lined, or, rather, had taken possession of, each side. Their enthusiasm was immense.' Aldersey White, *Adventurous Life of Lavallette*, II, p. 87. That said, the general point holds good: Jacobinism was on the march. As Hobhouse remarked in a letter written on 19 May, 'Although the cap of liberty is not hoisted, the eagle is held as its substitute. The Imperial Guard march to the Marseillaise, and it was remarked to me the other day at the Tuileries that, for the first time since the early days of the Republic, the troops passed in review to the tune of the once famous *Ça ira*.' Hobhouse, *Substance of Some Letters*, I, p. 207.

9. For the relevant clip, cf. Youtube: 'Waterloo (1970).; full movie (Part 3).', accessed 23 August 2015. In fairness, the film's depiction of the scenes that took place at Grenoble is not entirely unrepresentative: at the little town of Nontron, for example, the news of Napoleon's disembarkation was greeted by a popular rising that persuaded the sub-prefect to declare for the imperial cause. Cf. J. Lhomer, *Les cent jours et la terreur blanche en Dordogne* (Paris, 1904), p. 8.

10. That this was the case was recognized even by the Bourbons: as the news of Napoleon's progress grew steadily more alarming, so the government of Louis XVIII rushed to make good the damage of the past year, restoring all officers who had been placed on half-pay to the active list, advancing a considerable amount of pay to the rank and file and holding a series of parades in Paris at which Louis XVIII even went so far as to heap praise on Napoleon's victories. Cf. E. de Waresquiel, *Cent jours: la tentation de l'impossible, mars-juillet, 1815* (Paris, 2008), pp. 214–16.

11. Lhomer, *Cent jours*, p. 8.

12. Stiegler (ed.), *Memoirs of Marshal Oudinot*, p. 296.

13. E. Rousset (ed.), *Recollections of Marshal Macdonald, Duke of Tarentum* (London, 1892), II, p. 248. Still more embarrassing was the response of a veteran of the Thirteenth Dragoons who was personally enjoined by the Comte d'Artois to shout 'Long live the King!'. Thus: 'No, Sir: no soldier can fight against his father. I can only answer you by crying, "Long live the emperor!"' Cf. V. Develay, *La Bourgogne pendant les cent jours* (Paris, 1860), p. 9.

14. J. Tulard, *Napoleon: the Myth of the Saviour* (London, 1984), p. 328.

15. P. Lévêque, 'La "révolution de 1815": le mouvement populaire pendant les cent jours', in L. Hamon (ed.), *Les cent jours dans l'Yonne: aux origins d'un bonapartisme liberal* (Paris, 1988), p. 53. An important contribution to the debate, Lévêque's article is worth analysing in some detail. In brief, it is claimed that the soldiers did not move of their own accord but rather responded to the ever-growing wave of popular pressure manifested by the crowds that flocked to greet Napoleon, and that to classify the movement as a *pronunciamiento* is inappropriate, since the impetus came not from the upper ranks but rather the lower. However, whilst this is all very well, the author admits that no revolutionary movement can be discerned except in areas where the *acte additionnel* got a substantial 'yes' vote in the plebiscite, together with towns that found themselves isolated amidst substantial peasant revolts, and has to spend most of his time defending the failure of the *fédérés* and their allies to achieve any significant success (we learn, for example, that the bulk of the bourgeoisie had turned its back on revolution; that the radicals were denied arms and excluded from positions of power; that, where they had not sold out to the propertied classes, the great leaders of the past were either dead or in retirement; and that there was insufficient time to rebuild the political machine that had stood the radicals in such good stead in 1793). All

this, of course, is very true, but the effect is essentially to condemn Lévêque out of his own mouth. Cf. *ibid*, pp. 51–73.

16. Develay, *La Bourgogne pendant les cent jours*, p. 10. Across Burgundy and other parts of central France – precisely the area on which feudalism and the rights of the Church had weighed most heavily in 1789 – the rural population undoubtedly responded to the return of Napoleon with considerable excitement. More than that, indeed, there were numerous attacks on churches, *chateaux* and parish priests, the atmosphere being so tense in some areas that it recalled the *grande peur* of 1789. Cf. Waresquiel, *Cent jours*, p. 326. Forced to spend the night in the cottage of a humble peasant near Auxonne when the coach in which he was travelling slid into a deep ditch, Frédéric Rillier provides us with an interesting snapshot of popular feeling in the area. Thus: 'Our gallant host did not make the slightest effort to hide the joy that he felt at the return of the emperor. He believed that a golden age would follow in its train that for himself would begin with him receiving compensation for the losses he had suffered in the blockade of Auxonne the previous year. When we raised a number of doubts in respect of this flattering picture, the most important of which was the danger of conscription, he responded with great complacency: conscription, or so it seemed, had been very agreeable to the poor as it allowed them both to rid their families of useless mouths and make a bit of money through the hire of substitutes. Alien to all political calculation, the opinion of this humble peasant was probably that of a great many of his peers, including perhaps many of those who a year before would have trembled at the very mention of the word "conscription".' Cf. Rillier, 'Les cent jours en Belgique et en France', p. 253. Whatever the truth of this last observation, that the area was more in favour of Napoleon than many other parts of the country is clear from the results of the plebiscite organized in respect of the *acte additionnel*: the Department of the Yonne, for example, returned the fourth highest total of 'yes' votes in the entire country. Cf. J.P. Rocher, 'L'espirit public das l'Yonne pendant les cent jours', in Hamon (ed.), *Les cent jours dans l'Yonne*, p. 1.

17. Hobhouse, *Substance of Some Letters*, I, pp. 40–1.

18. A. Pigeard, 'La conscription sous le premier empire' <http://www.napoleon.org/fr/salle_lecture/articles/files/conscription_le_Premier_Empire1.asp>, accessed 22 April 2015.

19. Alison, *Travels in France*, II, p. 15.

20. Hobhouse, *Substance of Some Letters*, I, p. 40. In this respect, it is also worth quoting Alison: 'In conversation one evening with one of the *noblesse*, who had suffered in the Revolution, he told me that this military spirit extended not only to all ranks and professions, but to all ages. He said that the young men in the schools refused to learn anything but mathematics and the science of arms; and that he recollected many instances of boys ten and twelve years of age daily entreating their fathers and mothers to permit them to join Napoleon. It was in vain to represent to them the hardships they must suffer; their constant reply was, "If we die, we will at least find glory."' Cf. Alison, *Travels in France*, II, p. 111.

21. Cf. Hobhouse, *Substance of Some Letters*, I, pp. 43–5. Wisely enough, Napoleon was dismissive of such acclaim. As he remarked to his erstwhile Minister of Finance, Nicolas Mollien, when he received him in the Tuileries, 'The time for compliments is over: they have received me in the same way as they let me go.' *Cit.* N. Mollien, *Mémoires d'un Ministre du Trésor Publique, 1780–1815* (Paris, 1845), IV, p. 187.

22. W.H. Ireland, *The Life of Napoleon Bonaparte* (London, 1827), IV, pp. 260–1.

23. On this point Guizot is particularly interesting. As he says, 'Napoleon, in quitting Elba, deceived himself as to the disposition of Europe towards him ... But, once arrived in Paris and informed of the proceedings of the Congress, he beheld his position in its true light, and his clear and comprehensive judgement at once grappled with it in all its bearings. His conversations with the thinking men who were then about him, M. Molé and the Duke of Vicenza, confirm this opinion. He sought still to keep the public in the uncertainty which

he no longer felt. The manifesto … of the 13th of March was not published in the *Moniteur* until the 5th of April, and the treaty of the 25th March only on the 3rd of May. Napoleon added long commentaries to these documents to prove that it was impossible they could express the final intentions of Europe.' Guizot, *Memoirs*, I, pp. 64–5.

24. Hobhouse, *Substance of Some Letters*, pp. 179, 205. That this was the case is also pointed by an apologium that was written by Carnot a short time after the second restoration. 'I believed, and I still do believe, that Napoleon returned with the sincere desire of preserving the peace and governing in a paternal fashion. I believed, too, that the Allies would not inflict fresh devastation on a country which had expressed its desire to maintain the tranquillity of Europe so strongly. The general feeling was that the emperor could not have left Elba without the agreement of at least a part of the members of the Congress of Vienna and that in a few days we would see the return of the empress and her son. That the powers would leave us, as they had so often promised, to choose the government which we desired there was not the slightest doubt so long as we remained loyal to the stipulations of the Treaty of Paris.' *Cit.* Carnot (ed.), *Mémoires sur Carnot*, II, p. 415. Whether Carnot can be believed here is a matter of judgement, but it is by no means implausible that at least some of the crowds who cheered Napoleon really believed that they could both have the emperor and go on enjoying a state of peace.

25. Aldersey White, *Adventurous Life of Count Lavalette*, II, p. 87.

26. *Ibid,* p. 88.

27. Guizot, *Memoirs of my Time*, I, pp. 59–60

28. Aldersey White, *Adventurous Life of Count Lavallette*, II, pp. 76–9.

29. Hobhouse, *Substance of Some Letters*, I, pp. 445–7.

30. Alison, *Travels in France*, II, pp. 61–2.

31. *Ibid,* pp. 64–5.

32. Hobhouse, *Substance of Some Letters*, I, p. 57.

33. Rillier, 'Les cent jours en Belgique et en France', pp. 262–3.

34. Dallas, *The Final Act*, pp. 334–5; Schom, *One Hundred Days*, pp. 146–7.

35. J. Cornillon, *Le Bourbonnais pendant les cent jours* (Moulins, 1925), pp. 24–8.

36. Anon, 'Relation of the events that took place at Bordeaux towards the end of March 1815', in B. O'Meara (ed.), *Historical Memoirs of Napoleon* (Philadelphia, 1820), pp. 258–61.

37. Stiegler (ed.), *Memoirs of Marshal Oudinot*, pp. 307–9.

38. L. Carnot to Napoleon, 15 April 1815, *cit.* L. Carnot (ed.), *Correspondance inédite du Général Carnot avec Napoléon pendant les cent jours* (Paris, 1819), p. 72.

39. Mollien, *Mémoires*, IV, pp. 189–90.

40. Schom, *One Hundred Days*, p. 178.

41. *Ibid.*

42. Cf. G. D'Arcy-Wood, *Tambora: the Eruption that Changed the World* (Princeton, New Jersey, 2014). There is some suggestion that this event did not just wreak havoc with the harvest of 1816, but also had a direct influence on the campaign, it having been claimed that the disruption that it caused to the climate was the cause of the deluges of 17–18 June.

43. Alison, *Travels in France*, II, p. 75.

44. *Ibid,* II, pp. 83–4.

45. Anon, 'Relation of the events that took place at Bordeaux towards the end of March 1815', pp. 261–9.

46. *Ibid,* II, p. 80.

47. For a detailed account of these events, cf. O. Monge, *La capitulation de La Palud: campagne de Duc d'Angoulême en Vaucluse* (Paris, 1894). Also very helpful is E. le Gallo, *Les cent jours: essai sur l'histoire intérieure de la France depuis le retour de l'île d'Elbe jusqu'a la nouvelle de Waterloo* (Paris, 1924), pp. 164–78. According to Waresquiel, meanwhile, the murders were

the work not of *fédérés*, but of Protestant villagers and National Guards. Cf. Waresquiel, *Cent jours*, pp. 323–4.

48. This is not the place to embark on a discussion of the complex historiography of the Vendéen insurrections. Suffice to say that, thanks to the influence of the American historian Charles Tilly in particular, specialists in the field now generally accept that that the Vendéen revolt of 1793 and the lower-level Breton phenomenon that broke out at the same time known as the *chouannerie* – together essentially the root cause of all that followed – were the fruit not of ideology, but rather long-standing tensions between town and countryside, dissatisfaction with social and economic policies that in effect left the region infinitely worse off than it had been prior to 1789, and, above all, the introduction of conscription.

49. For a general survey of the revolt in Brittany and the Vendée, cf. R. Grand, *La chouannerie en 1815: les cent jours dans le ouest* (Paris, 1943). That it posed a serious threat is all too apparent from Napoleon to L. Davout, 22 May 1815, *cit.* Plon and Dumaine, *Correspondance de Napoléon I*, XXVIII, pp. 245–8.

50. For all this, see E. Gabory, *Les guerres du Vendée* (Paris, 2009), pp. 808–76. For eyewitness accounts of the campaign, cf. S. Canuel, *Mémoires sur la guerre de la Vendée en 1815* (Paris, 1817) and C. de Beaumont d'Autichamps, *Mémoires pour servir a l'histoire de la campagne de 1815 dans la Vendée* (Paris, 1817), whilst a detailed narrative may be found in A. Johannet, *La Vendée en trois époques: de 1793 jusqu'a l'empire, 1815–1832* (Paris, 1840), II, pp. 1–113.

51. P.V.J. de Bourniseaux, *Histoire des guerres de la Vendée et des chouans depuis l'année 1792 jusqu'au 1815* (Paris, 1815), III, pp. 131–92. M.P. du Breil du Pontbriand, *Un chouan: le general du Boisguy* (Paris, 1904) is a useful biography.

52. Cf. Hobhouse, *Substance of Some Letters*, I, pp. 20–5, 398. This, of course, is perfectly true, but it should not be forgotten that the fighting in the west and south diverted many thousands of troops who might otherwise have taken part in the Waterloo campaign.

53. *Cit.* Champollion-Figeac (ed.), *Fourier et Napoléon*, p. 218. The younger brother of the man who deciphered the Rosetta stone, Champollion-Figeac eventually became the curator of the manuscript section of the Bibliothèque Nationale. The words that he places in Napoleon's mouth on this occasion are worth recording as an indication of the emperor's self-image at this point. 'People talk a lot about my wars. In reality, the enemies of France sold her out. If I had wanted to make peace, I would have had to make shameful sacrifices … and I was not prepared to deprive her of anything I had not given her myself [a reference to Belgium and the left bank of the Rhine, both of which had been acquired prior to the coup of 18 Brumaire]. The legislative body, the council of state, the senate, all of them supported me. Indeed, they gave me 200,000 men when I had only asked for 100,000: the flatterers went further than I wanted. I will get rid of them, then: what I want is new men, men who are devoted patriots. Look how I was led from one misfortune to the next from Moscow all the way to Fontainebleau. I could have continued the war on the Loire, but I did not want civil strife. Rather than risk this, I stepped down, and look what they did. My rights are no other than those of the people: the populace should be told this and assured that I desire neither servitude nor empire, and that we will keep the peace. We must forget that we were the masters of other nations … [and] revise the structures of the state for the good of the people.' *Cit. ibid*, p. 219.

54. Carnot (ed.), *Mémoires sur Carnot*, II, p. 452. For a general discusión, cf. I. Collins, *Napoleon and his Parliaments, 1800–1815* (London, 1979), pp. 157–8.

55. *Ibid*, p. 159.

56. D. Melgari (ed.), *Journal intime de Benjamin Constant et letters a sa famille et ses amis* (Paris, 1895), p. 151.

57. Cornillon, *Le Bourbonnais pendant les cent jours*, pp. 29–30.

58. Lhomer, *Cent jours*, pp. 11–12. As more than one historian has pointed out, there was much comedy in the manner in which all round the country mayors and prefects issued proclamations enjoining the population to accept the authority of Napoleon only a matter of days after issuing proclamations enjoining the population to resist him to the death. For example G. d'Hauteclocque, 'Les cent jours dans le Pas-de-Calais, 20 mars-8 juillet 1815', *Mémoires de l'Académie des Ciences, Lettres et Arts d'Arras*, XXXVI, No. 1 (January 1895), p. 38.

59. Cornillon, *Le Bourbonnais pendant les cent jours*, pp. 40–4; d'Hauteclocque, 'Les cent jours dans le Pas-de-Calais, 20 mars-8 juillet 1815', pp. 41–2.

60. The idea of a general purge of the administration, had already been mooted by Napoleon as early as 26 March, but in the first instance it had been left to the existing prefects (hence, perhaps, the apparent failure to make much progress. Cf. Napoleon to L. Carnot, 26 March 1815, *cit.* Plon and Dumaine (eds.), *Correspondance de Napoléon*, XXVIII, p. 44.

61. Aldersey White, *Adventurous Life of Count Lavallette*, II, p. 97. For a good example of the danger of a purge one might cite the case of the Pas de Calais, where the post of prefect was eventually given to André Dumont, a sometime regicide who inaugurated his term of office by openly threatening his Department with a fresh Terror. Cf. D'Hauteclocque, 'Les cent jours dans le Pas de-Calais', pp. 54–5.

62. Cf. Champollion-Figeac (ed.), *Fourier et Napoléon*, pp. 252–4.

63. Collins, *Napoleon and his Parliaments*, p. 164. The failure of the administration in 1815 is revealed all too clearly by Napoleon's correspondence with Carnot. Thus, in letter after letter, we read bitter complaints in respect of this or that prefect or mayor. Cf. Anon, *Lettres et notes de Napoléon Bonaparte a Carnot, son Ministre de l'Interieure pendant les Cent Jours* (Brussels, 1819). In fairness to Carnot, it has to be said that from the start he had warned Napoleon against a sudden purge of the administration: change, he agreed was necessary, but it should be gradual, and as limited as possible, not least because of the circumstances in which France was placed: 'In the crisis which approaches, it will be the strong who are needed: every functionary who accepts the charge must accept that he is going into the breach.' L. Carnot to Napoleon, 2 April 1815, *cit.* L. Carnot (ed.), *Correspondance inédite*, p. 37.

64. Cf. Marquis de Noailles (ed.), *The Life and Memoirs of Count Molé, 1781–1855* (London, 1923), I, pp. 210–25. Pressed hard by Napoleon to accept his offers, Molé initially claimed that he was not fitted for either the Ministry of Foreign Affairs or the Ministry of the Interior, and, further, that even had this not been the case his health was 'almost ruined' and he himself 'incapable of continuous work'. However, eventually he came clean: 'I see revolution threatening France once more with terror and proscriptions … I see the men who produced the Law of Suspects and proposed the deportation of the nobles, men who are all ready to resume and renew our long series of disasters … I do not feel equal to coping with such men, and my sole thought is to let them forget me.' *Ibid*, pp. 221–2.

65. Mollien, *Mémoires*, IV, pp. 487–8.

66. *Cit.* Tulard, *Napoleon*, p. 335.

67. Napoleon to L. Carnot, 10 May 1815, *cit.* Plon and Dumaine (eds.), *Correspondance de Napoléon I*, XXVIII, p. 198; cf. also Napoleon to L, Carnot, 8 June 1815, *cit. ibid*, p. 308. In general, Napoleon's dispatches are a poor source for the events of 1815. In his letters, the vast majority of which are about such matters as the details of military organization or the provision of sufficient muskets and cannons, all is activity and decision, and the focus is very much the immense personal efforts which Napoleon made to ready France for war. Only very occasionally do we hear even of the fighting in western France, let alone the unrest and discontent that gripped much of the rest of the country. Yet, traditionally, it is Plon and Dumaine to whom those wishing to touch upon the French home front have tended to turn.

68. Hanoteau (ed.), *Mémoires de la Reine Hortense*, p. 354.

69. Hobhouse, *Substance of Some Letters*, I, p. 188. Such was the clamour at the *acte additionnel* that Napoleon was forced to issue a decree advancing the timetable for the convocation of the new assembly and implying that it would be permitted to revise the *acte* as it wished.

70. Champollion-Figeac (ed.), *Fourier et Napoléon*, pp. 264–5.

71. For all this, cf. Crook, "'Ma volonté est celle du people": voting in the plebiscite and parliamentary elections during Napoleon's Hundred Days, May-June 1815'; Crook, 'Uses of democracy: elections and plebiscites in Napoleonic France'. The standard French account is F. Busche, *Le plébescit des cent jours, avril-mai, 1815* (Geneva, 1974).

72. There are, however, some dissonant voices here. Herewith the account of Captain Coignet, for example: 'Backed by the whole of his general staff, the emperor made a speech. He had had the eagles brought to the ceremony to distribute to the army and the national guard. In his most stentorian voice, he cried to them, "Swear to defend your eagles! Do you swear it?" But the vows were made with little warmth. There was but little enthusiasm: the shouts were not like those of Austerlitz and Wagram, and the emperor perceived it.' Larchey (ed.), *Cahiers du Capitaine Coignet*, pp. 394–5. With regard to the new standards issued to the army, cf. T. Wise, *Flags of the Napoleonic Wars (I): Colours, Standards and Guidons of France and her Allies* (London, 1978), p. 10.

73. Poumiès de la Siboutie, *Recollections of a Parisian*, p. 148. For an excellent description of the assembly of the *champs de mai*, cf. Hobhouse, *Substance of Some Letters*, II, pp. 400–17.

74. Cf. Collins, *Napoleon and his Parliaments*, pp. 165–8.

75. Méneval, *Memoirs*, III, p. 455.

76. J.B. Bory de Saint Vincent, *Mémoires sur les cent jours pour servir d'introduction aux souvenirs de toute ma vie* (Paris, 1838), pp. 90 *champ de mai* 1.

77. The reappearance in France of several members of the Bonaparte family including Joseph, Lucien and Jerome did Napoleon no favours whatsoever. 'It was feared,' wrote Hortense de Beauharnais, 'that they still entertained pretensions to their old kingdoms, and did not believe that it would cost France anything to get them back.' Hanoteau (ed.), *Mémoires de la Reine Hortense*, II, p. 355.

78. Hobhouse, *Substance of Some Letters*, I, p. 466. For a general discussion of events in the new assembly prior to Waterloo, cf. *ibid*, I, pp. 434–44, 458–68. Cf. also Collins, *Napoleon and his Parliaments*, pp. 169–70.

79. There were doubters, however. Amongst them was Molé, who later claimed that he had told the emperor to his face that it was at best extremely foolhardy: 'The declaration embodies principles worthy of 1793: it begins with the words "all sovereignty resides in the people". With a principle such as that, the people can change its government and sovereign every day: it can give and take back the crown as it thinks fit; it could refuse it to your son.' Noailles, *Life and Memoirs of Count Molé*, I, p. 221.

80. For the full text of the *acte additionnelle*, cf. Plon and Dumaine (ed.), *Correspondance de Napoléon I*, XXVIII, pp. 140–7.

81. Collins, *Napoleon and his Parliaments*, p. 158.

82. *Cit.* Guizot, *Memoirs*, I, p. 67.

83. *Ibid*, p. 63. A further point to note here is the impact of Napoleon's return to power on business confidence. To quote Lazare Carnot, for example, 'The mere fear of war is already impacting on the fate of our manufactures in a most singular fashion: these have only ever been directed at the internal market, and in times of crisis this diminishes considerably.' *Cit.* L. Carnot to Napoleon, 30 April 1815, *cit.* Carnot (ed.), *Correspondance inédite*, p. 122.

84. R. Toombs, *France, 1814–1914* (London, 1996), p. 334.

85. R.S. Alexander, *Bonaparte and Revolutionary Tradition: the Fédérés of 1815* (Cambridge, 1991), pp. 21–106. The appointment of Joseph Fouché to the administration was

problematic in another sense. The archetypal political survivor, except for that of Louis XVIII (a failure that did not come about for want of trying), Fouché had served under, and, indeed, conspired against, every single regime that had ruled France since 1792: though strongly republican at heart, he was not a man to let ideological principle stand in the way of survival and personal advancement. To include him in the administration, then, was to include within its ranks a figure who could not be relied upon were things to go wrong, and Waterloo was in fact to see Fouché take a leading role in excluding Napoleon from power: indeed, within a matter of days he was head of the new provisional government. That said, it is absurd to argue that Fouché was somehow the architect of the emperor's downfall: at best, he can be seen as a figure who was ideally placed to take charge of the cause of revolt once it had manifested itself. What does beg the question, however, is the issue of why so calculating a figure as Fouché supported so obviously hopeless an adventure as the Hundred Days: one can only presume here that he believed that possession of the Ministry of General Police would enhance his chances of survival in the event of a French defeat. For a recent biography, see R. Mirante, *Medusa's Head: the Rise and Survival of Joseph Fouché, Inventor of the Modern Police State* (Richmond, British Columbia, 2014).

86. Guizot, *Memoirs*, I, p. 63.
87. Hobhouse, *Substance of Some Letters*, I, pp. 209–12. In fact, Hobhouse was mistaken: the origins of the *fédérés* lay not in Paris, but rather in such towns as Nantes and Rennes and, more particularly, fears of the resurgence of *chouannerie*. Cf. Tulard, *Napoleon*, p. 336.
88. Poumiès de la Siboutie, *Recollections of a Parisian*, p. 147.
89. Waresquiel, *Cent jours*, pp. 332–3.
90. Mollien, *Mémoires*, IV, p. 491. What makes the situation still more extraordinary is that Napoleon was behaving entirely cynically. As he told an ever more alarmed Molé, 'At the moment we shall certainly have to accept the the help of the Jacobins to ward off the most pressing of our dangers. But you may be easy in your mind: I am here to control them, and they will never make me go further than I want to go.' Noailles, *Life and Memoirs of Count Molé*, I, p. 222.
91. Alexander, *Bonapartism and Revolutionary Tradition*, p. 57.
92. *Cit. ibid*, p. 109. It should be noted that, terrified of the crowd as he was, Napoleon was intensely hostile to the idea of the organization of a popular militia of a specifically political character that would be outside the structures of the army and the National Guard and is reputed to have witnessed the demonstration of 14 May with the utmost repugnance. That said, on 22 April he had sanctioned the formation of volunteer guerrilla bands in all the frontier departments. Cf. decree of Napoleon, 22 April 2015, *cit.* Plon and Dumaine (ed.), *Correspondance de Napoléon I*, XXVIII, pp. 131–3. Whether any such bands came to fruition is another matter, however. Meanwhile, a letter to Marshal Davout of 1 May had spoken of a the organization of a *levée en masse*, but, reading on it becomes clear that the use of the term is disingenuous, the emperor being quite specific that what he was talking about was really nothing more than an amalgam of the National Guard, the country's thousands of gamekeepers and the *gendarmerie*, together with those men of good will who might choose to offer it their services. Cf. Napoleon to L. Davout, 1 May 1815, *cit. ibid*, pp. 171–4. Following the demonstration of 14 May, the emperor decreed the formation of twenty-four battalions of *tirailleurs fédérés* but the command of these units was given to retired or supernumerary army officers, and it is clear that he envisaged them as nothing more than an extension of the Paris National Guard – that what was afoot was nothing more than a manoeuvre designed to guide popular excitement into safer channels. Cf. decree of Napoleon, 15 May 1815, *cit. ibid*, pp. 216–17. Just a fortnight later, indeed, he was writing to Davout that he had no intention of arming the *tirailleurs fédérés* whilst there were still regular units of the National Guard without sufficient arms. Cf. Napoleon to L. Davout, 29 May 1815, *cit. ibid*, p. 276.

93. For example, P. Britten Austin, *1815: the Return of Napoleon* (London, 2002), pp. 152–60.

94. Champollion-Figeac (ed.), *Fourier et Napoléon*, p. 204.

95. M.H. Beyle (aka Stendhal), *A Life of Napoleon*, ed. A. Lentin (London, 2004), p. 211. Unlike Champollion-Figeac, Beyle was not an eyewitness to Napoleon's entry into Grenoble. That said, he was a native of the region, and it may be assumed that his remarks were based on accounts that he received from friends or relatives who did see what went on.

96. J. Fourier to F. de Montesquieu, 4 March 1815, *cit.* Champollion-Figeac (ed.), *Fourier et Napoléon*, p. 190. In a letter written the next day, Fourier goes still further and claims that the inhabitants were in a state of consternation and that many of them had come to him and proclaimed their outright opposition to Napoleon. Even accepting that there is a degree of whistling in the dark here, it is at least clear that many of the *notables* in particular were horrified at the turn which events had taken. Cf. J. Fourier to F. de Montesquieu, 4 March 1815, *cit. ibid*, pp. 194–5.

97. *Cit.* P. Leuilliot, *La premiere restauration et les cent jours en Alsace* (Paris, 1958), p. 182. Notwithstanding this claim, Strasbourg still witnessed a popular uprising in favour of Napoleon when news arrived that he had reached Paris, whilst there were anti-Bourbon riots in many other towns and villages; as in parts of the south, part of the issue appears to have been Protestant fear and resentment. Cf. *ibid*, pp. 191–201.

98. Aldersey White, *Adventurous Life of Count Lavallette*, II, p. 94. According to Lucien Bonaparte, this want of positive enthusiasm even extended to many Jacobins, plenty of whom 'saw Napoleon as just another monarch and in their republican ardour believed him to be just as bad as Louis XVIII'. Bonaparte, *La verité sur les cent jours*, p. 40.

99. Rillier, 'Les cent jours en Belgique et en France', pp. 253–4.

100. W. Scott, *Paul's Letters*, pp. 41–2.

101. Develay, *La Bourgogne pendant les cent jours*, p. 128.

102. Leuilliot, *La première restauration et les cent jours en Alsace*, pp. 234–50. Yet even here there were problems. For example, newly appointed to the command of the Army of the Rhine, on 14 May General Rapp had to complain to the prefect of Bas-Rhin that 'deaf to the voice of honour and *la patrie* alike', large numbers of national guards had either failed to turn up at the designated rendezvous or immediately returned to their homes. Cf. J. Rapp to J. de Bry, 14 May 1815, *cit.* F.C. Heitz, *Strasbourg pendant ses deux blocus et les cent jours: recueil des pieces officielles accompagnés d'une relation succinctes dans les années 1813, 1814 et 1815* (Strasbourg, 1861), p. 157. Equally, on 5 June the mayor had to issue 'a last warning' to the many members of the two battalions of élite companies of the Guard that had been permanently mobilised to help garrison the city who were currently absent without leave that troops would be billeted on their families unless they returned to their duty immediately. Cf. proclamation of the mayor of Strasbourg, 5 June 2015, *cit. ibid*, p. 169.

103. Hobhouse, *Substance of Some Letters*, II, pp. 3–5.

104. Bonaparte, *La verité sur les cent jours*, p. 60; W. Scott, *Paul's Letters*, p. 351.

105. Cf. proclamation of the mayor of Strasbourg, 10 May 1815, *cit.* Heitz, *Strasbourg pendant ses deux blocus*, p. 154.

106. *Cit.* Cornillon, *Le Bourbonnais pendant les cent jours*, p. 43. According to Cornillon, so widespread was discontent in the Department of the Allier that by the time that Waterloo was fought it was on the brink of insurrection. *Ibid*, pp. 52–6. It should be noted that the general disaffection did not mean that there was no support for the emperor: on the contrary, the arrival of the news of Waterloo led to serious rioting in the capital. *Ibid*, pp. 101–9.

107. *Cit.* D'Hauteclocque, 'Les cent jours dans le Pas-de-Calais', pp. 142–3.

108. A. Lignereux, *La France rébellionnaire: les résistances a la gendarmerie, 1800–1859* (Rennes, 2008), pp. 81–5.

109. Guizot, *Memoirs*, II, p. 74.

110. *Ibid*, p. 82.
111. Mercer, *Journal of the Waterloo Campaign*, I, pp. 366–7. As Mercer later points out, it is but fair to note that the warm welcome given British troops was not unconnected with the simple fact that they were not Prussian, and therefore on the whole treated the civilian populace with courtesy and respect whilst at the same time paying for everything that they requisitioned. *Ibid*, II, p. 28.
112. *Ibid*, II, pp. 8–20 *passim*. Liberated by the handful of troops that had throughout remained loyal to Louis XVIII, Armentières witnessed particular jubilation: 'What a reception did we receive! We were so swamped by the crowd ... that there were quite literally moments – I am not exaggerating in the slightest – when my horse was lifted off the ground.' Cf. Rillier, 'Les cent jours en Belgique et la France', p. 322.
113. Fellowes, *Paris during the Interesting Month of July 1815*, p. 11.
114. W. Scott, *Paul's Letters*, pp. 272–3.
115. *Ibid*, p. 351.
116. *Ibid*, p. 353.
117. Noailles, *Life and Memoirs of Count Molé*, I, pp. 242–3.
118. B. Liddell Hart (ed.), *The Letters of Private Wheeler, 1809–1828* (London, 1951), p. 178. As in 1814, there was doubtless much cynicism in all this. As William Lawrence of the Fortieth Foot observed, for example, 'We continued on our march to within a few miles of ... Paris, where we remained for a short time, coming up here with our allies the Prussians. They had already opened fire on that city of despotism, which was returned faintly by the enemy, but once the balance is turned, and once a man, however great, is defeated, all seem to forsake him, and he immediately becomes a usurper as was shown to be true in this Napoleon's case. There is not a doubt that the population would have held to him if he had been a conqueror, but, as it was, the whole city now changed its sentiments from Napoleon to Louis XVIII.' Bankes (ed.), *Autobiography of Sergeant William Lawrence*, pp. 218–19. This, however, is by-the-by: what matters is simply that the inhabitants of the capital were not willing to fight for Napoleon.
119. S. Monick (ed.), *Douglas' Tale of the Peninsula and Waterloo* (London, 1997), p. 104. In other cases French women who had married British soldiers returned home with them to Britain, two such cases being the wives of William Lawrence of the Fortieth Foot and Edward Costello of the Rifles.
120. Cf. W. Scott, *Paul's Letters*, pp. 156–9.
121. *Ibid*, pp. 50–1.
122. Hobhouse, *Substance of Some Letters*, II, pp. 6–10.
123. For example, Mercer, *Journal of the Waterloo Campaign*, II, p. 40.
124. W. Scott, *Paul's Letters*, pp. 346–7.
125. *Cit*. J. Scott, *Visit to Paris in 1814*, pp. xlvii–xlix. Disturbances involving the *fédérés* continued for the next month or so – on 16 July, for example, large numbers came out on the streets of various *faubourgs* wearing medals awarded by the emperor, and there were even a handful of acts of more-or-less individual armed resistance. However, tales that were circulating amongst English visitors who arrived in Paris in the immediate wake of Waterloo of pitched battles between the *fédérés* and the National Guard involving thousands of combatants – for a good example, see Fellowes, *Paris during the Interesting Month of July 1815*, p. 37 – are all too clearly wild exaggerations, while trouble of any sort became increasingly sporadic, the movement for the most part eventually allowing itself to be disarmed whereupon it quietly melted away. For all this, see Alexander, *Bonaparte and the Revolutionary Tradition*, pp. 209–12; Fellowes, *Paris during the Interesting Month of July 1815*, pp. 78–9.

126. Mercer, *Journal of the Waterloo Campaign*, II, p. 55; Thiry, *Les débuts de la seconde restauration*, p. 121.

127. W. Scott, *Paul's Letters*, pp. 155–6.

128. *Ibid*, p. 385.

129. Develay, *La Bourgogne pendant les cent jours*, pp. 204–5; D'Hauteclocque, 'Les cent jours dans le Pas-de-Calais', pp. 161–9.

130. W. Scott, *Paul's Letters*, p. 156.

131. Mercer, *Journal of the Waterloo Campaign*, II, p. 15.

132. For a lively account of these events, cf. Anon, *Memoirs of the Personal and Private Life of Napoleon Bonaparte with Copious Historical Illustrations and Original Anecdotes from the Manuscript of Count Labédoyère, interspersed with Extracts from M.V. Arnault, Counts Rapp, Montholon, Las Cases, Gourgaud, Ségur, etc, preceded by an Interesting Analysis of the French Revolution* (London, 1835), II, pp. 880–6. Cf. also Bonaparte, *La verité sur les cent jours*, pp. 41–56.

133. For a recent study, cf. J.D. Markham, *The Road to Saint Helena: Napoleon after Waterloo* (Barnsley, 2008). Cf. also G. Martineau, *Napoleon Surrenders* (London, 1971).

134. *Cit*. Maizeau, *Vie du Maréchale Ney*, pp. 170–1. The reference to the Guard was prompted by perhaps the most preposterous claim ever put forward by a Frenchman in respect of the battle of Waterloo, namely an allegation on the part of General Drouot that the last French attack had not been defeated at all, the panic on the western part of the field at the close of the day rather being produced by that fact that the Guard lost such heavy casualties that the wounded started emerging from the clouds of smoke occasioned by the fighting on top of the ridge in such crowds that it was mistakenly assumed that the attackers had been forced to retreat. Whether any sort of stand could really have been made is a moot point. In theory, France still had at least 100,000 men under arms, but among the troops who had escaped from Belgium morale and discipline alike were exceedingly poor, while many of the men concerned were serving in second-line formations that could not be relied upon: taking the example of Paris, for instance, 18,000 of the 40,000 defenders were improvised *tirailleurs fédérés*. Cf. Thiry, *Les débuts de la seconde restauration*, p. 3.

135. Coote, *Napoleon and the Hundred Days*, p. 241.

136. The best study of the emergence of the Napoleonic legend by far is constituted by S. Hazarreesingh, *The Legend of Napoleon* (London, 2004).

137. For the twists and turns of French historiography from 1815 up until the years immediately before the Second World War, cf. Geyl, *Napoleon For and Against*.

138. For an eloquent (and extremely amusing) statement of this case, cf. Clarke, *How the French won Waterloo (or think they did)*.

Select Bibliography

Printed Primary Sources

Adeane, J.H., and Grenfell, M. (eds.), *Before and after Waterloo: Letters from Edward Stanley, sometime Bishop of Norwich* (London, 1907).

Alison, A., *Travels in France during the Years 1814 and 1815 comprising a Residence at Paris during the Stay of the Allied Armies and at Aix during the Landing of Bonaparte* (Edinburgh, 1815).

Anon, *Lettres et notes de Napoléon Bonaparte à Carnot, son Ministre de l'Interieure pendant les cent jours* (Brussels, 1819).

Anon, *The Journal of the Three Days of the Battle of Waterloo, being my own Personal Journal of what I saw and of the Events in which I played a Part in the Battle of Waterloo and Retreat to Paris* (London, 1816).

Anon (ed.), *Memoirs of the Personal and Private Life of Napoleon Bonaparte with Copious Historical Illustrations and Original Anecdotes from the Manuscript of Count Labédoyère, interspersed with Extracts from M.V. Arnault, Counts Rapp, Montholon, Las Cases, Gourgaud, Ségur, etc, preceded by an Interesting Analysis of the French Revolution* (London, 1835).

Anon (ed.), *Memorials of the Late War* (Edinburgh, 1831).

Anon, *Personal Narrative of a Private Soldier who served in the Forty-Second Highlanders for Twelve Years during the Late War* (London, 1821).

Anon, *Some Particulars of the Battle at Waterloo in a Letter from a Sergeant in the Guards* (London, 1816).

Bankes, G.N. (ed.), *The Autobiography of Sergeant William Lawrence, a Hero of the Peninsular and Waterloo Campaigns* (London, 1886).

Batty, R., *Campaign of the Left Wing of the Allied Army in the Western Pyrenees and the South of France in the Years 1813–1814 under Field-Marshal the Marquess of Wellington* (London, 1823).

Bausset, L. de, *Private Memoirs of the Court of Napoleon and some Public Events of the Imperial Reign from 1805 to the First of May 1814* (Philadelphia, 1828).

Beauchamp, M. de, *An Authentic Narrative of the Invasion of France in 1814* (London, 1815).

Beaumont d'Autichamps, C. de, *Mémoires pour servir a l'histoire de la campagne de 1815 dans la Vendée* (Paris, 1817).

Beugnot, J.C., *Mémoires du Comte Beugnot, ancien ministre, 1783–1815*, ed. A. Beugnot (Paris, 1868).

Beslay, P. (ed.), *Un officier d'état-major sous le premier empire: souvenirs militaires d'Octave Levavasseur, officier d'artillerie, aide de camp du Maréchal Ney, 1802–1815* (Paris, 1914).

Bentley, N. (ed.), *Selections from the Reminiscences of Captain Gronow* (London, 1977).

Beyle, H. (aka Stendhal), *A Life of Napoleon*, ed. A Lentin (London, 2004).

Birkbeck, M., *Notes on a Journey through France from Dieppe through Paris and Lyons to the Pyrenees and back through Toulouse in July, August and September, 1814* (London, 1815).

Birks, M. (ed.), *The Young Hussar: the Peninsular-War Journal of Colonel Thomas Wildman of Newstead Abbey* (Brighton, 2007).

Blayney, A., *Narrative of a Forced Journey through Spain and France as a Prisoner of War in the Years 1810 to 1814* (London, 1814).

Blaze, S., *Mémoires d'un apothicaire sur le guerre d'Espagne pendant les années 1808 à 1814* (Paris, 1828).

Bonaparte, L., *La verité sur les cent jours* (Paris, 1835).

Bory de Saint Vincent, J.B., *Mémoires sur les cent jours pour servir d'introduction aux souvenirs de toute ma vie* (Paris, 1838).

Bourachot, C. (ed.), *Souvenirs militaires du Captaine Jean-Baptiste Lemonnier-Delafosse* (Paris, n.d.).

Bowdler, T., *A Postscript to the Letters written in France in 1814* (London, 1815).

Brett-James, A. (ed.), *Europe against Napoleon: the Leipzig Campaign, 1813, from Eyewitness Accounts* (London, 1970).

Bunbury, T., *Reminiscences of a Veteran, being Personal and Military Adventures in Portugal, Spain, France, Malta, New South Wales, Norfolk Island, New Zealand, the Andaman Islands and India* (London, 1861).

Butler, A.J. (ed.), *The Memoirs of Baron Thiébault, late Lieutenant-General in the French Army* (London, 1896).

Canuel, S., *Mémoires sur la guerre de la Vendée en 1815* (Paris, 1817).

Carnot, H.L. (ed.), *Mémoires sur Carnot par son fils* (Paris, 1863).

Carnot, L. (ed.), *Correspondance inédite du Général Carnot avec Napoléon pendant les cent jours* (Paris, 1819).

Chamand, A.M. *The Adventurous Life of Count Lavallette, Bonaparte's Aide-de-Camp and Postmaster-General, by Himself,* ed. L. Aldersey White (London, 1936).

Champollion-Figeac, J.J. (ed.), *Fourier et Napoléon: Egypte et les cent jours – mémoires et documents inédits* (Paris, 1844).

Channing, W.E., *Memoirs of Napoleon Bonaparte* (London, 1840).

Chateaubriand, F.R. de, *The Memoirs of François René, Vicomte de Chateaubriand, sometime Ambassador to England* (London, 1902).

Cooke, J.H., *A Narrative of Events in the South of France and of the Attack on New Orleans in 1814 and 1815* (London, 1835).

Costello, E., *Adventures of a Soldier written by Himself, being the Memoirs of Edward Costello, K.S.F, formerly a Non-Commissioned Officer in the Rifle Brigade, late Captain in the British Legions and now one of the Wardens in the Tower of London, comprising Narratives of the Campaigns in the Peninsula under the Duke of Wellington and the Subsequent Civil Wars in Spain* (London, 1852).

D'Espinchal, H., *Souvenirs militaires, 1792–1814*, ed. F. Masson and E. Boyer (Paris, 1901).

Dobbs, J., *Recollections of an Old Fifty-Second Man* (Waterford, 1863).

Donaldson, J., *Recollections in the Eventful Life of a Soldier* (Edinburgh, 1852).

Drouet, J.B., *Le Maréchal Drouet, Comte d'Erlon: vie militaire écrit pour lui-même* (Paris, 1844).

Dufour de Pradt, D., *The Congress of Vienna* (London, 1816).

Fain, A.J.F., *The Manuscript of 1814: a History of Events which led to the Abdication of Napoleon written at the Command of the Emperor* (London, 1823).

Fain, A.J.F., *Memoirs of the Invasion of France by the Allied Armies and of the Last Six Months of the Reign of Napoleon* (London, 1834).

Fée, A.L.A., *Souvenirs de la guerre d'Espagne, dite de l'independance, 1809–1813* (Paris, 1856).

Fellowes, W.D., *Paris during the Interesting Month of July 1815: a Series of Letters addressed to a Friend in London* (London, 1815).

Fézensac, Duc de, *Souvenirs militaires de 1804 a 1814* (Paris, 1863).

Firmin-Didot, G. (ed.), *Royauté ou empire? La France en 1814 d'après les rapports inédits du Comte Angles* (Paris, n.d.).

Fletcher, I. (ed.), *A Guards Officer in the Peninsula: the Peninsular-War Letters of John Rous, 1812–1814* (Staplehurst, 1997).

Fleury de Chaboulon, P., *Memoirs of the Private Life, Return and Reign of Napoleon in 1815* (London, 1820).

Franklin, J. (ed.), *Waterloo: Netherlands Correspondence* (Ulverston, 2010).

Giraud, P., *Des Bourbons et des puisances étrangeres le 20 mars 1815* (Paris, 1815).

Giraud, P., *Campagne de Paris en 1814 précédée d'un coup d'oeil sur celle de 1813* (Paris, 1814).

Giraud, P., *The Campaigns of Paris in 1814 and 1815 with a Sketch of the Campaign of 1813, or a Brief and Impartial Relation of Events from the Invasion of France by the Foreign Armies in 1814 to the Capitulation of Paris and the First Dethronement and Abdication of Bonaparte with a Concise History of the Events of the 15th, 16th, 17th and 18th of June 1815 or the Termination of his Political Life* (London, 1815).

Glover, G. (ed.), *An Eloquent Soldier: the Peninsular War Journals of Lieutenant Charles Crowe of the Inniskillings, 1812–1814* (Barnsley, 2011).

Glover, G. (ed.), *Eyewitness to the Peninsular War and the Battle of Waterloo: the Letters and Journals of Lieutenant-Colonel the Honourable James Stanhope, 1803 to 1825* (Barnsley, 2010).

Glover, G. (ed.), *A Guards Officer in the Peninsula and at Waterloo: the Letters of Captain George Bowles, Coldstream Guards, 1807–1819* (Godmanchester, 2008).

Glover, G. (ed.), *A Hellish Business: the Letters of Captain Kinloch, 32nd Light Infantry, 1806–16* (Godmanchester, 2007).

Glover, G. (ed.), *A Lifeguardsman in Spain, France and at Waterloo: the Memoirs of Sergeant-Major Thomas Playford, Second Lifeguards, 1810–1830* (Godmanchester, 2006).

Glover, G. (ed.), *Wellington's Lieutenant, Napoleon's Gaoler: the Peninsula and St Helena Diaries and Letters of Sir George Rideout Bingham, 1809–21* (Barnsley, 2005).

Glover, G. (ed.), *Wellington's Voice: the Candid Letters of Lieutenant-Colonel John Fremantle* (Barnsley, 2012).

Glover, G. (ed.), *The Waterloo Archive, II: German Sources* (Barnsley, 2014).

Guizot, F., *Memoirs to Illustrate the History of my Time* (London, 1858).

Hanoteau, J. (ed.), *Mémoires de la Reine Hortense* (Paris, 1927).

Henegan, R., *Seven Years' Campaigning in the Peninsula and the Netherlands from 1808 to 1815* (London, 1846).

Hobhouse, J.C., *The Substance of Some Letters written by an Englishman Resident in Paris during the Last Reign of the Emperor Napoleon* (London, 1816).

Jackson, Lady (ed.), *A Further Selection from the Diaries and Letters of Sir George Jackson, K.C.H, from 1809 to 1816* (London, 1873).

Johnston, R.M. (ed.), *In the Words of Napoleon: the Emperor Day by Day* (London, 2002).

Jones, P. (ed.), *In Napoleon's Shadow: being the First English-Language Edition of the Complete Memoirs of Louis-Joseph Marchand, Valet and Friend of the Emperor, 1811–1821* (San Francisco, 1998).

Jurgensen, J., *Travels through France and Germany in the Years 1815, 1816 and 1817 comprising a View of the Moral, Political and Social State of those Countries* (London, 1817).

Kincaid, J., *Adventures in the Rifle Brigade in the Peninsula, France and the Netherlands from 1809 to 1815* (London, 1830).

Ladrait de Lacharrière, J., *Journal inédit de Madame de Marigny, augmenté du journal de T.R. Underwood* (Paris, 1907).

La Garde-Chambonnas, A.L.C., *Anecdotal Recollections of the Congress of Vienna*, ed. A.D.V.M. Fleury (London, 1902).

Lamarque, M., *Mémoires et souvenirs du Général Lamarque* (Paris, 1835).

Lamothe-Langon, E.L., *Private Memoirs of the Court of Louis XVIII* (London, 1830).

Larchey, L. (ed.), *Les cahiers du Capitaine Coignet* (Paris, 1883).

Leach, J., *Rough Sketches in the Life of an Old Soldier during a Service in the East Indies, at the Siege of Copenhagen in 1807, in the Peninsula and the South of France in the Campaigns from 1808* to 1814 with the Light Division, in the Netherlands in 1815, including the Battles of Quatre Bras and Waterloo, with a Slight Sketch of the Three Years passed by the Army of Occupation in France (London, 1831).

Lecky, E. (ed.), Un général hollandais sous le premier empire: mémoires du Général Baron de Dedem de Gelder, 1774–1825 (Paris, 1900).

Lejeune, L., Memoirs of Baron Lejeune, Aide-de-Camp to Marshals Berthier, Davout and Oudinot, ed. A. Bell (London, 1897).

Lenormand, M., Réflexions impartiales sur le gouvernement de Louis XVIII et sur les fautes qui en ont entrainé le décadence (Paris, 1815).

Lequin, G. (ed.), Memoirs of the Comte de Rambuteau (London, 1904).

Liddell Hart, B. (ed.), The Letters of Private Wheeler, 1809–1828 (London, 1951).

Londonderry, Viscount, Narrative of the War in Germany and France in 1813 and 1814 (London, 1830).

Maitland, F., Narrative of the Surrender of Buonaparte and of his Residence on Board HMS Bellerophon with a Detail of the Principal Events that occurred in that Ship between the 24th of May and the 8th of August 1815 (London, 1826).

Maizeau, L.R.B., Vie du Maréchal Ney, Duc d'Elchingen, Prince de la Moskowa (Paris, 1816).

Marbot, M. de, The Memoirs of Baron de Marbot (London, 1892).

Mauduit, H., Les dernier jours de la grande armée ou souvenirs, correspondence et documents inédites de Napoléon en 1814 et 1815 (Paris, 1848).

Melgari, D. (ed.), Journal intime de Benjamin Constant et lettres a sa famille et ses amis (Paris, 1895).

Méneval, C.F. de, Memoirs to Serve for the History of Napoleon I from 1802 to 1815, ed. R.H. Sherard (London, 1895).

Mennechet, E., Lettres sur la restauration: seize ans sous les Bourbons, 1814–1830 (Paris, 1832).

Mercer, A.C., Journal of the Waterloo Campaign kept throughout the Campaign of 1815 (London, 1870).

Metternich, R. (ed.), Memoirs of Prince Metternich (New York, 1881).

Mikaberidze, A. (ed.), Russian Eyewitness Accounts of the Campaign of 1814 (London, 2013).

Mikhailofsky-Danilevsky, A, History of the Campaign in France in 1814 (London, 1839).

Mollien, N., Mémoires d'un Ministre du Trésor Publique, 1780–1815 (Paris, 1845).

Monick, S. (ed.), Douglas' Tale of the Peninsula and Waterloo (London, 1997).

Monick, S. (ed.), The Iberian and Waterloo Campaigns: the Letters of Lieutenant James Hope, 92nd (Highland). Regiment, 1811–1815 (Heathfield, 2000).

Moore-Smith, G.C. (ed.), The Autobiography of Sir Harry Smith, 1787–1819 (London, 1910).

Morris, T., Recollections of Military Service in 1813, 1814 and 1815 through Germany, Holland and France including some Details of the Battles of Quatre Bras and Waterloo (London, 1845).

Muffling, P. von, Passages from my Life, together with Memoirs of the Campaign of 1813 and 1814 (London, 1853).

Neithardt von Gneisenau, A.W., The Life and Campaigns of Field-Marshal Prince Blücher of Wahlstatt from the Period of his Birth and First Appointment in the Prussian Service down to his Second Entry into Paris in 1815 (London, 1815).

Noailles, Marquis de, The Life and Memoirs of Count Molé, 1781–1855 (London, 1923).

O'Meara, B. (ed.), Historical Memoirs of Napoleon (Philadelphia, 1820).

O'Meara, B., Napoleon in Exile or a Voice from Saint Helena: the Opinions and Reflections of Napoleon on the Most Important Events of his Life and Government in His Own Words (London, 1822).

Palmerston, Viscount, Selections from Private Journals of Tours in France in 1815 and 1818 (London, 1871).

Plon, H., and Dumaine, J. (eds.), Correspondance de Napoléon I publiée par ordre de l'Empereur Napoléon III (Paris, 1858–69).

Poumiès de la Siboutie, F.L., *Recollections of a Parisian (Docteur Poumiès de la Siboutie) under Six Sovereigns, two Revolutions and a Republic, 1789–1863*, ed. A. Branche and A. Dagoury (London, 1911).

Rapp, J., *Memoirs of General Count Rapp, first Aide-de-Camp to the Emperor* (London, 1823).

Rillier, F., 'Les cent jours en Belgique et en France', in Jullien, A. (ed.), *Soldats suisses au service étranger* (Geneva, 1910), IIII, pp. 237–347.

Robertson, I. (ed.), *The Subaltern: the Diaries of George Gleig during the Peninsular War* (Barnsley, 2013).

Rochefoucauld, L.F. de, *Mémoires du Duc de la Rochefoucauld* (Paris, 1817).

Rousset, E., *Recollections of Marshal Macdonald, Duke of Tarentum* (London, 1892).

Saint-Chamans, A. de, *Mémoires du Général Comte de Saint-Chamans, ancien aide de camp du Maréchal Soult, 1802–1832* (Paris, 1896).

Saint-Léon, L.B. de, *Mémoires et souvenirs de Charles de Pougens* (Paris, 1834).

Saint-Marcellin, M. de, *Rélation d'un voyage de Paris à Gand en 1815* (Paris, 1823).

Schlumberger, G. (ed.), *Journal du route du Capitaine Robinaux, 1803–1832* (Paris, 2009).

Scott, J., *Paris Revisited in 1815 by Way of Brussels including a Walk over the Field of Battle at Waterloo* (London, 1816).

Scott, J., *A Visit to Paris in 1814, being a Review of the Moral, Political, Intellectual and Social Condition of the French Capital* (London, 1816).

Scott, W., *Paul's Letters to his Kinsfolk* (Edinburgh, 1816).

Seaton, R.C. (ed.), *Notes and Reminiscences of a Staff Officer chiefly relating to the Waterloo Campaign and to Saint-Helena Matters during the Captivity of Napoleon* (London, 1903).

Shaw-Kennedy, J, *Notes on the Battle of Waterloo* (London, 1865).

Siborne, H.T., (ed.), *Waterloo Letters: a Selection from Original and Hitherto Unpublished Letters Bearing on the Operations of the Sixteenth, Seventeenth and Eighteenth June 1815* (London, 1891).

Stiegler, G. (ed.), *Memoirs of Marshal Oudinot, Duc de Reggio compiled from the Hitherto Unpublished Souvenirs of the Duchesse de Reggio* (New York, 1897).

Stuart, B. (ed.), *Soldier's Glory, being* Rough Notes of an Old Soldier *by Sir George Bell arranged and edited by his Kinsman, Brian Stuart* (London, 1956).

Underwood, T.T., *A Narrative of Memorable Events in Paris preceding the Capitulation and during the Occupancy of that City by the Allied Armies in the Year 1814, being Extracts from the Journal of a* Detenu *who continued a Prisoner on Parole in the French Capital from the Year 1803 to 1814, also Anecdotes of Bonaparte's Journey to Elba* (London, 1828).

Weigall, R. (ed.), *Correspondence of Lord Burghersh, afterwards Eleventh Earl of Westmorland, 1808–1840* (London, 1912).

Secondary Sources

Alexander, R.S., *Bonaparte and Revolutionary Tradition: the Fédérés of 1815* (Cambridge, 1991).

Artz, F., *France under the Bourbon Restoration, 1814–1830* (New York, 1963).

Ashby, R., *Napoleon against Great Odds: the Emperor and the Defenders of France, 1814* (Oxford, 2010).

Atteridge, A.H., *Joachim Murat: Marshal of France and King of Naples* (London, 1911).

Baker-Smith, V., *Wellington's Hidden Heroes: the Dutch and Belgians at Waterloo* (Oxford, 2015).

Barbero, A., *The Battle: a History of the Battle of Waterloo* (London, 2005).

Bergeron, L., *France under Napoleon* (Princeton, New Jersey, 1981).

Berthier de Sauvigny, G. de, *The Bourbon Restoration* (Philadelphia, 1966).

Black, J., *The Battle of Waterloo: a New History* (New York, 2010).

Bourniseaux, P.V.J. de, *Histoire des guerres de la Vendée et des chouans depuis l'année 1792 jusqu'au 1815* (Paris, 1815).

Breil du Pontbriand, M.P. du, *Un chouan: le general du Boisguy* (Paris, 1904).

Broers, M., *Europe under Napoleon* (London, 1996).

Bryant, A., *The Age of Elegance, 1812–1822* (London, 1950).

Bury, J.P.T., *France, 1814–1940* (sixth edition; London, 2003).

Busche, F., *Le plébescit des cent jours, avril–mai, 1815* (Geneva, 1974).

Caldwell, G., and Cooper, R., *Rifle Green at Waterloo* (revised edition; Leicester, 2015).

Chandler, D.G., *The Campaigns of Napoleon: the Mind and Method of History's Greatest Soldier* (London, 1966).

Chandler, D.G. (ed.), *Napoleon's Marshals* (London, 1986).

Chapman, T., *The Congress of Vienna: Origins, Processes and Results* (London, 1998).

Chesney, C., *Waterloo Lectures: a Study of the Campaign of 1815* (second edition, enlarged; London, 1869).

Clark, C., *Iron Kingdom: the Rise and Downfall of Prussia, 1600–1947* (London, 2006).

Clarke, S., *How the French won Waterloo (or think they did)* (London, 2015).

Clayton, T., *Waterloo: Four Days that Changed Europe's Destiny* (London, 2014).

Collins, I., *Napoleon and his Parliaments, 1800–1815* (London, 1979).

Connelly, O., *Blundering to Glory: Napoleon's Military Campaigns* (Wilmington, Delaware, 1987).

Coote, S., *Napoleon and the Hundred Days* (New York, 2004).

Cornillon, J., *Le Bourbonnais pendant les cent jours* (Moulins, 1925).

Cornwell, B., *Waterloo: the History of Four Days, Three Armies and Three Battles* (London, 2014).

Craig, G.A., *The Politics of the Prussian Army, 1640–1945* (Oxford, 1955).

Cronin, V., *Napoleon* (London, 1971).

Crook, M., '"Ma volonté est celle du people": voting in the plebiscite and parliamentary elections during Napoleon's Hundred Days, May–June 1815', *French Historical Studies*, XXXII, No. 4 (Fall 1989), pp. 619–45

Crook, M., 'Uses of democracy: elections and plebiscites in Napoleonic France' in Grosse, M, and Williams, D. (eds.), *The French Experience from Republic to Monarchy, 1792–1824: New Dawns in Politics, Knowledge and Culture* (Basingstoke, 2000), pp. 58–71

Dallas, G., *The Final Act: the Roads to Waterloo* (New York, 1996).

Daly, G., *Inside Napoleonic France: State and Society in Rouen, 1800–1815* (Aldershot, 2001).

Develay, V., *La Bourgogne pendant les cent jours* (Paris, 1860).

Develay, V., *La France devant les deux invasions, 1814–1815* (Paris, 1864).

D'Hauteclocque, G., 'Les cent jours dans le Pas-de-Calais, 20 mars–8 juillet 1815', *Mémoires de l'Académie des Ciences, Lettres et Arts d'Arras*, XXXVI, No. 1 (January 1895), pp. 28–185.

Dickinson, H.T. (ed.), *Britain and the French Revolution, 1789–1815* (London, 1989).

Divall, C., *Redcoats against Napoleon: the Thirtieth Regiment during the Revolutionary and Napoleonic Wars* (Barnsley, 2009).

Doulcet de Pontécoulant, P.G. le, *Napoléon à Waterloo, 1815, ou précis rectifié de la campagne de 1815 avec des documents nouveaux et des pièces inédites*, ed. C. Bourachot (Paris, 2004).

Dry, A., *Reims en 1814 pendant l'invasion* (Paris, 1902).

Dupuy, R., *La Bretagne sous la révolution et l'empire* (Paris, 2004).

Dwyer, P., *Citizen Emperor; Napoleon in Power, 1799–1815* (London, 2013).

Ellis, G., *The Napoleonic Empire* (second edition; Houndmills, 2003).

Elting, J.R., *Swords Around a Throne: Napoleon's Grande Armée* (London, 1988).

Esdaile, C.J., 'De-constructing the French Wars: Napoleon as anti-strategist', *Journal of Strategic Studies*, XXXI, No. 4 (August 2008), pp. 515–52.

Esdaile, C.J., *Napoleon's Wars: an International History, 1803–1815* (London, 2007).

Esdaile, C.J., *The Wars of Napoleon* (Harlow, 1995).

Field, A.W., *Prelude to Waterloo: Quatre Bras – the French Perspective* (Barnsley, 2014).

Field, A.W., *Waterloo: the French Perspective* (Barnsley, 2012).

Fisher, H.A.L., *Napoleon* (London, 1912).

Fitzpatrick, B., *Catholic Royalism in the Department of the Gard* (Cambridge, 1983).

Forrest, A., *Napoleon: Life, Legacy, Image – a Biography* (London, 2012).

Fremont-Barnes, G., *Waterloo, 1815: the British Army's Day of Destiny* (Stroud, 2014).

Gabory, E., *Les guerres du Vendée* (Paris, 2009).

Gallagher, J.G., *Napoleon's* Enfant Terrible*: General Dominique Vandamme* (Norman, Oklahoma, 2008).

Gallo, E. le, *Les cent jours: essai sur l'histoire intérieure de la France depuis le retour de l'ile d'Elbe jusqu'a la nouvelle de Waterloo* (Paris, 1924).

Gates, D., *The Napoleonic Wars, 1803–1815* (London, 1996).

Geyl, P., *Napoleon For and Against* (London, 1949).

Glover, G., *Waterloo: Myth and Reality* (Barnsley, 2014).

Glover, G., *Waterloo: the Defeat of Napoleon's Imperial Guard: Henry Clinton, the Second Division and the End of a 200-Year-Old Controversy* (Barnsley, 2015).

Grand, R., *La chouannerie en 1815: les cent jours dans le ouest* (Paris, 1943).

Guillaume de Vaudoncourt, F., *Histoire des campagnes de 1814 et 1815 en France* (Paris, 1826).

Hamilton-Williams, D., *The Fall of Napoleon: the Final Betrayal* (London, 1994).

Hamilton-Williams, D., *Waterloo: New Perspectives: the Great Battle Revisited* (London, 1993).

Hamon, L. (ed.), *Les cent jours dans l'Yonne: aux origins d'un bonapartisme liberal* (Paris, 1988).

Haythornthwaite, P., *The Armies of Wellington* (Leicester, 2000).

Hazarreesingh, S., *The Legend of Napoleon* (London, 2004).

Henderson, E.F., *Blücher and the Uprising of Prussia against Napoleon, 1806–1815* (London, 1911).

Heitz, F.C., *Strasbourg pendant ses deux blocus et les cent jours: recueil des pieces officielles accompagnés d'une relation succincte des années 1813, 1814 et 1815* (Strasbourg, 1861).

Hofschroer, P., *1815, the Waterloo Campaign, I: Wellington, his German Allies and the Battles of Ligny and Quatre Bras* (London, 1998).

Hofschroer, P., *1815, the Waterloo Campaign, the German Victory, II: from Waterloo to the Fall of Napoleon* (London, 1999).

Hofschroer, P., *Prussian Napoleonic Tactics* (Oxford, 2011).

Hourtoulle, F.G., *1814: the Campaign for France – the Wounded Eagle* (Paris, 2005).

Houssaye, H., *Napoleon and the Campaign of 1814* (London, 1914).

Houssaye, H., *1815: Waterloo* (London, 1900).

Houssaye, H., *1815: the Return of Napoleon* (London, 1934).

Ireland, W.H., *The Life of Napoleon Bonaparte* (London, 1827).

Jarrett, M., *The Congress of Vienna and its Legacy: War and Great-Power Diplomacy* (London, 2013).

Johannet, A., *La Vendée en trois époques: de 1793 jusqu'a l'empire, 1815–1832* (Paris, 1840).

Josselson, M. and D., *The Commander: a Life of Barclay de Tolly* (Oxford, 1980).

Juhel, P., *De l'île d'Elbe à Waterloo: la garde impériale pendant les cent jours, 1815* (Paris, 2008).

Lefebvre, G., *Napoleon, 1807–1815* (London, 1969).

Leggiere, M.V., *Blücher: Scourge of Napoleon* (Norman, Oklahoma, 2014).

Leggiere, M.V., *The Fall of Napoleon: the Allied Invasion of France, 1813–1814* (Cambridge, 2007).

Leuilliot, P., *La première restauration et les cent jours en Alsace* (Paris, 1958).

Lhomer, J., *Les cent jours et la terreur blanc en Dordogne* (Paris, 1904).

Lieven, D., *Russia against Napoleon: the Battle for Europe, 1807 to 1814* (London, 2009).

Lignereux, A., *La France rébellionnaire: les résistances a la gendarmerie, 1800–1859* (Rennes, 2008).

Lipscombe, N., *Bayonne and Toulouse, 1813–1814: Wellington Invades France* (Oxford, 2014).

Lipscombe, N., *Wellington's Guns: the Untold Story of Wellington and his Artillery in the Peninsula and at Waterloo* (Oxford, 2013).

Mackenzie, N., *The Escape from Elba: the Fall and Flight of Napoleon, 1814–1815* (Oxford, 1982).

Maiseau, R.B., *Vie du Maréchal Ney, Duc d'Elchingen, Prince de la Moskowa* (Paris, 1816).

Markham, J.D., *The Road to Saint Helena: Napoleon after Waterloo* (Barnsley, 2008).

Martineau, G., *Napoleon Surrenders* (London, 1971).

Mikaberidize, A., 'The Russian army', in Fremont-Barnes, G. (ed.), *Armies of the Napoleonic Wars* (Barnsley, 2011), pp. 36–56.

Mirante, R., *Medusa's Head: the Rise and Survival of Joseph Fouché, Inventor of the Modern Police State* (Richmond, British Columbia, 2014).

Monge, O., *La capitulation de La Palud: campagne de Duc d'Angoulême en Vaucluse* (Paris, 1894).

Muir, R., *Britain and the Defeat of Napoleon* (London, 1996).

Muir, R., *Wellington: Waterloo and the Fortunes of Peace* (London, 2015).

Nicholson, H., *The Congress of Vienna: a Study in Allied Unity, 1812–1822* (London, 1948).

North, J. (ed.), *The Napoleon Options: Alternate Decisions of the Napoleonic Wars* (London, 2000).

Oman, C., *A History of the Peninsular War* (Oxford, 1902–1930).

Pigeard, A., *Les étoiles de Napoléon* (Paris, 1996).

Pilbeam, P., *The Constitutional Monarchy in France, 1815–1848* (Abingdon, 2000).

Petre, F.L., *Napoleon at Bay, 1814* (London, 1913).

Plack, N., 'Napoleon's land-grab', *History Today*, LXIII, No. 3 (March 2013), pp. 6–7.

Price, M., *Napoleon: the End of Glory* (Oxford, 2014).

Richard, J.F., *Histoire du département des Deux-Sèvres sous le consulat, l'empire, la première restauration et les cent jours* (Saint Maixent, 1848).

Roberts, A., *Napoleon and Wellington* (London, 2001).

Roberts, A., *Napoleon the Great* (London, 2014).

Robertson, I., *Wellington Invades France: the Final Phase of the Peninsular War, 1813–14* (London, 2003).

Rothenberg, G., *Napoleon's Great Adversaries: the Archduke Charles and the Austrian Army, 1792–1814* (London, 1982).

Rowe, M., 'Between empire and home town: Napoleonic rule on the Rhine, 1799–1814', *Historical Journal*, XLII, No. 3 (September 1999), pp. 643–74.

Rowe, M., 'France, Prussia or Germany? The Napoleonic Wars and shifting allegiances in the Rhineland', *Central European History*, XXXIX, No. 4 (December 2006), pp. 611–40.

Sale, N., *The Lie at the Heart of Waterloo: the Battle's Hidden Last Half Hour* (Stroud, 2014).

Schama, S., *Patriots and Liberators: Revolution in the Netherlands, 1780–1813* (London, 1977).

Schmidt, O., 'The Prussian army' in Fremont-Barnes, G. (ed.), *Armies of the Napoleonic Wars* (Barnsley, 2011), pp. 98–126.

Schom, A., *One Hundred Days: Napoleon's Road to Waterloo* (London, 1992).

Schroeder, P., *The Transformation of European Politics, 1763–1848* (Oxford, 1994).

Scott, W., *The Life of Napoleon Buonaparte, Emperor of the French with a Preliminary View of the French Revolution* (London, 1827).

Seeley, J.R., *Life and Times of Stein or Germany and Prussia in the Napoleonic Age* (Cambridge, 1878).

Shanahan, W., *Prussian Military Reforms, 1786–1813* (New York, 1945).

Siborne, W., *The Waterloo Campaign, 1815* (fourth edition; Birmingham, 1894).

Simon, W.M., *The Failure of the Prussian Reform Movement, 1807–1819* (New York, 1971).

Sutherland, D.M.G., *The French Revolution and Empire: the Quest for a Civic Order* (Oxford, 2003).

Teffeteller, G.L., *The Surpriser: the Life of Rowland, Lord Hill* (Newark, Delaware, 1983).

Thiry, J., *Les débuts de la seconde restauration* (Paris, 1947).

Thoral, M.C., *From Valmy to Waterloo: France at War, 1792–1813* (Houndmills, 2011).

Toombs, R., *France, 1814–1914* (London, 1996).

Tulard, J., *Dictionnaire Napoléon* (Paris, 1989).

Tulard, J., *Napoleon: the Myth of the Saviour* (London, 1984).

Uffindell, A., *Napoleon, 1814: the Defence of France* (Barnsley, 2009).

Uffindell, A., *The Eagle's Last Triumph: Napoleon's Victory at Ligny, June 1815* (London, 1994).

Walter, D., 'Meeting the French challenge: conscription in Prussia, 1807–1815', in Stoker, D., *et al* (eds.), *Conscription in the Napoleonic Era: a Revolution in Military Affairs?* (Abingdon, 2009), pp. 24–45.

Ward, A., *et al* (eds.), *Cambridge Modern History, IX: Napoleon* (London, 1902–10).

Waresquiel, E. de, *Cent jours: la tentation de l'impossible, mars–juillet, 1815* (Paris, 2008).

Webster, C., *The Foreign Policy of Castlereagh, 1812–1815* (London, 1931).

Weller, J., *Wellington at Waterloo* (London, 1992).

Wise, T., *Flags of the Napoleonic Wars (I): Colours, Standards and Guidons of France and her Allies* (London, 1978).

Woloch, I., 'Napoleonic conscription: state power and civil society', *Past and Present,* No. 111 (May 1986), pp. 101–29.

Zamoyski, A., *Rites of Peace: the Fall of Napoleon and the Congress of Vienna* (London, 2007).

Index